A Shared Destiny

Community Effects
of Uninsurance

Committee on the Consequences of Uninsurance

Board on Health Care Services

INSTITUTE OF MEDICINE
OF THE NATIONAL ACADEMIES

THE NATIONAL ACADEMIES PRESS
Washington, D.C.
www.nap.edu

THE NATIONAL ACADEMIES PRESS • 500 Fifth Street, N.W. • Washington, DC 20001

NOTICE: The project that is the subject of this report was approved by the Governing Board of the National Research Council, whose members are drawn from the councils of the National Academy of Sciences, the National Academy of Engineering, and the Institute of Medicine. The members of the committee responsible for the report were chosen for their special competences and with regard for appropriate balance.

Support for this project was provided by The Robert Wood Johnson Foundation. The views presented in this report are those of the Institute of Medicine Committee on the Consequences of Uninsurance and are not necessarily those of the funding agencies.

International Standard Book Number 0-309-08726-0

Library of Congress Control Number 2003100538

Additional copies of this report are available for sale from The National Academies Press, 2101 Constitution Avenue, N.W., Box 285, Washington, DC 20055. Call (800) 624-6242 or (202) 334-3313 (in the Washington metropolitan area); Internet, http://www.nap.edu.

For more information about the Institute of Medicine, visit the IOM home page at **www.iom.edu.**

Printed in the United States of America.

The serpent has been a symbol of long life, healing, and knowledge among almost all cultures and religions since the beginning of recorded history. The serpent adopted as a logotype by the Institute of Medicine is a relief carving from ancient Greece, now held by the Staatliche Museen in Berlin.

"Knowing is not enough; we must apply.
Willing is not enough; we must do."
—Goethe

INSTITUTE OF MEDICINE
OF THE NATIONAL ACADEMIES

Shaping the Future for Health

THE NATIONAL ACADEMIES
Advisers to the Nation on Science, Engineering, and Medicine

The **National Academy of Sciences** is a private, nonprofit, self-perpetuating society of distinguished scholars engaged in scientific and engineering research, dedicated to the furtherance of science and technology and to their use for the general welfare. Upon the authority of the charter granted to it by the Congress in 1863, the Academy has a mandate that requires it to advise the federal government on scientific and technical matters. Dr. Bruce M. Alberts is president of the National Academy of Sciences.

The **National Academy of Engineering** was established in 1964, under the charter of the National Academy of Sciences, as a parallel organization of outstanding engineers. It is autonomous in its administration and in the selection of its members, sharing with the National Academy of Sciences the responsibility for advising the federal government. The National Academy of Engineering also sponsors engineering programs aimed at meeting national needs, encourages education and research, and recognizes the superior achievements of engineers. Dr. Wm. A. Wulf is president of the National Academy of Engineering.

The **Institute of Medicine** was established in 1970 by the National Academy of Sciences to secure the services of eminent members of appropriate professions in the examination of policy matters pertaining to the health of the public. The Institute acts under the responsibility given to the National Academy of Sciences by its congressional charter to be an adviser to the federal government and, upon its own initiative, to identify issues of medical care, research, and education. Dr. Harvey V. Fineberg is president of the Institute of Medicine.

The **National Research Council** was organized by the National Academy of Sciences in 1916 to associate the broad community of science and technology with the Academy's purposes of furthering knowledge and advising the federal government. Functioning in accordance with general policies determined by the Academy, the Council has become the principal operating agency of both the National Academy of Sciences and the National Academy of Engineering in providing services to the government, the public, and the scientific and engineering communities. The Council is administered jointly by both Academies and the Institute of Medicine. Dr. Bruce M. Alberts and Dr. Wm. A. Wulf are chair and vice chair, respectively, of the National Research Council.

www.national-academies.org

IOM Staff

Wilhelmine Miller, Project Co-director
Dianne Miller Wolman, Project Co-director
Lynne Page Snyder, Program Officer
Tracy McKay, Research Associate
Ryan Palugod, Senior Project Assistant

Consultants

Darrell J. Gaskin, Deputy Director, Center for Health Disparities Solutions
and Research Scientist, Johns Hopkins Bloomberg School of Public Health
Jack Needleman, Assistant Professor of Economics and Health Policy,
Department of Health Policy and Management, Harvard University

Reviewers

This report has been reviewed in draft form by individuals chosen for their diverse perspectives and technical expertise, in accordance with procedures approved by the NRC's Report Review Committee. The purpose of this independent review is to provide candid and critical comments that will assist the institution in making its published report as sound as possible and to ensure that the report meets institutional standards for objectivity, evidence, and responsiveness to the study charge. The review comments and draft manuscript remain confidential to protect the integrity of the deliberative process. We wish to thank the following individuals for their review of this report:

BRENT ASPLIN, Assistant Professor of Emergency Medicine, University of Minnesota, Research Director and Director of Public Policy Research, Regions Hospital, St. Paul, MN

JOHN BILLINGS, Director, Center for Health and Public Service Research, New York University

GEORGE D. GREENBERG, Executive Advisor, U.S. Department of Health and Human Services, Washington, DC

SANDRAL HULLETT, Acting Chief Executive Officer, Jefferson Health System, Birmingham, AL

JUDITH R. LAVE, Interim Chair, Department of Health Policy and Management, Graduate School of Public Health, University of Pittsburgh

ROBERT A. LOWE, Associate Professor, Emergency Medicine Research, Oregon Health Sciences University, Portland

ALAN NELSON, Special Advisor to the Executive Vice President, American College of Physicians-American Society of Internal Medicine, Fairfax, VA

THOMAS RICKETTS, Director, North Carolina Rural Health Research Program, Cecil G. Sheps Center for Health Services Research, Chapel Hill, NC
LEIYU SHI, Associate Professor, Associate Director, Johns Hopkins Primary Care Policy Center for the Underserved, Johns Hopkins University, Baltimore, MD

Although the reviewers listed above have provided many constructive comments and suggestions, they were not asked to endorse the conclusions or recommendations nor did they see the final draft of the report before its release. The review of this report was overseen by **Hugh H. Tilson, Clinical Professor, School of Public Health, University of North Carolina, Chapel Hill**, appointed by the Institute of Medicine and **Joseph P. Newhouse, John D. MacArthur Professor of Health Policy and Management, Harvard University,** appointed by the NRC's Report Review Committee, who were responsible for making certain that an independent examination of this report was carried out in accordance with institutional procedures and that all review comments were carefully considered. Responsibility for the final content of this report rests entirely with the authoring committee and the institution.

Foreword

A Shared Destiny: Community Effects of Uninsurance is the fourth in a series of six reports planned by the Institute of Medicine (IOM) and its Committee on the Consequences of Uninsurance. Since we issued the third report last September, the Census Bureau has reported that the *number* of uninsured people in the United States as well as the *rate* of uninsurance have risen again after slight dips in 1999 and 2000. More than 41 million people went without any health insurance during calendar year 2001, and the number probably increased in 2002 because of the slowdown in the economy. Forty-one million uninsured people, virtually all of whom are under age 65, translates into an uninsured rate of 16.5 percent for the population in that age range.

Lacking or losing health insurance can have effects that extend beyond the individual without coverage. The Committee's last report, *Health Insurance Is a Family Matter,* showed that all members of a family can be adversely affected if even one member lacks coverage. In *A Shared Destiny,* we learn that the rate of uninsurance in a community can affect the health and health services available to all members of that community, insured and uninsured alike. This report demonstrates that we share a common interest in ensuring that our neighbors, as well as members of our own families, are covered by health insurance.

When the Committee's first report, *Coverage Matters,* was issued in the fall of 2001, the country was reeling from the effects of the 9/11 attacks and the threat of bioterrorism. Americans felt a sense of community with the victims' families in New York and Washington. Many of us offered blood, donated money, and helped in other ways with the recovery effort. Since that time, we have gained a deeper appreciation of the value of public health and emergency services. As the country rebounds and rebuilds, we have a clearer sense of the importance of strong social bonds within our communities.

A Shared Destiny looks with fresh eyes at the effects of uninsurance and sees the numerous ways in which *all* of us are affected when many lack health insurance coverage. By adopting a community perspective, the report shows how the quality, quantity, and scope of health services within the community can be adversely affected by the presence of a large and growing population of uninsured. Because this is a groundbreaking approach, the Committee highlights fruitful areas for future research. It also presents its own conclusions, based on the existing literature and original research that the Committee undertook.

The members of the Committee on the Consequences of Uninsurance represent expertise in a broad variety of disciplines, including economics, public health, health services research and management, epidemiology, strategic planning, small business management, clinical medicine and nursing, and health communications. This report presents a number of important findings about the documented impacts of the lack of health insurance on communities throughout the United States. It charts an ambitious research agenda for the development of information that policy makers and the American public need if we are to understand more completely the implications and consequences of the choices we are making about the financing of health care. The conclusions in this report are consistent with those of the Committee's earlier reports: health insurance has benefits for all of us.

Harvey V. Fineberg, M.D., Ph.D.
President, Institute of Medicine
February 2003

Preface

A Shared Destiny: Community Effects of Uninsurance examines whether the presence of a large uninsured population in a community can affect the health of and health services available to all in the community. The spillover effects of uninsurance go beyond the individual who lacks coverage to touch those who have adequate insurance as well.

This is the fourth of six reports that will be issued by the Committee on the Consequences of Uninsurance, a major three-year effort of the Institute of Medicine (IOM) supported by The Robert Wood Johnson Foundation. The Committee continues to follow the research design outlined in its first report, *Coverage Matters: Insurance and Health Care*. This report, *A Shared Destiny*, builds on the Committee's previous three reports by expanding the perspective from the consequences of uninsurance on individuals and their families to entire communities. The Committee's first report, *Coverage Matters*, presented background information about who is uninsured and why and underscored the persistence of a large uninsured population in the United States during both good and bad economic times. The second report, *Care Without Coverage: Too Little, Too Late*, analyzed clinical research documenting the health effects on adults of being uninsured. The literature shows conclusively that uninsured adults tend to suffer worse health and risk dying sooner than individuals who are insured. The Committee broadened the focus beyond the individual to the family in its third report, *Health Insurance Is a Family Matter*. The report concluded that if even one family member is uninsured, the entire family faces an increased risk of financial catastrophe, poorer health, and diminished well-being.

A Shared Destiny widens the Committee's perspective from the family to entire communities. It explores the complex interrelationships between populations of insured and uninsured, the financial viability of local health care institutions and practitioners, the financing mechanisms that support provision of health care services at the community level, and the effects that loss of key health care providers or institutions has on the overall health of a community. This relatively new and innovative approach to examining the broader consequences of health insurance disparities for populations overall presents a coherent historical and policy context for understanding how we all can be adversely affected by the lack of coverage within our communities.

The report that follows this one will examine the economic costs (as described in the Committee's first four reports) to society of maintaining an uninsured population of more than 41 million. The sixth and final report in this series will consider models, strategies, and policy options designed to expand coverage and will suggest principles to guide policy analysts and policy makers as they craft solutions to the problem of uninsurance in America.

Mary Sue Coleman, Ph.D.
Co-chair
Arthur L. Kellermann, M.D., M.P.H.
Co-chair
February 2003

Acknowledgments

A Shared Destiny: Community Effects of Uninsurance is the result of collaborative effort. The Committee acknowledges and thanks the individuals whose work made this publication what it is.

The Committee especially recognizes the members of the Subcommittee on Community Effects of Uninsured Populations that developed this report: Christopher Queram, who served as its chair, David Baker, Regina Benjamin, Sandra Hernández, Ichiro Kawachi, Ronda Kotelchuck, Keith Mueller, Mary Tierney, Reed Tuckson, and Mary Wakefield. These members of the drafting subcommittee constitute a group with especially broad scope and depth of practical and research expertise in health care. They gave much time and thoughtful advice over the course of the report's development.

Darrell Gaskin, Johns Hopkins University, and Jack Needleman, Harvard University, conducted two original analyses examining the effect of local uninsured rates on hospital services and financial status as consultants to the Committee. In addition to preparing these research monographs (Appendix D of this report), Darrell and Jack served as expert resources to the Subcommittee, Committee, and project staff. Eugene Moyer, senior economist with the Department of Health and Human Services (retired), also served as consultant, providing expertise on the federal health insurance programs. Vic Miller, senior fellow with Federal Funds Information for States, volunteered his time and expertise on issues of intergovernmental finance and provided data on state-level spending and revenues to the Committee.

The Committee and Subcommittee benefited from presentations from a number of experts on various issues covered in *A Shared Destiny* made during their meetings over the past year. Mohammad Akhter, president, American Public

Health Association; Robert Bitterman, University of North Carolina; E. Richard Brown, University of California at Los Angeles; Andrew Coburn, University of Southern Maine; Christopher Conover, Duke University; Jonathon Fielding, director of public health and health officer, Los Angeles County Department of Health Services; Irene Ibarra, Alameda Alliance for Health; Vic Miller, Federal Funds Information for States; Paul Offner, Georgetown University; and Hugh Waters, Johns Hopkins University, shared their research analyses, management experience, and perspectives with the Committee. The Committee also wishes to thank Paul Fronstin of the Employee Benefit Research Institute, Bill Finerfrock of the National Association of Rural Health Clinics, Michael Davern of the State Health Access Data Assistance Center, and Alicia Gable and Douglas Weihl of the Institute of Medicine's Board on Health Promotion and Disease Prevention for contributing their time and expertise to this project.

The Committee recognizes the hard work of staff at the Institute of Medicine. Program officer Lynne Snyder served as principal staff to the Subcommittee and conducted much of the literature review and fact gathering on which this report is based. Lynne worked tirelessly and resourcefully to pursue information and formulate issues for consideration by the Subcommittee and Committee in this relatively novel area of inquiry. Project co-director Wilhelmine Miller managed the work of the consultants and the overall drafting of *A Shared Destiny*. Co-director Dianne Wolman reviewed and edited multiple drafts of the report. Research associate Tracy McKay provided research assistance and prepared the manuscript for publication. Senior project assistant Ryan Palugod maintained the project's research database and supported communications with Committee members and meetings logistics. This work is being conducted within the Board on Health Care Services, Janet Corrigan, director.

Funding for the project comes from The Robert Wood Johnson Foundation (RWJF). The Committee extends special thanks to Risa Lavisso-Mourey, president, and Anne Weiss, senior program officer, RWJF, for their continuing support and interest in this project.

Contents

A Shared Destiny

Community Effects of Uninsurance

Executive Summary

A COMMUNITY PERSPECTIVE

In its first three reports, the Committee has shown that the lack of health insurance is widespread and enduring in the United States and that there are adverse health, psychosocial, and economic impacts on uninsured individuals and members of families with at least one uninsured member. By removing or lowering financial barriers to access to health care, health insurance can and does make a positive difference in the lives of insured persons when they need health care. This report sets the experiences of uninsured individuals and families in the context of the communities in which they live, work, and seek health care. It considers another aspect of health insurance's importance, namely, as a predictable and stable revenue source for health care service providers.

In *A Shared Destiny: Community Effects of Uninsurance,* **the Committee finds that the adverse effects of uninsurance that accrue to uninsured individuals and families in a community, as well as the financial strain placed on the community's health care system, have important spillover effects on community health care institutions and providers.** In communities with higher uninsured rates, access to health services and consequent benefits are compromised for persons other than those who lack coverage. The community effects of uninsurance are often difficult to see at a national level but can be quite vivid at the local level. The great heterogeneity in the organization of health care services locally and in the ways that care for uninsured persons is financed affects how uninsurance interacts with local health services, a community's social and economic fortunes, and may even affect the health of its members. *A*

Shared Destiny documents a number of these interactions and presents working hypotheses about many more.

Health care practitioners and institutions are an important part of most local communities, knitting together the lives of individual community residents as providers facilitate access to care, contribute to local economic vitality, and protect and improve the health of community members. Even for healthy community members, having a regular health care provider and more advanced medical services and resources available has real value. These health care relationships and resources enhance the quality of our lives and peace of mind.

The failure to insure all members of American communities can distort and even disrupt these relationships between health care providers and the people they serve. Uninsured persons have much more trouble finding health care providers who will see them, use health care services much less often when they need care than do insured persons, and are more likely to incur high unreimbursed costs when they do obtain care (IOM, 2001a, 2002b). As a result, the presence of a sizable or growing population of uninsured persons may impose destabilizing financial stresses on the health care providers that serve all community members and on the public and private sources that finance local health care. Lack of access to health care results in adverse economic, social, and health consequences for uninsured persons and their family members (IOM, 2001a, 2002a, 2002b). Ripple or spillover effects of these consequences on uninsured persons may be felt by their insured neighbors. For example, an uninsured breadwinner's lack of health care can lead to disability and loss of income that necessitates public support payments.

This fourth report of the Committee on the Consequences of Uninsurance explores the ways in which many others may be affected by the lack of health insurance of some of us. The Committee hypothesizes a series of spillover effects of uninsurance, effects that extend beyond the adverse health and financial impacts on uninsured individuals and families documented in *Coverage Matters, Care Without Coverage,* and *Health Insurance Is a Family Matter. A Shared Destiny* establishes an analytic framework for thinking about the causal pathways hypothesized to lead to the more widespread impacts of uninsurance, assesses the limited empirical evidence that exists about community effects, and proposes a research agenda to better demonstrate the presence or absence of these effects.

Given the large, persisting population of uninsured persons in the United States, the current economic environment and state government fiscal situations make the problems of uninsurance even more urgent and in need of remedy. The national uninsured rate of 16.5 percent among persons under age 65 masks substantial variation in state and local uninsured rates, median durations of uninsured spells of individuals, and the sizes and concentrations of uninsured groups within different populations (Mills, 2002). Uninsured rates vary across the states from 8.7 percent in Iowa to 26 percent in Texas (see Figure ES.1).

Over the past two decades the uninsured rate and total number of uninsured nationally has grown slowly but steadily (with only a slight dip during 1999 and 2000). With the current combination of higher unemployment and rapidly rising

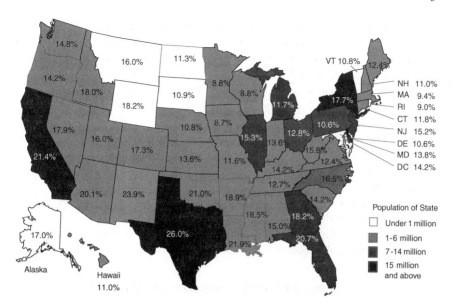

FIGURE ES.1 Probability of being uninsured for population under age 65, by state, 2001.

SOURCE: Fronstin, 2002, estimates based on March 2001 Current Population Survey.

costs of health care and insurance premiums, absent major public policy reforms, the national uninsured rate can be expected to rise more rapidly in future years (Chernew et al., 2002; Cutler, 2002).

Assessing Community Effects

For the purposes of this report, the Committee defines a community as a group of people who (1) live in a particular geographic area and (2) have access to a specific set of health resources for which information about financial and health-related outcomes exists. Geographical entities (e.g., rural counties, metropolitan statistical areas) are the units for which epidemiological, demographic, and economic data are collected most often, and they serve as rough approximations for health services market areas. The limited availability of research about community-level attributes, for example, the availability of specialty care within a neighborhood, constrains the Committee's analysis. Findings are often based on cross-sectional comparisons among states, metropolitan areas, and rural counties with differing uninsured rates as well as on illustrative case studies and other qualitative evidence. Because of the limited data with which to characterize and monitor community effects and the challenges of distinguishing effects that stem from the extent of uninsurance from effects of related community-level characteristics (e.g., income structure), the Committee developed a research agenda as part of its work.

The Committee hypothesizes that the experiences of uninsured individuals and of families within a community influence the collective and aggregate effects of uninsurance on their community. The causal pathways hypothesized for community effects incorporate the experiences of uninsured individuals and families as well as the performance of health care institutions and providers. Figure ES.2 depicts the Committee's conceptual framework for thinking about the breadth and scope of community effects and the pathways through which those effects are exerted. The framework builds on a widely used behavioral model of access to health services (Andersen, 1995; Andersen and Davidson, 2001) and focuses primarily on the economic, financial, and coverage-related factors that affect outcomes of health care services and their impact on communities. These hypothesized pathways and effects are noted in the sections that follow. Some of these effects on local health care services, local economies, and population health have been documented. Other effects are not well understood and require more extensive and systematic data collection and analysis.

CONTEXT FOR COMMUNITY EFFECTS

Financing the Delivery of Health Services

Over the past 25 years, federal and state policies to control health care costs and an increasingly competitive private market for health care services and coverage have constrained reimbursement rates for care, eroding previous levels of subsidy for uncompensated care costs associated with care delivered to uninsured persons. The effects of this erosion have been felt more strongly in communities with large or growing uninsured populations and by providers (e.g., public hospitals) that serve a high number or proportion of uninsured persons. Although the mainstream health care system provides most of the services that uninsured persons receive, the uninsured rely disproportionately on safety-net arrangements for care (Cunningham and Tu, 1997; Lewin and Altman, 2000). In urban areas, multiple tiers of providers and services tend to segregate patients by income level and coverage status, isolating insured patients from the experiences of uninsured patients. In rural areas, insured and uninsured patients may have more in common because a more limited set of providers typically serves all community members and safety-net arrangements tend to be less formal.

Responsibility for financing and providing health care to uninsured persons in the United States is fragmented and ill defined. State, county, and municipal facilities are, often by default, the providers of last resort for uninsured patients. The so-called safety net is a highly diverse set of frequently ad hoc local arrangements to accommodate patients without the ability to pay for their own care. The incomplete patchwork of federal, state, and local mandates that minimal services be provided does not typically specify a scope of benefits to which a medically indigent person is entitled, nor are there guarantees that providers will be reimbursed. The particular local configuration of safety-net arrangements—for ex-

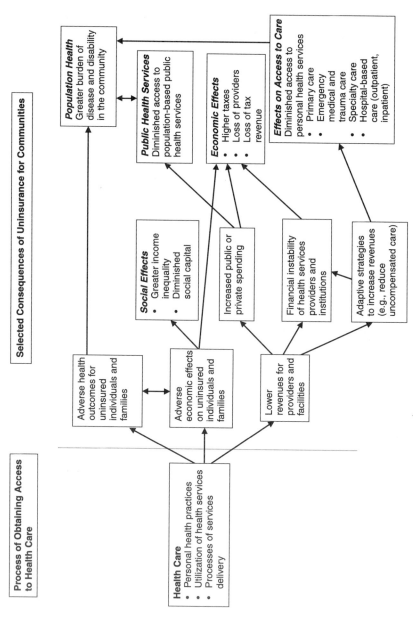

FIGURE ES.2 A conceptual framework for community effects.

ample, whether it is centralized or dispersed—and its effectiveness in caring for the community's uninsured residents influences the range and extent of community effects related to uninsurance.

The current amalgam of service arrangements and the mix of public and private funding sources was not designed as an integrated system; rather, it has resulted from the aggregation, over time, of initiatives and developments in both the private and the public sectors. Because the organization and delivery of care are closely linked to health insurance, the needs of persons who lack health insurance have been of secondary interest, often only as afterthoughts in the development of public policy.

Who Pays for Care for Uninsured Persons?

Public support of the health care expenses of uninsured Americans accounts for as much as 85 percent of the estimated $34–$38 billion (for 2001) in uncompensated care costs that they incur (Hadley and Holahan, 2003). To address the health needs of a relatively large low-income population, state and local jurisdictions may find themselves under considerable financial pressure, supporting health services both directly, through public hospitals and clinics, and indirectly, through public insurance programs such as Medicaid.

Federal, state, and local governments play different roles in financing care for uninsured persons. The federal government's primary role is financing health care services through insurance mechanisms (e.g., the State Children's Health Insurance Program [SCHIP]), grant programs for service delivery (e.g., community health centers), and programs of direct care (e.g., Department of Veterans Affairs facilities). States determine eligibility standards and provide funding for Medicaid, SCHIP, and similar state programs that serve populations that do not qualify for federal matching funds. Local governments operate public clinics and hospitals and frequently provide personal health care services directly or through contracts to uninsured residents. Physicians in solo and group practices, practicing in clinics and in hospital settings, provide an estimated $5.1 billion in free or reduced-price charity care to uninsured patients (Hadley and Holahan, 2003).

COMMUNITY EFFECTS ON ACCESS TO CARE

Insurance facilitates access to health care by removing or diminishing financial barriers faced by individuals and families. It also supports the stable operations of health care providers and institutions. The Committee hypothesizes that the burden of financing care for uninsured persons affects the health services available to all community residents, especially in urban areas where providers treat large numbers of uninsured persons and in rural areas where providers treat relatively high proportions of them. The pathway proposed is that of lower provider revenues resulting from the combination of the lower use of health services by uninsured persons (compared with use by insured persons), as well as the uncompensated costs incurred when uninsured persons do receive health care. **The Committee finds that low- to moderate-income[1] and uninsured residents have worse access to health care in communities with high uninsured rates than they do in communities with relatively low rates, although the causal influence of the local uninsured rate on access is unclear.** Health care providers in rural and urban settings both experience financial pressures related to lower revenues but may adopt different strategies for coping with them. In an effort to avoid the burden of uncompensated care for uninsured residents or to minimize its financial impact, physician practices and hospitals may cut back services, reduce staffing, relocate or close.

Three recent studies examine the relationship between self-reported access to care and community uninsurance in urban areas (Cunningham and Kemper, 1998; Brown et al., 2000; Andersen et al., 2002). All of the studies rely on survey data about self-reported access to care, using measures such as difficulty obtaining care or not having seen a physician in the previous 12 months, and include limited analytic adjustments for the many covariates of insurance status. These studies find that, unadjusted for the major covariates of local uninsured rate, the uninsured rate in urban areas is inversely associated with the ability of uninsured and of low- to moderate-income residents to obtain needed and regular health care. Such measures of access to health services are basic markers of effective, quality care that improves health outcomes (Millman, 1993; IOM, 2002a, 2002b).

Primary Care

Aside from the studies of access to care described above, there are few studies of uninsurance's effects on primary care. Shortages of physicians in rural and urban areas with relatively high uninsured rates can mean less access to primary care for all residents. Over the 1990s, the proportion of physicians who have provided charity care (whether to uninsured or insured persons) has declined, a decrease that is explained as a response to declining provider revenues (Reed et al., 2001; Cunningham, 2002). In rural areas, physicians are more likely to treat Medicaid and uninsured patients and have higher proportions of Medicare patients. Reimbursement levels in rural areas are lower than in urban areas and safety net arrangements tend to be less formal and not supported with public funds (Taylor et al., 2001; Coburn, 2002).

In urban areas, public clinics play a key role. One survey of primary care access at four types of ambulatory care sites in New York City in 1997 finds that public sites provide the most comprehensive care for low-income patients and

---

[1]Defined as persons in families with income less than 250 percent of the federal poverty level.

concludes that serving increasing numbers of uninsured persons may weaken ambulatory sites' capacity to provide primary care to all members of the community (Weiss et al., 2001).

Community health centers (CHCs) face financial pressures on a number of fronts: from reduced income from Medicaid patients, from reduced public subsidies, and from an increased proportion of their patient mix that is uninsured (Lewin and Altman, 2000). These pressures have adversely affected CHCs' capacity to serve all of their patients (Shi et al., 2001; Rosenbaum et al., 2002). A longitudinal study of 588 CHCs between 1996 and 1999 finds that reductions in capacity appear to be concentrated among subsets of health centers with a sizable number or share of uninsured patients or those that have experienced a recent increase in uninsured patients (McAlearney, 2002).

Reduced access to primary care may increase demand for services in already overcrowded hospital emergency departments. In turn this may reduce access to care and the quality of care received, regardless of insurance status.

Emergency Medical Services and Trauma Care

Emergency departments and trauma centers are key examples of how market pressures and public policies interact in ways that create incentives for hospitals to reduce their exposure to financial losses associated with serving uninsured patients. For example, the federal Emergency Medical Treatment and Labor Act (EMTALA) requires that emergency deparments (EDs) maintain an "open door" policy, serving all comers without regard to their ability to pay. The service areas of highly specialized and resource-intensive trauma centers extend across populous metropolitan areas and multicounty regions in rural areas, transcending local neighborhood boundaries that often separate wealthier, insured groups from less wealthy, uninsured ones. In many urban and rural areas, hospital emergency departments are often filled beyond capacity, affecting all who rely on them (Richards et al., 2000; Derlet et al., 2001; Lewin Group, 2002).

ED overcrowding is primarily caused by an insufficient number of staffed inpatient beds into which ED patients can be admitted (Brewster et al., 2001). This bed shortage is in part a result of market and related financing pressures on hospital operating margins, pressures that include the relative amount of uncompensated care provided by the hospital, some of which is delivered to uninsured patients. Overcrowding adversely affects the quality of care for all emergency department patients (Bindman et al., 1991; Kellermann, 1991; Rask et al., 1994). Members of medically underserved groups are particularly likely to suffer because they have fewer options to obtain primary care outside EDs, compared with insured persons, although they use EDs less frequently than do insured persons (Felt-Lisk et al., 2001; IOM, 2002a; Weinick et al., 2002).

Specialty Care

Evidence about the relationship between the uninsured rate and access to specialty services other than emergency medical care is limited. A consequence of the on-call obligations that hospitals may require of affiliated specialists, under EMTALA, is the relocation of orthopedists, neurosurgeons, and other specialists out of the area, leading to local shortages of particular specialty services (Bitterman, 2002). In addition, in rural areas, all residents may experience lessened access to specialty care (as with primary care) if providers leave the community because of financially unviable practice conditions (Ormond et al., 2000a). Rural areas tend to have shortages of specialty physicians, and referrals are often to specialists in urban areas, which may deter some patients from obtaining care or result in their seeking it later than advisable. The inability of primary care providers to make specialty referrals for their patients may be an effect of a relatively high local uninsured rate.

Urban safety-net hospitals and academic health centers (AHCs), major sites for specialty care in their communities, are also likely to be affected by high levels of uninsured patients (Gaskin, 1999). A study of 125 public and private academic health centers between 1991 and 1996 finds that in local markets with high managed care penetration, care for uninsured persons had been increasingly concentrated at a subset of AHCs, resulting in less aggregate revenue for the AHCs. For private AHCs, particularly those that are *not* located in neighborhoods with high uninsured rates (e.g., central city), one strategic response of hospitals to such cost pressures has been to eliminate specialty services with relatively poor rates of reimbursement, such as burn units, trauma care, pediatric and neonatal intensive care, emergency psychiatric inpatient services, and HIV/AIDS (Gaskin, 1999; Commonwealth Fund, 2001).

Hospital-Based Care

Hospitals treating uninsured patients must contend with the cumulative effects of inadequate care for chronic conditions, exacerbated acute illnesses, and delayed treatment (IOM, 2002a). In addition, hospital outpatient departments and their satellite clinics are an important source of both primary and specialty care for medically underserved populations, including uninsured persons and their families. As discussed above, one way that hospitals have responded to increasing financial pressures is to reduce the availability of certain services known to attract persons who are more likely than average to be uninsured (Gaskin, 1999). The reduced availability or complete loss of these services (e.g., trauma, burn care, care for HIV/AIDs) may be expected to affect everyone in the health services market who needs them. In urban areas, this community effect is likely to affect access for low-income residents, who have few options for care other than their local public or private safety net hospitals. In contrast, in rural areas, where health services are less segmented, adverse effects on hospital operating margins are more likely to affect the care of residents across income levels (Sutton et al., 2001).

Financial pressures may also motivate a local hospital's governing body to merge, to convert from public to private ownership status, or from private non-profit to for-profit status, or to close (Meyer et al., 1999; Needleman, 1999). Local uninsured rates and the burden of uncompensated care costs to local and state government have contributed to the conversions of some large urban public hospitals (Bovbjerg et al., 2000b). The conversion, merger, or closing of a hospital may lead to improved and less costly health services locally. However, the loss of a physical plant and with it the relatively automatic support that a bricks-and-mortar institution commands may also result in a net loss of public dollars for indigent health care, and the proposed closing of a public hospital may be perceived by other local providers as threatening the financial stability of their own institutions by spreading the burden of uncompensated care more broadly.

New Analysis of Hospital Services and Financial Margins

The Committee commissioned analyses of hospital services and financial margins across the 85 largest metropolitan statistical areas and across nonmetropolitan (rural) counties in seven states in the 1990s. Compared to urban areas with relatively low uninsured rates, the analyses show that hospitals in urban areas with relatively high uninsured rates:

- have fewer beds per capita (except for intensive care unit beds);
- offer fewer services for vulnerable populations, including psychiatric, alcohol and chemical dependence, and AIDS care; and
- are less likely to offer trauma and burn care (Gaskin and Needleman, 2002).

In comparison to rural areas with relatively low uninsured rates, hospitals in rural areas with relatively high uninsured rates:

- have lower financial margins,
- have fewer intensive care unit beds, and
- offer fewer psychiatric inpatient services (Needleman and Gaskin, 2002).

ECONOMIC AND SOCIAL IMPLICATIONS OF UNINSURANCE WITHIN COMMUNITIES

Over the past two decades the uninsured rate nationally has grown slowly but steadily, despite an increasingly tight labor market that expanded employment-based coverage and yielded tax revenues to expand public coverage. Present economic trends have changed from boom to economic recession and, absent major policy interventions, indicate a continuing rise in this rate. Health care cost and health insurance premium increases are projected to add to the ranks of the uninsured (Chernew et al., 2002; Cutler, 2002).

Health insurance is not the solution to all communal ills; nevertheless, the Committee hypothesizes that its presence or absence can make a substantial difference for a community's economic fortunes. The costs of care for uninsured Americans are passed down to taxpayers and consumers of health care in the forms of higher taxes and higher prices for services and insurance. Locally, residents are likely to subsidize care for their uninsured neighbors through taxes and higher prices for health services and health insurance in their community. The tax burdens of funding care for uninsured residents is more concentrated locally than is the burden of Medicaid finance or other insurance-based public programs in which the federal government participates.

For communities as for individuals and families, uninsurance can be associated with a loss of income and increased expenditures that weaken shared economic and social foundations. Increased public sector support for or reimbursement of providers for uncompensated care delivered to uninsured persons requires that additional public revenues be raised, resources be diverted from other public purposes, or budget cuts be imposed, adversely affecting all members of the community and potentially increasing the number of uninsured persons.

State and local governments' capacity to finance health care for uninsured persons tends to be weakest at times when the demand for such care is likely to be highest, namely, during economic recessions. While health insurance programs such as Medicaid also make claims on state tax revenues, the incidence of the tax burden for federal or shared federal–state financing programs falls more broadly upon American taxpayers and can alleviate some of the financial demands that uninsurance places on disproportionately affected communities. As a result, the communities most in need of tax-subsidized assistance to health services institutions and providers may be the least likely to be able to afford to finance care for uninsured and underserved persons (Lewin and Altman, 2000).

Budget Implications for States and Localities

During the 1990s, the fiscal capacity and resources of the states for spending on health programs grew. Starting in 1999, states have increasingly been experiencing hard times, with economic recession, federal cuts to Medicare and Medicaid, and public resistance to raising taxes (Dixon and Cox, 2002; Lutzky et al., 2002). Many states plan to cut Medicaid spending in the coming years (Smith et al., 2002). The consequences of these responses are likely to result simultaneously in lower public funding for health insurance, fewer public funds available for other purposes, and higher taxes. States' ability to levy taxes and their tax structures constrain revenue increases to support care for uninsured persons. The federal-state financing structure of Medicaid places great demands on state budgets even as it provides federal monies to the states. Medicaid's federal match is designed to provide relatively greater federal support to those states with lower average personal income; however, it only imperfectly reflects relative state needs (Miller, 2002b).

Economic Base and the Potential for Development

How health care contributes to the economic vitality of communities and how uninsurance within a community affects the local economy overall are poorly documented (Doeksen et al., 1997). A high uninsured rate may both indicate and contribute to an area's economic challenges as it reflects the relative availability of employment-based coverage. Coverage is less likely to be available in areas with a lower-waged labor force.

A high uninsured rate and the corresponding burden of uncompensated care on the local health care system may threaten the survival of individual providers or hospitals, reducing the viability of the economic base of the community. These hypothesized effects are easier to measure in rural than in urban areas because of the smaller scale and simpler scope of rural economies and the influential economic role of local hospitals in rural areas (Doeksen et al., 1997; Cordes et al., 1999; Colgan, 2002). Public financing, particularly through Medicare and Medicaid, is especially important for the rural health services infrastructure (Cordes, 1998). These dollars, spent locally, can be a source of new jobs, population growth, and tax revenues, making hospitals a form of economic development that brings outside dollars into the community (Cordes et al., 1999). Rural hospital closings are also associated with the loss of community physicians, and the jobs and tax revenues that private practices generate (Hartley et al., 1994; Doeksen et al., 1997).

UNINSURANCE AND COMMUNITY HEALTH

The health of the community itself, including its insured as well as uninsured residents, may be compromised by high levels of uninsurance. The sheer number of uninsured persons in an area contributes disproportionately to the community's burden of disease and disability, because of the poorer health of uninsured community members and from spillover effects on other residents. The mechanisms for this can be as diverse as the spread of communicable diseases and the paucity or loss of primary care service capacity as a result of physicians' location decisions, cutbacks in clinic staffing and hours, or outright closures.

Area-wide rates of potentially avoidable hospitalizations serve not only as indicators of access to care but also as measures of the acuity of illness experienced within a population and the efficiency with which health care is provided overall. Uninsured patients are more likely to experience avoidable hospitalizations than are privately insured patients when measured as the proportion of all hospitalizations, and studies consistently report substantially higher rates of these hospitalizations in lower-income areas (Billings et al., 1993, 1996; Millman, 1993; Bindman et al., 1995; Pappas et al., 1997). Uninsurance is likely to contribute to these higher rates.

Public Health and Community Uninsurance

The intentional dispersal of anthrax through the U.S. mail in late 2001 exposed yet another way in which uninsurance could threaten community health, when the impaired access to care of uninsured persons means delays in detecting, treating, and monitoring the transmission of infectious diseases linked to bioterrorism (Wynia and Gostin, 2002; IOM, forthcoming 2003). As public and policy attention turned to the country's emergency preparedness, the weaknesses of the highly fragmented public and private health care systems became apparent. This fragmentation and minimal capacity for communication across systems and types of care hamper the ability of a community to respond rapidly and effectively to an unfamiliar threat to the public's health.

Public health includes the key functions of assessing population health, developing policy solutions for problems identified, and ensuring that problems are addressed by the solutions devised (IOM, 1988). Many health departments also care for uninsured residents who have difficulty gaining access to care in other settings. In many parts of the country, health department officials have expressed their perceptions of being caught between the increasing demand and need for care of growing numbers of uninsured persons and diminished budgets (IOM, 1988, forthcoming 2003; Lewin and Altman, 2000).

Efforts to meet the personal health care needs of uninsured residents place considerable demands upon local health department resources and may divert funds from population-based public health activities. This diversion of resources undermines communities' capacity to prepare for emergencies and bioterrorist threats. National planning for the vaccination of some or all of the U.S. population against smallpox is coming up against the capacity limitations of public health departments, unless there is an infusion of new federal funds.

Communicable disease control is a core function of public health departments. The Committee hypothesizes that the presence of sizable uninsured populations without reliable access to care means that both population immunization levels and communicable disease rates are likely to be worse than they otherwise would be if everyone in the United States had health insurance. For example, underimmunization of children increases the vulnerability of entire communities to outbreaks of diseases such as measles, whooping cough, and rubella (IOM, 2000). Because uninsured families and children tend to live in neighborhoods with higher-than-average uninsured rates and are likely to go without immunizations, all who live in these communities are at greater risk.

Another consequence of community uninsurance may be a greater risk of the transmission of the virus that causes HIV/AIDS especially for members of groups that are already at greater risk for becoming infected. Almost 20 percent of all persons with HIV infection are uninsured and they tend to experience greater difficulties in obtaining access to timely and appropriate care (Sorvillo et al., 1999; Kates and Sorian, 2000; IOM, 2002a). Persons who are HIV positive and uninsured are also more likely to be unaware of their infectious state than are seropositive persons with health insurance, either public or private (Bozzette et al., 1998).

SUMMARY

The Committee draws two conclusions based on its expert judgement and the sufficiency of the evidence base.

1. A community's high uninsured rate has adverse consequences for the community's health care institutions and providers. These consequences reduce access to clinic-based primary care, specialty services, and hospital-based care, particularly emergency medical services and trauma care.

2. Research is needed to more clearly define the size, strength, and scope of adverse community effects that are plausible consequences of uninsurance. These include potentially deleterious effects on access to primary and preventive health care, specialty care, the underlying social and economic vitality of communities, public health capacity, and overall population health.

What we don't know *can* hurt us. There is much that is not understood about the relationships between health services delivery and financing mechanisms and even less about how the current structure and performance of the American health care enterprise affect communities' economies and the quality of social and political life in this country. Because policy makers and researchers have not asked or examined these questions through comprehensive and systematic research and analysis, there is a limited body of evidence of mixed quality on community effects.

The Committee believes, however, that it is both mistaken and dangerous to assume that the prevalence of uninsurance in the United States harms only those who are uninsured. It calls for further research to examine the effects of uninsurance at the community level but nonetheless believes there is sufficient evidence to justify the adoption of policies to address the lack of health insurance in the nation (Corrigan et al., 2002). Rather, the call for more research is to say that, as long as we as a nation tolerate the status quo, we should more fully understand the implications and consequences of our stalemated national health policy.

1

Introduction

In *A Shared Destiny: Community Effects of Uninsurance*, the fourth report of the Institute of Medicine (IOM) Committee on the Consequences of Uninsurance, the Committee expands its focus from the adverse impacts of lack of health coverage on uninsured individuals and their families to examine the potential and likely indirect effects of the failure to insure all on their community. The Committee hypothesizes that the community overall experiences these effects largely through the problems that uninsurance poses for local health care institutions and services. In its phased study of the widespread and persistent lack of health insurance in the United States, the Committee has tried to convey the interrelated and systemic nature of the problems related to uninsurance. That perspective is especially important for this report, in which the Committee develops a series of hypotheses about community effects, assesses the evidence pertaining to these hypotheses, and proposes a research agenda to better document and understand those effects that cannot now be quantified or are poorly documented.

The towns, cities, and rural areas of the United States are home to a substantial number of uninsured persons. In 2000, an estimated 58 million people lived in families in which at least one member was uninsured (IOM, 2002b). In 2001, approximately 41 million Americans lacked health insurance coverage (Mills, 2002). The proportion of uninsured Americans rose steadily between the late 1970s and the late 1990s (IOM, 2001a). After a slight dip in 1999 and 2000, the national uninsured rate and number are increasing once again, with one out of six (16.5 percent) of those under age 65 lacking health care coverage.

The South and West, the most populous regions in the United States, are home to the greatest numbers of uninsured persons (an estimated 16.6 million and 11.2 million, respectively) (Mills, 2002; all numbers are for persons under 65 years old and for the year 2001). The West South Central, Pacific, and Mountain regions, with uninsured rates of 24.3 percent, 19.7 percent, and 18.6 percent, respectively, have uninsured rates well above the national average (16.5 percent). The states with the highest number of uninsured persons tend to be those with the largest populations, including California (6.7 million uninsured), Texas (4.9 million), New York (2.9 million), and Florida (2.8 million). Uninsured rates show less of a direct relationship with population size; the border state of New Mexico, for example, is home to just 1 percent of the uninsured population nationally (an estimated 400,000 uninsured persons) but has one of the highest uninsured rates (23.9 percent) of all the states. Reflecting the predominantly urban location of the U.S. population, 82 percent of uninsured persons live in urban areas. However, urban and rural (non-urban) residents are about equally likely to be uninsured (rates of 16.5 percent and 16.8 percent, respectively). See Tables C.1, C.2, and C.3 for more information about the regional distribution of the uninsured population.

Coverage Matters: Insurance and Health Care, the Committee's first report, shows that uninsured persons in the United States are predominantly workers or members of families in which someone had paid employment. It finds that many Americans lacked coverage because their employers did not offer it and workers were unable to afford policies without an employer contribution. *Coverage Matters* also identifies the unstable nature of health insurance coverage for Americans younger than 65—those with coverage today could lose it tomorrow for any number of reasons. However, at age 65, virtually everyone becomes permanently entitled to Medicare coverage.

The second report, *Care Without Coverage: Too Little, Too Late,* compares health outcomes for insured and uninsured adults, concluding that the lack of health insurance results in consistently worse health outcomes, including premature death, for adults. These poor outcomes result from deficits in access, use, and quality of health care across the spectrum of preventive, acute, and chronic care services.

Health Insurance Is a Family Matter, the Committee's third report, breaks new ground in examining the effects of a lack of coverage by anyone in a family on the family as a whole and the implications for children's health when they or their parents do not have coverage. The Committee concludes in its third report that the health, emotional well-being, and financial stability of families are at risk when even one member is uninsured. Thus, at a time when an estimated 38 million Americans lacked coverage (2000), another 20 million insured family members shared the financial risk and threats to peace of mind and even to their own health.

The lack of health insurance coverage within a population is frequently understood as a problem only for those who are immediately affected, namely, those without coverage and their families. *A Shared Destiny* explores whether and how many of us can be affected by the stark differences in financial access and resources available to those who have and those who don't have health insurance. Our health care institutions and the vitality of our neighborhoods, cities, towns, and rural communities can be imperiled by the lack of financing for and access to health services for some of us. Our major medical institutions of care and healing are not, nor should they be, gated communities. They should serve everyone.

The provision of health insurance is both a private and a public undertaking. Fully 25 percent of Americans have insurance through public programs.[1] More than three-fifths of the population is covered by employment-based health plans (Mills, 2002). Despite the characterization of Americans as proudly self-reliant and individualistic, we nonetheless participate in each other's fate in sickness and in health. This report contributes to our understanding of how this sharing occurs.

A SYSTEMS APPROACH TO THE PROBLEMS OF UNINSURANCE

Statements of value and purpose articulated by the IOM Committee on the Quality of Health Care in America in *Crossing the Quality Chasm* provide a unifying focus for this report (IOM, 2001b, pp. 1,6):

> Americans should be able to count on receiving care that meets their needs and is based on the best scientific knowledge … the single, overarching purpose of the American health care system as a whole … is to continually reduce the burden of illness, injury and disability, and to improve the health and functioning of the people of the United States.

These goals for the nation's health care system are not conditioned on having health insurance; *all* Americans should be able to receive needed and effective care. *Care Without Coverage* and *Health Insurance Is a Family Matter* have documented the lesser effectiveness of health care received by uninsured persons, notably for those with chronic conditions, which are a major priority for quality improvement efforts. Yet uninsured populations undermine health systems' quality improvement for reasons beyond the kind of care that uninsured persons themselves receive. To the extent that health care institutions have uncompensated care burdens, investments in state-of-the-art information technology, creating multi-disciplinary care teams, and other aspects of the health services infrastructure are less feasible (IOM, 2001b).

The importance of understanding the health care enterprise as a complex system is a contribution of the recent national movement to improve the quality and safety of health care services. This joint public–private effort has focused on increasing the reliability of ever more complex medical care and broadening the understanding of effective health care interventions to encompass the patient or consumer at the center, teams of professionals, and community-based health-related activities.

---

[1]This includes 11 percent of the U.S. population that has both public and private health insurance, for example, Medicare plus a private supplemental insurance policy (Mills, 2002).

The Institute of Medicine's recent work in quality of care—*Primary Care: America's Health in a New Era* (Donaldson et al. 1996), *To Err Is Human* (Kohn et al., 1999), *Crossing the Quality Chasm* (IOM, 2001b), and *Envisioning the National Health Care Quality Report* (Hurtado et al., 2001)—contribute comprehensive and system-focused visions of the proper and attainable goals of the American health care enterprise. These reports also propose strategies for achieving such goals. Likewise, *Unequal Treatment: Confronting Racial and Ethnic Disparities in Health Care* (Smedley et al., 2002) and a related report, *Guidance for the National Healthcare Disparities Report* (Swift, 2002) examines systemic biases and inequities in health services delivery and proposed strategies and diagnostic tools to remedy them. The capacity and performance of the nation's public health infrastructure have also been the subject of a comprehensive assessment and prescription for improvement in *The Future of the Public's Health in the 21st Century* (IOM, forthcoming 2003).

A *Shared Destiny* extends these diagnoses of systemic weaknesses and opportunities for improvements in American health care to consider the effects of uninsurance and of the current strategies for addressing it. These factors present both challenges to the quality and equity of health care and opportunities to improve the sector's performance for all Americans.

This report makes three contributions that advance the understanding of health insurance dynamics at the population level. First, it identifies what is known and assesses the strength of evidence about possible health, institutional, and economic consequences of sizable uninsured populations for communities. Meeting this first objective engaged a second, more ambitious task, namely, to articulate a new analytic framework that traces plausible causal pathways from uninsurance to a number of effects on population groups or communities. This conceptual work allows the Committee to identify probable steps involved in moving from a hypothesized causal factor, such as a metropolitan area's higher-than-average uninsured rate, to effects such as changes in the area's health services capacity. Questions that emerge from such an examination include the following:

- Which services and facilities do those who have health insurance and those without it share, and how does the degree of integration or segregation of these two populations within particular institutions affect health care service quality and capacity throughout the community?
- Who ultimately pays for the care that uninsured Americans receive?
- How and to what extent are health care facilities and, more broadly, civic institutions and community economic development affected by the presence of a sizable uninsured population?
- How does the health status and access to health services of uninsured community residents affect the health and access of others within the same community?

The Committee hypothesizes that indirect and sometimes obscure "spillover" or "secondhand" effects of uninsurance on the community at large can be considerable. These spillover effects have not been fully articulated or well documented in studies and evaluations, however. Many of these questions about community-level impacts of uninsurance cannot be answered satisfactorily with currently available statistical information and studies. Hence, the third contribution of this report is to propose an agenda for additional conceptual and empirical research that would examine community-level effects of uninsurance more directly and thoroughly.

DEFINITION OF "COMMUNITY"

Just which collective of people is considered to be a community depends on what activities or interests are at issue. In health policy analysis, the term "community" has evoked a variety of social, political, and economic concerns that have changed over time (Schlesinger, 1997; Ricketts, 2002). Communities may be defined broadly along a number of dimensions, alone or in combination:

- Geographically (in terms of patterns of settlement)
- Politically (in terms of government units or jurisdictions)
- Socially (in terms of schools, clubs, voluntary associations)
- Economically (in terms of market or health services areas)
- Culturally and historically (in terms of shared identities or interests)

The size of an area defined as a community, and what characteristics are taken into consideration in this definition, ideally are related to the questions of concern and influence the ability to observe the processes and outcomes hypothesized to be taking place (Diez-Roux, 2001). The units in which data about health care utilization, health status, and health resources are collected and reported shape the Committee's approach to assessing community effects. In practical terms, the particular unit of analysis specified as a community also reflects issues of data availability. Throughout this report, the actual unit of analysis is noted in discussing the results and findings of specific studies.

For the purposes of this report, the Committee defines a community as a group of people that (1) lives in a particular geographic area and (2) has access to a specific set of health resources for which there are data about financial and health-related outcomes. Most statistical information is collected and organized around politically and economically defined communities that are also geographically distinct, for example, single political jurisdictions (cities, counties, states) or the catchment area of a hospital. Consequently, much of the information available about uninsured people is aggregated into these units of analysis. In addition, like many forms of services, health care is delivered and received in person; thus, geographically defined communities are the predominant unit of analysis in this report.

Because of the variation in existing evidence regarding community effects, the Committee uses the term community in this report to refer to locations as small as neighborhoods and as large as states. How expansive a community is specified to be depends partly on the patterns of social and economic interaction that are being analyzed and also on population density. For example, the community that shares primary care resources such as physician practices and clinics may be relatively small and local, while the community sharing an advanced trauma care facility may encompass an entire metropolitan area and adjacent rural counties.

CONCEPTUALIZING COMMUNITY EFFECTS OF UNINSURANCE

Although we often think of the impact of an injury in very personal terms, an injury to one may also be an injury to all. Consider the following examples. When a local hospital can no longer absorb the costs of serving uninsured patients in need of care and cuts back on staffed inpatient beds as a result, all members of the community served by the hospital are likely to experience reduced access to care. The effects do not stop there. In an effort to keep beds staffed, the hospital may contain costs by cutting staff in other departments, or, if the hospital cuts back its nursing staff, patient safety and the quality of care would be reduced for all patients. Alternatively, the hospital may turn to local, state, or federal governments for revenue to offset the costs of caring for uninsured persons, thereby increasing the tax burden on all residents or reducing other public services. Also, if public health department funds are diverted from communicable disease control programs to support hospital services for medically indigent residents, the health of all community members is put at risk. As these scenarios illustrate, the effects of uninsurance can be wide-ranging and significant.

The experiences of uninsured individuals and of families *within* a community influence the collective and aggregate effects of uninsurance *on* their community. These collective and aggregate effects are the subject of this report. This section first illustrates how these collective and aggregate effects can be distinguished from individual and family effects and presents the broader conceptual framework in which this report's analysis is grounded. The next section discusses research methods used in this report, and the section following that sets out the working hypotheses about specific community effects that guided the Committee's investigation.

The Committee's analysis in each of its reports has been based on a general framework presented in *Coverage Matters.*[2] This framework links individual and collective factors, including health status, financial resources, and health services capacity to the use of health care services and ultimately to a variety of health-related and financial outcomes. These include aggregate community characteristics

---

[2]The precursors of this model can be found in Andersen and Aday (1978) and Andersen and Davidson (2001).

such as population health and uninsured rate, as well as ecological characteristics such as economic vitality and social cohesion, measures that are not reducible to individuals' characteristics. Factors at both the individual and the community levels determine the extent and quality of individuals' access to health care (Andersen et al., 2002). Appendix A depicts both the general conceptual framework and the Committee's modification of it to guide the analysis in this report.

The causal pathways hypothesized for community effects incorporate the experiences of uninsured individuals and families as well as the performance of health care institutions and providers. The Committee's conceptual framework for hypothesizing about pathways through which community effects are exerted and the breadth and scope of community effects builds selectively on a widely used behavioral model of access to health services (Andersen, 1995; Andersen and Davidson, 2001; see Figure 1.1).

The conceptual framework focuses primarily on the economic, financial, and coverage-related factors that facilitate or impede access to health services. The health, social, and economic consequences of delayed or forgone health care for uninsured individuals and families (as depicted in the two boxes labeled "adverse health outcomes for uninsured" and "adverse economic effects") can result in a greater burden of disease and disability for the community overall as well as erosion of the capacity for timely and appropriate health services delivery in the community. To the extent that uninsured individuals and their families obtain health services, the uncompensated care burden on local providers and facilities (as depicted in the box labeled "lower revenues for providers and facilities") serves as another pathway to community effects because it leads to (1) pressures to increase public spending to subsidize care for uninsured persons, (2) increased costs for health care and for health insurance, and (3) financially destabilized local health services. As a result, *all* members of the community may potentially experience diminished access to and quality of health services, as well as a greater burden of disease and disability. These hypothesized pathways and effects will be discussed in greater depth in the sections that follow; see Appendix A for a more detailed discussion of the conceptual framework.

The Committee's definitions of health insurance and uninsured status are consistent with those adopted in its previous reports. Health insurance is defined by the Committee as financial coverage for basic hospital and ambulatory care services provided through employment-based indemnity, service-benefit, or managed care plans; individually purchased health insurance policies; public programs such as Medicare, Medicaid, and the State Children's Health Insurance Program, and other state-sponsored health plans for specified populations. Uninsured refers to persons without any form of public or private coverage for hospital and outpatient care for any length of time. The Committee does not attempt to address the condition of underinsurance, by which is meant individuals or families whose health insurance policy or benefits plan offers less than adequate coverage. The problems faced by the underinsured are in some respects similar to those faced by the uninsured, although they are generally less severe. Uninsurance and underin-

22

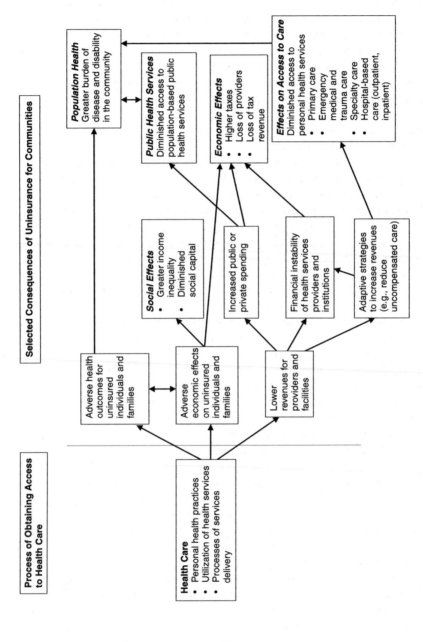

FIGURE 1.1 A conceptual framework for community effects.

surance, however, involve distinctly different policy issues, and the strategies for addressing them may differ. Throughout the Committee's series of reports, the main focus is on persons with no health insurance and thus no assistance in paying for health care beyond what is available through charity and safety net arrangements.

This report looks at what happens, and what reasonably may be expected to happen, to a community when one community-level variable, namely, the local uninsured rate, is relatively high or on the rise. Of course, the uninsured rate within a community is closely related to a number of other aggregate characteristics that affect health or economic outcomes such as educational attainment, family income, and industrial composition (Shi, 2000, 2001; IOM, 2001a). Studies that attempt to measure the impact of uninsurance on community-level outcomes face the challenge of factoring out or analytically accounting for these covariates of health insurances that can be expected to affect the outcomes of interest. Throughout this report, the extent and nature of any analytic controls for covarying community characteristics are included in the descriptions of studies cited.

Figure 1.2 graphically depicts the overlap and interplay of individual characteristics, including health insurance status, with community-level factors, including the local uninsured rate, with another factor, the quality of the health care system, to determine individual and population-wide access to appropriate health care and other health outcomes. Insurance status functions as both a community-level and an individual-level characteristic that influences receipt of appropriate care in conjunction with characteristics of the health care system. The shaded portion of the figure, where all three spheres overlap, represents individual and aggregate population outcomes for a particular health condition. As depicted in this diagram, the outcome at the individual level is affected not only by the individual's own features but also by those of the community collectively. The outcome at the population level is more than the summation of individuals' independent experiences; it includes the effect of community factors such as the local uninsured rate.

Figure 1.3 presents two graphs for comparison to illustrate the phenomenon of a community-level effect of the local uninsured rate on individuals' access to care, over and above the effect of personal health insurance status. This pair of diagrams simplifies what is a much more complicated set of relationships among multiple individual and community factors that affect measures of access such as a physician visit within the year (e.g., those shown in Figure 1.2), but its simplicity allows for a clearer depiction of the hypothesized community-level effect. Graphs A and B each chart the percentage of two distinct population groups, Insured and Uninsured, that have a physician visit within a year (an outcome variable) against the local uninsured rate for a number of different communities (e.g., metropolitan areas). In both graphs, Insured populations are more likely to have had a physician visit than are Uninsured populations. Graph A represents the case in which there is *no* community effect on this outcome variable (a relatively crude measure of access to health care) because the lines plotted are parallel to the horizontal axis.

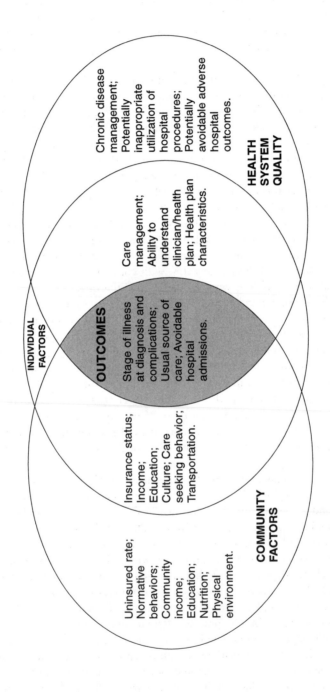

FIGURE 1.2 Relationship among individual factors, community factors, and health system quality as affecting health outcomes.
SOURCE: Adapted from Lurie 2002.

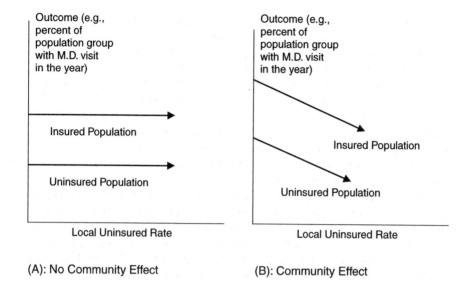

FIGURE 1.3 Community effects diagram.

The outcome for each group, Insured and Uninsured, remains constant as the local uninsured rate increases. Graph B represents the case in which there *is* a community effect on the outcome variable because, as the local uninsured rate increases, the percentage of both the Insured and the Uninsured with a physician visit within a year decreases, indicated by the downward-sloping line.

METHODS

Despite the acknowledged importance of community effects of uninsurance, they have rarely been studied directly. As a result, the research literature is slim on some topics and non-existent on others, making a systematic literature review impractical for the purposes of this report. Instead, the Committee has chosen to work from its conceptual framework, discussed above, modified from the framework used for the series of reports and first presented in *Coverage Matters*.

Search terms for use with PubMed were identified for the topics described in a background paper prepared for the Committee (Needleman, 2000) and articles were gathered for the years from 1985 onward, with reference articles and books included from earlier years. In addition to the bibliography collected for and cited in the Committee's previous three reports, a non-systematic literature review was conducted, using the following terms, singly and in combination: academic medical centers; charity care; community health centers; cost control; cost-shifting; costs and cost analysis; crowding; economic development; economics, hospital; emergency medical services; health facility merger; hospitals, urban; managed care; Medicaid; medical indigency; primary care; public assistance; public hospitals; rural health services; rural population; social capital; state government; trauma centers; uncompensated care. In addition, copies of relevant studies were collected from foundation, research center, and trade association websites.

For historical framing of current issues, interpretive weight was given to publications covering the period from the late 1970s through the mid-1990s. For interpretation of current issues, more interpretive weight was given to publications covering the period since the mid-1990s, given the changes in the organization and financing of health services delivery, for example, the advent of Medicare prospective payment in the early 1980s and the spread of state Medicaid managed care contracting in the early 1990s.

The variation in state and local uninsured rates offers one of the best opportunities to detect the effects of uninsurance on community health care services, institutions, and population health. The Committee attempts to identify the nature, size, and significance of these community effects by comparing geographically defined communities in which differing proportions of the population lack health insurance, focusing in particular on areas (municipalities, metropolitan areas, rural counties, states, and regions) that have disproportionately large uninsured populations. Because the impacts on rural communities are likely to differ from those in urban areas, rural areas are examined separately and in some detail throughout the report. In addition, states and larger geographic regions exhibit different patterns of health insurance coverage and uninsurance, with some states having relatively uniform uninsured rates throughout and others encompassing communities and substate areas with highly disparate uninsured rates. Appendix B describes and provides examples of distinctive patterns of uninsurance within and among states across the country.

The Committee has described and noted the limitations of the major national databases and surveys that provide information about health insurance coverage, health care expenditures, service utilization, and access to health care in its previous three reports. The reader is referred to those sources, particularly *Coverage Matters*, Appendix B (IOM, 2001a), and *Care Without Coverage*, Chapter 2 (IOM, 2002a), for reviews of the data sets that are the basis for much of the national-level research reported in this report. When particular studies are cited in this report, the accompanying discussion notes the relevant features and limitations of the data and methodology used.

WORKING HYPOTHESES ABOUT COMMUNITY EFFECTS

According to the Committee's conceptual framework (Figure 1.1), the components and users of the health care system are interrelated, with the process of health care influenced by individual, family, and community-level resources, characteristics, and needs and with feedback or adaptation as part of this process. On the basis of this framework, the Committee hypothesizes that a community with both insured and uninsured residents—that is to say, all American communities—is likely to be affected by the incomplete coverage status and diminished access to health care experienced by its uninsured population. In other words, uninsurance is likely to have spillover effects on the lives of people with insurance as well as those without it. For example, low- to moderate-income residents in cities with a higher-than-average uninsured rate report having less access to health services, compared to residents in cities with a lower-than-average uninsured rate (Brown et al., 2000; Andersen et al., 2002; see discussion in Chapter 2). At the same time, some members of a single community and some communities overall may be less subject to spillover effects from uninsured populations than others are. In the case of community-wide access to care cited above, it is *low-income* residents, not higher-income residents, whose access to care is affected by high community uninsured rates.

This section sets out the working hypotheses that motivate the lines of investigation the Committee pursued to determine whether and how communities as a whole are affected by the presence of substantial uninsurance among their populace. In each chapter that follows, the Committee specifies the strength and quality of the evidentiary base upon which its findings are drawn. Where there are few or no data or evidence on which to base conclusions about questions central to the Committee's hypothesis, questions meriting further research are proposed.

Availability of Health Care Services in the Community

How does uninsurance within a community affect the availability of local health services? As depicted in Figure 1.1, the Committee hypothesizes that when faced with uninsured persons who need care, providers such as physician practices, hospitals, clinics, health departments, and the state and local governments that fund and operate facilities take measures to increase revenues from other sources and to contain their costs in order to balance the effects of uncompensated care. In the case of privately sponsored providers, they may adopt management strategies that reduce their exposure to uncompensated care costs. Public and private providers have similar options. They may

- restrict access to or the general availability of health services for uninsured persons, leaving them to go elsewhere for care or to forgo care;
- raise the funds necessary to cover the uncompensated care costs incurred by uninsured patients (by means of taxes, higher prices charged to those who do pay for services, or philanthropy);
- reduce costs significantly, which can affect access (e.g., fewer hours of service), quality, or safety; or
- provide no care at all to anyone (e.g., close the service).

Any community resident may experience the results of decisions made about care for those without health insurance when they encounter the local public health infrastructure, need emergency medical services, seek primary or specialized health care, or use their local hospital for outpatient or inpatient care.

Especially for institutions that serve a high proportion of uninsured patients such as public hospitals, community health centers, and some academic health centers, a large or growing number of uninsured persons seeking health care may destabilize them financially and "tip" a hospital or clinic's financial margins from positive to negative. A health care provider's efforts to avoid this tipping or to respond in ways that protect the provider's financial viability may trigger a series of events, for example, a reduction in hours that services are available or in the number of staff or active beds (which can lead to increased waiting times or reduced responsiveness to patients). To protect their financial viability, health care providers might also eliminate certain services or close the practice or facility. These events may result in the loss of access to care or lesser quality care.

Primary Care

Does a high or increasing demand for uncompensated care by uninsured patients adversely affect the economic viability of ambulatory care clinics and of private physician practices or lessen the availability of primary care in a community? The Committee hypothesizes that it does. Community health centers and other nonprofit clinics depend on public subsidies as well as patient revenues, and many already are providing services at their capacity. Without new funds to support their operations, they may not be able to expand to serve new clients (Cunningham, 1996; McAlearney, 2002). In areas experiencing increasing or high uninsured rates, physicians may refuse to accept new patients who are uninsured or publicly insured (to limit their financial losses), decline to establish a practice in an area, or decide to leave the area, resulting in less availability of services for all community residents.

Emergency Medical Services

Do large numbers of uninsured patients within a community increase utilization of local hospital emergency departments? Does a heavy uninsured patient load lead hospitals to cut back on emergency and trauma services? The Committee hypothesizes that relatively high or increasing local uninsured rates could result in greater emergency department (ED) utilization and overcrowding. However, hospital ED overcrowding is also affected by a number of other factors (including, for example, the availability of staffed inpatient beds in the same hospital and fewer restrictions on the use of ED services by managed care plans), which makes it difficult to tease out any contribution that the use of EDs by those without insurance makes to overcrowding. Evidence from the 1980s suggests that some of the closings of hospital trauma services may be attributable to a high uncompensated care burden, in turn associated with a heavy uninsured patient load (Dailey et al., 1992; Fleming et al., 1992).

Specialty Services[3]

Do high uninsured rates jeopardize the availability of specialty services from physicians, clinics, and hospitals? The Committee hypothesizes that relatively high uninsured rates discourage the provision of specialty care in a community. In the 1980s, for-profit hospitals were less likely to offer unprofitable services viewed as community benefits, such as emergency and trauma services, and certain kinds of specialty care, such as burn units or pediatric intensive care, that are disproportionately used by uninsured patients and are also less likely to be reimbursed fully by insurers (Gray, 1986; Needleman, 1999). Similar strains on hospitals that disproportionately serve uninsured patients may adversely affect access to care for all community residents, since these hospitals, which are often public facilities or academic health centers, are more likely than other facilities to provide health professions training and specialty services (burn, pediatric neonatal intensive care, trauma, psychiatry, AIDS care). Many of these highly specialized services and community resources are particularly crucial when natural or man-made disasters strike and could be considered an aspect of "homeland security."

Hospital Outpatient and Inpatient Care

How are hospital outpatient services and inpatient care affected by the level of uninsurance within the community? The Committee hypothesizes that because hospitals are the locus of much of the more costly care provided to uninsured Americans, hospitals in communities with relatively high uninsured rates would show evidence of financial stress and fewer services as a result. Hospitals are particularly likely to be faced with the cumulative effects of inadequate care for chronic conditions, exacerbated acute illnesses, and delayed treatment among uninsured patients (IOM, 2002a). Many hospitals operate with narrow financial margins that leave little room to subsidize the uncompensated care associated with treating uninsured patients. A high uninsured rate over time or an increase in the number of uninsured patients is likely to reduce a hospital's financial margin or even result in operating losses. Without a source of public or private funds to cover the costs of uncompensated care, hospitals may trim the hours and availability of services, particularly of its emergency department, obtain private capital through conversion from public to private status (with the potential loss of access to care previously guaranteed at a public facility), or close some or all of their operations entirely, leaving all community residents to seek services elsewhere.

---

[3]Specialty services are defined as services other than primary care, general internal medicine, pediatrics, gerontology, obstetrics, and gynecology. Emergency medicine, radiology, neurology, orthopedics, and surgery are considered types of specialty services.

Economic Consequences

Taxation and Spending Implications for Localities, States, and the Nation

How does the uncompensated care provided to uninsured persons affect public revenues and spending? As depicted in Figure 1.1, the Committee hypothesizes that state and local tax rates are affected by the demands for uncompensated care within these jurisdictions. Because subsidized and free care is supported by government and philanthropic funds as well as by revenues generated from insured patients, economic effects on communities with relatively high uninsured rates may include higher taxes, fewer philanthropic dollars available for other purposes, and higher costs for health services. In some states, tobacco settlement dollars have been devoted to improving access to care for uninsured persons, providing a new revenue stream to subsidize uncompensated care and delaying the need to limit services if other revenues, such as increased taxes, are not forthcoming. However, tobacco settlement monies need not be spent on health programs, and states are increasingly using these funds for other purposes, including covering general budget deficits (Dixon and Cox, 2002).

Economic Base

If physicians, clinics, or hospitals cut their services or close their doors for reasons related to a high or growing uninsured rate, would employees in the health and local service sectors lose their jobs and is the local economy affected as a result? The Committee hypothesizes that local economies are affected by reductions in health services capacity and that such impacts are more easily documented in rural than in urban communities. In rural areas, the loss of local health professionals and jobs may mean less income generated and spent locally, with less tax revenue available for the entire range of public endeavors including education, social services, and health care. In urban areas, where there are more options for health services and a greater number of employers, the relationship between uninsurance and the local economy is likely to be mediated by many other factors and thus be harder to detect.

Community Health

How does the local or state uninsured rate affect the health of the whole population? As depicted in Figure 1.1, the Committee hypothesizes that communities with relatively high uninsured rates have worse overall population health than those with relatively low uninsured rates. Further, it hypothesizes that these differences can be attributed not only to the worse health status of uninsured persons within the population but also to spillover effects of uninsured populations on those with health insurance. Measures of population health that might be affected in this way include general health status, rates of communicable disease, disability rates, and hospitalizations for conditions amenable to treatment on an ambulatory basis.

A high or rising uninsured rate within a community may result in the reallocation of public funds and staff resources away from public health programs that serve all members of the community and toward direct services delivery urgently needed by low-income uninsured persons (IOM, 1988, forthcoming 2003). This is especially likely if there is little political support for raising state or local tax revenues to support direct services delivery and if other revenue sources (e.g., tobacco settlement monies) are not available.

The redeployment of public health agency resources away from population health activities to provide personal health care services to uninsured residents, along with the general underutilization of and limited access to care by uninsured members of the community can fuel the spread of disease and undermine communicable disease control efforts (e.g., tuberculosis, sexually transmitted diseases); prevention activities, such as immunization programs and antismoking educational campaigns; health protection activities such as food safety inspections and pollution control; and the increasingly essential surveillance of unusual disease outbreaks that can indicate the possibility of bioterrorism.

LIMITATIONS OF THIS STUDY

Identifying and interpreting potential community effects poses several analytical challenges. As noted above, many factors are correlated with both individual and community-level health insurance status (e.g., educational attainment, income, and job type). In addition, the relationships between a community's attributes (e.g., median educational attainment, income, employment opportunities) and the effects of uninsurance (e.g., population health status) are interdependent. Because the studies reviewed in this report are observational and (for the most part) cross-sectional in design, it is more difficult to infer causal relationships than to demonstrate statistical associations among these various factors. Throughout the report, the kinds of analytic controls and limits on interpretation that apply to cited studies are noted in the discussion.

Another important issue in considering the evidence base is that information about impacts of uninsurance on the community as a whole is often inferred rather than observed directly. For example, the inverse relationship between the funding of public health activities in relation to state and local health departments' provision of personal health services has been documented over several decades (IOM, 1988, forthcoming 2003; Fairbrother et al., 2000), but the extent of the provision of uncompensated care to medically indigent residents has not necessarily been analyzed as a function of local uninsured rates. It may take several logical steps or links to make a connection between the hypothesized cause and effects. One objective of this report is to describe these steps and point out the linkages that can be made with existing data and research.

The lack of empirically validated measures by which community-level attributes, such as the adequacy of specialty care resources within a neighborhood, can be identified also limits the characterization and recognition of effects of uninsurance on communities (Andersen et al., 2002). While individuals' demographic, social, economic, and health characteristics are commonly collected and *aggregated* for population-level analyses (e.g., rates of uninsurance or immunization), *ecological* variables, which are population-level characteristics that are not created by aggregation of individual-level measures, are much less frequently used in health services research (Sampson and Morenoff, 2000; Diez-Roux, 2001). One example of such an ecological variable would be the presence or absence of a trauma care center within a city to serve its residents. Another quite different ecological measure would be the degree of mutual trust among the city's residents, based on attitudinal surveys.

Assessing community-level impacts of uninsured populations is made more difficult by ongoing and rapid changes in the organization and financing of health services. Not only do changes in a community's uninsured rate affect the financial margins of community hospitals, but so do changes in Medicare payment policy and in the relative bargaining power of private insurers and health care institutions. Finally, institutional and program data often are not available for analysis until several years later, whereas economic and public policy environments are in constant flux. This dynamic environment makes it difficult to describe today's situation with yesterday's statistics, because policies, markets, and populations have changed in the interval.

Recognizing these limitations, the Committee nonetheless believes that the picture of community-level impacts of uninsured populations provided by this report, although tentative in some respects, is an important starting point for developing more definitive evidence in the future. The Committee also believes that the picture is clear enough to inform some policy choices now.

ORGANIZATION OF THE REPORT

This report provides a new framework for thinking about potential community effects of uninsurance. It assesses the evidence that exists and proposes the research that would be needed to determine the existence and magnitude of other population effects. In Chapter 2, the Committee describes the context for its exploration of potential community effects in the history and present functioning of health care system financing and care for uninsured persons. It presents the public policies and fiscal structures that support the care of uninsured Americans as they have evolved to their current form within the larger context of American health care financing. Chapters 3, 4, and 5 present the Committee's findings. Chapter 3 examines how the availability of health care for all members of a community is affected by local levels of uninsurance. The results of original analyses of hospital services and financial margins as affected by local uninsured rates are presented here. Chapters 4 and 5 discuss the hypothesized mechanisms for economic impacts on communities and explore likely effects on the health of the community. A sixth and final chapter presents the Committee's findings and conclusions and consolidates the data needs and research questions included in the earlier chapters into a research agenda.

2

Context for Community Effects: Uninsurance and the Financing and Delivery of Health Services

There is no guarantee that uninsured persons will be able to obtain the health care that they need and no guarantee that if they do get care, it will be adequate or affordable. Responsibility for financing and providing health care to uninsured persons in the United States is fragmented and ill-defined, to the extent that this responsibility exists at all. Many of the Committee's hypothesized effects of uninsurance on communities stem from the structure of health care finance and the patterns of service provision for insured and uninsured Americans that have emerged over the past half-century. The current structure of safety net and non-safety net arrangements, along with the mix of public and private funding sources, was not envisioned or designed as an integrated system; rather, it has resulted from the aggregation, over time, of multiple initiatives and developments in both the private and the public sectors. Because the organization and delivery of care are closely linked to health insurance, the health care needs of persons who lack health insurance have been of secondary interest, often only as afterthoughts in the development of public policy.

In this chapter, the Committee describes the ad hoc nature of health care financing and services for the more than 41 million uninsured Americans. This information is drawn from both descriptive and analytic, empirical research sources. It frames the discussions in subsequent chapters of pathways through which community uninsurance is hypothesized to affect health care institutions, local economies, and population health. The chapter also documents the magnitude and distribution among providers of uncompensated care to the uninsured and considers who, if anyone, is responsible for providing that care.

The chapter is divided into four sections. The first section gives a historical account of the development of the current programs and arrangements for financing and providing health care to those without the means to pay (the "medically indigent"), including people without health insurance. The second and third sections describe the current mix of public and private financing and delivery arrangements involved in caring for uninsured persons, including the roles of government, health care institutions and professionals, and philanthropies and the issue of shifting costs to, or getting subsidies from, private payers (insurers and employers). The fourth section is a summary of what is known and what remains to be learned about how the present arrangements for financing and providing health care generally, and uninsured care in particular, have made uninsurance a critical and destabilizing factor in local health care markets and community economies today. Readers who are familiar with this historical background and policy context may want to turn immediately to the fourth section, which identifies research questions and data needs and then to Chapters 3 through 6, which provide the Committee's findings and conclusions regarding community effects.

HISTORICAL AND ORGANIZATIONAL CONTEXT OF HEALTH CARE FOR UNINSURED AMERICANS

Over the past 25 years, federal and state policies to control health care costs and an increasingly competitive private market for health care services and coverage have constrained public payer and commercial reimbursement rates for care. As a result, there has been an erosion of the previous level of public support and private cross-subsidy for the uncompensated care costs associated with providing health services to uninsured persons. The effects of this erosion have been felt more strongly in communities with large or growing uninsured populations and by providers (e.g., public hospitals) that serve a high number or proportion of uninsured persons.

As health insurance has become more central both as a means to access care and to the support of health care providers and institutions, the presence of sizable uninsured populations in communities has become a common explanation for, or the most obvious proximal cause of, health system failings and inefficiencies. Understanding why and how this has happened requires some appreciation of the development of the present public and private structures for financing health services. This historical context also aids an objective appraisal of evidence as to what health system and community-wide effects can validly be attributed to local uninsured rates rather than to other aspects of the overall structure of health care finance.

The public–private amalgam of health insurance mechanisms and the mixed delivery system of private not-for-profit, private for-profit, and public health care institutions and services are a legacy of America's particular history and notions of the public good. Over the past century in the United States, the concurrent development of private and public approaches to financing health care (and the tension between them) have given shape to American health care services and institutions (Starr, 1982; Stevens, 1989).

The well-documented story of financing for hospitals illuminates the growing importance over time of health insurance as a revenue source for health care providers, the backdrop to the emergence of uninsurance as a health policy issue. Since the 1940s, hospitals have become increasingly reliant on revenues from patients to support their budgets and the financial margins on which their survival and development depend (Stevens, 1989). As health care costs have risen and coverage has become increasingly important for access to care by individuals and families, the presence of a sizable uninsured population has meant not only less access for uninsured persons but also the loss of potential revenues for health care providers. This section briefly traces the history of uninsurance in the context of changes in health care financing and delivery. The discussion is divided into three parts, following a typology proposed by Lynn Etheredge that includes an era in which health insurance became common (his era of fee-for-service reimbursement), an era of public regulation of pricing, and an era of managed care and market incentives (Etheredge, 2000).

The Rise of Health Insurance

Before the advent of Medicare and Medicaid in the mid–1960s, persons without the means to pay for their care relied for the most part on the charity of individual physicians, hospitals, and clinics in their communities. In the nineteenth century and into the early twentieth century, hospital dispensaries and public hospitals were important locations where medically indigent patients could obtain medical care, while patients with the means to hire physicians were treated in their homes. These practices reinforced a two-tier approach to medical care that was firmly established by the mid–1800s (Rosenberg, 1987).

During the first three decades of the twentieth century, profound changes in biomedical science and health professions education transformed hospitals into sites of care for middle-class persons, losing the stigma of the almshouse. The development of the new hospital and new standards of practice for providers brought higher prices for health care (Stevens, 1989). The financial consequences of paying for health care in hospitals became an issue for the middle class. In response, a variety of private health insurance plans were devised, some adapted from voluntary "sick funds" organized by immigrant benefit societies, fraternal orders, and unions. Others, such as Blue Cross, were newly created arrangements for individuals to pool their risk of incurring major hospital expenses through modest monthly payments that would relieve the individuals of further financial obligations should hospitalization be needed (Starr, 1982). Economic disparities in health services utilization among various income groups, documented by the Committee on the Costs of Medical Care in a series of studies between 1928 and 1931, were lessened by the 1950s, reflecting the expansion of health insurance more broadly among the population (Starr, 1982; Andersen and Anderson, 1999).

Enrollment in private health insurance plans expanded rapidly during the 1940s and 1950s, aided by workplace benefits and favorable federal tax treatment (Starr, 1982; Numbers, 1985; Gabel, 1999). By 1940, half of the states had enacted the legal framework for hospital service-benefit plans. These frameworks authorized state insurance commissioners to review the rates of such plans and also exempted the plans from taxes as charitable organizations. In that year, Blue Cross plans had a total enrollment of more than 6 million people and commercial insurers another 3.7 million subscribers (Starr, 1982). By the early 1950s, enrollment in commercial insurance plans and Blue Cross was comparable. In 1953, 29 percent of Americans were covered by commercial carriers, 27 percent by Blue Cross, and another 7 percent by independent plans, amounting to 63 percent of the U.S. population (Starr, 1982). Enrollment grew rapidly during the 1950s, then more slowly in the early 1960s.

As hospitals, physicians, and other providers of care during this era grew to rely on revenues generated from insurance payments, persons without insurance found themselves encountering arrangements for care that depended on public support or charitable donations to cover their unreimbursed expenses or on the ability of providers to cross-subsidize this care with revenues from insured patients. Then, as now, public and private nonprofit hospitals alike were widely considered to be obliged (ethically if not always legally) to provide community benefits, including uncompensated care to patients without the ability to pay, in exchange for their tax-supported or tax-exempt status (Clement et al., 1994; Buchmueller and Feldstein, 1996; Trocchio, 1996; Needleman, 2001). Another source of charitable care came from nonprofit community hospitals' participation in the federal Hill-Burton hospital construction program, which from the late 1940s through the early 1970s (through a successor program) provided grants, loans, and loan guarantees for building and renovation, particularly in rural areas. Support through this program entailed a legal obligation to serve all community residents without regard to ability to pay and to provide a percentage of the value of their original Hill-Burton grant as uncompensated care (Stevens, 1989).[1] A third source was federal vendor payments to the states to partially reimburse the care delivered to medically indigent persons, a predecessor to the Medicaid program (Stevens, 1989). Continued inflation in the costs of health care, however, brought new difficulties for uninsured persons in getting access to care and strained the capacity of these initiatives to accommodate growing volumes and costs of uncompensated care.

The passage of the Medicare and Medicaid programs as amendments to the

---

[1]Although bonds issued under the authorities of states and localities to finance the capital construction costs of hospitals (which may be public, nonprofit, or for-profit institutions) are federally tax exempt, this financial privilege does not entail any explicit community service obligation akin to the Hill-Burton requirement.

Social Security Act in the mid-1960s brought the promise of universal coverage and more stable financial footing for health care providers by filling significant gaps in coverage in the general population (Lewis, 1983; Stevens, 1989). Medicare and Medicaid expanded insurance-based financing for those over 65, the disabled, and single-parent families receiving income assistance. These programs preserved the ability of hospitals to charge and be reimbursed more than the direct costs involved in caring for the insured patient.[2] However, because Medicare and Medicaid reimbursed for what were called contractual allowances (negotiated rates) rather than whatever fees a hospital might choose to charge for its services, implementation of these public insurance programs brought with it new concerns on the part of private payers that they would end up cross-subsidizing the unreimbursed expenses of publicly insured patients (Stevens, 1989).

The two programs filled some but not all existing gaps in coverage, with Medicare limited to persons at least 65 years of age and with categorical and income limits for Medicaid. Medicare was a nationally uniform program administered initially by Blue Cross and modeled after commercial health insurance plans. A federal entitlement program tied to the Social Security retirement and disability insurance program, Medicare specifically addressed the failure of the private market to supply health insurance to the elderly and the impoverishment of older Americans and their families that followed hospitalizations among this population (Marmor, 2000). Medicaid was enacted in conjunction with Medicare as a joint federal–state program entitling the very poorest Americans, through their eligibility for public assistance, to a broad scope of health care services. There was and continues to be much variation from state to state in the size and characteristics of Medicaid programs. Because Medicare and Medicaid left tens of millions of Americans uninsured, hospitals, physicians, and other providers who treated uninsured patients continued to incur costs that went unreimbursed.

In addition to expanding public coverage, efforts were made to meet the needs of uninsured and other medically underserved persons through a combination of dedicated health facilities, health professions education subsidies, and a clearer articulation and enforcement of hospital's charitable obligations under Hill-Burton. Starting in the mid-1960s, the Office of Economic Opportunity awarded project grants to local community organizations to establish neighborhood health centers as innovative models of comprehensive health care delivery organized around primary care that also recognized the positive contributions of health care to local economic vitality and population health (Sardell, 1988). These neighborhood health centers eventually became community health centers. The National Health Services Corps, begun in the early 1970s, placed new physicians in medically underserved communities (Redman, 1973), and litigation in the early

---

[2]This was true for Medicare more than for Medicaid because, in 1969, Medicaid reimbursement policy was decoupled from Medicare's guarantee of "reasonable cost"-based reimbursement for hospitals and fee schedules for physicians based on "usual and customary" fees (Stevens and Stevens, 1974).

1970s led to the requirement that hospitals explicitly document fulfillment of their Hill-Burton service obligations to medically indigent patients, a significant source of free care through the 1980s, when most Hill-Burton obligations ended (Blumstein, 1986; Stevens, 1989).

Federal reimbursement and purchasing policies related to Medicare and Medicaid set the stage for the current state of health care finance and the impact of uninsured patients and uncompensated care on health care institutions (Stevens, 1989). Implementation of Medicare and Medicaid was followed by a rapid rise in health care costs, attributable to greater use of hospital services. Public and private hospitals alike scrambled to secure reimbursement from third-party payers sufficient to keep revenue ahead of expenditures. As one observer of the time period notes. (Stevens, 1989, pp. 318-319):

> Hospitals of all kinds made remarkable adjustments to changes in their environments in the years following Medicare and Medicaid. Some hospitals became aggressively profit-oriented, closing their emergency rooms and seeking maximum reimbursement rates. Others, seeking to maintain a traditional social role, became increasingly hard pressed. . . Taxing agencies, like their private counterparts, looked for ways to reduce demand for care by patients who were unable to pay. The dictates of the market seemed all-pervasive.

The influence of commercial payment, now joined by the interests of public payers, boosted the transformation of hospitals into vendors of services, with much potentially to be lost financially by caring for uninsured persons.

The role of public hospitals themselves was brought into question, as the availability of public financing through the Medicare and Medicaid program was posited to eliminate the need for tax-supported institutions (e.g., urban hospitals supported by local property taxes) to care for medically indigent persons who previously would not be seen by private hospitals or at least argue for the reallocation of public dollars for expanding coverage rather than expanding safety-net facilities (Blendon et al., 1986). Some have argued that, in fact, Medicaid actually fostered fragmentation of the health care system, for example, by not remedying existing racial segregation and segregation of the poor within health care facilities (Stevens, 1989).[3] In the 1970s, public hospitals, particularly in urban areas, found themselves with many uninsured patients and inadequate reimbursement for many services, leading to great financial stress. By the early 1970s there were also efforts to constrain the huge increase in hospital expenditures by limiting expansion of Medicaid and by price controls (Etheredge, 2000). The failure of national health insurance proposals meant that Medicaid, with its limited income eligibility standards and frequently inadequate payment rates, marked the limits of greater access for the poor (Stevens, 1989).

---

[3]In contrast to Medicaid, Medicare did promote racial integration in hospitals because, in order to participate in Medicare, hospitals had to agree to care for patients regardless of race.

Cost Controls Shape the Health Care Marketplace, 1983–1992

The federal government's reform of Medicare payments for hospital inpatient services from cost-based reimbursement to prospective payment in the early 1980s fundamentally transformed the economic incentives facing hospitals. Prospective payment was intended to standardize the payments made to hospitals all over the country so that reimbursement for an inpatient stay for a patient with a particular diagnosis (categorized under a diagnosis-related group, or DRG) would be tied to the average costs of treating that diagnosis and would be similar for every hospital. It was a response to the rapid increase in health care expenditures and resulting inflation in costs and health insurance premiums that had followed the introduction of Medicare and Medicaid 20 years earlier; Medicare and Medicaid spending increased by an average of 17 percent each year between 1965 and 1982 (Etheredge, 2000).

For hospitals, prospective payment exposed the economic differences between insured patients and uninsured patients even more starkly and heightened the importance of maximizing the hospital's revenues, and its market position, through a variety of adaptive strategies (e.g., altering how its case mix is classified to receive higher reimbursements, earlier discharge of patients, shifting from inpatient admissions to outpatient visits) (Stevens, 1989). Third-party insurers followed Medicare's lead in setting payment levels for services.

Prospective payment under Medicare had different economic impacts in different parts of the country and for different types of hospitals. Some hospitals found prospective payment to be profitable while others, for example public hospitals in large urban areas, lost revenue. With pressures on hospitals and providers to keep their costs low, the cross-subsidy or support of uncompensated care for uninsured patients became more difficult, especially for hospitals that disproportionately served the uninsured (Stevens, 1989). Public and private hospitals, and both nonprofit and for-profit hospitals, competed for patients whose health insurance coverage would yield the highest reimbursement for services and contribute the most to the facility's revenues. Access to care for vulnerable groups, including the uninsured, was diminished (Stevens, 1989).

The federal government has responded to this situation through a series of subsidies and regulations grounded in its financing programs, including the following:

• supplemental payments through the Medicare and Medicaid programs to hospitals serving a "disproportionate share" of low-income (and presumably higher-cost) program beneficiaries and for graduate medical education (these payments are discussed more fully later in this chapter) and
• prohibition of "patient dumping," the refusal to treat or the inappropriate transfer of patients unable to pay for their care, through the Emergency Medical Treatment and Labor Act (EMTALA), the federal law enacted as part of the

Consolidated Omnibus Budget Reconciliation Act of 1986 (COBRA). Structured as a hospital condition of participation in the Medicare program, EMTALA requires all hospitals with emergency departments to screen and stabilize all patients who present themselves for treatment, regardless of financial means or insurance status. Because EMTALA has not included provisions for reimbursing hospitals for the care they provide to uninsured patients, one consequence of the statute has been to make hospital emergency departments the providers of last resort and to place the departments at serious financial risk (Bitterman, 2002).

Since 1993: Hospital Margins Down, Number of Uninsured Persons Up

Prospective payment has proved unable to constrain costs in the long term (Etheredge, 2000; Aaron, 2002; Altman and Levitt, 2002). First private and then public purchasers have used managed care and selective contracting as ways to reduce their outlays for health services for their enrollees (Rundall et al., 1988; Etheredge, 2002). For example, state Medicaid programs have turned to managed care both to control costs and to provide enrollees in Medicaid with greater access to mainstream health care providers and potentially better integration of the delivery system. As Figure 2.1 shows, acute care, nonfederal hospitals saw their private payer surplus decline significantly over the course of the 1990s, from a high of nearly 12 percent in 1992 to about 5 percent in 2000. Over the same period, Medicare revenues first rose and then began to decline as a percent of Medicare costs. This contrasts with the trend for uncompensated care, which showed little change, while total margins for hospitals at first grew and then declined. There has been an erosion of the capacity of hospitals to cross-subsidize uncompensated care.

Figure 2.1 indicates a leveling off of the decline in hospital total margins, starting in 1999, reflecting a new period of growing inflation in the late 1990s in health care costs and health insurance premiums. In 2001, health care spending per capita increased by 10 percent (Strunk et al., 2002). More than half of this growth in total spending is attributable to spending on hospital inpatient and especially outpatient services. About one-third of the increasing spending on hospital services reflected higher payment rates and two-thirds reflected greater utilization of services (Strunk et al., 2002). Strunk and colleagues interpret the higher prices charged by hospitals as the outcome of hospital gains in market power (e.g., negotiating strength with health plans) and the loosening of managed care restrictions. They predict a slowing of growth in health care spending, as privately insured persons respond to increased cost-sharing (higher costs passed through their insurance plan) by dampening their use of services and as health care markets adjust to changes in managed care (Strunk et al., 2002).

Although this generation of cost-control efforts met with some success through the mid-to late 1990s, the number of uninsured persons has continued to increase, while remaining a relatively constant proportion of the general population. Health insurance coverage rates had first begun to increase substantially in

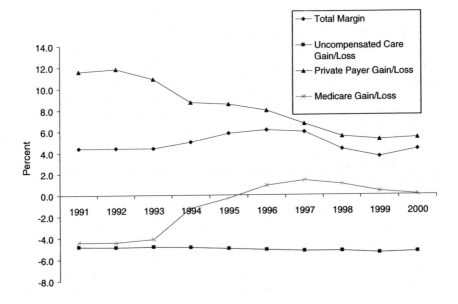

FIGURE 2.1 Hospitals' total margins, with percent gains or losses by source of payment (private payer, uncompensated care, Medicare), 1991–2000.
NOTE: Gains or losses are the difference between the cost of providing care and the payment received.
SOURCE: Adapted from Hadley and Holahan, 2003, based on MedPAC, 2002a, pp. 156, 157.

the 1940s and 1950s, with the expansion of private and public insurance programs. By 1976, the number of uninsured Americans fell to between 24 million and 25 million (approximately 12 to 13 percent of the population under age 65) before increasing once again (HIAA, 2002).

Health insurance has played key roles in facilitating access to care and in securing a revenue stream for health care providers, roles that are rooted in the historical development of a third-party financing approach to paying for personal health services in the United States. The Committee considers the effects of uninsurance upon communities as growing out of the changes over time in the relationship among health insurance coverage, access to care, and the financing of health care services.

SAFETY NET SERVICES, PROVIDERS OF LAST RESORT, AND MAINSTREAM HEALTH CARE

Finding: Although the health care institutions and practitioners that serve the larger community of insured persons provide most of the

services that uninsured persons receive, the uninsured rely disproportionately on so-called safety-net providers and arrangements for
care.

**Finding: Rural and urban areas differ in the organization and deliv-
ery of care for uninsured persons.** In urban areas, multiple tiers of
providers and services tend to segregate patients by income level
and coverage status, isolating insured patients from the experiences
of uninsured patients. In rural areas, insured and uninsured patients
may have more in common because a more limited set of providers
typically serves all community members and safety-net arrangements tend to be less formal. At minimum, mainstream health care
and safety-net arrangements are connected by their shared reliance
on public and private financing streams.

**Finding: Anticipated growth in the number and capacity of publicly
supported ambulatory care clinics (under the Consolidated Health
Centers program) is expected to be inadequate to meet the needs of
the existing, as well as the projected future, number of uninsured
persons.**

A widely held misperception is that there are special programs and public
facilities nationwide that give uninsured Americans adequate access to health care
(Blendon et al., 1999; IOM, 2001a). This is a comforting but invidious myth. The
provision and financing of health care for the uninsured are ill-defined, fragmented, and insufficient (Lewin and Altman, 2000; Hadley, 2002; IOM, 2002a).
Perhaps more importantly, the metaphor of a safety net does not highlight the fact
that all parts of this "net" are anchored, for better or worse, in the mainstream
health care system (see Box 2.1). However, the term safety net has become
established in public discourse about health services and other social welfare programs that serve vulnerable populations, including the uninsured. The Committee
uses the phrase safety net only as an adjective, to refer to health care facilities and
programs that disproportionately serve uninsured persons.[4]

Local safety-net arrangements commonly include services provided through
health departments; federally sponsored clinics (e.g., community, migrant); other
independent community, faith-based, or free clinics; hospital outpatient departments; public hospitals; and hospital emergency departments. In certain parts of
the country, private hospitals may participate in safety net arrangements (Lewin
and Altman, 2000). Like the broader health care market, the breadth and depth of

---

[4]One recent study of changes in the capacity of safety-net services over time operationalized the
designation as applying to providers that supplied a high volume or high proportion of services to
uninsured persons or whose caseload included a high proportion of uninsured clients (Felt-Lisk et al.,
2001).

BOX 2.1
One Definition of the Health Care Safety Net

Certain health care institutions, including public hospitals and academic health centers, community health centers, other clinics, and health departments, because of their explicit missions and prominent roles in serving medically underserved or indigent groups have been labeled "core" safety net institutions. The Institute of Medicine (IOM) Committee on the Changing Market, Managed Care, and the Future Viability of Safety Net Providers, authors of *America's Health Care Safety Net,* recognized both the unique role and mission of safety-net providers within communities and the highly variable configurations of safety-net services that exist across the country (Lewin and Altman, 2000, p. 47):

The concept of a health care safety net conjures up the image of a tightly woven fabric of federal, state, and local programs stretched across the nation ready to catch those who slip through the health insurance system. . . . America's safety net is neither secure nor uniform. Rather, it varies greatly from state to state, community to community. . . . These variations notwithstanding, most communities can identify a set of hospitals and clinics that by mandate or mission care for a proportionately greater share of poor and uninsured people.

This earlier IOM Committee concludes that safety net arrangements are "intact but endangered," threatened fiscally by a decline in support from public revenues, due particularly to the changes associated with state Medicaid managed care programs, and an increase in demand for services as reflected in an increasing number of uninsured persons nationally.

SOURCE: Lewin and Altman, 2000.

safety-net services are shaped by the local employment and tax base, the generosity of state Medicaid support, the community's own history and performance in providing services to vulnerable groups, and the demand for services (Baxter and Mechanic, 1997; Lewin and Altman, 2000). Neither the existence of core safety-net providers nor the volume of care delivered outside formal safety net arrangements guarantees that there will be sufficient or adequate care for uninsured persons. There is considerable unmet need for health care in general in many communities around the United States (IOM, 1988, forthcoming 2003; Bovbjerg et al., 2000b).

Despite having distinctive characteristics and being identifiable within communities, safety-net providers and service arrangements may be interrelated with and sometimes part of mainstream health care providers and institutions. This blending of safety-net and mainstream health care services is particularly likely in rural areas and for specialty care in general.

There is significant heterogeneity across localities in the financing, function, and scope of safety-net arrangements, depending on factors such as the size of the community and its uninsured population, population density, and state health services and financing programs (Baxter and Mechanic, 1997; Norton and Lipson, 1998; Lewin and Altman, 2000). Service configurations in rural areas differ from those in metropolitan areas, and urban center city safety-net arrangements differ from those that have emerged in suburban areas (Mueller et al., 1999; Ormond et al., 2000b; Taylor et al, 2001). The problems that rural communities face in terms of the absolute supply of services and further distances traveled to reach health care is magnified for uninsured rural residents, who may not have the economic means to travel out of their community in order to obtain greater access to care (Schur and Franco, 1999). Rural areas tend not to have dedicated safety net facilities. Physicians in private practice may provide the bulk of primary care to uninsured patients, and private hospitals may perform safety net functions that in a more urban community would be carried out by a public hospital (Taylor et al, 2001). In urban areas, in contrast, a tiered arrangement for health services tends to segregate patients by income level and coverage status, at separate institutions and through differential treatment within a single facility, such as a private nonprofit hospital. The sustainability of this tiered structure depends on patterns of insurance coverage within the community and additional support to reimburse providers for uncompensated care.[5] Indeed, the threshold requirements of subsidies such as disproportionate share hospital payments by Medicare and Medicaid may promote the concentration of lower-income patients in some hospitals. If the need for care by uninsured patients substantially exceeds the capacity of local safety net arrangements, other health care providers in the community may be drawn on, even if they do not customarily participate in safety net care.

Although providers and institutions commonly considered to be parts of local safety-net arrangements are more likely than others to treat uninsured persons and members of partially uninsured families, most uninsured persons and their families obtain care not from formal safety-net arrangements but from mainstream health services providers and institutions (Cunningham and Tu, 1997; Lewin and Altman, 2000). In terms of the distribution of reported uncompensated care in 1994 as a rough proxy for services delivered to uninsured and other medically underserved groups, for example, private hospitals provided $10.6 billion in uncompensated care costs, while public hospitals provided $6.2 billion (Cunningham and Tu, 1997). For this reason, efforts to expand the capacity of safety net facility arrangements are unlikely to be successful as the sole strategy for providing adequate access and health care to uninsured Americans.

---

[5]"Uncompensated care" is a broad and imprecise term, defined by the American Hospital Association as the combination of the cost attributable to bad debt and charity care (Blanchfield and Randall, 2000). In the literature it has been measured in a number of different ways and using a variety of units (Duncan, 1992). Hospital uncompensated care is discussed in more detail in later sections of this chapter.

Uninsured patients comprise a relatively large proportion (40 percent) of the client base of federally supported primary care clinics (Cunningham and Tu, 1997; Bureau of Primary Health Care [BPHC], 2002). However, uninsured clients served by these clinics represent a relatively small proportion (between 6.5 and 10 percent) of the total uninsured population, and most uninsured persons do not live in the vicinity of a community health center (Cunningham and Tu, 1997; Cunningham and Kemper, 1998; Carlson et al., 2001; BPHC, 2002). Funding for community health centers and other primary care clinics has been limited and piecemeal, and health centers and clinics do not have the physical capacity to meet the projected unmet primary care needs of all of the uninsured persons in their area (Lewin and Altman, 2000).

Although the expansion of the federally supported health centers is anticipated to improve their ability to meet a growing patient demand, given the limited capacity and geographical limits of community health centers (CHCs), providers such as hospital outpatient clinics and emergency departments are unlikely to be replaced by CHCs as providers of the greatest volume of primary care for uninsured persons. Through the Health Care Safety Net Amendments of 2002, the Bush Administration began a major effort to enlarge the CHC system, with a goal of doubling the capacity in CHCs from the current level of 11 million people served annually (4 to 5 million of whom are uninsured) to 22 million over a five-year period (NACHC, 2002). This expansion was accompanied by the defunding of Community Access Program grants to improve the coordination of safety-net services within communities.

Given a national uninsured population of 41 million persons as of 2001 and that 40 percent of CHC clients are uninsured, the projected capacity for CHCs is about one quarter of what would be needed, even if the number of uninsured Americans did not increase. This calculation assumes that all uninsured persons would receive primary and preventive care from CHCs and that CHCs would continue to serve both insured and uninsured clients as they do now. Over the next five to ten years, estimates of the projected number of uninsured persons range from a decrease to roughly 34 million in 2005, given a strong economic outlook, to an increase of up to 61 million uninsured by 2009 in the case of an economic recession (IOM, 2001a).

Major Providers of Safety-Net Care

In their participation in safety-net arrangements, physicians and health care institutions have taken some direct responsibility for providing care to the uninsured, on ethical as well as legal grounds. CHCs and public hospitals have mandates and some financial support earmarked for serving uninsured persons. Private hospitals are bound by the terms of their charters (e.g., provision of community benefits in exchange for tax-exempt status), by federal Hill-Burton grant and loan obligations, and by the requirements of the Emergency Medical Treatment and

Labor Act (EMTALA), to provide limited services regardless of patients' ability to pay.

Physicians working in private practice, nonprofit clinics (such as federally qualified health centers and free clinics), and hospitals all provide significant amounts of subsidized or free care to uninsured persons. Information about the financial cost of services rendered to uninsured patients is often incomplete. Of the information available, more is known about hospitals' provision of uncompensated care than about ambulatory care provided in doctors' offices and clinics.

The amount and sources of uncompensated care generated within a particular community reflect economic and other factors beyond the uninsured rate within the community. Not all uncompensated or even charity care is generated by the uninsured, and not all care to the uninsured is uncompensated or subsidized. Some is traceable to insured patients who do not pay their copayments or deductibles. Three studies based on data from the 1980s estimate the share of hospital uncompensated care costs attributable to uninsured patients. These studies of Florida, Indiana, and Massachusetts hospitals report that 72, 72, and 59 percent, respectively, of uncompensated care costs were for services to uninsured patients (Duncan and Kilpatrick, 1987; Saywell et al., 1989b; Weissman et al., 1992).

Changes in the mix of services offered by hospitals and the overall trend toward outpatient instead of inpatient treatment have affected the level of uncompensated care as well as its distribution among different types of providers. Nationally, during the first half of the 1990s, there was an increasing concentration of uncompensated care among safety-net (public and academic health center) hospitals and a shift of uncompensated care burden from hospitals to private physicians and community health centers (Cunningham and Tu, 1997; Commonwealth Fund, 2001). In many rural communities, the hospital remains the source of ambulatory as well as institutional acute care. Overall, hospitals reported little change in their relative burden, although hospital care overall represented a smaller share of the health care dollar.[6] Growing pressures on hospital financial margins due to competition within the private health insurance market and changing practice patterns contribute to this shift away from the hospital sector, as well as changes in the technology of medical care (Etheredge, 2000).

Physicians

By waiving or reducing fees to uninsured patients and others unable to pay the direct costs of their care and by donating their services in free clinics and

---

[6]In 1988, hospital services accounted for 42 percent of spending for personal health care services nationally and physician and other clinical services for 36 percent. By 1997, hospital services accounted for only 38 percent, while physician and other clinical services had increased slightly to 37 percent of total spending for personal health care services (Cowan et al., 2001).

similar settings, physicians provide a significant amount of free or reduced-price charity care. One estimate of the value of charity care provided to uninsured patients by private practice physicians is $5.1 billion in 2001 dollars (Hadley and Holahan, 2003). This estimate reflects an adjusted midpoint from a range of survey results on physician-provided free and reduced-price care.

Both the American Medical Association (AMA) and the American Academy of Pediatrics (AAP) have surveyed their members about the provision of uncompensated care.

• A recent AMA survey (1999) reports the responses of a nationally representative survey of nonfederal physicians involved in patient care (part of the AMA's Socioeconomic Monitoring System), defining charity care as services provided at free or reduced price in light of a patient's financial need. [7] Sixty-five percent of the surveyed physicians reported delivering charity care, averaging 8.8 hours per week or 14.4 percent of total patient hours among those who provide such care (Kane, 2002). Primary care physicians are less likely to provide charity care (62 percent) and provide fewer hours of care, on average (8.1 hours per week), than other physicians (67 percent, a weekly average of 9.3 hours); the latter category includes internal medicine subspecialties, surgeons, radiologists, psychiatrists, anesthesiologists, pathologists, and emergency medicine specialists. Emergency medicine physicians are reported to have experienced the greatest increase in the proportion providing charity care, from 48 percent in 1988 to 61 percent in 1999 (Kane, 2002). Of physicians in nonmetropolitan areas, 72 percent report providing charity care, compared with 64 percent of physicians in urban areas.

• The most recent AAP survey of primary care pediatricians involved in direct provision of care finds that approximately 8 percent of these physicians' patients are uninsured, on average, and that roughly 42 percent of services to uninsured patients are uncompensated (Yudkowski et al., 2000).

Another set of estimates comes from a nationally representative survey, the Community Tracking Study (CTS). CTS data show a decrease in the proportion of physicians providing charity care between 1997 and 2001, from 76.3 percent to 71.5 percent (Cunningham, 2002). Results from an earlier round of the CTS survey (1998-1999) indicate those physicians providing charity care report delivering an average of 2.5 hours weekly (Reed et al., 2001). Although the AMA and CTS survey results are quite disparate, both show a decrease in the number of physicians providing charity care in the mid-to-late 1990s (Cunningham et al., 1999).

---

[7]This analysis distinguishes charity care from bad debt but does not specify whether the recipients of charity care are uninsured.

Clinics

By mission, community health centers, other federally qualified health centers (FQHCs), and rural health clinics are devoted to improving access for medically underserved persons, including those who are uninsured. The FQHCs are considered "core" safety net institutions (Lewin and Altman, 2000). For the most part, FQHCs provide primary care and preventive and screening services, together with a small proportion of specialty services and referrals for specialty care.[8] They fill a special niche, not only because of their location in underserved neighborhoods and communities but also because they offer enabling or wraparound services, such as transportation, translation, and case management, that facilitate access to health care (Davis et al., 1999). In addition, they frequently employ community residents. The unmet health needs that justify placement of a community health center vary regionally and may include a rural or frontier community's isolation, resulting in lack of local physicians, an area's high uninsured rate, or other impediments to access to care for low-income persons and recent immigrants (Clemmitt, 2000).

As of 2001, there were approximately 750 private nonprofit grantees operating clinics at more than 4,000 sites that served some 10 million people, 39 percent of whom were uninsured (BPHC, 2002). These health center grantees received approximately $1.2 billion in federal grants to support their operations. Federal grants supply just 25 percent of the centers' operating funds, overall. Medicaid payments account for about 34 percent; state and local support, 14 percent; Medicare and other third-party payments, 15 percent; patient payments, 6 percent; and other sources, 6 percent (BPHC, 2002). There has been growth in the number of uninsured persons receiving free or reduced-price care from community health centers, from 2.2 million in the early 1990s to 4.0 million people in 2001.

Clinics have a limited capacity to care for their client base, and this capacity has been threatened in recent years. Many health centers and clinics that rely on federal section 330 grants for operating revenue are experiencing financial trouble (USGAO, 2000; McAlearney, 2002). Approximately 50 percent have fiscal or operating problems, with smaller clinics (those serving 5,000 or fewer patients annually) more likely to be experiencing trouble. In 1998, 50 percent of clinics had costs greater than or equal to revenues, and for 5 percent of clinics, costs exceeded revenues by 30 percent (USGAO, 2000). Since the 1970s, CHCs have become increasingly reliant on Medicaid reimbursement due to increasing enrollments in Medicaid. They have experienced little real increase in federal grants

---

[8]This section excludes hospital outpatient clinics, which are discussed in the following section on hospitals. Hospitals operate outpatient clinics for specialty care and care following hospitalizations and, particularly in urban, medically underserved communities, also operate ambulatory care clinics that provide ongoing primary care to a stable client population.

over the past 20 years. After a period of growth through the mid-1990s, CHCs have experienced severe fiscal pressures from the combination of declining Medicaid revenues, in part connected with the spread of state Medicaid managed care contracting, and a rising uninsured population (Hawkins and Rosenbaum, 1998).

Rural health clinics do not receive federal operating grants and are under no legal obligation to care for underserved groups, yet they often function in this capacity (Gale and Coburn, 2001; Finerfrock, 2002; NARHC, n.d.). Because these rural clinics receive cost-based reimbursement from the Medicare and Medicaid programs, they are able to provide the facilities and administrative structure for bringing physicians, nurse practitioners, and other clinicians into rural areas, where a limited economic base may make it hard to recruit and retain health professionals in the community. During 2000, 55 percent of independent rural health clinics (RHCs) and almost 70 percent of provider-based (e.g., owned by physician or physician assistant) RHCs had free or reduced-price care policies. Four out of five RHCs accepted applications for such care, and most RHCs reported writing off uncompensated care (Coburn, 2002).

Hospitals

Estimates of hospital uncompensated care may be presented in several ways (Duncan, 1992):

- the number of patients served
- the dollar amount of care or the volume or amount of services provided
- the total amount of care given that the patient does not pay for or the net dollar amount after a partial subsidy from other payers.

The estimates that result from these different metrics lead to varying interpretations of hospitals' relative efforts and burdens. Although uncompensated care is often measured in terms of the individual physician or hospital, another perspective is provided when the volume of such care is cast in terms of overall community resources. The burden of providing free care is likely to be distributed unevenly and depends both on what individual providers choose to offer and from which institutions patients seek care (Duncan, 1992). The relative performance of nonprofit and for-profit hospitals in providing charity care varies by state and locality and reflects market circumstances and demographics as well as ownership type and explicit mission. The ownership profiles of hospitals in urban and rural areas also differ. Box 2.2 gives a national overview of hospitals by type of ownership and the relationship between ownership type, hospital mission, and obligations to serve the community as a whole. Box 2.3 defines some of the accounting terms used in discussion of uncompensated care and hospital finance.

Data from AHA annual surveys are the basis for recent national estimates of hospital uncompensated care. Over the past decade, uncompensated care expenditures at hospitals nationally have been relatively stable at about 6 percent of costs

BOX 2.2
Hosptials by Ownership Status

Public hospitals may be sponsored directly by city, county, state, or federal governments or by local hospital districts independent of other government agencies or jurisdictions. In 1998, there were 651 city or county hospitals, 551 so-called district hospitals, 322 state hospitals, and 275 federal hospitals (Needleman, 2000). Federal hospitals usually are reserved for specific populations, for example, active and retired members of the military and their families through the Veterans Administration or American Indians through the Indian Health Service. State-owned facilities include psychiatric hospitals and university academic health centers.

Private hospitals are greater in number and less likely to receive direct government subsidies to reimburse the uncompensated care costs incurred by uninsured persons. In 1998, there were 3,200 nonprofit and 1,182 for-profit hospitals nationally (Needleman, 2000).

For-profit hospitals are assumed to set their prices with the goal of maximizing profits (Hoerger, 1991; Needleman, 1999; Zwanziger et al., 2000). They are less likely to serve as safety-net institutions or to provide care for uninsured persons (Hoerger, 1991; Mann et al, 1997). Because they are for profit, the prices charged to uninsured persons may be set differently than those charged by non-profit hospitals.

Nonprofit hospitals vary widely in their provision of charity care, which depends upon the health insurance coverage rates in their service area, their mission, and whether there are public hospitals in their communities.

Both public and private nonprofit hospitals are expected to provide *community benefits*, by virtue of their status as nonprofit and tax-exempt (Needleman, 2000; Nicholson et al., 2000). The term "community benefits" generally is understood to include

- charity or uncompensated care for medically indigent persons;
- the provision of Medicaid services (particularly in areas where Medicaid reimbursement does not fully cover the cost of care);
- the provision of certain kinds of services at a financial loss (e.g., emergency medical services and burn care);
- affiliation or involvement with graduate medical education; and
- direct connection to the community served through local ownership and governance.

(Hadley and Holahan, 2003). In 1999, this translated into roughly $20.8 billion of care that was reported provided to patients who could not or did not pay their bills (MedPAC, 2001).[9] The proportion of uncompensated care remained relatively

---

[9]Estimates in terms of the difference between what a hospital charges and what it is paid may overstate the extent of lost revenues, since hospitals may adjust their charges based on anticipated changes in reimbursement (Conover, 1998). Estimates in terms of the difference between a hospital's expenses or costs and what it is paid may be more reliable and accurate, although analytic adjustments

BOX 2.3
Health Care Accounting Definitions

- *Bad Debt:* Charges to patients who are billed for services but do not pay in full or part.
- *Charity Care:* Care rendered at no or reduced charge to patients deemed unable to pay for their own care.
- *Contractual Allowances:* The difference between charges and the amount actually paid by a third-party payer.
- *Cost-to-Charge Ratio:* An analytical adjustment used to evaluate the extent of a hospital's markup (charge) of the underlying cost of a service.
- *Financial or Operating Margin:* Revenues from sales minus current costs of goods sold.
- *Free Care:* Services given without any expectation of reimbursement; free to the recipient, although not free to the provider.
- *Uncompensated Care:* Most broadly, any type of charge for which no or partial payment is received.

steady throughout the 1990s, although the national estimate masks important regional and local variations and trends (Cunningham and Tu, 1997). Specifically, the overall uncompensated care burden has become more concentrated in fewer hospitals, especially public hospitals. This has been attributed to new market pressures on hospitals and, consequently, a lessened ability to shift uncompensated care costs to insured patients, both public and private (Cunningham and Tu, 1997). These authors project that if Medicaid managed care patients go to private hospitals and uninsured patients are concentrated in public facilities, public hospitals will face increased fiscal pressure due to the combined impact of reduced revenue and uncompensated care. Gaskin and colleagues (2001) have documented this phenomenon in the case of low-risk Medicaid maternity patients, who are financially attractive, shifting from urban public hospitals to private hospitals.

In rural areas, hospitals often anchor the web of relationships and institutions that comprise safety-net arrangements. Because there are fewer alternative providers of services in rural than urban areas, hospitals on average have greater burdens of uncompensated care and are more sensitive to fluctuations or changes in federal and state reimbursement policies for public insurance (e.g., Medicare, Medicaid,

---

may be needed, specific to the patient's characteristics and to local health services market conditions (Duncan, 1992; Conover, 1998). In addition, the dollar amount of uncompensated care may not give any indication of the number of medically indigent patients served because a relatively small proportion and number of patients may generate large expenditures.

State Children's Health Insurance Program [SCHIP]). In urban areas, public and large teaching hospitals play a major role in serving uninsured patients, providing levels of uncompensated care much greater than their overall market share. The relationships among practitioners and institutions are more extensive, however, given the greater number of sites at which uninsured persons may be able to receive care (Lipson and Naierman, 1996; Bovbjerg et al., 2000a; Commonwealth Fund, 2001).

Providers of Last Resort

No single public entity functions nationally as a "provider of last resort" in the United States. Legal and financial responsibility for at least some of the care that uninsured persons need varies by locality. To the extent that states, counties, or municipalities do designate a provider of last resort, the services to be provided usually are not specified.

Unlike most developed countries and many developing nations, the United States does not guarantee its citizens or residents access to personal health care services beyond treatment to stabilize an emergency condition and care at childbirth. The minimal national standard of access to health services that has been established by EMTALA, a provision of the Omnibus Budget Reconciliation Act of 1986, is described in Box 2.4.

The facilities of states, counties, and municipalities are, often by default, providers of last resort for patients without the financial means to pay for their own care. Some states explicitly assign responsibility for this role in their constitutions or by statute, while others acknowledge the obligation implicitly through annual budgetary appropriations for personal health care services. Local agencies are more likely than state programs to be involved in the delivery of health services. Some states reimburse local health departments, public hospitals, or clinics for the direct provision of care; some reimburse all hospitals in the state for a percentage of their expenditures; some finance state and county catastrophic care funds; and others subsidize packages of services that resemble an insurance plan (IOM, 1988).

WHO PAYS FOR CARE FOR UNINSURED PERSONS?

Finding: Public support for the uncompensated care expenses incurred by uninsured persons is substantial. The public sector is estimated to finance up to 85 percent of the $34 billion to $38 billion in uncompensated care estimated to have been rendered to uninsured persons in 2001. The exact amount is unknown, because states and providers do not consistently document or report these public expenditures in ways that tie spending directly on behalf of unin-

BOX 2.4
The Emergency Medical Treatment and Labor Act (EMTALA)

EMTALA was enacted in 1986 to counter the practice of hospitals turning away or inappropriately transferring patients who did not have the means to pay for their care (a practice known as patient dumping) (Schiff et al., 1986; Ansell and Schiff, 1987; Friedman, 1987; Kellerman and Hackman, 1990; Bitterman, 2002). As a condition for participating in the federal Medicare program, hospitals must adhere to the requirements of EMTALA, which directs them to medically screen and stabilize all patients who present themselves to the emergency department for treatment and prohibits prescreening with regard to a patient's insurance coverage or means to pay for care (Fields et al., 2001). The hospital is not precluded from billing the patient after the service has been provided, whether or not the patient has insurance or other resources to pay.

EMTALA does not require any care beyond screening, stabilization, and, if necessary, hospitalization. Thus, uninsured persons who seek care in hospital emergency departments are unlikely to achieve continuity in their care over time, one hallmark of high-quality care (IOM, 2001b, 2002a).

EMTALA is the single federal statutory provision that directly addresses the right to health care for uninsured persons (Fields et al., 2001). Most significantly for the financial viability of hospitals and emergency physicians, EMTALA does not authorize or appropriate any federal or other public funds to support its mandate. The requirements of EMTALA have ramifications not only for how emergency departments (EDs) function but also for the availability of inpatient beds and the willingness of specialists to serve on physician on-call panels to handle all cases within EDs and hospitals generally (Kamoie, 2000).

sured persons. Many of the sources that do pay for services delivered to uninsured persons are not explicitly authorized or appropriated to do so, contributing to the uncertainty about the extent of public support for such care.

Finding: Although a larger scale and scope of public insurance programs (e.g., Medicaid, SCHIP) is sometimes associated with lower uninsured rates at the state level, it is the size of an area's lower-income population (families with incomes of less than 200 percent of the federal poverty level, or FPL) that determines the relative need for public support for health care of all kinds (including both insurance and direct services). At the state level, higher uninsured rates tend to be associated with higher levels of public spending on coverage.

Finding: There is little direct evidence about the size of private payers' cross-subsidy of the unreimbursed costs of care for uninsured persons.

There is no uniform public responsibility to subsidize or pay for the care delivered to uninsured persons. The financing that exists is diffuse, spread unevenly, and varies by locality.

The financial and organizational ties that bind safety-net arrangements to mainstream health care mean that unreimbursed expenditures for health services delivered to uninsured persons are borne by both public and private payers and by federal taxpayers as well as state and local ones. These expenditures, charges, or costs contribute to the total burden of uncompensated care shouldered by local providers and governments at all levels. It is hard to estimate the extent of uninsurance's draw on public sector resources both because of the lack of explicit documentation and the lack of a comparison scenario (e.g., public expenditures if all uninsured persons were insured). It is likely that many of the same public funding streams would remain in place, especially because they do not target uninsured persons specifically. This topic, as well as the issue of what "true" costs of uninsurance may be estimated for the nation as a whole, will be discussed in greater depth in the Committee's fifth report. It is introduced briefly here to give a more complete overview of health care financing for uninsured persons.

Even though individuals without health insurance are estimated to use only two-thirds of the care of comparable insured populations, the costs of the services that they do use are considerable (Marquis and Long, 1994–1995). Uninsured persons are more likely to forgo care until health conditions deteriorate, leading to more costly and less effective courses of treatment (IOM, 2002a, 2002b). Faced with a need for health care, some people without health insurance seek the care they need and pay for it out of pocket, and some try to obtain the care at subsidized rates or at public expense. Most people probably adopt some combination of these strategies. Given the limited incomes of most uninsured persons and the cost of health care, the costs borne societally (e.g., by taxpayers) for the care of uninsured persons is likely to be substantial.

One recent analysis of uncompensated care provided to uninsured Americans derived and compared estimates from two independent sources of information, one, the Medical Expenditures Panel Survey (MEPS) and the other, provider reports of uncompensated care. The authors of this study estimate the value of such care for 2001 in the range of $34 billion to $38 billion (Hadley and Holahan, 2003). For the estimate based on MEPS, the authors used reported expenditures, pooled for the years 1996 through 1998 and adjusted for an undercount of uninsured persons (care that is not billed is not recorded by MEPS) to arrive at an estimate of $34.5 billion in free care and $26.4 billion in out-of-pocket expenditures, for a total of $60.9 billion spent, in 2001 dollars. Their series of estimates about the providers and sources of financing for the proportion of uncompensated care delivered to uninsured persons is summarized in Table 2.1.

As described in Table 2.1, combined federal, state, and local spending is estimated at $30.6 billion, which the authors calculate equals about 5 percent of estimated public spending for Medicare, Medicaid, and the tax benefit of employment-based insurance plans in 2001 (Hadley and Holahan, 2003). The discussion

TABLE 2.1 Summary, Estimated Amounts and Sources of Payment for Free Care Delivered to Uninsured Persons, 2001

Provider Type	Source of Funds	Est. Spending for Uninsured Persons ($$, billions)			
		Federal	State and Local	Private	Total
Physicians (independent of health care facilities)	Charity/practitioners			5.1	5.1
Clinics and Government (direct care)	Veterans Administration	3.89			3.89
	BPHC (e.g., CHCs)	0.47	0.26	0.11	0.84
	Indian Health Service	0.67	0.02		0.69
	HIV/AIDS Bureau	0.59	0.09		0.68
	Local health departments		0.58		0.58
	MCHB	0.06	0.23	0.02	0.31
	NHSC	0.01	0.11		0.12
Totals, Support for Clinics		5.69	1.29	0.13	7.11
Hospitals (nonfederal)	Medicaid DSH	6.7	1.7		8.4
	Medicare DSH	5.0			5.0
	State and local indigent care		4.3		4.3
	State and local appropriations to hospitals		3.1		3.1
	Private (hospital surplus revenues)			1.5-3.0	1.5-3.0
	Medicare IME	1.6			1.6
	Private (philanthropy)			0.8-1.6	0.8-1.6
	Medicaid UPL	0.9	0.3		1.2
Totals, Support for Hospitals		14.2	9.4	2.3-4.6	25.9-28.2

NOTES: Definitions of acronyms follow; see glossary for explanations of programs. BPHC = Bureau of Primary Health Care; DSH = Disproportionate Share Hospital; IME = Indirect Medical Education; MCHB = Maternal and Child Health Bureau; NHSC = National Health Services Corps; UPL = Upper Payment Limit.
SOURCE: Hadley and Holahan, 2003.

and Table 2.1 that follow are not meant to be a comprehensive assessment of the adequacy or cost-effectiveness of current financing arrangements but rather to provide a sense of the magnitude of public and private supports for care to the uninsured persons.

Persons who are without health insurance for the entire year pay out of pocket an average of about 35 percent of the charges and payments for health care made on their behalf (Hadley and Holahan, 2003).[10] The proportion paid out of pocket varies by the type of service (e.g., physician, inpatient hospital, prescriptions) (IOM, 2002b). If the provider who delivers the service is to remain financially viable, some or all of the remainder must be covered by federal, state, and local governmental funds or by charity.

While a significant proportion of the health care that uninsured persons receive is paid for by the uninsured themselves, an even greater share is subsidized either explicitly or implicitly. The distribution of this subsidy varies by locality, reflecting the different configurations of health services markets both among and within states, including which public entity or level of government, if any, has the responsibility to serve as a provider of last resort. The proportion of the subsidy borne by government, providers, and philanthropy also varies by type of service.

Explicit subsidies include public sources such as operating grants to community health centers and public hospitals and private sources such as philanthropic grants and hospital endowments for charity care. Examples of indirect subsidies include public subsidies for health professional education and research at safety net hospitals (e.g., Medicare graduate medical education payments), as well as higher charges for services provided to patients who are insured. Medicare and Medicaid disproportionate share hospital (DSH) payments are nominally *implicit* subsidies of care for uninsured persons because their explicit justification is the greater cost of caring for lower-income federal program beneficiaries; however, these payments are widely understood as compensating hospitals for the costs of their nonpaying patients as well.[11]

Public Payers

The role of federal, state, and local governments in supporting personal health services for uninsured persons is substantial:

• Federal programs, funding, and regulation create the financial, legal, and organizational contexts within which care to the uninsured is provided. The federal government's primary role is in financing health care services. It accom-

---

[10]This estimate is lower than the out-of-pocket spending reported in *Health Insurance Is a Family Matter* (41 percent) (IOM, 2002b), which was also based on MEPS data, because the authors adjusted the MEPS results for undercounting of uncompensated care by private practitioners and hospitals.

[11]The following section describes the Medicare and Medicaid DSH programs.

plishes this function largely through insurance mechanisms such as Medicare, Medicaid, and SCHIP and also through grant programs for service delivery (e.g., the Community Health Center program) and direct delivery (e.g., Department of Veterans Affairs facilities, Indian Health Service). These various programs are administered independently of each other, by different agencies within the Department of Health and Human Services and even by different departments (Veterans Affairs).

• States determine eligibility standards and provide funding for health insurance programs (Medicaid, SCHIP, and similarly structured programs serving populations that do not qualify for federal matching funds) that directly affect the number and characteristics of uninsured residents.

• Local governments, through the operation of public hospitals and clinics (and, increasingly, by contract) directly serve uninsured community members and, in some jurisdictions, also contribute to the financing of the state Medicaid program.

The sections that follow discuss the contributions of federal, state, and local governments in turn.

Federal Government

Through a variety of programs and funding mechanisms, different federal agencies support a portion of the health care services delivered to uninsured people and others unable to pay for their care. This support includes categorical and unrestricted grants; loans to public and private agencies, organizations, companies, and individuals; and the direct provision of care. Box 2.5 lists the major federal sources and mechanisms.

Monies for the care of uninsured people are provided largely through special financing provisions of the Medicaid program and by state and local tax revenues that subsidize uncompensated care for lower-income persons. States have employed a variety of approaches to raise the maximum amount of dollars that can be used to obtain federal matching funds through the Medicaid program, including the DSH payments (discussed below) and other financing mechanisms such as provider taxes and donations, administrative claims for school-based services, intergovernmental transfers, upper payment limits, and tobacco settlements (see Figure 2.2) (Schneider, 2002). In addition, federal Medicaid waivers to state governments have allowed states to redirect Medicaid monies toward the care of uninsured persons (Coughlin and Liska, 1997).

Even though uninsured persons by definition are not enrolled in Medicaid, their care is subsidized by Medicaid payments, a substantial portion of which are made to public hospitals, academic health centers, and other hospitals that disproportionately serve uninsured people. In addition, there is considerable overlap between the uninsured and Medicaid-enrolled populations, given the high turnover rates in the enrolled population and the similar demographic characteristics

BOX 2.5
Sources of Federal Support for Care of Uninsured Persons

Subsidies Through Public Insurance Programs

- Medicare and Medicaid DSH payments
- Medicare payments to academic medical centers for graduate medical education
- Medicare Critical Access Hospital program (rural hospitals)
- Tobacco master settlement payments through the Medicaid program

Programs Targeted at the Uninsured and Medically Underserved

- Operating grants for ambulatory care centers and clinics (e.g., community health centers, migrant health centers, health care for the homeless, public housing, primary care)
- Grants for technical assistance to organize and improve care for medically underserved persons, including the uninsured (e.g., community access program, state planning grants)
- Loan and grant obligations under the Hill-Burton hospital construction program[1]
- Area health education center residency training
- Support for physicians, nurses, and other health professional to be trained and to serve for varying lengths of time in counties formally designated as medically underserved or health professions shortage area

Direct Provision of Health Services to Entitled Categories of People

- Department of Veterans Affairs health system
- Indian Health Service

Grants for Categorical Services

- Maternal and child health
- Development health (for children with special needs and the developmentally disabled)
- Mental health services
- HIV/AIDS care
- Immunization services
- Family planning
- Sexually transmitted disease services

---

[1] Obligations under the Hill-Burton program have largely expired.

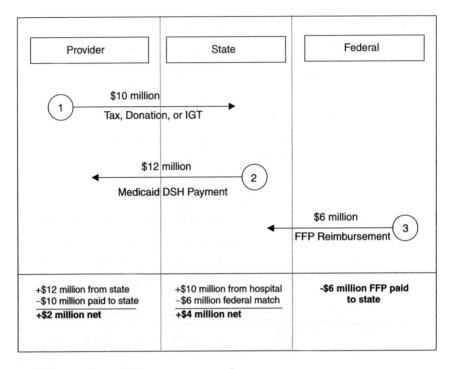

FIGURE 2.2 How a DHS program can work.
NOTE: IGT = intergovernmental transfer, FFP = federal financial participation.
SOURCE: Coughlin and Liska, 1997.

for Medicaid enrollees and uninsured people (e.g., family or household income of less than 200 percent FPL).

Both the Medicare and the Medicaid programs are significant sources of indirect financing for care to the uninsured. The Medicare and Medicaid DSH provisions, which provide for additional payments to hospitals that serve a "disproportionate share" of low-income patients, are particularly important in this context. The Medicare DSH payment provision (see Box 2.6) was authorized originally by the 1983 legislation establishing prospective payment for hospital inpatient services under Medicare, to allow payment adjustments to take account of the special needs of public and other hospitals serving low-income patients (Schneider, 2002). The Medicaid DSH (see Box 2.7) program was created in 1981 as part of the Omnibus Budget Reconciliation Act (Schneider, 2002). It required hospitals to establish payment rates that take into account the situation of hospitals serving a disproportionate share of low-income patients. Although the nominal purpose of Medicare and Medicaid DSH payments was to compensate hospitals for the additional costs of serving low-income program beneficiaries, the original impetus for the programs included a recognition of the need for additional rev-

BOX 2.6
Medicare Disproportionate Share Hospital Payments

In fiscal year 2001, Medicare DSH payments to hospitals amounted to an estimated $5.0 billion (Hadley and Holahan, 2003). Medicare DSH payments are allocated among hospitals according to an index that sums two ratios: the share of total patient days represented by Medicaid patients and the share of Medicare patient days represented by patients receiving Supplemental Security Income (and who are thus also Medicaid enrollees) (Nicholson, 2002). Hospitals with index values that exceed certain thresholds (different for rural and urban hospitals and for hospitals of varying size) are eligible for DSH payments. One recent analysis of Medicare DSH payments concludes that, although the Medicare DSH formula rewards hospitals for high proportions of Medicaid and Medicare patients, it does not result in higher payments to hospitals that actually have relatively high uninsured patient loads (Nicholson, 2002). The Medicare Payment Advisory Commission (MedPAC) has recommended that the Medicare DSH index be revised to take uncompensated patient careloads directly into account (Nicholson, 2002).

BOX 2.7
Medicaid Disproportionate Share Hospital Payments

Medicaid DSH payments, both federal and state shares, amounted to $15 billion in 1998, of which $9 billion were federal funds (Schneider, 2002). For 2002, the federal share of DSH payments is projected to exceed $9 billion (Miller, 2002a). Only about 75 percent of federal DSH payments are estimated to go to general hospitals, however, since a significant portion of these monies support state mental hospitals and some of the monies are returned by the institutions receiving them to state treasuries in the form of provider tax payments (Schneider, 2002). States have a great deal of discretion in determining how Medicaid DSH payments are distributed among hospitals. Federal statute requires that states have a program of DSH payments and that, at a minimum, they make such payments to hospitals whose share of Medicaid patient days is at least one standard deviation above the average (mean) for the state or whose low-income patient use rate is 25 percent or more (Coughlin et al., 2000). However, states may make DSH payments to hospitals with Medicaid patient day shares as low as 1 percent.

enues by hospitals caring for a high volume of uninsured patients and a relatively low volume of privately insured patients (Coughlin and Liska, 1997; Fagnani and Tolbert, 1999; Coughlin et al., 2000; Nicholson, 2002).

Medicaid and Medicare DSH payments shape local capacity to provide services for uninsured persons, even though the number of uninsured patients and the amount of care provided them are not taken directly into account when allocating these funds (Fagnani and Tolbert, 1999). Past decreases in DSH funding levels due to the Balanced Budget Amendments of 1997 have increased the financial pressures on hospitals that disproportionately serve Medicaid and uninsured patients, while recent legislative changes in the Medicare, Medicaid, and SCHIP Benefits Improvement and Protection Act of 2000 are likely to lead to increased DSH payments.

States vary greatly in their participation in Medicaid DSH, the extent to which they draw down the maximum amounts they are allowed under the program, and their reallocation of other public funds in response to DSH payments. On average, Medicaid DSH payments account for 6.6 percent of federal Medicaid grants to the states. Eight states have federal DSH grants that account for more than 10 percent of federal grants for Medicaid inpatient services, while 19 states have DSH grants amounting to less than 3 percent of that total (Miller, 2002a). Only a small proportion of state Medicaid DSH payments is assumed to be funding available to cover uncompensated care (Ku and Coughlin, 1995). If states or localities reduce their own support of hospitals for uncompensated care and simply allow federal payments to replace what they had previously supported, the value of the DSH payments to providers is obviously less than if the federal support augments state and local funding. Table 2.2 represents a regional summary of federal payments to the states under the Medicare and Medicaid DSH programs in 1998, compared to the relative size of the target population (uninsured persons and Medicaid enrollees) within the region. See Table C.4 in Appendix C for a summary by state.

TABLE 2.2 Combined Federal Medicare and Medicaid Disproportionate Share Hospital (DSH) Payments by Census Region, 1998

	Population <65 yrs, 1998 (millions)	No. of Uninsured, 1998 (millions)	Uninsured Rate, 1998 (%)	No. of Medicaid, 1998 (millions)	Medicaid Rate, 1998 (%)
Total	238.6	43.9	18.4	24.9	10.4
New England	11.7	1.5	12.6	1.3	11.1
Middle Atlantic	33.5	5.7	17.0	4.0	12.0
East North Central	39.4	5.7	14.6	3.7	9.4
West North Central	16.3	1.9	11.6	1.4	8.8
South Atlantic	41.4	7.8	18.9	3.7	9.0
East South Central	14.4	2.5	17.6	2.0	13.7
West South Central	26.8	6.7	25.2	2.6	9.8
Mountain	15.5	3.3	21.5	1.2	7.4
Pacific	39.6	8.7	22.0	5.0	12.6

SOURCE: Fronstin, 2000; Wynn et al., 2002.

The table gives a rough approximation of the marked variation across regions in state participation in the DSH programs, participation that may not necessarily correlate with the need for public support, as indicated by the size of the target population:

• The West South Central region has the highest proportion of the target population for public support (35 percent either uninsured or enrolled in Medicaid, which is 122 percent of the average nationally), and states in this region receive on average 104 percent of the national average combined DSH payment per member of the target group ($301). The Pacific region has almost as high a proportion of the target population as the West South Central region (34.6 percent either uninsured or enrolled in Medicaid), and states in this region receive on average 96 percent of the national average combined DSH payment ($276).

• The New England states, whose proportion of uninsured and Medicaid-enrolled persons (23.7 percent) is 82 percent of the national average, receive on average 172 percent of the national average DSH payment ($495).

• For states in the Mountain region, the proportion of the target population is comparable to the national average (28.9 percent), but the combined DSH payments per member of the target group fall short, with the region's states receiving on average 40 percent of the national average DSH payment ($114).

Sum No. (Uninsured and Medicaid), 1998 (millions)	Sum Rate (Uninsured and Medicaid), 1998 (%)	Sum Rate/ Total, (%)	Combined Medicare and Medicaid DSH Payment, 1998 (millions)	Combined DSH/Sum No. ($$)	Combined DSH/ Sum No./ Total (%)
68.8	28.8	100	19,844	288	100
2.8	23.7	82	1,387	495	172
9.7	29.0	100	4,391	453	157
9.4	24.0	83	1,843	196	68
3.3	20.4	71	961	291	101
11.5	27.9	97	3,012	262	91
4.5	31.3	109	1,154	256	89
9.3	35.0	122	2,795	301	104
4.5	28.9	100	514	114	40
13.7	34.6	120	3,787	276	96

State Government

Health activities within a state reflect budgetary priorities set by both the state and the federal government. The federal government supports almost half of all health care spending by state governments, with the proportion of federal funds varying by program (NACCHO, 2001). Federal grant dollars are a large part of state public health budgets (50 to 85 percent in the mid-1990s in the 13 states studied in the Urban Institute's Assessing the New Federalism project) (Wall, 1998).[12] For state governments as for the federal government, health care is the single largest budget item (NACCHO, 2001).

In addition to state constitutional or delegated responsibilities for public health and welfare, state budget decisions have important implications for all of the health activities within the state. States administer and share the financing of their own Medicaid program, in conjunction with the federal government. Each state has its own health department, as well as local health departments. While state agencies may provide health services directly to vulnerable populations, including uninsured persons, they more often provide financial support, both through the operation of public insurance programs such as Medicaid and SCHIP and through grants and revenue sharing to counties and other jurisdictions. Forty-two states have general assistance programs for medically indigent persons, including the uninsured, and fourteen states have other subsidy programs (Rajan, 1998). A recent study divides state-supported programs into two groups: (1) those that pay for or subsidize coverage of uninsured persons, including subsidy of employment-based coverage, and support for persons who are not eligible for public coverage or who are deemed medically uninsurable, and (2) those that pay subsidies directly to health care providers, using general revenues or dedicated taxes (Seifert, 2002).

State Policy Choices for Public Insurance Programs

The choices states make about Medicaid influence the size of their uninsured population. Although the federal government provides well over half of the costs of Medicaid and SCHIP, states have discretion in their programs' eligibility criteria, benefits, and payment rates beyond minimum federal standards.[13] In addition to determining what proportion of their low-income population is eligible for Medicaid, states vary widely in payment rates for services. Both the extensiveness of their public insurance programs and the level of payments for services under these programs affect the financial status of health care providers that serve unin-

---

[12]The 13 states in this ongoing study include Alabama, California, Colorado, Florida, Massachusetts, Michigan, Minnesota, Mississippi, New Jersey, New York, Texas, Washington, and Wisconsin.

[13]See the Committee's previous report, *Health Insurance Is a Family Matter,* for a fuller discussion of Medicaid and SCHIP and state eligibility standards for these programs (IOM, 2002b).

sured persons. They also affect whether hospitals and physicians serve the unin-sured at all because if Medicaid payment rates are too low, providers cannot afford to offer uncompensated care. Box 2.8 describes the distinctive experiences of Medicaid waiver programs in Oregon and Tennessee that extended coverage to previously ineligible state residents, ostensibly financed in both cases by reduced payments for services.

Although local (county, city, district) tax revenues are the primary source of support for public hospitals and clinics, state dollars may also come from separate payments for medical education (supplementing those made by Medicare), appro-priations to medical schools, and state-sponsored uncompensated care pools (dis-cussed below) that reimburse hospitals. The state and local tax base, along with the state's level of "fiscal effort," account for much of the funding differences among states (Trenholme and Kung, 2000). See Appendix B for further discussion of how differences in state spending contribute to differences in uninsured rates.

State Uncompensated Care Pools

In Maryland, Massachusetts, New Jersey, and New York, an *uncompensated* or *free care pool* redistributes some of the disproportionate burden of uncompensated care borne by some hospitals more equitably among all hospitals in the state (Needleman, 1999; Bovbjerg et al., 2000a). Box 2.9 describes the operation of Massachusetts' pool as a case in point. Pools have the potential to facilitate greater access to care for uninsured persons who do not live near public hospitals (Bovbjerg et al., 2000a). The pool of funds for uncompensated care is raised by surcharges on payments to hospitals by insurers and patients.

Uncompensated care pools began in the 1970s, in response to growing un-compensated care costs and health care inflation spurred by an economic reces-sion. They were incorporated into these four states' hospital rate-setting regula-tions during the 1980s (Bovbjerg et al., 2000a). With the deregulation of hospital payment practices in the early 1990s (except in Maryland), the states turned to Medicaid DSH payments and Medicaid waivers as additional revenue sources for their pools. States have narrowed the scope of the care that qualifies for payment through the pools, targeting only charity (rather than all) uncompensated care and only those hospitals providing the greatest volume of such services. As uncompen-sated care expenditures continued to rise during the 1990s, pool resources were exhausted.

Like Medicaid DSH payments, state uncompensated care pools are an indirect means of financing care for uninsured persons and, as such, have similar problems with inefficiencies. Increasingly competitive hospital markets have spurred greater resistance by hospitals to assessments levied by the state, and fair and efficient targeting of pool funds is made more difficult by lack of information about actual amounts of charity care provided to uninsured patients. Hospitals that provide uncompensated care but are not recognized as safety-net institutions (i.e., are not public or teaching hospitals) are less likely to receive compensation from pools.

BOX 2.8
Expanding Medicaid Coverage to Reduce Uninsurance:
Two Examples

In 1994, Oregon and Tennessee each began a major expansion of their Medicaid programs, using federal waivers (which required that the new program be budget neutral) and managed care contracting. All persons at or below 100 percent of the federal poverty level became eligible for public coverage or for employer-subsidized coverage. Expanding Medicaid to decrease uninsurance has involved hard choices for these demonstration states, and their success has been mixed and limited. In 2001, both states had uninsured rates below the national average. Still, each had a sizable uninsured population: 443,000 uninsured persons in Oregon (12.8 percent of the state's population of 3.5 million persons) and 640,000 uninsured persons in Tennessee (11.3 percent of the state's population of 5.7 million) (Mills, 2002).

Oregon

Since the 1980s, health reformers have attempted to implement universal coverage in the state incrementally, by means of a series of coordinated measures. These include the Oregon Health Plan, which is a Medicaid expansion to all persons at or below 100 percent of FPL, an employer mandate (which has not been implemented), a public subsidy for workers to purchase employment-based coverage, and a state high-risk pool for persons unable to purchase coverage privately due to their medical conditions (medically uninsurable persons).

The immediate spur to action was the highly publicized death of a 7-year-old boy from leukemia following the state Medicaid program's rejection of a proposed transplant to treat the child's disease. A unique political and technical strategy for engaging public and legislative discussion about the cost of the Medicaid expansion was to make decisions about the scope of Medicaid benefits explicit. Conditions for which treatment would be covered under the program were ranked in order of priority, an approach described as rationing care. Ostensibly, the goal of this approach has been a budget-neutral program expansion. In reality, there is little evidence of cost savings under the new list-based approach to Medicaid benefits, given federal limits placed on changes to Medicaid's benefit package and anecdotal evidence that uncovered care has been provided, if not reimbursed, through other means. The Medicaid expansion has been underwritten by new state general revenues and proceeds from a new tax on cigarette sales.

The Oregon Health Plan has lowered the state's uninsured rate, covering an estimated additional 130,000 low-income persons who would otherwise be uninsured, improved access to care and quality of care for low-income residents, and reduced uncompensated care. In addition, the process of developing and revising the list of benefits that Medicaid covers has fostered social cohesion, building popular support for the Medicaid program.[1]

Tennessee

Tennessee's reforms were motivated by an imminent fiscal crisis in the state's Medicaid program after challenges to its use of a provider tax to raise state matching funds for Medicaid (a situation somewhat unique to Tennessee, which does not levy an income tax). A federal Medicaid waiver moved all of the state's Medicaid enrollees into private sector managed care, doubled the size of the Medicaid program to make eligible all persons at or below 100 percent of FPL; and extended public coverage to all uninsured children through age 17. Benefits were made more generous than under the Medicaid program, with some cost-sharing and premiums tied to income.

Despite the large increase in enrollment that followed expanded eligibility and the greater volume of services delivered by providers at lower reimbursement rates, there was a relatively small increase in new funds to support TennCare. Dollars have come from federal and a variety of state and local revenue streams, including DSH payments to hospitals and annual insurer assessments that had been supporting a state high-risk pool. Capitation resulted in lower per-enrollee payments. One study estimates that during the TennCare's first five years, state and federal government spent about $700 million less than would have been predicted for the Medicaid program without the waiver but that TennCare's expansion of eligibility cost approximately $3.8 billion more, when predicted changes in charity care, patients' cost-sharing, and local government spending were considered.

In the first year after TennCare began, the state's uninsured rate shrank by one-third to one-half, putting the state well below the national average uninsured rate, and there was greater coverage of medically uninsurable persons. This dramatically lower rate has not been maintained, although Tennessee continues to have a lower-than-average uninsured rate. After the first year, fiscal constraints led state officials to close further enrollment of uninsured persons ineligible for Medicaid. In the years since, problems related to TennCare's relatively low capitation rates and potential for adverse risk selection of chronically ill patients have meant further financial stresses and less progress in reducing uninsurance. Lower reimbursement rates have contributed to financial losses that have fiscally destabilized public hospitals and academic health centers, community health centers, and physicians in private practice that serve Medicaid and uninsured patients, and uncompensated care has continued to grow. Although TennCare has improved access to care, quality of care, and consumer satisfaction, and has introduced some efficiencies, it has also fueled tensions between providers and state Medicaid administrators and among beneficiaries, providers, and the state. This has resulted in a decline in social cohesion and a relative lack of popular support that have made it more difficult to secure funding for the program.[2]

---

[1] SOURCES: Jacobs et al., 1999; Leichter, 1999.
[2] SOURCE: Conover and Davies, 2000.

BOX 2.9
State Uncompensated Care Pools: Massachusetts

The Commonwealth of Massachusetts has operated an uncompensated or free care pool since 1985. The goal of the pool is to lighten the burden of uncompensated care related to charity at hospitals and freestanding community health centers that serve large numbers of uninsured and medically indigent persons, by redistributing a portion of the costs incurred in providing these services across all hospitals in the state. For persons judged to be medically indigent (medical expenses greater than 30 percent of income and insufficient assets to cover the expenses) and for lower-income uninsured patients (less than 200 percent of FPL), care is free to the patient and eligible to be fully reimbursed through the pool if funds are available. Care provided to moderate-income (between 200 and 400 percent of FPL) uninsured patients is partially free to the patient and eligible for reimbursement. Although both clinics and hospitals participate in the pool, hospitals are the primary beneficiary, for both inpatient and outpatient services. Allowable free care does not include prescription drugs, physician care outside of what is billed through hospitals or clinics, or services provided by nonacute care hospitals.

The pool is financed by hospital assessments ($170 million in fiscal year 2002); surcharges on payments for hospital and ambulatory surgery center services by private payers (e.g., health plans), including individuals with medical bills over $10,000 ($100 million); and annual state appropriations comprised of federal matching dollars through the Medicaid DSH program ($30 million; the remaining $120 million to $130 million in matching Medicaid DSH dollars goes into state general revenues). Additional state contributions to the pool may also include in-

---

Finally, the pool may unintentionally encourage poor management practices or poor quality of care at hospitals, for example, by offering financial incentives to provide hospital inpatient rather than outpatient care for conditions that may not require hospitalization (Dunn and Chen, 1994; Spencer, 1998; Bovbjerg et. al, 2000a).

City and County Governments

There are approximately 3,000 local health agencies across the country. These include county, city, combined city–county, township, and district or regional organizations. Sixty percent of local public health agencies are at the county level, and 69 percent of local agencies are in jurisdictions of fewer than 50,000 persons (NACCHO, 2001). Annual spending varies from zero to more than $836 million (1999–2000 figures), with median annual expenditures of $621,000 in 1999 dollars (NACCHO, 2001). The largest proportion (average of 44 percent) of total budgets for these health departments comes from local funds (county, city, town), with an average of 30 percent from state funds and federal funds passed through by

tergovernmental transfers from public hospitals in Boston and Cambridge ($70 million in fiscal year 2002), surplus funds from a payroll tax-supported Medical Security Trust Fund that finances coverage for unemployed workers ($90 million), and proceeds from the Tobacco Settlement Fund. On a monthly basis, hospitals submit information to the state about charges incurred by private sector payers, bad debt connected with the provision of emergency department services, and free care delivered to persons qualified to receive such care on the basis of income and residency criteria. Each hospital is credited or reimbursed a portion of the costs, adjusted for an assessment based on the proportion of private sector charges and a proportion of the fund's anticipated shortfall.

Demands on the pool have outpaced available funds in all but two of the past ten years, and current budget trends indicate continuing pressures from state fiscal cutbacks and pressures related to the functioning of the pool and its relationship to the state's Medicaid program (MassHealth). Unanticipated stress on pool resources may result from unintended incentives for hospitals to turn to the pool as a first-dollar payer rather than as a payer of last resort, despite pool regulations stipulating that hospitals screen patients for public coverage eligibility, because of higher reimbursement for services compared with public health insurance reimbursements. The pool's viability also depends in part on the status of MassHealth. For the first three years following expansion of MassHealth in the latter part of the 1990s, draws on the free care pool declined, although increasing health care inflation countered this decline in subsequent years. Also, a planned cutback in MassHealth eligibility, expected to result in 50,000 newly uninsured adults in 2003, is likely to result in greater demand on free care pool resources as well as the loss of federal Medicaid DSH matching dollars available to the pool.

SOURCES: Bovbjerg et al., 2000a; Bovbjerg and Ullman, 2002; Seifert, 2002.

the state to localities. Three percent comes to localities directly from the federal government. Overall, local health departments receive an average of 19 percent of their budgets as reimbursement for direct health services delivery (Medicare, Medicaid, third-party insurers, fees) (NACCHO, 2001).

Local health departments deliver primary care and categorically funded services that are both public health activities and personal health care services (e.g., maternal and child health, immunizations, family planning clinics). In areas with a high uninsured rate, local health departments frequently have absorbed the increases in demand for services from medically indigent residents. Since the late 1980s, health departments have shifted away from the direct provision of personal health services and toward privatizing or contracting out services delivery (Wall, 1998; NACCHO, 2001). At the same time, health departments have become more reliant on Medicaid reimbursements for services they previously provided without charge. However, this source of funds began to decline in the early 1990s, as Medicaid programs entered into managed care contracts with private sector health care providers (Martinez and Closter, 1998; Wall, 1998; Fairbrother et al., 2000).

The degree to which health departments directly provide or arrange for the delivery of health services varies by region and urban versus rural location. Urban health departments are more likely than rural agencies to be involved in the delivery of primary care services and often provide primary care, maternal and child health services, and sexually transmitted disease screening and treatment. Thirty-seven percent of health departments serving more than 500,000 people are involved in direct delivery of health services, compared with 11 percent of agencies serving fewer than 25,000 people (NACCHO, 2001). County health departments in California and Florida and in the South are more likely than health departments in other areas of the country to be involved in direct provision of service. In California and Florida, this involvement stems from the sizable unmet need due in part to high levels of uninsurance, while in the South it reflects historical shortages of private health facilities and providers, particularly in lower-income and rural communities (Needleman et al., 1999).

Public hospitals receive much of their nonoperating revenue from local (municipal and county) dollars (Bovbjerg et al., 2000b). State support may be less important than local public funding for public and other facilities that disproportionately serve uninsured patients. In one study of safety-net capacity in five urban areas, four of the sites had city or county subsidies for general health services (in addition to support for the local health department) through contracts with a city health department or academic health center to provide services, a managed care program sponsored by the county, or support for a public hospital (Felt-Lisk et al., 2001). Box 2.10 details the financing and organization of care for uninsured persons in a number of states and localities to illustrate the variety of arrangements and extensiveness of programs across locales.

Interactions Between Coverage and Services for the Uninsured

As discussed earlier, the size and impacts of a community's uninsured population are closely related to the scope and scale of the state's Medicaid program, as well as its spending on direct services and the size of its lower-income population. For example, Massachusetts' expansion of its Medicaid program to cover childless adults (MassHealth) is estimated to have contributed to a 10 percent decrease in the state's uninsured rate between 1997 and 1999 (Zuckerman et al., 2001b).

Medicaid payments underpin the financial operations of providers that serve the uninsured and public program beneficiaries alike. Yet the extent of employment-based health insurance coverage has an even greater effect on state-level uninsured rates than does the expansiveness of the state's Medicaid program (Holahan, 2002). Some researchers have investigated whether the availability of publicly provided services within a community influences local uninsured rates. Rask and Rask (2000) found, using 1987 data, that counties with public hospitals also had higher uninsured rates than counties that did not have their own hospitals. The direction of causality in this study cannot be determined. Another study using more recent national survey data found that, as measured by a composite of aggregate uncompensated hospital care, physician charity care, and presence of community health centers, low-income workers in cities with a greater safety net capacity to provide charity care are less likely to have an offer of workplace health insurance coverage, although they are just as likely to take up coverage if offered by their employer (Herring, 2001).

Community health centers and other federally supported clinics are in a double bind with regard to Medicaid managed care. Because they have grown to rely on Medicaid revenues in lieu of operating grants, they have an incentive to serve patients who are Medicaid beneficiaries. However, when costs of providing care under Medicaid managed care contracts exceed their capitation payments, the centers' financial condition worsens. Consequently, they have less revenue with which to provide care to uninsured patients (Shi et al., 2001; Rosenbaum et al., 2002). Financial losses and the loss of capacity are likely to diminish access for all health center clients, insured as well as uninsured—for example, pregnant women and young children covered through SCHIP, low-income members of racial and ethnic minority groups, and low-income seniors enrolled in Medicare.

When legislation in the late 1980s established special cost-based reimbursement for FQHCs, these centers were able to increase their capacity to serve uninsured clients substantially, by 1.6 million persons between 1989 and 1999 (BPHC, 2001). In 1997 the Balanced Budget Act stipulated that the special FQHC provision be phased out. However, consequent to the Benefits Improvement and Protection Act of 2000 (BIPA), the federal government adopted a prospective payment system for Medicaid managed care contracts with CHCs, based on each center's cost experience, which is expected to ameliorate some of the adverse effects of managed care contracting for health centers (USGAO, 2001; Schneider, 2002).

Private Payers

Philanthropy

Private charitable contributions play a small but important role in financing health care services for uninsured and other medically indigent individuals. Private nonprofit hospitals and health care networks operated by charitable organizations (e.g., Catholic Health Association members) constitute one type of philanthropic support (Catholic Health Association, 2002). Hospital charity care funds also include the endowments of and relatively small contributions to not-for-profit institutions and community foundations established in the conversion of not-for-profit hospitals and health plans to for-profit status (Grantmakers in Health, 2002b). One estimate puts the total value of private philanthropy at between 1 and 3 percent of hospital revenues, of which only a portion is available for the care of uninsured patients (Davison, 2001).

Regional, community-based, and national foundations also play a role in underwriting care to those who are uninsured. For example, the W.K. Kellogg

BOX 2.10
State, County, and Local Financing of Care
for Uninsured Persons

Texas

In Texas, counties can discharge their duty as provider of last resort by participating in a hospital taxing district (87 counties) that raises funds for indigent care, operating a public hospital (32 counties) or an indigent care program (138 counties), or some combination of these options. Hospital districts levy local property taxes, which account for about one-quarter of the revenue devoted to indigent care, with the remainder financed by the state, out-of-pocket payments, and third-party payers (including Medicaid and Medicare). The state's Tertiary Care Fund (unclaimed lottery prizes) partially reimburses hospital districts for trauma care provided to residents from outside the district and is received mostly by larger urban districts. Federal Medicaid DSH and Medicare graduate medical education (GME) dollars also support hospital districts—again, often larger urban teaching hospitals. In addition, counties and cities may operate their own public hospitals, without the benefit of a hospital district's taxing authority or dedicated local tax revenues, and some rural counties operate their own indigent care programs.

Texas also has an array of publicly supported safety net arrangements similar to those found in other parts of the country, involving academic health centers, state tuberculosis and psychiatric hospitals, and the criminal justice system (about $270 million spent annually on health care, funded solely by state general revenue because prisoners are ineligible for public coverage). Federal matching and block grants, together with state dollars, support specialty services for uninsured persons as well as for the underinsured, chiefly in the areas of family planning ($65 million annually), substance abuse treatment ($85 million annually), and HIV/AIDS treatment ($56 million annually). Finally, uninsured persons are served by 163 federally qualified health centers (FQHCs), an undetermined number of free clinics, more than 450 rural health clinics, and clinics operated or contracted for by local health departments.[1]

Colorado

With its relatively high 17.8 percent uninsured rate in 1998, the 2.2 million person Denver metropolitan area includes the 500,000 residents of the city and county of Denver as well as five adjacent suburban counties. Financing for services for uninsured residents is more secure in the city and county of Denver and less stable in the suburbs, which are experiencing population growth. In both urban and suburban areas, state Medicaid DSH funds and local funds are critical sources of support for this care.

The state finances health care for uninsured persons through the Medicaid DSH program ($174.9 million in 2001), grants for primary and preventive care and for essential community providers ($4.8 million), and the state's indigent care programs (Denver Indigent Care, University Hospital, and Outstate Medically Indigent Care, $79.6 million altogether), which are also supported through the Medicaid DSH program. The indigent care programs are open to uninsured residents or migrant workers who are either U.S. citizens or legal residents and who meet certain income and assets guidelines (sliding scale for copayments). They reimburse up to 30 percent of costs for a broad range of services delivered by qualified providers and are supported by the state's Medicaid program. During 1999, 150,000 Coloradans participated in the state's indigent care programs.

The city and county of Denver support an integrated set of safety-net arrangements through the Denver Health and Hospitals authority, which includes a hospital, 11 FQHCs, a local health department, and 12 school-based clinics, with coordination of services and information across the system. In 1999, Denver's hospital authority provided close to 40 percent of all inpatient visits under the state's indigent care program and more than 40 percent of all indigent care program outpatient visits, delivering about half of all uncompensated care in the larger metropolitan area. The state's Medicaid DSH program and support from the city or county of Denver are major and essential revenue sources for the authority. In 2000, net revenues came from the Medicaid program (33 percent), private insurers (22 percent), the city (11 percent), and Medicare (10 percent). Other sources (e.g., grants, teaching funds) comprised smaller percentages. The city's annual payment to Denver Health in recent years has averaged about half of Denver Health's charity care expenses (not including bad debt, expenses reimbursed through Medicaid DSH, federal operating grants, and revenue from patients). In 1999, Denver contributed $26 million toward Denver Health's estimated $57 million in uncompensated care expenditures. In addition, Denver Health has cultivated new revenue streams from Medicaid managed care (as a partner in statewide Medicaid managed care contracting through Colorado Access); from contracts to care for state and local prisoners and to provide local indigent care and emergency medical services; and from payments made by SCHIP enrollees and paying patients from outside the combined city and county jurisdiction.

Compared with the city of Denver, the suburban counties surrounding it have been less successful in financing care for uninsured persons. Safety-net arrangements include three nonprofit clinic networks at 11 sites (coordinated through the Colorado Community Health Network), county health departments, and private hospitals, with University Hospital as the provider of last resort for inpatient care. Population growth has been more rapid in the suburbs than in the city of Denver itself, and with this growth have come relatively greater numbers of uninsured persons who are ineligible for the indigent care programs (undocumented immigrants). In recent years, University Hospital has accumulated losses that administrators attribute to an increasing load of uninsured patients without a sufficient increase in funding, leading to the rationing of available sources and plans for future cutbacks in the amount of charity care to be given.[2]

Idaho

In Idaho, both the state and the counties finance care for the medically indigent. The state operates a Catastrophic Health Care Cost program that reimburses hospitals for individual patients' bills greater than $10,000 in a one-year period, drawing on a state general fund and a $4.50 per capita fee assessment on each county. Each county functions as the provider of last resort for residents and operates a Medical Indigency Care Program (MICP), supported by local property taxes. At the discretion of the county commissioners, the local MICP may pay bills for less than $10,000 to reimburse necessary care for eligible county residents who apply and are accepted into the program. The structure of the program, eligibility guide-

Continued

BOX 2.10   Continued

lines, and reimbursement amounts and schedules vary from county to county. Recipients are expected to reimburse the MICP for at least a portion of their covered expenses according to a payment schedule. To enforce this provision, at the time a resident applies to MICP, a lien is placed on the recipient's real and personal property and future potential insurance benefits that remains until the payback is completed.

A survey of 11 Idaho counties finds that between 1995 and 1999, few of the counties spent the full amount that had been budgeted for MICP, limited reimbursement was collected, and there were no foreclosures on property. In 1999, budgets for 10 of these counties ranged between $123,000 and $5.8 million, with expenditures of between 50 and 90 percent and paybacks of between 4 and 53 percent.[3]

New Mexico

In New Mexico, a state with a high uninsured rate (and no state income tax), some care for uninsured persons is covered through County Indigent Fund programs. Although participation is not required, most of New Mexico's 33 counties take part in the state's County Indigent Fund program, which finances payments for health care largely through a gross receipts tax. The counties also collect funds and may use their County Indigent Fund program to support county Medicaid (25 percent of County Indigent Fund expenditures overall) and Sole Community Provider (40 percent of expenditures) programs, both of which receive federal matching funds. The eligibility criteria (including residency and documentation of legal immigration status) and benefits vary from county to county and tend to be limited. County indigent hospital and health care boards have administrative oversight of the funds.

In state fiscal year 2001, the participating counties collected about $26.3 million and spent about $28.5 million (including funds carried over from previous years), with a median expenditure of about $570,000 and a range in expenditures from $55,000 for De Baca County to $3.8 million for Dona Ana County on the southwestern border and $3.7 million for San Juan County. In addition, six counties finance indigent care outside the County Indigent Fund, drawing for the most part on property taxes and collecting about $46.1 million in 2001.

A closer look at one county gives a sense of the balance of funding streams and expenditures. In urban Bernalillo County, for example, which includes the Albuquerque metropolitan area, during state fiscal year 2001 the county collected $1

Foundation's six-year program of grants to 13 communities through its Community Voices program supports collaborative efforts to expand access to care through expanded insurance coverage (Kellogg Foundation, 2002). Local foundations in California, Rhode Island, New Hampshire, New York, and Kansas have funded programs to expand coverage, both alone and together with national foundations including The Robert Wood Johnson Foundation (Grantmakers in Health, 2002a).

One new source of support for regional or statewide charitable health foun-

million in gross receipts tax to pay providers under its County Indigent Fund. In addition, the county collected $31.4 million in property taxes and $5.1 million in a General Fund Health Care Account, which were applied toward support for the University of New Mexico's County Medical Center, a county mental health center, health care at the county's detention denter, and service for the debt on a public health facility bond.[4]

Indianapolis, Indiana

Marion County, Indiana, which is contiguous with the city of Indianapolis, operates a managed care program, Wishard Advantage, that enrolls 20,000 of an estimated 40,000 to 60,000 lower-income uninsured persons (earning less than 200 percent of FPL) living in the county. The municipal Health and Hospital Corporation, which oversees the county health department, the county public hospital (Wishard Memorial Hospital), and affiliated health clinics, began this program in 1997 as a way to improve access to primary and preventive services, reduce inappropriate and often costly utilization of the hospital's emergency department, and put the public hospital on a more sound financial footing in an increasingly competitive hospital market. The number of uninsured persons in the county was also increasing at the time the program began.

Benefits are similar to those offered through Indiana's Medicaid managed care programs, although enrollees have access only to providers in the Wishard Advantage network (e.g., a physicians group practice affiliated with Indiana University Medical School, Wishard Memorial Hospital, a neighborhood health clinic).

The Corporation has the authority to levy property taxes and generates roughly $70 million annually in revenues, of which $56 million supports Wishard Advantage. State and federal dollars through the Medicaid DSH payment amounted to almost $52 million in 1997. Funding is considered stable, given the stable tax rate since 1992 and rising property values.[5]

---

[1] SOURCE: Fenz, 2000 et al.
[2] SOURCES: Matherlee, 2001; Ormond and Lutzky, 2001; Tilly, 2002; State of Texas Comptroller's Office, 2000.
[3] SOURCES: Borden et al, 2001; State of Idaho, 2002.
[4] SOURCES: State of New Mexico, 2000, 2002.
[5] SOURCES: Bruen et al., 2001; Katz et al, 2001.

---

dations is the conversion of nonprofit health plans to for-profit status (analogous to the conversion of nonprofit hospitals) and the creation of local foundations (Grantmakers in Health, 2002b). In California, not-for-profit health plans converting to for-profit status are required by the state to transfer the not-for-profit's assets into a charitable foundation (California Wellness Foundation, n.d.). A number of foundations have been created in this way, including The California Wellness Foundation (established in 1992 with the assets from the conversion of the Health Net health maintenance organization [HMO]) and two foundations created from the 1996 conversion of Blue Cross of California into WellPoint Health Networks (The California Endowment and the California HealthCare Foundation) (California Endowment, n.d.; California HealthCare Foundation, 2001; California Wellness Foundation, n.d.). These foundations have supported care to the uninsured through operating grants, but some devote the bulk of their funding to research, technical support, and education.

The pro bono services of physicians and other health professionals in treating uninsured patients, both within their private practices and at specially established clinics, also fall within the category of philanthropy. The extent of such care provided by physicians has been discussed in a previous section.

Privately established free clinics, sponsored variously by faith-based institutions, medical societies, and community coalitions, provide a growing but poorly documented share of services to uninsured persons (Grantmakers in Health, 2002a). A study of changing safety-net capacity in the mid-1990s finds volunteer-staffed free clinics at three of five sites studied (Detroit, Michigan; Columbus, Ohio; and Oklahoma City, Oklahoma) (Felt-Lisk et al., 2001). The clinics have limited hours, are supported by donations, tend to provide primary care and pharmaceuticals for adults, and are often connected with churches. They may be affiliated with local hospitals, but the relationship can be tenuous, with the hospital unwilling to accept referrals. These clinics provide greater access for vulnerable groups, particularly uninsured persons who are ineligible for public coverage (i.e., undocumented immigrants) but are limited in resources and unlikely to be able to sustain continuity of care. Like soup kitchens in church basements for homeless people, the need for and existence of community free clinics point up the inadequacies of local public services and provisions for vulnerable community residents.

Third-Party Payers and Cross-Subsidization

An earlier section of this chapter describes the public subsidies that reimburse some of the uncompensated care expenditures incurred by uninsured persons. Private sector payers may also contribute to the reimbursement of providers' uncompensated care costs. This section explores how one might think about such a private "cross" subsidy from commercial or private sector payers (e.g., insurers, employers who sponsor employment-based coverage, and covered workers, whose insurance represents part of their compensation package). The extent of private cross-subsidy of the uninsured has not been systematically investigated. Aside from Massachusetts, where provider surcharges finance a free care pool for hospitals and some clinics (Seifert, 2002), such cross-subsidy is expected to be implicit rather than explicit. There is, however, research literature about physician and hospital pricing policy with regard to the "shifting" of incurred costs from public to private payers that suggests how a similar mechanism for private cross-subsidy of a portion of the unreimbursed costs of the uninsured would work.

The term *cost-shifting* has been defined in a number of ways. Some studies consider shifting in a static sense (e.g., price discrimination, when a hospital charges different prices of different payers, without any particular relationship between the different prices). Others, which look at shifting in a dynamic sense (e.g., when the price charged to one payer is higher because a lower price is charged to another payer or because of a shortfall in revenue from the other payer), are more relevant to understanding potential cross-subsidies of uncompensated care (Morrisey, 1996). In the early 1980s, the term described how, after the advent of Medicare prospective payment, hospitals sought to "shift" what they considered unreimbursed expenditures for Medicare patients to private payers by means of higher billed rates for health services (Morrisey, 1994; Clement, 1997–1998). In the first half of the 1990s, attention focused on cost-shifting from private (managed care contracting for employment-based coverage) to public payers.

Changes in hospital margins over time give a rough sense of the extent to which private cross-subsidies affect hospitals' capacity to absorb uncompensated care expenditures. Figure 2.1 depicts the simultaneous decline in private payer surpluses for hospital payments over the past 10 years with little change in reported (net) uncompensated care and change in hospitals' financial margins; the trends could be interpreted as evidence that hospitals have actually been able to raise their charges to private payers in order to cover uncompensated care costs. It is difficult to interpret the changes in hospital pricing because published studies have examined individual hospitals, rather than the overall relationship between uncompensated care, uninsured rates, and pricing trends in the hospital services market overall.

There is little published evidence about cross-subsidizing uncompensated care among for-profit hospitals. To the extent that such institutions conform to standard economic models of profit maximization, they would be predicted to minimize their provision of uncompensated care (Needleman, 2000; Zwanziger et al., 2000). One analyst argues that there was little or no cross-subsidization from private payers during the 1990s, despite the potential for it, because of "price sensitive employers, aggressive insurers, and excess capacity in the hospital industry," all of which imply a relative lack of market power on the part of hospitals (Morrisey, 1996). Older data (from the 1980s) yields somewhat more evidence for cross-subsidization among nonprofit hospitals than among for-profit hospitals (Hadley and Feder, 1985; Frank and Salkever, 1991; Morrisey, 1993, 1994; Gruber, 1994; Hadley et al., 1996; Dranove and White, 1998; Needleman, 1999). Hospitals have been less able to shift costs among payers as health services markets have become more competitive (Morrisey, 1993; Bamezai et al., 1999; Keeler et al., 1999). In some circumstances (e.g., California in the 1980s and early 1990s), uncompensated care has declined in response to increased market pressures and to public policy (Gruber, 1994; Rundall et al., 1988; Mann et al., 1995). Instead of *shifting* costs, hospitals are *cutting* costs and reducing uncompensated care (Campbell and Ahern, 1993; Gruber, 1994; Zwanziger et al., 1994; Hadley et al., 1996;

Morrisey, 1996; Dranove and White, 1998). Some analysts argue, however, that the ability to cross-subsidize care remains substantial (Zwanziger et al., 2000).

Institutional efforts to reduce private cross-subsidy can result in the transfer of the burden of uncompensated care from private hospitals to public institutions, which has been facilitated by the increasingly competitive market for hospital services and managed care contracting (Morrisey, 1996). As discussed earlier in this chapter, in some urban areas there is evidence that uninsured patients are being even more concentrated at safety-net facilities and that, as a result, there is less opportunity for private cross-subsidy of their care. The closing or ownership conversion to private status of public hospitals, a topic to be taken up in Chapter 3, can effect a reverse transfer, from public to private institutions, depending on local public financing arrangements.

Efforts to increase, decrease, or maintain private cross-subsidies may have a particular impact in rural areas. The smaller the provider, the less ability it has to cross-subsidize. Coburn (2002) argues that physicians in private practice are able to provide the 20 to 40 percent of uncompensated care in rural communities that they do because they are supported or subsidized by their community's hospital. For employers in rural areas, the importance of cross-subsidy is a function of scale. It is a greater burden in small towns, where there are fewer employers across whom to spread the financial burden when it occurs in the form of higher costs for health care and health insurance premiums. As a result, there is a competitive disadvantage that accrues to employers who offer more generous or greater subsidies of their employment-based coverage (Morrisey, 1994). A hospital's ability to cross-subsidize uncompensated care costs is affected by the percentage of the revenue base to which uncompensated expenses may be shifted. Rural hospitals tend to have a smaller-than-average private payer revenue base because Medicare constitutes a higher-than-average proportion of their payer mix (MedPAC, 2001). Similarly, hospitals that disproportionately serve Medicaid and uninsured patients by definition have a smaller private payer base that could potentially cross-subsidize the care provided to uninsured patients.

RESEARCH QUESTIONS

2.1 Local Patterns of Unmet Need and Utilization by Uninsured Persons
What are the unmet needs for care of uninsured persons and families? Do they differ geographically both within and among states?

Basic to almost all the proposed research in this chapter is the need for reliable and current local estimates of uninsured rates and measures of the dispersion or concentration of uninsured persons within local health services markets and among the providers within a market. Until the late 1990s most estimates of uninsured rates were available only at the national, state, or major metropolitan statistical area (MSA) level, most notably through the U.S. Census Bureau's March Current

Population Survey (CPS).[14] In recent years, the Health Resources and Services Administration's State Planning Grant program, together with the State Health Access Data Assistance Center (SHADAC), has facilitated the creation of uninsured rate surveys at the county or regional level within states, although these estimates tend not to be comparable across surveys. Enhanced data collection and coordination of existing surveys are needed, as well as the development of new methods to allow generation of more precise and reliable local uninsured rates and for the comparison of these estimated rates across jurisdictions.

A local uninsured rate can be the basis for estimating the unmet need or health services utilization of uninsured persons, but more direct measures are preferable. Programs to provide and pay for uninsured care are often stretched to their resource limits, with existing dollars outstripped by the perceived health needs of this population (Lewin and Altman, 2000; Felt-Lisk et al., 2001; IOM, forthcoming 2003). Evaluative research is needed to understand how uninsurance at a local level influences the organization and delivery of health care. How have communities that have been substantially effective in meeting the needs for health care of uninsured and other underserved populations proceeded, and what financing and services strategies have they employed?

2.2 Public Subsidy of Health Services Delivered to Uninsured Persons
What are the sources of public support for care to uninsured persons? How much does each source contribute and how efficiently are the funds allocated?

The Committee relies on Hadley and Holahan (2003) for a working set of rough estimates about the extent of public subsidy. More complete and consistent documentation of existing federal, state, and local supports for the provision of care to uninsured persons is needed. The levels of such payments to hospitals alone, for example, are substantial and may even be adequate in total to cover the costs of uncompensated hospital care for those completely without health insurance (Hadley and Holahan, 2003). However, more research is needed to pinpoint administrative barriers and inefficiencies in the allocation of funds that result in inadequate or poorly targeted subsidies for the care of uninsured persons. For example, the formulas used to calculate Medicare and Medicaid DSH payment rates do not take the number of uninsured patients into account. In addition, it is difficult if not impossible to compare the relative amounts spent by states through the Medicaid DSH program because states use a variety of methods to generate their match (e.g., tax revenues, intergovernmental transfers from public hospitals) and report different types of data.

---

[14]Appendix B in the Committee's first report, *Coverage Matters*, reviews the major surveys that give estimates of uninsured rates (IOM, 2001a).

2.3 *Private Subsidy of Care Delivered to Uninsured Persons*

To what extent does uncompensated care by doctors, hospitals, and other entities support care for uninsured persons? To what degree do private cross-subsidies support the care of uninsured persons?

It is widely assumed that private payers (e.g., employers, insurers) and private sector health care providers (e.g., nonprofit hospitals, physician practices) cross-subsidize the costs of care for uninsured patients. However, the size of this subsidy is difficult to estimate and the mechanisms through which this uncompensated care is subsidized are complex and not explicitly addressed or documented in the research literature. To the extent that private cross-subsidies occur, what are the implications for health care costs, for local businesses and employers who offer employment-based coverage, and for economic activity in the community?

The literature on hospital cost-shifting presents a useful approach to proposed research on private cross-subsidy. One way to gauge the extent of cross-subsidy, for example, is depicted in Figure 2.1, which compares the contributions of uncompensated care, Medicare margins, and private payer surpluses to hospitals' total margins over time. A longitudinal analysis of changes in payment-to-cost ratios or prices for each payer to an individual provider, correlated with changes in the provider's total margin and in the cost of unreimbursed care provided to uninsured persons, would yield more precise information about the amount and sources of private subsidy (Dobson, 2002; Morrissey, 2002). Both quantitative and qualitative studies would likely be needed to tease out the extent of private cross-subsidy, with much regional and market variation related to the market position of both insurers and health care providers (e.g., ability to negotiate discounted charges, anticipated revenue from a hospital's patient case mix, the amount of hospital revenues across which an uncompensated care burden could be spread).

SUMMARY

As one historian of health care financing in twentieth-century America has observed, hospitals have proven to be quite efficient in their adaptive responses to changed fiscal incentives but not nearly as efficient in meeting changing public needs for health care (Stevens, 1989). The growth of insurance-based means for financing care, the federal government's approach to shaping health policy through payment policies, increasing price competition in the market for health services, and erosion of the cross-subsidies afforded by private payer reimbursements for care have meant that persons who lack health coverage are less able than insured persons to gain access to affordable care and to be able to pay for the care that they receive. As a result, health care providers who treat uninsured persons are likely to accumulate uncompensated costs that may impair their ability to continue delivering care.

Governments, health care practitioners and institutions, philanthropies, and private payers all play a part in serving or paying for the care of uninsured Americans. The implicit subsidies are considerable, and their target efficiency and adequacy are difficult to judge. Ultimately, there is no comprehensive or coordinated approach to caring for uninsured persons. The financial implication of this reality—namely, uncompensated care—sets into motion a number of potential community effects of uninsurance.

The growth over the past several decades in the importance of health finance in the U.S. economy and government finances magnifies market distortions and inequities and inefficiencies in the allocation of public resources. Hospital uncompensated care was much easier for both governments and the institutions themselves to address when Medicaid and Medicare together accounted for much less of the national spending on hospital care than the 48 percent that they currently do (Cowan et al., 2001). The DSH payments under those two federal programs, although substantial and essential supports for institutions that are major providers of care to the uninsured, are blunt tools.

Mainstream health services delivery and the provision of care to and financing of care for uninsured Americans are fundamentally interrelated. Although these two components of the health care enterprise are often treated as separate entities with distinct constituencies governed by separate policies, they cannot be understood in isolation from one another. This is especially evident when tracing the funding streams that pay for the care the uninsured receive and the impacts on health care institutions and providers locally when the proportion of uninsured residents is relatively high or increasing. Despite the relatively stable proportion of the national population without health insurance over the past two decades, major changes in the financing and organization of health care services in both the public and the private sectors have changed the significance and impact of uninsured populations for health care providers and governments at all levels.

The next three chapters examine community health care services and access, social and economic institutions, and population health in conjunction with local uninsurance.

3

Community Effects on Access to Care

The Committee hypothesizes that the burden of financing care for uninsured persons affects the health services available within the community, especially in urban areas where providers treat large numbers of uninsured persons and in rural areas where providers treat relatively high proportions of uninsured. The strategies taken may be different in rural and urban areas, but the Committee finds plausible the idea that providers in rural and urban settings respond to financial pressures related to uninsurance in similar ways. In an effort to avoid this burden or to minimize its impact on a provider's bottom line, services may be cut back, relocated, or closed. Staffing may be reduced. This may further strain the capacities of already overcrowded hospital emergency departments, and physicians' offices or even hospitals may be relocated away from areas of town or entire communities that have concentrations of uninsured persons. Such disruptions may reduce people's access to care and the quality of care they receive, regardless of their insurance status.

In this chapter, the Committee explores the consequences of community uninsurance for access to care in the context of the present era of rapid change in public and private health care financing. As discussed in Chapter 1, the Committee has chosen to interpret its task as concerning community effects of uninsurance but not of underinsurance, despite the difficulties of disentangling the likely mutual influences of uninsurance and underinsurance and the limits of the existing literature. After a brief discussion of access to care considered in general, the chapter is organized by type of service, examining primary care, emergency medical services and other specialty care, and hospital-based care in turn. The chapter concludes with a discussion of questions for further research and a summary.

Although many of the data and studies are organized by institution or profession, the Committee takes the perspective of community residents as consumers of health care and reports on local health services arrangements as typically encountered by someone seeking care. Focusing on the types of services as they may be affected by uninsured rates, rather than on providers and institutions, allows a more systematic perspective on the adequacy of health services throughout the community (see IOM, 2001b). In addition, the mere survival of particular institutions may not be a good proxy for the availability of high-quality care (particularly primary care) or for judging the impacts of uninsurance in a rapidly changing health care system or market. Nonetheless, the value of a hospital or clinic may include contributions to a community's social and economic base or serve as a source of community identity. Thus, changes related to uninsurance may have additional effects beyond those related to access and quality of care. These values are discussed in the next chapter, which addresses some potential social and economic effects of uninsurance.

ACCESS TO CARE

Finding: Persons with low to moderate incomes (less than 250 percent of the federal poverty level), nearly one-third of whom are uninsured, and uninsured persons have worse access to health care services in communities with high uninsured rates than they do in communities with lower rates. The causal influence of the local uninsured rate on measures of access is unclear.

While insurance facilitates access to health care by removing or diminishing financial barriers faced by individuals and families, it also secures a revenue stream for health care providers and institutions (IOM, 2001a, 2002a, 2002b). The Committee hypothesizes that when this revenue stream is diminished by higher local uninsured rates, providers may opt to change their patterns of service provision within the community in an effort to preserve revenues. Depending on the local organization of health services, this provider phenomenon would be expected to affect the opportunities of insured residents to obtain health care. Lower-income residents are particularly likely to be affected by loss of access to care because of their limited economic ability, for example, in rural areas to travel long distances to obtain services unavailable locally or to pay higher costs for care.

Three recent studies examine the relationship between self-reported access to care and community uninsurance in urban areas (Cunningham and Kemper, 1998; Brown et al., 2000; Andersen et al., 2002). All of the studies rely on survey data about self-reported access to care, using a number of different measures (e.g., difficulty obtaining care, not having seen a physician in the previous 12 months).

The first study, based on the nationally representative 1996–1997 Community Tracking Study (CTS) Household Survey, examines the differences among metropolitan statistical areas (MSAs) larger than 200,000 population in the rates that uninsured residents reported forgoing, postponing, or having difficulty obtaining needed medical care as a function of the community uninsured rate (Cunningham and Kemper, 1998). The authors show that the rates at which uninsured residents reported difficulties in obtaining care differed more than twofold over the range of high-uninsured-rate and low-uninsured-rate communities, from about 41 percent (Lansing, Michigan) to 19 percent (Orange County, California), with a national average of 30 percent.[1] Only about 15 percent of the variation among the communities in rates of difficulty in accessing care is related to measured differences in the health needs or other population characteristics of the uninsured respondents, indicating that most of this variation is related to unmeasured factors. Concluding that an uninsured person's place of residence plays a key role in determining ease of access to care, the authors hypothesize that differences in access may reflect the economic make-up of the uninsured person's community (e.g., providers in wealthier areas may be better able or inclined to deliver free or reduced-price care) or the availability of health care outside of the community (e.g., proximity of multiple health care markets in the larger MSAs) (Cunningham and Kemper, 1998).

Although the first of the three studies discussed focuses only on uninsured residents, it points up how their ability to obtain care depends on their relative numbers within the overall community. Further, the possibility remains that insured residents are affected by local uninsurance in ways not measured in the analysis. The authors report no relationship (correlation) across the 60 communities studied between the proportion of privately insured respondents reporting difficulty obtaining access to care and the proportion of uninsured respondents with access difficulties, as well as different reasons for difficulties, with 90 percent of uninsured respondents citing cost as the key constraint, compared with 48 percent of insured respondents. Yet the often separate experiences of uninsured and privately insured with the organization and delivery of care in urban areas (as described in Chapter 2) may be linked through the effects that uninsurance exerts on the local health care market.

The second study considers the aggregate experiences of all low- to moderate-income residents (earning less than 250 percent of the federal poverty level [FPL]), under age 65 in the 85 largest MSAs in 1997, without distinguishing between insured and uninsured respondents (Brown et al., 2000). The authors examine measures of health care access including forgone or delayed care, no physician visit within the year, and having a regular source of care, as a function of uninsured rate (Brown et al., 2000, data for 1997). Residents of the 12 MSAs with

---

[1]This analysis was unadjusted for the many individual and community-level covariates of uninsured rate. Adjusting for health care need (health status, age, gender) and socioeconomic and demographic characteristics (income, education, family size, race and ethnicity, whether Spanish language interview) narrowed the range in reported difficulty in obtaining access to care to between 36 percent for Cleveland, Ohio, and 22 percent for Newark, New Jersey.

significantly higher uninsured rates (at least one standard deviation above the mean for all 85 MSAs) reported greater difficulty obtaining health care than did residents of the 17 MSAs with significantly lower uninsured rates, unadjusted for any covariates of unin-surance: 22 percent reported delaying or going without needed health care in MSAs with high uninsured rates, compared to 8 percent in MSAs with substantially lower uninsured rates; the comparable figures for those who reported no physician visit in the past year were 39 and 14 percent in MSAs with high and low uninsured rates, respectively. Since almost one-third of persons under age 65 who earn less than 200 percent of FPL or who are members of families that earn less than 200 percent of FPL are uninsured (Fronstin, 2002), it is likely that a proportion of the effect observed of local uninsured rate reflects the experiences of the uninsured rather than the insured study participants.

The third study complicates conclusions that might be drawn from the findings of Cunningham and Kemper about what unmeasured community-level characteristics may influence the access of uninsured persons to care and the findings of Brown et al. about the relative influence of community uninsurance on insured versus uninsured residents. In a multivariate, cross-sectional study of the likelihood (odds) that low-income children and adults under age 65 have seen a physician in the past year in the 25 largest MSAs nationally, the authors show that a number of individual-level and community-level covariates may better explain differences in access to care than does the community uninsured rate (Andersen et al., 2002). While analytically adjusting for measures of community demand for care (percentage in poverty, uninsured rate, and percentage enrolled in Medicaid) did not change the odds that low-income children and adults would have seen a physician in the past year, taking into account differences in a community's financial and structural capacity to deliver care (e.g., higher per capita income, lower unemployment, greater income inequality, number of public hospital beds per thousand population, number of community health centers per thousand population, lower degree of managed care penetration) did improve the odds of seeing a physician in the past year (Andersen et al., 2002). Echoing the hypothesis laid out by Cunningham and Kemper, the authors suggest that a possible explanation for their findings is that greater community wealth may strengthen the financial viability of safety-net arrangements, either directly or through the support of higher levels of eligibility for public coverage or higher spending on related public programs.

Together, these three studies provide evidence that, with limited analytic adjustments for the many covariates of insurance status and uninsured rate, an urban area's uninsured rate is associated with the ability of uninsured and of moderate- and lower-income residents to obtain needed and regular health care. Such measures of access to health services are basic markers of effective, quality care that improves health outcomes (Millman, 1993; IOM, 2002a, 2002b). Longitudinal studies are needed, with adjustments for covariates of insurance status and uninsured rate, to better distinguish whether and how community uninsurance influences the access experiences of insured and uninsured community members in different ways and to a greater or lesser extent.

PRIMARY CARE

Except for the studies of access to care described in the preceding section, which include measures that can be interpreted as measures of access to primary care, there is little empirical documentation of the relationship between community uninsurance and access to primary care. In this section, the Committee draws on the literature about primary care providers and sites of care, for the most part, physicians and clinics, to develop background information about potential mechanisms and outcomes of community effects.

Uninsurance may compromise access for many community residents to preventive, screening, and primary care services. These services are provided in diverse settings, ranging from general primary care and specialized health department clinics (e.g., immunization, family planning), private physician offices, community health centers, hospital outpatient and emergency departments, and dedicated hospital primary care outpatient clinics (Donaldson et al., 1996). See Box 3.1 for the Committee's working definition of primary care. Particularly for low-income residents and members of other medically underserved groups, clinics and health centers play a special role in primary health care services delivery due to their close geographical proximity to underserved populations, their cultural competence and history in the community, and their provision of supportive "wrap-around" services that facilitate access to care and quality care (Hawkins and Rosenbaum, 1998). As a result, when uninsurance results in fiscal pressures on community facilities, insured as well as uninsured clients may be affected by reductions in health center services. To make up for the provision of uncompensated care, clinics and health centers may cut back on available services, lengthen waiting times for all patients, and cease operations altogether in some communi-

---

BOX 3.1
Definition of Primary Care

The Institute of Medicine Committee on the Future of Primary Care defines primary care "as the provision of integrated (that is to say, comprehensive, coordinated, and continuous over time), accessible health care services by clinicians who are accountable for addressing a large majority of personal health care needs, developing a sustained partnership with patients, and practicing in the context of family and community" (Donaldson et al., 1996). Primary care clinicians typically are physicians, physician assistants, or nurse practitioners, sometimes working together in a team. The ongoing personal relationship between provider and patient that is the ideal in primary care is an integral element of quality health care (IOM, 2001b).

ties. In Los Angeles County in the latter half of the 1990s, for example, in a survey of private providers who contracted with the county to care for medically indigent patients, respondents reported finding themselves at financial risk, with the potential loss of the provider's services to the entire community (Grazman and Cousineau, 2000). See Box 3.2 for case studies of uninsurance and primary care in two of the country's largest urban areas.

Shortages of physicians in rural and urban areas with relatively high uninsured rates can mean less access to primary care for all residents. Access for rural residents is particularly sensitive to reductions in available care, because residents have limited choices to begin with and are likely to face long travel times and distances to reach providers outside their community. Furthermore, rural residents, who tend to be in poorer health and older than residents of suburban and urban areas, are likely to experience greater difficulty traveling these longer distances (Ormond et al., 2000a).

Physicians

Physicians' decisions about the nature and location of their practice may be influenced by the uninsured rate of the community among other factors (e.g., malpractice insurance costs, the availability of specialty support, the option to practice in large tertiary care hospitals, the safety and overall attractiveness of the community as a place to live). Considerations about where to locate a new practice are likely to differ from those regarding an ongoing practice because established practices may be better able to accommodate charity or other uncompensated care. Many rural areas and lower-income and economically depressed urban neighborhoods have a harder time recruiting and retaining primary care practitioners than do more populous and affluent communities.

For communities in rural areas, uninsurance may make it more difficult for a private physician to maintain a financially viable practice. Physicians in rural areas are more likely to treat Medicaid and uninsured patients and have higher proportions of Medicare patients due to rural demographics (Mueller et al., 1999). As a result, rural physicians may face lower levels of reimbursement. This can place further financial drains on their practices (Coburn, 2002). At the same time, in such areas, safety net arrangements for primary care tend to be informal and not publicly subsidized, especially in the smallest towns (Taylor et al., 2001). A convenience survey of informal safety net arrangements in eight towns across the country (less than 5,000 population) finds that rural hospitals are particularly important in this regard (Taylor et al., 2001). Many rural physicians work in affiliation with or are supported by their community hospital, through either a rural health clinic or the hospital itself. For example, a family practice in Deer Island, Maine, a fishing community in which 60 percent of the residents were uninsured, alleviated its financial problems by affiliating with a local hospital as a rural health clinic (Finger, 1999).

Physicians who serve uninsured patients encounter ethical and legal dilemmas

BOX 3.2
Effects on Primary Care: Los Angeles and New York City

Los Angeles County, California

Los Angeles County is home to 10 million people, roughly one-quarter of whom (2.5 million persons) are uninsured. Financial pressures on the county health department related to the care of medically indigent and uninsured persons are leading to a reduction in primary care and preventive services and the closing of sites of care for all county residents. The county health department serves an estimated 800,000 patients each year, many of whom are uninsured.

Broad cuts in services were averted during a county budget crisis in the mid-1990s through an increase in federal Medicaid payments for outpatient services (totaling more than $2 billion) under a five-year program waiver from the federal government. This waiver was renewed once and is scheduled to expire in 2005. Under the waiver, county health services were reconfigured to emphasize primary care and preventive services, which improved access to care but did not reduce hospital inpatient utilization significantly or result in appreciable cost savings.

Recent years' state Medicaid budget troubles are shared by Los Angeles County. Despite the county's Board of Supervisors' efforts to balance the department's $2.9 billion dollar budget and voter support of a property tax increase earmarked to support hospital trauma centers ($168 million expected annually), a $700 million to $800 million deficit is anticipated in 2003. To reduce this deficit, the county has made cuts in primary care rather than in specialty services, hospital inpatient services, or emergency medical services. According to one news account, decision makers justified this choice by explaining that primary care services are more affordable for the clinics' clients than specialty services, even though one of the anticipated consequences is increased emergency department (ED) use for non-urgent, primary care. Like hospital EDs elsewhere, those operated by public hospitals in Los Angeles are precluded by the Emergency Medical Treatment and Labor Act (EMTALA) from limiting the use of their services to persons with health insurance.

In June 2002, the county closed 11 of its 18 public health clinics and 1 of its 6 public hospitals. It also scaled back support for 100 private clinics and cut 18 percent of employees (5,000 jobs). This was done as part of efforts to trim the deficit in preparation for negotiations for additional federal or state subsidies. Further downsizing and closings are anticipated to be announced in the coming months.[1]

New York City

New York's municipal Health and Hospitals Corporation (HHC) is the largest public hospital system in the country, overseeing 11 acute care public hospitals and more than 100 local clinics among its varied responsibilities to provide health care to medically underserved groups. HHC serves approximately 1.3 million persons a year, 43 percent of whom are uninsured. About half of all hospital-based care is delivered to uninsured and underinsured residents, and HHC facilities provide a disproportionate share of services more likely to be used by vulnerable populations (e.g., tuberculosis, HIV/AIDs, psychiatric, trauma, alcohol and substance abuse, emergency medical services).

Since 1994, HHC has responded to several financial challenges by cutting back funds and shifting patients from hospitals to primary care clinics. During 2001, HHC experienced its first deficit in five years. News accounts attribute part of the $300 million deficit to a 30 percent increase since 1996 in the number of uninsured persons (totaling more than 564,000 uninsured patients in 2000). Other factors include changes in patient mix and volume (e.g., loss of market share to other hospitals), competition for Medicaid patients to fill inpatient beds (given declining inpatient utilization) from private nonprofit hospitals, and a growing gap between uncompensated care and public subsidies (e.g., indigent care dollars from the state, Medicare disproportionate share hospital payments, and appropriated city tax revenue). Uninsured patients account for 10 percent of hospitalized patients and 30 percent of ambulatory care patients in HHC facilities. As Medicaid payments lag behind health care cost inflation, especially for clinic visits, and private sector facilities compete successfully for Medicaid managed care enrollees, Medicaid revenues to HHC facilities have declined. Because patients have been shifted from hospitals to primary care clinics, there has been a 9 percent increase in clinic visits and a 12.5 percent decrease in inpatient admissions since 1992. Because Medicaid managed care payments to primary care clinics are lower than those for hospital care or for specialty services, HHC facilities have been squeezed financially.

Despite the known benefits of primary care, HHC has closed and merged preventive and primary health care sites over the past year, including eight neighborhood health centers. After receiving additional funds from the city, HHC decided to keep open 15 school-based clinics slated for closure, although their operations will result in an anticipated $2.7 million loss in 2001. For the most part, the clinics selected for closing are located in immigrant and low-income neighborhoods where roughly two-thirds of the patients are uninsured. Clinics to be closed include 9 of 42 that specialize in children's health. Overall, the loss of capacity is estimated as 100,000 children served annually. Other cost-control measures include cutting staff and downsizing capacity—for example, decreasing the capacity of the renovated Queens Hospital Center from 300 to 200 beds. These changes have resulted in overcrowding and longer waits at public hospital emergency departments and waiting areas, longer waiting times to get appointments, higher fees for pharmacy services, and lower quality of care. [2]

---

[1]SOURCES: Cornwell et al., 1996; Grazman and Cousineau, 2000; Andersen et al., 2002; Cohn, 2002; Larrubia, 2002; Lutzky and Zuckerman, 2002; Riccardi, 2002a, 2002b; Riccardi et al., 2002; Rundle, 2002.

[2]SOURCES: Siegel, 1996; Prinz et al., 2000; Ramirez, 2001; Sengupta, 2001; Steinhauer, 2001a, 2001b; United Hospital Fund, 2002.

that physicians who do not see the uninsured (either by choice or by practice location) can avoid. Anticipating little or no reimbursement for their services, they may have to decide between reducing the amount or nature of the services they provide to patients from whom they do not expect any compensation or seeing fewer uninsured patients in their practices (Weiner, 2001). The decision to limit service for uninsured persons may preserve the financial basis for individual or group practice, but it presents an ethical or moral conflict for many physicians (Weiner, 2001).

Over the 1990s, the proportion of physicians who provided charity care (whether to uninsured or insured persons) declined. The CTS results presented in Chapter 2 show a decline in the proportion of physicians reporting giving charity care from 76.3 to 71.5 percent between 1997 and 2001 (Reed et al., 2001; Cunningham, 2002). The proportion of physicians devoting more than 5 percent of their clinical practice time to charity care also decreased over this period from 33.5 to 29.8 percent, while the proportion devoting less than 5 percent of their practice time to charity care increased from 66.5 to 70.2 percent (Cunningham, 2002). This change is thought to be related to health care market changes, including the shift of physicians from solo and group ownership of practices to becoming employees of larger health services institutions. It may also be related to the financial strain on physician practices and increased time pressures. According to the results of a 2000 CTS survey, even at academic health centers (which serve a safety-net function in many urban areas), 63 percent of affiliated medical school faculty surveyed report that they are discouraged from seeing uninsured patients, by either inadequate payment, their teaching hospital, or their practice group (Weissman et al., 2002).

Physicians who provide charity care also have concerns about malpractice liability that may affect their provision of such care. A random sample survey of California generalist physicians ($n = 124$) finds that these practitioners' decisions about accepting new uninsured patients were influenced by the concern that they would be more likely to be sued (49 percent) (Komaromy et al., 1995). This study reported that just 43 percent of those surveyed accepted new uninsured patients compared with 77 percent who accepted new privately insured patients.

Community Health Centers and Clinics

Finding: Serving a high or increasing number of uninsured persons reduces a community health center's capacity to provide ambulatory care to all of its clients, insured as well as uninsured.

By mission, community health centers (CHCs) are located in areas with limited access to primary care (Davis et al., 1999). For uninsured persons, there is evidence that CHCs provide better access to primary health care, as measured by having a regular source of care and having a physician visit in the previous year, and higher-quality care, as measured by patient satisfaction and meeting *Healthy*

People 2000 goals for health promotion, prevention, and screening than other ambulatory care providers (Carlson et al., 2001). Expanding the number of CHCs or their capacity to provide services is likely to improve access to primary care for medically underserved groups (Forrest and Whelan, 2000). One survey of primary care access at four types of ambulatory care sites (public facilities, private nonprofits, federally qualified health centers, and other freestanding health centers) in New York City in 1997 found that public sites have the strongest performance for low-income patients in terms of coverage for uninsured persons, services available after business hours, and the availability of wraparound services.[2] This study concluded that serving increasing numbers of uninsured persons, in the context of fiscal pressures from Medicaid managed care and fewer Medicaid patients overall, may weaken ambulatory sites' capacity to provide primary care to all members of the community (Weiss et al., 2001). The loss of ambulatory care clinical services would be particularly damaging to vulnerable populations because these clinics serve higher proportions of low-income and minority group members under age 65 and have safety net missions (e.g., serving farmworkers, homeless persons, or undocumented immigrants) or patients with specific high-risk diagnoses (e.g., tuberculosis, sexually transmitted diseases, substance abuse).

CHCs face financial pressures on a number of fronts: from reduced income from Medicaid patients, related to the growth of state Medicaid managed care contracting; from reduced public subsidies; and from an increased proportion of their patient mix that is uninsured (Lewin and Altman, 2000). As discussed in Chapter 2, since the 1980s, Medicaid revenues have become more central to supporting clinics and supporting, indirectly, primary care for uninsured persons. During the 1990s, however, the rapid growth of state Medicaid managed care contracting destabilized this revenue stream for CHCs. Between 1980 and 2000, inflation-adjusted federal grant support for CHCs actually dropped 30 percent, even as the number of centers increased 22 percent and the number of uninsured patients served by CHCs grew by 54 percent (Markus et al., 2002). As a result, changes in the Medicaid program both influence uninsured rates and affect the capacity of CHCs to serve all of the members of their target community. For example, when a CHC is not included in a local Medicaid managed care network or when substantial discounts are negotiated as a part of its contract with a managed care network, the CHC's scope of operations may be compromised (Cunningham, 1996; IOM, 2000a).

---

[2]As part of their mission, CHCs offer wraparound or enabling services that facilitate access to care for members of medically underserved groups. These services include transportation, translation, social services and assistance in enrolling in public assistance and other programs, community outreach and health education and promotion, and environmental health; commonly used services that are easier to access at one site (e.g., pharmacy, radiology, and laboratory services); and specialty services targeting the special needs of the client population (e.g., nutrition, prenatal care, dedicated services for HIV/AIDS, substance abuse treatment, and mental health services) (Davis et al., 1999; USGAO, 2000).

The increasing proportion of CHC clients who are uninsured may reflect not only greater numbers of uninsured persons but also the practice, becoming more common, of health care providers' referring uninsured patients to CHCs rather than accepting such patients for treatment themselves (Hawkins and Rosenbaum, 1998). This phenomenon is akin to "patient dumping," the transfer of medically indigent patients from private hospitals to public facilities. The result is likely to be the concentration of uninsured patients in safety-net institutions, including CHCs.

Over the long term, the increasing reliance of CHCs on Medicaid revenues, often through managed care contracting, has adversely affected CHCs' capacity to serve all of their patients, insured as well as uninsured (Shi et al., 2001; Rosenbaum et al., 2002). A survey of CHCs between 1996 and 2000 found that participation in Medicaid managed care contracts was associated with financial losses for CHCs. Still, health centers' participation in managed care, particularly for Medicaid enrollees, increased more than 50 percent over this four-year period (Rosenbaum et al., 2002). As a result, federal operating grants awarded to CHCs to support care for uninsured persons actually may be compensating the centers for losses incurred from treating insured patients enrolled in Medicaid managed care programs.

The financial difficulties experienced by community health centers may result in narrowing the scope of services offered at these sites and a decrease in the center's capacity to deliver primary care, including wraparound services that facilitate access to care, for all members of a center's target population (Hawkins and Rosenbaum, 1998).

Because wraparound services are, for the most part, not reimbursed by Medicaid or other third-party payers, federal grants support these services (McAlearney, 2002). In light of this fact, any increase in the number and proportion of uninsured users at a health center may create financial strains that result in the reduction or elimination of one or more of these enabling services. This is likely to decrease both access to care and quality and continuity of care (USGAO, 2000).

The degree to which CHCs have lost capacity to provide primary care is not uniform nationally. A longitudinal study of 588 CHCs between 1996 and 1999 found that reductions in capacity appear to be concentrated among subsets of health centers with a sizable number or share of uninsured patients or those that have experienced a recent increase in uninsured patients (McAlearney, 2002). Nationally, one-fifth of federally funded CHCs (130 of 700) have a high proportion of uninsured clients (62 percent or higher, rather than the national average of 41 percent). More than half are located in the South, West, or other areas with high uninsured rates (Markus et al., 2002).

EMERGENCY MEDICAL SERVICES AND TRAUMA CARE

Finding: Although hospital emergency department (ED) overcrowding is not primarily a consequence of uninsurance within a community, rising uninsured rates can worsen ED overcrowding and the

financial status of ED operations. As a result, community unin-surance is likely to result in lessened availability of hospital emer-gency services within a community, including reduced availability of on-call specialists.

Finding: A significant source of financial stress on regional trauma centers is the high proportion of uninsured patients that they serve. Hospitals may decline to open a trauma center or may decide to close an existing trauma center in response to this financial stress.

The fates of uninsured and insured community residents meet in the waiting room of their local hospital emergency department. Emergency departments are a key example of how market pressures and public policies (e.g., EMTALA require-ments that EDs maintain an "open door" policy, serving all comers without regard to their ability to pay) interact in ways that create incentives for hospitals to reduce their exposure to financial losses associated with serving uninsured patients. The Committee hypothesizes that hospitals' adaptive strategies with respect to contain-ing financial losses have consequences for all community residents served by the hospital's emergency department.

Perhaps more so than with hospital emergency departments, the closure of hospital regional trauma centers puts at greater risk the health of everyone in the communities the centers serve. Reliance on the highly specialized and resource-intensive care provided by trauma centers extends throughout populous metropoli-tan areas and multicounty regions in rural areas, transcending more local neighbor-hood boundaries that often separate wealthier, insured groups from less wealthy, uninsured ones. The lack of adequate financing for the care of uninsured persons with traumatic injuries thus poses the risk of diminished access to care for all residents of a region. See Box 3.3 for the Committee's working definition of trauma care.

The following sections discuss the hypothesized community effects on emer-gency medical services and trauma care for all members of a community with a sizable or growing uninsured population.

Hospital Emergency Departments

Hospital emergency medical services often do not, and frequently are not, expected to make a positive contribution to a hospital's overall financial margins, particularly as hospital accounting practices do not credit patient revenues from persons admitted through the emergency department, as some 40 to 60 percent of all admissions are (Bonnie et al., 1999). Typically, hospital emergency departments and trauma centers provide what are considered community benefits, often unre-munerative services offered in exchange for a hospital's nonprofit status and tax exemption (Kane and Wubbenhorst, 2000; Nicholson et al., 2000) (see discussion of community benefits in Chapter 2). Hospitals' ability to cross-subsidize commu-nity benefits have been limited by an increasingly competitive market for hospital services during the 1990s. In addition, as managed care plans have negotiated

BOX 3.3
Definition of Trauma Care

• Trauma centers provide highly specialized care, ideally in the first hour after an injury, when health care is most likely to make a difference. Care is coordinated regionally by the states and includes prehospital emergency medical services (e.g., paramedic care, ambulance transport), acute care at hospital-based trauma centers, and rehabilitation (Bonnie et al., 1999).

• The American College of Surgeons designates a hospital emergency department as a trauma center based on qualifying criteria related to staffing, resources, and services (Bonnie et al., 1999). There are four designations: Level 1, with the most stringent requirements, for providing tertiary care on a regional basis; Level 2, providing services similar to a Level 1 center but without clinical research and prevention activities; Level 3, for emergency services, often in a rural area, with fewer specialized services and resources than Level 1 or 2 centers; and Level 4, usually in a rural area, describing hospitals and clinics that perform a triage function.

• In 2000, about 37.4 percent of the 108 million emergency department visits were for injuries (McCaig and Ny, 2002). About 10 to 12 percent of injury visits are classified as receiving trauma care services (Bonnie et al., 1999).

contracts for hospital services, some have excluded high-cost providers (including those that offer advanced trauma care) from networks or restricted enrollee's use of them to cases in which the technologically advanced care was clearly needed, thereby undercutting hospitals' ability to spread the costs of expensive service capacity across many (lower-severity) patients (Malone and Dohan, 2000).

In many urban and rural areas, hospital emergency departments are often filled beyond capacity. A recent survey of 1,501 hospitals (approximately 36 percent of all hospitals nationally with EDs) finds that 62 percent report their EDs to be at or over capacity (Lewin Group, 2002). A survey of California ED directors in a range of settings (university, county, and private hospitals) finds that virtually all respondents cited overcrowding as a problem (Richards et al., 2000). Ninety-one percent of ED directors responding to a recent national survey report overcrowding problems in their departments, with 39 percent reporting overcrowding on a daily basis and little difference between overcrowding in academic health centers and in private hospitals (Derlet et al., 2001).

A key cause of ED overcrowding appears to be an insufficient number of active or staffed inpatient beds into which ED patients can be admitted.[3] This bed

---

[3]Hospitals have reduced staffed beds over the last decade. This downsizing is a function of multiple pressures and trends, including the shift of diagnostic and treatment procedures to outpatient settings; third-party reimbursements for care that have not kept pace with inflation in the costs of health care; staffing shortages, particularly nursing; and consequences of the Balanced Budget Act of 1997 that have led to the loss of beds in community-based facilities (e.g., nursing homes) to which to discharge patients who need ongoing care (Brewster et al., 2001).

shortage is in part a result of market and related financing pressures on hospital operating margins, pressures that include the relative amount of uncompensated care provided by the hospital, some of which is delivered to uninsured patients. When an ED cannot move seriously ill or injured patients into inpatient beds in a timely fashion, a logjam or backup of patients boarded in the ED can be created. If this backup becomes severe, the ED may temporarily close its doors to new patients who arrive by ambulance, diverting them to other area hospitals (Brewster et al., 2001). When a hospital is on diversion status, ED services are unavailable, although ambulatory (walk-in) patients may continue to arrive and wait to be seen.

The pressures on EDs created by a shortage of available inpatient capacity have been intensified by an increasing demand for ambulatory care services at hospital emergency departments, by both insured and uninsured patients, as a consequence of inadequate access to primary care in the community (Derlet, 1992; Grumbach et al., 1993; Baker et al., 1994; Billings et al., 2000). In addition, EMTALA has unintentionally fostered the use of scarce ED resources for non-urgent care (Fields et al., 2001).[4] The costs of care provided through EDs often are not reimbursed in full (e.g., claims for urgent care may be challenged or rejected by managed care plans, and uninsured patients are estimated to pay only a percent-age of their bills for ED care) (Johnson and Derlet, 1996; Kamoie, 2000).

In the late 1980s and early 1990s, the rising number of uninsured persons was clearly identified as contributing to the overcrowding of hospital emergency de-partments (Melnick et al., 1989; USGAO, 1993; McManus, 2001). Their growing numbers resulted in diminished access to emergency medical services, at least at large urban teaching hospitals. Overcrowding in the past few years, however, reflects a more complex set of interactions and is likely to reflect the effects of a community's rising number or concentration of uninsured persons only in specific instances, for example, in the case of a large urban public hospital without ad-equate funding to support care for the greater number of uninsured patients. Overall, the number or proportion of uninsured patients in a community is likely to contribute to ED overcrowding only indirectly (USGAO, 2000; Derlet, 2002). See Box 3.4 for a case study of uninsurance and EDs in Arizona.

Overcrowding adversely affects the quality of care for all emergency depart-ment patients through longer waits to be seen and admitted and longer transport times to the hospital if some area emergency departments have been temporarily closed (Bindman et al., 1991; Kellermann, 1991; Rask et al., 1994). The problems ED patients then face range from dissatisfaction to needless suffering and adverse health outcomes. A survey of 30 emergency departments in Los Angeles County in 1990 found that about one of every twenty patients left before receiving treatment (Stock et al., 1994). In overcrowded EDs, staff experience greater

---

[4]See Chapter 2 for a brief discussion of EMTALA.

BOX 3.4
Access to Emergency Medical Services: Arizona

Like all hospitals, those in Arizona are subject to EMTALA, and like many other hospitals around the country, Arizona facilities have had to cope with a relatively high uninsured rate locally, a high degree of managed care penetration in local health services markets, and a rising patient volume at hospital emergency departments. In addition, Arizona hospitals also face the highest burden nationally of uncompensated emergency care, reflecting a rapid growth in the size of the local low-income population and the fact that a sizable proportion consists of undocumented immigrants, meaning that they are ineligible for Medicaid (MGT of America, 2002). Although hospitals do not formally document the immigration status or ethnicity of their patients, one recent study indicates that 16 Arizona hospitals along the Mexican border provided $44 million in expenditures over a three-month period in 2001 to treat uninsured, medically indigent immigrants. Overall, in 2001, Arizona's 10 hospitals reported providing $525 million in uncompensated care. Hospital officials attribute the growth in uncompensated care expenses to a number of developments: the sheer number of low-income undocumented immigrants living and working in the state, the lack of reimbursement from the federal Immigration and Naturalization Service for health care services delivered to persons apprehended but not officially in custody, difficulty discharging patients out of the country for follow-up care, and the humanitarian practice of parole, or allowing Mexican residents in need of emergency medical services to obtain them at facilities on the U.S. side of the border, given the lack of trauma centers in nearby Mexico.

After a November 2001 clarification of federal Medicaid regulations resulted in the disqualification of undocumented immigrants from receiving kidney dialysis and other treatments previously considered emergency services, the state legislature allocated $2.8 million in temporary Medicaid funding, from tobacco settlement dollars, to pay for dialysis and related care needed by approximately 150 uninsured, medically indigent immigrants. The state's funding meets both humanitarian and fiscal needs, since access to care is anticipated to reduce patients' utilization of the costly hospital emergency services expected to be needed if they could no longer afford regular dialysis.

SOURCES: Associated Press, 2001, 2002; Duarte, 2001; Taylor, 2001; Arizona Daily Star, 2002; Erikson, 2002; Gribbin, 2002; MGT of America, 2002.

frustrations and lower productivity, which may create an unsafe workplace (Derlet and Richards, 2000; Brewster et al., 2001). Emergency departments are expected to treat emergency conditions only and are not rewarded by their parent institutions for providing comprehensive care. Emergency department physicians and other personnel are thus caught between professional ethical standards and ideals of excellence and institutional pressures to minimize uncompensated care expenses. A financially unstable ED may even put its affiliated hospital in danger of closing (Malone and Dohan, 2000).

Although both insured and uninsured members of the community are likely to be adversely affected by overcrowded emergency departments, members of medically underserved groups are particularly likely to suffer because they have fewer options to obtain primary care outside EDs, compared with insured persons (Felt-Lisk et al., 2001; Weinick et al., 2002). The promise of EMTALA, that an uninsured person will at least be seen and medically stabilized, and the generally high quality of acute care and its around-the-clock accessibility, make the hospital emergency department a logical choice for uninsured patients (Kellermann, 1994; Young et al., 1996). For some, it may be their only option for receiving medical attention. However, despite the greater likelihood that uninsured persons will use EDs relative to other ambulatory care settings, they still use EDs less frequently than do Medicaid and privately insured patients (Cunningham and Tu, 1997; Billings et al., 2000; IOM, 2002a).

Financial stresses on hospitals related to EDs also contribute to the difficulty that many hospitals are experiencing in recruiting medical specialists to serve on on-call panels that EMTALA requires hospitals to maintain (Asplin and Kropp, 2001).[5] Specialists may decline to serve on these panels because of the high numbers of uninsured patients they would be obligated to treat without any assurance of compensation (Johnson et al., 2001). When a hospital cannot summon an appropriate on-call specialist, the emergency department is forced to transfer the patient needing specialty care to another facility, adding to the cost of care, delaying needed care, and potentially leading to needless suffering, disability, or even death.

For example, in Phoenix, Arizona, which has a 17 percent uninsured rate (2001), some specialty physicians (e.g., orthopedists, neurosurgeons) have ended their hospital affiliation or refused to participate in on-call panels of area hospital EDs, in order to avoid treating uninsured patients for whom they do not expect to be reimbursed (Draper et al., 2001b). This has resulted in a shortage of specialty services both in emergency departments and within the community generally, as some specialists have organized their own group practices and hospitals on a for-profit basis or have collectively negotiated for higher payments from hospitals (Taylor, 2001). Likewise in California, nonprofit hospitals and academic health centers have experienced a shortage of specialists willing to serve in an on-call capacity to emergency departments (Johnson et al., 2001). A number of factors influence the reluctance of physicians to serve on on-call panels (e.g., coverage and payment limitations from both public and private insurance plans, high malpractice insurance rates). High levels of uninsured patients, together with the legal mandate of EMTALA, may represent the last straw and lead specialist physicians to drop participation in on-call panels.

---

[5]The Centers for Medicare and Medicaid Services are expected to issue a new final rule governing EMTALA requirements early in 2003 that will address on-call requirements among others.

Preserving the adequacy of the capacity for emergency and trauma care is a community-wide concern. Ideally, services should be coordinated regionally as well as within health services markets (Bonnie et al., 1999). When an individual hospital responds to ED overcrowding by diverting ambulances to other hospitals, it can trigger a wave of ED closures and ambulance diversions. When this occurs, the access to emergency medical care for all community residents is adversely affected. The Institute of Medicine (IOM) Committee on Assuring the Health of the Public in the 21st Century has identified the limited capacity of the nation's hospitals to accommodate "surges" or sudden influxes of severely ill or injured patients as a system weakness that remains to be addressed by public health policy (IOM, forthcoming 2003).

Trauma Centers

Trauma centers often are "loss leaders" within hospitals, with the explanation for this attributed to rising health care costs, inadequate reimbursement for services provided, and unfavorable changes in health services financing (Dailey et al., 1992; Bonnie et al., 1999; Selzer et al., 2001). The successful organization of regional trauma systems, specifically the use of prehospital triage, has resulted in the most severely injured patients being admitted to trauma centers (Eastman et al., 1991; Rhee et al., 1997). The greater proportion of sicker patients at Level 1 trauma centers (who require more expensive care for which payment may not be automatic or complete), the greater proportion of uninsured patients, and the greater likelihood of seeing low-income patients, given their urban location, affiliation with safety net institutions, and type of injury, have each been identified as factors contributing to financial losses (Saywell et al., 1989a; Bazzoli et al., 1996; Fleming et al., 1992; Selzer et al., 2001). Trauma centers that have positive revenue margins tend not to be located in urban areas or tend to see patients who have health insurance (Taheri et al, 1999).

Trauma patients are more likely to be uninsured, compared with all hospital patients. One national but nonrepresentative survey of 25 Level 1 or 2 trauma centers in the late 1980s reported that 31 percent of trauma patients were uninsured, compared with 9 percent of hospital patients overall (Eastman et al., 1991). This large share of uninsured patients in trauma centers resulted in an overall negative financial margin (revenues less than costs) of nearly 20 percent. In addition, the expenses of uninsured patients related to trauma care are, almost by definition, less likely to be reimbursed. In a four-year study of one community hospital's trauma registry, 211 patients with penetrating injuries related to assault (e.g., firearms, knives) generated more than $2 million in hospital charges (Clancy et al., 1994). Two-thirds of these charges were incurred by uninsured patients; only 30 percent of the $2 million was reimbursed.

Furthermore, along with the rest of the hospital industry, the financial margins for regional trauma center systems have been narrowed since the early 1990s, particularly in urban areas, with the transition in public program financing from fee-for-service to prospective payment and managed care and with commercial managed care for private payers. According to one recent literature review, during the 1990s, trauma centers were able to bring in revenue to cover 71 percent of their estimated costs, when a cost-to-charge ratio was used as the base for calculations (Fath et al., 1999). In an analysis of regional trauma system development in 12 urban areas during the 1990s, Bazzoli and colleagues (1996) credited Medicare and Medicaid disproportionate share hospital (DSH) payments, along with state and local subsidies to trauma centers, with sustaining trauma services within communities.

The high proportion of uninsured patients found in a trauma center can threaten its financial viability. A study of trauma care costs in a large urban teaching hospital in Detroit, Michigan, looked at all trauma patients over a one-year period (1996–1997), calculating actual costs for 667 *insured* patients ($10.3 million) and estimating costs for 96 *uninsured* patients ($1.6 million), for whom financial data were missing (Fath et al., 1999). Insured and uninsured patients had similar demographic characteristics and injury severity. For patients who stayed a relatively short time (seven days or fewer), hospital revenues exceeded costs by 17 percent, but for trauma patients as a group, revenues were only 87 percent of costs. Overall, the trauma center lost money. Citing other case studies as well as their own work, Fath and colleagues suggest that the urban location of many trauma centers means that their patient base will be more likely to be uninsured and at higher risk for trauma. A study of an urban Level 1 trauma center in Indiana over a six-month period included all 553 trauma patients for whom billing records were available (Selzer et al., 2001). Over six months, charges for these cases exceeded direct reimbursements by $2.1 million. Self-pay or charity patients, presumed to be uninsured, comprised 41 percent of the trauma patients in the study (224 persons), including 32 percent of the blunt injury patients, 37 percent of the penetrating injury patients, and 38 percent of the burn patients.

SPECIALTY CARE

Finding: Relatively high uninsured rates are associated with the lessened availability of on-call specialty services to hospital emergency departments, and the decreased ability of primary care providers to obtain specialty referrals for patients who are members of medically underserved groups.

Evidence about the relationship between uninsured rate and access to specialty services other than emergency medical care is limited. In the section that follows on hospital-based care, the Committee presents the results of its commissioned analyses, which include quantitative findings about the influence of community uninsurance on specialty services. As background to that discussion, this section describes likely mechanisms or pathways through which specialty care may be affected, drawing on examples from the literature on specialist provider location and on specialty care provided by academic health centers.

Emergency medical services constitute one type of specialty care that is likely to be less available to all community members as a result of a community's relatively high uninsured rate. As discussed earlier in this chapter, physicians (including generalists as well as specialists) are devoting fewer hours to charity care, which as measured does not distinguish between insured and uninsured recipients of this free and reduced-price care. This means that there are fewer referrals available for both uninsured patients and lower-income insured patients who share the same set of medical facilities and practitioners. This effect is more likely to occur in rural communities and central city neighborhoods, where the local economy may not sustain private physician practices. Another consequence of on-call obligations that hospitals may require of affiliated specialists may be the relocation of orthopedists, neurosurgeons, and other specialists out of the area, leading to local shortages of particular specialty services. EMTALA places the burden of maintaining on-call panels on hospitals, rather than physicians, feeding a dynamic where hospitals pressure specialists to participate as a condition of the provider's continued affiliation (Bitterman, 2002). This dynamic accelerates the movement of specialists to relocate or, more often, drop their medical staff privileges in favor of opening an ambulatory surgical center or a boutique specialty hospital that does not include an emergency department.

Insured and uninsured rural residents alike may experience lessened access to specialty care (as with primary care) if providers leave the community because of financially unviable practice conditions (Ormond et al., 2000a). Rural areas tend to have shortages of specialty physicians, and referrals are often to specialists in urban areas, which may deter some patients from obtaining care or result in their seeking it later than advisable. Specialists who see patients at rural hospitals are key in preventing the loss of privately insured patients to larger urban hospitals, maintaining a broader payer mix to counterbalance the financial effect of patients for whom reimbursement is lower or absent (e.g., publicly insured and uninsured patients) at the rural hospital (Ormond et al., 2000b).

The inability of primary care providers to make specialty referrals for their patients may be an effect of relatively high local uninsurance. For example, while community health centers may have relationships with hospitals in the community that enable them to make specialty referrals for uninsured patients more easily than physicians in private practice, referrals may not come easily. In a study of access to care at 20 CHCs in 10 states, respondent providers reported that they had difficulty obtaining specialty referrals for all their patients, not only those who were uninsured (Fairbrother et al., 2002). Another descriptive study of rural counties in five states also reports that community health centers have difficulty obtaining specialty referrals for their patients, many of whom are uninsured (Ormond et al., 2000b).

Urban safety-net hospitals and academic health centers (AHCs), major sites for specialty care in their communities, are also affected by high levels of uninsured patients (Gaskin, 1999). A study of 125 public and private AHCs between 1991 and 1996 concludes that a small increase in the proportion of uncompensated care provided by AHCs (as a proportion of gross patient revenues) reflects the combination of a decrease in bad debt and a 40 percent increase in the amount of charity care provided (Commonwealth Fund, 2001). Over that period, in local markets with high managed care penetration, care for uninsured persons had been increasingly concentrated at a subset of AHCs, resulting in less revenue overall. For private AHCs, particularly those that are *not* located in neighborhoods with high uninsured rates (e.g., central city), one strategic response of hospitals to such cost pressures has been to eliminate specialty services with relatively poor rates of reimbursement, such as burn units, trauma care, pediatric and neonatal intensive care, emergency psychiatric inpatient services, and HIV/AIDS (Gaskin, 1999; Commonwealth Fund, 2001). Public academic health centers or safety net hospitals in central city neighborhoods often are the only source of specialty care for local residents and may find it difficult to reduce or eliminate such services. A study of urban safety-net hospitals during the 1990s finds a decline in the provision of specialty services. However, because the hospitals' initial array of specialty services was greater than at other hospitals, the volume and proportion of some of these services in safety net hospitals remained relatively high (Zuckerman et al., 2001a). In addition, to the extent that AHCs trim or eliminate certain specialty services, their teaching mission may be adversely affected.

HOSPITAL-BASED CARE

Finding: Community uninsurance can put financial stress on hospital outpatient and inpatient departments, sometimes resulting in lessened availability of services or the closing of a hospital. When public jurisdictions respond to this and other financial pressures by converting their hospitals to private ownership status, the availability of services may be adversely affected, especially for members of medically underserved groups.

In addition to the impacts of uninsured clients on EDs and hospital-based specialist services, hospital inpatient care is also affected by the level of uninsurance within the community. Hospitals treating uninsured patients must contend with the cumulative effects of inadequate care for chronic conditions, exacerbated acute illnesses, and delayed treatment among uninsured patients (IOM, 2002a). The more intensive and costly care that uninsured patients may eventually require because of having forgone care earlier in the course of their illness is frequently provided by hospitals. In addition, hospital outpatient departments and their satellite clinics are an important source of both primary and specialty care for medically underserved populations, including uninsured persons and their families.

Hospital Services

One way that hospitals have responded to increasing financial pressures is to stem the use of certain services known to attract persons who are more likely than average to be uninsured. The reduced availability or complete loss of these services (e.g., trauma, burn care, care for HIV/AIDs) may be expected to affect everyone in the health services market who needs them. As described in a previous section on emergency medical services, one dynamic seen recently within hospitals is a relative shortage of staffed inpatient beds, compared with the overall demand for admissions. When ED patients requiring admission end up waiting in the emergency department for a staffed inpatient bed that is open, ED capacity is limited and subsequently access to care for all members of the community is diminished. Favoring elective admissions over those from the ED reduces the hospital's inpatient uncompensated care "exposure" because patients admitted from the ED tend to involve more costly care and are less likely to be well insured, if insured at all.

A survey of urban, nonfederal, acute care hospitals ($n = 2,668$) between 1990 and 1997 finds that the 498 safety-net hospitals (defined as hospitals with a high proportion of uncompensated care expenses relative to other hospitals in their market, a high percentage of total expenses that are uncompensated, or both) reported slower growth in the numbers of patients admitted and fewer births, on average, compared with non-safety-net hospitals (Zuckerman et al., 2001a). This trend reflects the impact of Medicaid managed care competition for patients, as well as the adverse financial effects of serving a sizable uninsured population.

New Analysis of Hospital Services and Financial Margins

Finding: Higher uninsured rates in urban areas are associated with lesser total inpatient capacity and fewer population-adjusted medical-surgical, psychiatric, and alcohol and chemical dependence beds. In rural areas, higher uninsured rates are associated with a lower number of population-adjusted intensive care unit (ICU) beds, especially where uninsured patients are not concentrated at specific hospitals within the area.

Finding: Higher uninsured rates in urban areas are associated with a smaller proportion of hospitals offering services for vulnerable populations, including psychiatric inpatient, psychiatric emergency, psychiatric outpatient, alcohol and chemical dependence, and AIDS services. In rural areas where uninsured patients are not concentrated at specific hospitals, higher uninsured rates are associated with a decreasing proportion of hospitals offering psychiatric inpatient services.

Finding: Higher uninsured rates in urban areas are associated with smaller proportions of hospitals offering trauma care, burn care, and tomography (SPECT). In rural areas where uninsured patients are not concentrated at specific hospitals, higher uninsured rates are associated with smaller proportions of hospitals offering transplants, magnetic resonance imaging (MRI), radiation therapy, and lithotripsy (ESWL).

Finding: Higher uninsured rates in urban areas are associated with smaller proportions of hospitals offering such community services as community outreach and Meals on Wheels. In rural areas where uninsured patients are not concentrated at specific hospitals, higher uninsured rates are associated with smaller proportions of hospitals providing Meals on Wheels.

Finding: For urban areas, higher uninsured rates are associated with lower inpatient capacity and fewer services but not lower financial margins. In comparison, hospitals in rural areas with relatively high uninsured rates are more likely to maintain inpatient capacity and services provision but to have lower financial margins.

The Committee commissioned two analyses of hospital services and financial margins as a function of local uninsured rates, which are included in Appendix D. Because of the limited data available and identified limitations in the modeling and analytical adjustments, these analyses are exploratory rather than definitive. They are first steps toward testing the hypothesis that uninsurance adversely affects access to hospital-based care for community residents. Figure 3.1 depicts the hypothesized relationship between the independent variable (community uninsured rate) and one of several dependent variables (level of psychiatric inpatient services) tested in the analyses, with analytic adjustments for measured covariates of a community's uninsured rate.

Both analyses use data from four years (1991, 1994, 1996, 1999) considered cross-sectionally as multiple data points rather than longitudinally, to assess relationships between uninsured rates, hospital services and financial margins. The first of the two analyses looks at the experiences of nonfederal, short-term (acute care) hospitals in the largest 85 MSAs (Gaskin and Needleman, 2002).[6] The second analysis looks at hospitals in rural (defined as all nonmetropolitan) counties in an opportunity sample of seven states (California, Massachusetts, New Jersey, New

---

[6]In the urban (MSA-level) analysis, *financial margin* is defined as the net hospital income within the MSA divided by total hospital revenues in the MSA. In the rural analysis, this margin is defined as the net hospital income within the county divided by total hospital revenues in the county.

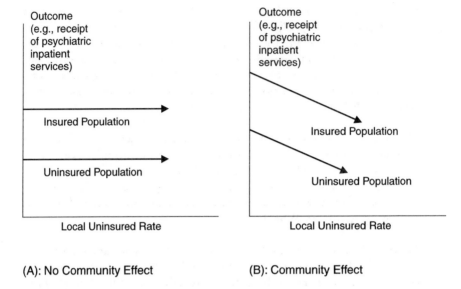

FIGURE 3.1 Community effects diagram.

York, Pennsylvania, Washington, and Wisconsin), using hospital discharge data to approximate uninsured rates at the county level (Needleman and Gaskin, 2002). Five types of dependent variables were chosen, to better understand the potential relationship between community uninsured rate and access to care not only for medically underserved, low-income or vulnerable populations but also for all community residents. These included measures of inpatient capacity, services generally offered by hospitals and those typically offered by safety net hospitals, and financial margin (Reuter and Gaskin, 1997; Gaskin, 1999).

The economic or policy significance of statistically significant associations seen between the community uninsured rate and access to services depends on the average number of beds and services for the hospitals in the areas studied. For example, a 5 percentage-point decrease in the availability of a high technology service associated with a 1 percentage-point higher uninsured rate may be expected to have more of an adverse effect on rural communities, where the level of services provision is lower than in urban areas. For a rural area, such a decrease may mean the loss of the service entirely and the need for local residents to travel to a neighboring urban area to obtain the service. Table 3.1 presents the means and standard deviations for the independent and dependent variables used in the two analyses. Except for two measures of inpatient capacity (total number of beds and number of medical-surgical beds), the bed, services, and margin variables all have higher means in the urban areas studied than in the rural areas. The confidence intervals for most of the dependent variables in the rural analysis are broader than for the urban analysis, with many including zero; the broad variation in measures of beds, services, and margins reflects the heterogeneity of rural health services markets.

Area-Level Analyses

Table 3.2 displays the statistically significant findings from the urban and rural area analyses. Interpretation of these results is limited by their imprecision due to insufficient variation in the sample and model; see Appendix D for more discussion.

Urban Areas

For the 85 urban areas examined (the MSA analysis), higher uninsured rates are associated with fewer beds per capita, lower levels of services, and a lower financial margin. Analytically adjusting (weighting) the analysis to take into account hospital size changes some of these findings, yielding an association of higher uninsured rates with greater availability of neonatal intensive care units (NICUs) and angioplasty and erasing the association with financial margin. These findings are discussed in more detail below.

The urban area analysis of services and margins includes weighting for hospital size, as measured by a hospital's share of beds as a proportion of hospital beds in the MSA. In the case of the service variables, for example, the unweighted model gives equal emphasis to smaller and larger MSAs and to smaller and larger hospitals. The weighted model examines the proportion of beds in hospitals that offer the service, attaching greater weight to larger hospitals. This is based on the rationale that changes in the level of services offered by a larger hospital are more likely to affect a community more broadly, compared with the offerings of a smaller hospital.

Reading across Table 3.2, for measures of inpatient capacity, an uninsured rate 1 standard deviation (5.3 percentage points) above the mean uninsured rate (14.6 percent) for the 340 MSA observations is associated with a 4.5 percentage-point decrease in the total number of beds per 100,000 population, a 6.1 percentage-point decrease in medical–surgical beds, a 17.5 percentage-point decrease in psychiatric beds, and a 25.8 percentage-point decrease in alcohol and chemical dependency beds. Interpreting these changes in terms of the number of beds in the "average" urban area, a 5.3 percentage-point higher uninsured rate is associated with a decrease in total beds per 100,000 population from 316.2 beds (the mean number) to 302 beds and the loss of 1 of almost 4 alcohol and chemical dependency beds.

For services disproportionately used by vulnerable populations, a 5.3 percentage-point higher uninsured rate is associated with a 14.7 percentage-point lower proportion of hospitals in the MSA that offer psychiatric inpatient services, a 23.2 percentage-point lower proportion offering alcohol and chemical dependence services, and a 4.6 percentage-point lower proportion offering AIDS services. In

TABLE 3.1 Means and Standard Deviations for Independent and Dependent Variables

| | Urban (MSA)[1] | | | | |
| | Unweighted | | | Weighted | |
Variable	N	Mean	S.D.	Mean	S.D.
Percent Uninsured	340	14.6	5.3		
Percent Uninsured Discharges					
Beds per 100,000 Population					
Total	340	316.2	106.6		
Medical-surgical	340	173.2	78.0		
ICU	340	29.7	10.3		
Psychiatric	340	18.5	12.1		
Alcohol and chemical dependence	340	3.9	4.3		
Services for Vulnerable Populations (%)					
Psychiatric inpatient	340	39.6	18.1	59.2	21.6
Psychiatric emergency	340	40.5	19.4	58.4	22.1
Psychiatric outpatient	340	32.5	16.7	49.3	21.8
Alcohol and chemical dependence	340	25.8	16.7	37.8	22.4
AIDS	340	54.1	21.0	73.7	18.9
High-Technology Services (%)					
Trauma	340	22.3	13.8	38.5	19.8
NICU	340	25.8	12.6	42.9	17.9
Transplant	340	16.5	11.2	32.2	17.3
Burn	340	5.2	4.9	11.1	11.0
MRI	340	47.2	20.6	66.2	23.3
Radiation therapy	340	37.2	15.3	61.0	18.5
Angioplasty	340	34.2	14.9	60.4	18.8
SPECT	340	41.2	16.8	57.3	19.4
ESWL	340	14.5	10.7	26.0	19.0
Community Services (%)					
Community outreach	255	56.9	17.8	75.4	17.5
Transportation	255	24.8	15.6	33.7	22.0
Meals on Wheels	255	12.3	12.7	14.2	15.7
Margin (%)	340	3.4	4.8		

NOTES: For the urban analysis, services are weighted by a hospital's share of beds as a proportion of hospital beds in the MSA (a measure of availability). For the rural analysis, services measures are weighted by the percentage of hospitals offering the service.
SOURCES: [1]Gaskin and Needleman, 2002; [2]Needleman and Gaskin, 2002.

Rural (County)[2]					
Unweighted			Weighted		
N	Mean	S.D.	N	Mean	S.D.
426	4.4	4.4			
422	423.3	392.3			
396	186.8	146.5			
396	17.8	22.1			
396	10.0	19.1			
396	4.2	16.0			
396	21.7	37.2	396	23.7	39.0
396	35.1	43.7	396	37.4	44.9
396	15.7	33.5	396	16.5	34.5
396	17.3	33.1	396	17.7	34.1
400	39.6	44.1	396	42.4	45.9
396	16.1	33.4	396	16.6	34.1
426	2.7	12.9	422	3.7	16.7
400	6.0	21.8	396	6.4	22.8
n/a	n/a	n/a	n/a	n/a	n/a
396	20.1	36.0	396	21.3	37.4
400	13.4	29.9	396	15.5	32.6
396	3.6	16.0	396	4.5	18.5
396	20.6	36.6	396	21.6	37.8
396	6.6	21.9	396	7.4	23.8
258	51.8	44.4	258	52.5	45.1
258	9.9	25.0	258	10.5	27.1
258	18.9	35.2	258	18.5	35.8
414	1.8	5.9			

TABLE 3.2 Selected Regression Coefficients of Hospital Services and Financial Margins on Percent Uninsured, Area Analyses[a]

Dependent Variables	Urban (MSA)[1]			
	Unweighted		Weighted[c]	
	Coeff.	Change associated with uninsured rate 1 S.D. above the mean[b] (%)	Coeff.	Change associated with uninsured rate 1 S.D. above the mean[b] (%)
Inpatient Capacity (beds per 100,000 population)				
Total	−2.67	−4.5		
Medical–surgical	−2.00	−6.1		
ICU				
Psychiatric	−0.61	−17.5		
Alcohol and chemical dependence	−0.19	−25.8		
Services for Vulnerable Populations				
Psychiatric inpatient	−1.10	−14.7	−1.10	−9.8
Psychiatric emergency	−1.40	−18.3	−1.30	−11.8
Psychiatric outpatient	−1.27	−20.7	−1.36	−14.6
Alcohol and chemical dependence	−1.13	−23.2	−1.31	−18.4
AIDS	−0.47	−4.6		
High-Technology Services				
Trauma	−0.62	−14.7	−0.63	−8.7
NICU			0.61	7.5
Transplant				
Burn	−0.17	−17.2		
MRI				
Radiation therapy				
Angioplasty			0.46	4.0
SPECT	−0.65	−8.4		
ESWL				
Community Services				
Community outreach	−1.15	−10.7	−0.77	−5.4
Transportation				
Meals on Wheels	−0.52	−22.4		
Margin	−0.14	−21.8		

[a]Results (coefficients) are reported if they are statistically significant at $p<0.05$.

[b]Percent change is calculated as the value of the coefficient, multiplied by the value of 1 standard deviation from the mean of the independent variable (percent uninsured for the urban analysis, percent uninsured discharges for the rural analysis), divided by the mean value of the dependent variable.

[c]For the urban analysis, inpatient capacity and services are weighted by a hospital's share of beds as

| Rural (County)[2] | | | |
| Weighted and unadjusted for concentration | | Weighted and adjusted/not concentrated[d] | |
Coeff.	Change associated with % uninsured discharges 1 S.D. above the mean[b] (%)	Coeff	Change associated with with % uninsured discharges 1 S.D. above the mean[b] (%)
−0.45	−11.1	−0.54	−13.3
		−0.64	−15.8
		−1.38	−25.6
		−0.96	−66.0
Not studied		Not studied	
−1.67	−34.5	−1.99	−41.1
		−1.41	−40.0
−0.91	−54.1	−1.04	−61.8
		−1.27	−30.2
−0.17	−37.4	−0.22	−48.4

a proportion of hospital beds in the MSA (a measure of availability). For the rural analysis, inpatient capacity is weighted by average county population and services by the percentage of hospitals offering the services.

[d]Adjusting for the relative concentration of uninsured patient discharges, or the relative degree of clustering of uninsured patients at hospitals within the area, as measured by the ratio of the Herfindahl index for uninsured discharges over the Herfindahl index for all discharges.

SOURCES: [1]Gaskin and Needleman, 2002; [2]Needleman and Gaskin, 2002.

the case of psychiatric inpatient services, this association translates into a decline in the proportion of hospitals offering this service from 39.6 percent (the mean across all MSA observations) to 33.8 percent. Adjusting the analysis by hospital size, a 5.3 percentage-point higher uninsured rate is associated with between a 9.8 percentage-point and 14.6 percentage-point lower proportion of psychiatric beds in hospitals offering these services and an 18.4 percentage-point lower proportion of alcohol and chemical dependence beds in hospitals that offer that service. Compared with an urban area with the "average" uninsured rate, a 5.3 percentage-point higher uninsured rate is associated with a decline from 37.8 percent to 30.9 percent of alcohol and chemical dependence beds in hospitals offering this service.

For high-technology services, a 5.3 percentage-point higher uninsured rate is associated with a 14.7 percentage-point lower proportion of hospitals offering trauma services, a 17.2 percentage-point lower proportion offering burn services, and an 8.4 percentage-point lower proportion offering tomography (SPECT). These changes translate into a decline from 22.3 to 19.0 percent of hospitals offering trauma services, from 5.2 to 4.3 percent of hospitals offering burn services, and from 41.2 to 37.7 percent of hospitals offering SPECT. Adjusting the analysis for hospital size, a 5.3 percentage-point higher uninsured rate is associated with an 8.7 percentage-point lower proportion of trauma beds in hospitals offering the service, a 7.5 percentage-point *higher* proportion of neonatal intensive care, or NICU, beds and a 4 percentage-point *higher* proportion of angioplasty beds in hospitals offering these services. The case of greater NICU availability may reflect the greater relative need for neonatal intensive care in communities with higher uninsured rates, the fact that this need is usually accompanied by eligibility for public coverage, and the more extensive coverage of pregnant women and newborns by public insurance programs, compared with public coverage of the population overall (Howell, 2001; IOM, 2002b). The finding of greater availability of angioplasty services in higher uninsured rate urban areas may reflect regional differences in practice patterns (e.g., the procedure is more common in the South and West, which also have higher uninsured rates) that are unmeasured and unadjusted for in the analyses (Pilote et al., 1995; Krumholz et al., forthcoming 2003).

Rural Areas

The associations between uninsurance in rural counties (measured as the percent of all hospital discharges in the county that are uninsured) and measures of beds, services, and financial margins follow a pattern similar to that seen in the urban area analysis. In addition, the rural analysis includes an adjustment for the degree to which uninsured patients were clustered at particular hospitals within a given county. The concentration of patients may reflect competitive strategic interactions among hospitals. For example, a hospital may eliminate a service it cannot support with its patient and payer mix. This could allow a competing hospital to add to its caseload while lowering per-patient costs and making a profit on the service. Table 3.2 includes two sets of coefficients for the rural area analysis, one in which a general effect is found related to the uninsured rate and a second set in which a significant association is observed only when uninsured patients are not clustered at particular hospitals within the county; see Appendix D for details.

For the rural counties studied, higher uninsured rates are associated with lower inpatient capacity for ICU services and, where uninsured patients are not concentrated at specific hospitals, psychiatric inpatient services. A 4.4 percentage-point higher uninsured rate (one standard deviation above the mean percent uninsured discharges of 4.4 percent for the 426 nonmetropolitan county observations) is associated with a 11.1 percentage-point decrease in the number of ICU beds per 100,000 population. When patients are not concentrated at hospitals (adjusted model), the size of the effect increases. A 4.4 percentage-point higher uninsured rate is associated with a 13.3 percentage-point decrease in the number of ICU beds per 100,000 population and a 15.8 percentage-point decrease in the number of psychiatric beds. Viewing the adjusted percentage changes in terms of the number of beds in the "average" rural county, the findings indicate a decrease from 423.3 ICU beds (the mean number) to 367 ICU beds and a decrease from 10 to 8.4 psychiatric beds per 100,000 population.

Both the urban and the rural analyses show a consistent association between higher uninsured rates and lower levels of provision of high-technology services and community services. In rural areas, a 4.4 percentage-point higher uninsured rate is associated with a 34.5 percentage-point lower proportion of hospitals offering magnetic resonance imaging (MRI) and a 54.1 percentage-point lower proportion of hospitals offering lithotripsy (ESWL). Compared with the "average" uninsured rate rural county, this difference results in a decrease from 20.1 to 13.9 percent of hospitals offering MRI and a decrease from 6.6 to 3.0 percent of hospitals offering ESWL. When patients are not concentrated at specific hospitals, the size of the effect increases and additional findings become statistically significant, including decreased availability of transplant services, MRI, radiation therapy, ESWL, and Meals on Wheels.

In contrast to urban areas, for rural counties there is a strong association between higher uninsured discharges and lower financial margins, whether or not the analysis is adjusted for the concentration of uninsured patients. Unadjusted, a 4.4 percentage-point higher uninsured rate is associated with a 37.4 percentage-point lower margin, which translates into a decrease from a 2.0 percent to a 1.3 percent aggregate margin. With the adjusted model, a 4.4 percentage-point higher uninsured rate is associated with a 48.4 percentage-point lower financial margin, representing an even larger decline in aggregate margin, from 2.0 percent to 1.0 percent. The lower margins may account in part for the lower likelihood that hospitals offer specific costly high- technology services. They may also affect quality and staffing in ways not observable in the analysis.

Hospital-Level Analysis

One would expect that the findings in the area-level analyses reflect the strategic behavior of hospitals within urban and rural markets, in response to financial incentives and disincentives to offer services and maintain staffed beds as well as to each hospital's mission and history in its community. For example, inpatient and emergency psychiatric and transplant services have the potential to bring in uninsured patients whose care is likely to be very expensive. In the case of NICUs, for example, state Medicaid programs almost always cover the costs of care for the newborn of previously uninsured women, so that the burden of uncompensated care is likely to be less. Hospitals may choose not to offer psychiatric services for fear that they will not be reimbursed for a significant portion of the expensive care they provide (Gaskin, 1999). Alternatively, some hospitals may offer these services because there are few other sources of such care in the community and they are willing to absorb the losses in lower margins.

While analyses by hospital rather than area ideally should capture information about these relationships, data limitations precluded the development of appropriate models that would have done so. The hospital-level analysis for urban areas (described in Appendix D but not presented here) makes fewer untested assumptions about the interactions among hospitals than do the area analyses, yet the Committee considers the hospital-level findings to be less reliable than the MSA-level findings. The hospital-level model indicates how the average individual hospital may respond to increased demand for hospital care from uninsured persons as measured by the MSA-wide uninsured rate. However, it is unlikely that the overall market response to uninsurance is merely the weighted average of individual hospital responses in the market. This would assume that hospitals neither behave strategically nor respond to the actions of their competitors. For example, a safety-net hospital may eliminate a high-tech service because they cannot support it with their payer mix. This may pave the way for a competing hospital to offer the service. Alternatively, this may reduce the availability of the service to the uninsured and insured populations who use that hospital. Neither of these potential outcomes is observable in the hospital-level model, while the MSA-level models allow for the observation of the overall association of uninsurance and the availability of hospital services, net of the strategic behavior of individual hospitals.

The hospital-level findings for urban hospitals indicate that all the measures of inpatient bed capacity are negatively and significantly associated with the area uninsured rate, except for ICU beds, which are positively and significantly associated. Of the other variables, only alcohol and chemical dependency services (services disproportionately utilized by vulnerable populations) are negatively and significantly related in the hospital-level analysis. See Appendix D for a more detailed discussion of findings and the limitations of the analysis.

Hospital Financial Margins

As with health departments and ambulatory care clinics, many hospitals operate with financial constraints that leave little room for cross-subsidizing the costs of care for uninsured patients, who on average pay a small proportion (7 percent) of their total inpatient hospital bills (IOM, 2002b; MedPAC, 2002a). During the early and mid-1990s, the average total operating margins for public academic health centers, which disproportionately serve uninsured patients, were approximately zero (Commonwealth Fund, 2001). Despite a significantly increasing average total margin for all hospitals from 1.8 to 3.7 percent between 1991 and 1996, among those that provided the equivalent of at least 6 percent of their gross patient revenues in charity care, margins declined by 1.2 percentage points (Commonwealth Fund, 2001).

In urban areas, the adverse financial effects on hospitals are more likely to have an impact on low-income residents who have few options for care other than their local public or private safety net hospitals. For example, urban hospitals in Newark, New Jersey, serve a much higher proportion of uninsured patients, compared with hospitals in the surrounding suburbs. This means that these inner city hospitals face great financial pressure to cut their costs by cutting services, but neighboring hospitals that do not serve such a large number or proportion of uninsured patients may continue operations as usual (Draper et al., 2001a).

In rural areas, in contrast, there is less opportunity to segment the market and serve only a portion of the community, given the limited supply of health care practitioners and the smaller economic base to support hospitals. As a result, the adverse effects on hospital operating margins are more likely to affect the care of all community residents in rural areas than in suburban or urban communities (Sutton et al., 2001). Within rural communities, however, whether or not uninsured patients are more concentrated in one or a few hospitals than is the general population will determine how their presence affects the hospitals' financial positions. However, in rural counties where uninsured patients are relatively more concentrated in one or a few hospitals than is the county population overall, hospital margins—both in the aggregate and by hospital—are less affected by rural or county uninsured rates than those in counties where uninsured patients are more widely dispersed among local hospitals (Needleman and Gaskin, 2002).[7]

---

[7]This finding may be weakened by the fact that many rural counties have only one hospital, especially in western states. Alternatively, if a county has more than one hospital, the concentration of uninsured patients in a single facility may be associated with that hospital having an external source of funding to care for uninsured persons. As a result, the hospital may have a positive total margin, while the other hospitals in the county might be suffering financially and in danger of further financial decline if the burden of caring for the uninsured were to be dispersed among all hospitals in the county.

Hospital Closures and Conversions

A community's high uninsured rate or an increasing demand for care by uninsured persons may influence decisions by a local hospital's governing body to merge; to convert from public to private ownership status, or from private non-profit to for-profit status; or to close.

These major changes are usually prompted by a variety of factors. A hospital's decision to convert its ownership status may be motivated by the need for funds to continue operating, either independently or as one of a group of hospitals, or by the need to raise capital (Meyer et al., 1999; Needleman, 1999). Local uninsured rates and the burden of uncompensated care costs to local and state government contributed to the conversions of three large urban public hospitals—in Milwaukee, Wisconsin, Boston, Massachusetts, and Hillsborough County, Florida—to private ownership during the 1990s (Bovbjerg et al., 2000b). The conversions were spurred by changing market conditions and political decision making, particularly localities' interest in cutting expenses (Meyer et al., 1999; Bovbjerg et al., 2000b).

The conversion, merger, or closing of a hospital may lead to improved and less costly health services locally. It may also promote greater access to higher-quality care by making ambulatory primary care more available with the resources freed up from support of an unviable and inefficient inpatient facility (Needleman, 2000). Chapter 4 discusses such transitions in the case of rural hospitals. However, some changes bring with them the risk that the whole community will end up with less access to services or lower-quality care. For example, the loss of a physical plant and with it the relatively automatic support that a bricks-and-mortar institution commands may result in a net loss of public dollars for indigent health care (Bovbjerg et al., 2000b). A study of three public hospital closings in the 1990s finds that the basic lack of capacity to finance needed services for local underserved populations was not addressed, although the delivery of health services was better integrated through managed care arrangements that followed the closures (Bovbjerg et al., 2000b). For the most part, local public funders did not reward providers who inherited the patient base of the closed public hospitals for the cost savings and improved quality of care that came out of the conversion process, which led to a decline in local dollars for services to uninsured persons within these communities following the closings. In addition, a change in ownership status or operations can result in the relocation of a hospital from a neighborhood with a high uninsured rate to an area with a lower uninsured rate. This was the case in one Florida hospital, where, as part of its reorganization, a public hospital affiliated with a medical school shifted its base of operations to a new campus away from its inner city location and opened new outpatient facilities in more prosperous neighborhoods (Meyer et al., 1999; Bovbjerg et al, 2000b).

The proposed closing of a public hospital may be perceived by other providers in the area as threatening the financial stability of their own institutions by potentially spreading the effects of uninsurance more broadly throughout the community. As a result, some closings may be successfully opposed. In Los Angeles County in the mid-1990s, for example, uncompensated care costs attributed in part to a sizable uninsured population led the county's Board of Supervisors to consider closing a public hospital affiliated with the University of Southern California (one of many public hospitals in the county and the largest). Neighboring private hospitals threatened to close if faced with the public hospital's patients, and this political resistance was sufficient that the county decided to keep its public hospital open (Cornwell et al., 1996). The heterogeneity from community to community in the degree of concentration or dispersion of safety net arrangements is described briefly in Chapter 2. The relative influence of greater or lesser dispersion of uninsured patients on uninsured rate is hinted at in the Committee's commissioned papers and is likely to depend on the local configuration of health services organization and financing.

When public hospitals convert to private ownership, however, the availability of services for all community residents is more likely to be adversely affected, as documented in two studies. The first is the previously cited study of hospital conversions in Florida between 1981 and 1996 (Needleman et al., 1999). The authors conclude that public hospitals provided less care after conversion. Although converting public hospitals provided lower levels of uncompensated care on average (9.1 percent) before their change in status, compared to public hospitals that did not convert (14.7 percent), they provided even less after conversion (6.8 percent). For the two converting hospitals in counties with other hospitals, their market share of uncompensated care declined significantly, from 65 percent to 39 percent (Needleman et al., 1999). The second study followed 52 privatizations of public hospitals to nonprofit or for-profit status in California, Florida, and Texas between 1980 and 1997 (Desai et al., 2000). The authors find a statistically significant 23 percent decrease in the level of uncompensated care given by public hospitals that converted to for-profit status, compared with care provided by comparable hospitals that did not convert, and greater decreases in uncompensated care among converting hospitals in lower-income areas compared with those in higher-income areas (Desai et al., 2000).

There are regional variations in the level of uncompensated care in converted hospitals after such changes. In California, for example, private hospitals have lower uncompensated care levels, on average, than Florida, reflecting both a greater availability of public hospital services and more extensive Medi-Cal eligibility and enrollment (Needleman et al., 1999). Accounting for differences in size, teaching status, and urban or rural location, levels of uncompensated care at 15 Florida private nonprofits that converted to for-profit status between 1981 and 1996 remained relatively stable, at a lower-than-average rate compared with all private nonprofit hospitals in the state. The hospitals that converted, however, provided lower levels of unprofitable services such as emergency and trauma services after the conversion (Needleman, 1999).

In contrast to public hospital conversions, for nonteaching hospitals, the shift from private nonprofit to for-profit status resulted in little change in the amount of uncompensated care delivered, the level of community benefits, and the price of care for all community residents (Mark and Cheng, 1997; Young et al., 1997; Needleman et al., 1999; Young and Desai, 1999; Hadley et al., 2001). Conversions of 137 hospitals from private nonprofit to for-profit status between 1985 and 1996, compared with similar hospitals that did not convert, resulted in few changes in the numbers of hospital births or emergency department visits, but the numbers of total outpatient visits and Medicaid inpatient discharges increased more slowly (Hadley et al., 2001). Neighboring hospitals (within 5 miles) of conversions reported larger (but not statistically significantly larger) increases in the volume of publicly insured patients (Medicare and Medicaid), no significant change in the number of emergency or outpatient visits, a significant increase in the number of births (particularly in public and large teaching hospitals), and a shift in the pattern of emergency department visits to large teaching hospitals, with a decline at neighboring public hospitals (Hadley et al., 2001).

RESEARCH QUESTIONS

3.1 Access to Care Across the Community
Does the local uninsured rate, independent of other factors, affect residents' access to care throughout the community?

Existing studies of the relationship between community uninsurance (state or MSA uninsured rate) and access to care offer preliminary evidence that, particularly for low- to moderate-income and uninsured populations, higher local uninsured rates are associated with worse access to care. These provocative findings should be corroborated with additional studies that include more refined measures of access as outcome variables. Well-controlled, longitudinal study designs could allow researchers to tease out the difference between the effects of the uninsured population as exerting an *aggregate* influence on local health services (e.g., because the uninsured constitute a large portion of the population being studied) as compared with having an ecological impact (e.g., the independent effect of uninsured rate on access to care for insured persons). Is the supply of services in more affluent urban neighborhoods and suburbs affected by proximity to large or small populations of uninsured persons, and how?

3.2 Access to Primary and Preventive Services
How does the local uninsured rate affect the availability of primary and preventive services for the community's insured as well as uninsured residents?

Because primary and preventive services are often considered elective by patients (unlike emergency medical services and hospital inpatient care), use of these services may fall off more quickly when patients lack the financial means to pay for care. When the number or proportion of uninsured patients increases within a primary care practice, the combination of decreasing patient utilization and an increasing proportion of uninsured visits may also adversely affect the financial position of the practice. As a result, primary care practices may become financially unviable. A conservative estimate of the amount of charity care that physicians provide annually to uninsured patients is roughly $5 billion (Hadley and Holahan, 2003). Better information about the distribution and impact of the burden of providing uncompensated care among physician practices and its implications for the availability of high-quality, stable primary care services is needed in order to understand the dimensions of the problems that uninsurance poses for communities.

3.3 Access to Specialty Care, Including Emergency Medical Services

How does the local uninsured rate affect the availability of specialty services, including emergency medical services and trauma care for the community's insured as well as uninsured residents?

The legal duty of hospital EDs and trauma units to screen and medically stabilize all patients regardless of ability to pay is one source of financial stress on hospitals. What is less clear is how important the financial demands of providing care to uninsured patients are compared with other reasons for emergency department overcrowding and causes of financial strain (Tsai et al., forthcoming 2003). Further study is needed to understand the degree to which ED overcrowding and financial instability could be ameliorated by reductions in the number of uninsured persons, the restructuring of financial subsidies for their care, or the strategic diversion of emergency department patients to alternative sites for primary care. In addition, more research is needed to understand the degree to which administrative and staffing decisions made within hospitals (e.g., the specialized services such as psychiatric inpatient care) reduce community access and what alternatives exist to address the problem without jeopardizing the financial health of hospitals. While emergency medical services and trauma care provide some of the strongest evidence about access to specialty care, the Committee's findings about the difficulty community health center physicians have obtaining referrals for their uninsured and other patients, and about hospital-based specialty services suggest that further investigation of the availability throughout a community to a wide range of specialty services is merited. How does the institutional setting (e.g., AHC) influence or moderate the effect of uninsurance on access to other specialty services? And what impacts does uninsurance have on the other related missions of these institutions, for example, medical education in academic health centers?

3.4 Access to Hospital-Based Services

How does the local uninsured rate, in conjunction with public institutional support such as DSH payments, affect hospital service offerings, financial stability, and decisions to close?

The limitations and preliminary findings of the Committee's commissioned analyses of hospital inpatient capacity, services, and financial margins suggests a number of ways that community effects on access to care might be explored.

Perhaps most important is the examination of strategic or competitive responses of hospital administrators and their boards to local market conditions, including the decisions of competing hospitals to expand or shrink inpatient capacity and boost or trim the provision of services, and the relationship between these responses and individual hospital financial margins. More refined studies, based on market areas smaller than MSAs, are needed to understand better the impacts of uninsured populations on hospital services and operations. For example, findings for rural areas that the concentration of uninsured patients may lessen the size of the effect of local uninsured rate on inpatient capacity, services, and margins of all hospitals in the county, on average, suggests that such concentration of uncompensated care caseload among a few providers may be beneficial to the health care system as a whole. On the other hand, concentrating all care for uninsured persons in one facility, such as a county hospital, may both limit access to care, compared with more dispersed safety net arrangements, and lead to poor quality of care. Further research is needed to assess the overall effect of concentration and dispersion on access to hospital-based care.

Although there were hundreds of hospital closures during the 1980s and 1990s, there has been little documentation of the role that a community's uninsured rate may have played in these closures. Most studies of hospital closings do not directly address the influence of uninsurance because of the limited information about local uninsured rates and about hospital payer mix. Closures of public hospitals are of particular concern because these hospitals often serve as providers of last resort. Studies that examine reasons for these closings and the impacts of these closings or conversions are needed.

3.5 Quality of Care

How does uninsurance within communities affect the quality of care available to and provided to all residents, insured and uninsured alike?

An important and underexamined potential impact of uninsurance within a community is on the quality of care provided to all residents. The Committee's earlier reports document problems of quality (based on measures of process and outcome) in the care of uninsured patients. This report focuses more holistically on the effects on a provider's performance overall when uninsured patients or uncompensated care overwhelm or impair the provider's capacity to provide quality services. No studies have directly assessed the correlation of community uninsured rates with hospital quality of care.

There are at least two areas in which high uninsured rates could adversely affect quality of care for all patients. First, if high rates of uninsurance adversely affect hospital margins, this could lead to cutbacks in nursing staff, which in turn threaten quality of care (Needleman et al., 2002). Second, if high uninsured rates contribute significantly to emergency department overcrowding at certain facilities, those hospitals may deliver poorer quality of care during times of patient overload. Detailed studies at the level of the patient are needed to understand the relationship between overcrowding, patient safety, and quality of care.

SUMMARY

The Committee's hypothesized effects of uninsurance on access to health care services are borne out by evidence that, although preliminary, offers reason for concern. For primary and specialty care delivered by physicians in private, clinic, and hospital settings and in hospital emergency, outpatient, and inpatient settings, the burden of providing unreimbursed care to uninsured patients threatens and impairs the capacity of a community's health care institutions and providers. Based on the evidence developed in this chapter, the Committee concludes that moderate- to lower-income residents of communities with higher uninsured rates are more likely than all residents to experience adverse spillover effects of uninsurance. The findings of the Committee's commissioned analyses, while preliminary, indicate that residents with moderate or higher incomes may also be at risk for diminished access to care.

Health care professionals and institutions exist in social and economic relationships with the rest of the community that go beyond their roles as providers of health services. Community effects related to these relationships are the subject of Chapter 4.

4

Economic and Social Implications of Uninsurance Within Communities

For individuals and for families, being uninsured can be associated with a loss of income. A family's breadwinner may lose a job that included health insurance coverage, or an individual's inability to work because of poor health may be prolonged or made worse by a lack of coverage for treatment that would improve the individual's health (IOM, 2002a, 2002b). For the communities in which uninsured individuals and families live, the lack or loss of health insurance coverage by some may undermine the shared economic and social foundations of the entire community. For example, uninsurance may result in higher prices charged to everyone for health services and health insurance premiums or higher state and local taxes levied in order to support local hospitals that provide substantial amounts of uncompensated care. Health insurance is not the solution to all communal ills; nevertheless, the Committee hypothesizes that its presence or absence can make a substantial difference for a community's economic fortunes. While public health insurance programs such as Medicaid also make claims on state tax revenues, the incidence of the tax burden for federal or shared federal–state financing programs falls more broadly upon all American taxpayers and can alleviate some of the financial demands that uninsurance places on disproportionately affected communities.

The impact of uninsurance on the social and economic "glue" that binds a community together is difficult to assess because a community's social and economic resources are as likely to affect uninsured rates as the converse. In addition, the hypothesized relationships between the local uninsured rate and community resources may feed back on themselves in a cycle that amplifies their adverse impacts. For example, declining economic stability and prosperity can foster a sense of social isolation and loss of confidence in public institutions and services, making those who are relatively better off, namely workers with health insurance coverage, feel vulnerable and less prepared to share scarce resources with those who lack a job or health insurance by, for example, extending public benefits to them (Ehrenreich, 1989; Rubin, 1994). Communities with relatively high uninsured rates may experience economic difficulties when uninsurance places new financial demands on local health services providers who make significant contributions to the local economy. As a result, the communities most in need of tax-subsidized assistance to health services institutions and providers may be the least likely to have the tax revenues and be able to afford to finance care for uninsured and underserved persons (Lewin and Altman, 2000).

In this chapter the Committee discusses several probable economic consequences of uninsurance, first characterizing these varied potential community effects as hypotheses and then distinguishing between those for which adequate evidence exists and those requiring further documentation and research. The chapter is organized into five parts. The first three sections consider potential effects of uninsurance on the local economy, through (1) the relationship between uncompensated care locally and increases in health care costs and spending, (2) the increased pressures on states and localities to support greater public spending on health care in response to high or rising uninsured rates, and (3) the loss of fiscal stability by health care institutions, due to high uncompensated care burdens, that may lead to the loss of this major component of the local economy. The fourth section explores new ways to think about potential effects of uninsurance on a community's social bonds and its social institutions in the context of the recent research literature on income inequality, social capital, and health. The fifth section draws together a discussion of key research questions that, once addressed, will fill in the details about economic consequences of uninsurance for communities.

THE CONTEXT: INCREASING HEALTH CARE COSTS AND TAXPAYER SUPPORT

Over the past two decades the uninsured rate nationally has grown slowly but steadily, despite an increasingly tight labor market that expanded employment-based coverage and yielded tax revenues to expand public coverage. Present economic trends have changed from boom to economic recession and, absent major policy interventions, indicate a continuing rise in the uninsured rate. Projected health care cost and health insurance premium increases are likely to add to the ranks of the uninsured (Chernew et al., 2002; Cutler, 2002). It is probable that rising numbers of the uninsured, in turn, will result in further increases in the costs of care and coverage for those with health insurance. In the face of renewed health care inflation, employers have not yet dramatically dropped coverage for their employees but have increased cost-sharing and pared benefits (Strunk et al., 2002). The Committee's observations in *Coverage Matters* remain valid:

- The rising uninsured rate since the late 1970s is directly related to increasingly unaffordable health insurance premiums, as health care inflation has advanced more rapidly than increases in real income or purchasing power (Cooper and Schone, 1997; Holahan and Kim, 2000). After a period of stability in the mid-to-late 1990s, health care costs are again increasing at a rapid rate (Heffler et al., 2001).
- The decade of the 1990s saw a slowing of this inflationary trend, with economic prosperity and relatively low rates of increase in health care costs accompanied by increases in employment-based coverage. Declines in public coverage (reflecting declining Medicaid enrollment particularly after welfare reform), continued until public coverage increased in the late 1990s with implementation of the State Children's Health Insurance Program (SCHIP) (Holahan and Pohl, 2002).
- The first recession of the new century has already erased the gains in private coverage made in recent years. Current estimates released by the Census Bureau indicate that between 2000 and 2001, an additional 1.4 million persons became uninsured, raising the national uninsured rate for persons under age 65 from 15.8 percent to 16.5 percent, or a total of 41 million uninsured persons (Mills, 2002).

The Committee hypothesizes that those with health insurance pay more for it than they otherwise would if fewer people lacked coverage. Public support (e.g., disproportionate share payments to hospitals, subsidy of public hospitals and clinics, federal grants to health centers) and private subsidy (e.g., charity care at private nonprofit hospitals, cross-subsidy provided by employment-based coverage insurance payments) covers an estimated 85 percent of the value of the health care delivered to uninsured persons that is not paid for by the uninsured themselves (Hadley and Holahan, 2003). These costs are passed down to all taxpayers and consumers of health care in the form of higher taxes and higher prices for services and insurance. The Committee's fifth report will take up this subject in greater depth, showing the economic effects of these costs and expenditures on society.

Locally, residents are likely to subsidize care for their uninsured neighbors (though in an arguably inefficient and invisible manner) through taxes and higher prices for health services and health insurance in their community. Because directly provided health services are largely a function of state and local governments, the tax burdens of funding that direct care for uninsured residents is more concentrated locally than is the burden of Medicaid financing or other public programs in which the federal government participates.

Current financing structures for health services are also regressive. One study of health care costs in South Carolina in 1996 finds that persons in households that earned less than 100 percent of the federal poverty level (FPL) had per capita health care costs that were, on average, 70 percent lower than those of persons in households earning more than 400 percent of FPL, yet they paid four times as high a proportion of their income for health care services in taxes and direct spending

(Conover, 1998).[1] In counties with hospital taxes or other subsidy-generating revenues tied to health care use, the uninsured likely bear fewer of these costs than do low-income people in general because they use fewer services.

BUDGET IMPLICATIONS FOR STATES AND LOCALITIES

Finding: Public subsidy of uncompensated care delivered to uninsured persons requires that additional public revenues be raised, resulting in a higher tax burden at the local level, the receipt of monies from federal coffers, or the diversion of resources from other public purposes. If additional revenues are not generated, budget cuts may be imposed, either for health care or across the board, that can adversely affect all members of the community and even increase the number of uninsured persons locally.

Finding: State and local governments' capacity to finance health care for uninsured persons tends to be weakest at times when the demand for such care is likely to be highest (i.e., during periods of economic recession).

Public support for health care services for uninsured persons places demands on state and local governmental budgets. Although the discussion in the previous section assumes that the increasing cost of health care and coverage will be met by increased spending, this is not always the case. States and localities may respond to greater health-related pressures on public budgets in a variety of ways. They may change the state's Medicaid eligibility, benefits, or reimbursement policies; raise taxes (within the limits on their capacity to do so); or use one-time sources of revenue such as tobacco settlement dollars to meet demands for serving uninsured residents.

States' abilities to levy taxes and their tax structures affect state responses to financing care for the uninsured. Box 4.1 provides a broad overview of the diversity among the federal and state tax systems and the proportion and nature of the expenditures by the federal and state governments, respectively. The preeminence of the federal government in raising public revenues suggests that any public finance solution to uninsurance will need to rely in large part on federal financing.

Community residents subsidize care for uninsured patients through their tax dollars. Like the private sector, public funders of health care currently have to cope with increased costs for health services in a time of economic recession. In comparisons among states, relatively higher levels of state spending on Medicaid

---

[1] In 2002, the federal poverty level for an individual was $8,860 and for a family of four was $18,100 for the 48 contiguous states and the District of Columbia (USDHHS, 2002).

BOX 4.1
Federal and State Tax Spending Structures

A brief overview of the structure of the U.S. federal system will give an appreciation of the resources available for health care at the local level. The federal government is the overwhelmingly dominant fiscal presence; it collects two-thirds of the governmental revenue in this country (Miller, 2002b). Even with recently enacted tax cuts, the federal personal income tax will yield as much revenue as all state and local taxes combined.

The tax structures of the different levels of government vary widely. Eighty-five percent of federal revenue in fiscal year 2001 came from direct taxes on individuals—the personal income tax or Social Security taxes. By comparison, state and local governments collect less than half of their revenues by directly taxing individuals. More than half of their revenues comes from indirect business taxes; some combination of sales and property taxes; and other licenses, taxes, and fees (Miller, 2002b). There are simply no generalizations to describe the different state systems: some states have no income taxes, some have no sales tax, others have neither.

The federal government does not use most of its revenue to participate in the economy as a purchaser of goods and services. Its budget is primarily a transfer mechanism—direct transfers to individuals such as Social Security and Medicare (49 percent), indirect transfers through state governments for programs such as Medicaid and child nutrition (11 percent), other grants to state and local governments (6 percent), and net interest (9 percent) (Miller, 2002b). Slightly more than one-fourth of the federal budget can be considered direct spending, divided between national defense (17 percent) and domestic expenditures (9 percent) (Miller, 2002b). By comparison, most state and local spending is either direct spending or transfers from states to local jurisdictions.

The levels of government also have very different debt constraints. State and local governments primarily borrow to finance capital construction. While there is a great deal of misunderstanding surrounding states' balanced budget requirements, these generally can be described as forbidding borrowing for operating expenditures. The federal government, in general, does not describe the purpose of most borrowing but rather borrows to finance an overall unified federal budget deficit.

These differing governmental finance systems produce very different impacts and requirements. The federal and various state tax systems respond very differently to the changes in the business cycle. States that depend on income taxes usually tie either their definition of income or their tax liability to federal definitions and consequently are substantially exposed to changes in federal law. States with sales taxes are highly sensitive to changes in consumption patterns but also benefit when reductions in interest rates produce strong sales of durables. They have been constrained by federal prohibitions on taxing Internet and mail-order sales. Jurisdictions (mostly local) that depend on property tax revenue generally experience a lag in receipts, reflecting the delay between increases in property values and increases in assessments.

are not necessarily associated with lower uninsured rates. (This depends on the number and proportion of low-income and medically needy persons in the state, and on the breadth and generosity of the state's Medicaid program [Holahan, 2002]). However, for a given state, lower rates of public coverage are likely to result in fewer insured persons and a higher uninsured rate. Decreasing enrollment in public insurance (due to tightened or otherwise constrained eligibility) in an environment where employment-based coverage rates are flat or declining will result in less use of health services overall (because uninsured persons use fewer services, on average). However, when uninsured persons do use services, they are likely to need more costly health services because of delays in seeking care (IOM, 2002a, 2002b). The lesser use of services by uninsured persons and their relatively high out-of-pocket spending for health care suggest that aggregate public spending would increase if they gained health insurance coverage.

Given the range of strategies employed to finance uncompensated care and safety-net arrangements from community to community there is no generalized, simple relationship between a community's uninsured rate and its tax burden. An increase in uninsurance would be expected to be met by pressures to increase taxes and reallocate public funds (to the extent that legal structures of taxation and spending allow) devoted to activities other than the provision of personal health services. Thus, a relatively greater uninsured rate may result in higher state and local tax burdens. Because 57 percent of national Medicaid expenditures are paid for by the federal government (and 70 percent of SCHIP spending nationally has been paid for by the federal allocation),[2] when states provide coverage and health care through federally matched insurance programs, the demands on local funds for uncompensated care are likely to be decreased.

Over the previous decade, the fiscal capacity and resources of the states for spending on health programs have grown, due to both the general economic boom in the mid-to-late 1990s and revenues from tobacco lawsuit settlements with the states. Most recently, however, particularly since 2001, states are increasingly experiencing hard times, with economic recession, federal cuts to Medicaid (limiting DSH payments) and Medicare, and public resistance to raising taxes (Dixon and Cox, 2002; Lutzky et al., 2002). States are in a bind because of budget shortfalls, and many plan to cut Medicaid spending in the coming years (KCMU, 2002; Smith et al., 2002). The consequences of these responses are likely to result simultaneously in lower public funding for health insurance, fewer public funds available for other purposes, and the need for higher taxes.

---

[2]Estimate based on unpublished analysis of Vic Miller, Federal Funds Information for States, Washington, D.C., 2002.

Medicaid Financing

State and local programs and policies affecting services for the uninsured are mediated by state Medicaid program policies. Medicaid represents 20 percent, on average, of states' budgets, and the financial incentives of the federal match as well as federal program requirements draw state funds away from more discretionary spending on the uninsured and into the Medicaid program. Total Medicaid program expenditures have increased throughout the 1990s, accounting for almost 15 percent of national health spending in 1998. At the same time, the state and local share of total health spending remained constant over the decade and was about 6 percentage points lower than the share of national health care spending that state and local governments accounted for in 1970 and 1980 (Miller, 2001). This means that there was relatively less of state and local budgets available for all non-Medicaid health spending than in earlier decades.

Changes in a state's spending on Medicaid are likely to affect the level of community uninsurance and the demand for uncompensated care. For example, in Massachusetts, the decision by state officials to trim Medicaid costs by eliminating an expansion that had covered 50,000 adults is predicted to add to the unreimbursed expenses accumulated by hospitals (Goldstein, 2002; Powell, 2002). These hospitals will continue to provide care to at least some of the now newly uninsured state residents and will not be able to draw on the state's uncompensated care pool, which is depleted of funds.

Medicaid program spending often takes priority over state health programs of direct services, including services for uninsured residents, in state budget allocation decisions because of its structure as an individual entitlement and the federal financial match for program expenditures by the state. Medicaid's federal match is designed to provide relatively greater federal support to those states with lower average personal incomes. However, it only imperfectly reflects relative state needs. States still have to cope with reduced tax revenues and higher uninsured rates at the same point in the economic cycle.

Much of the federal government's economic presence is designed to be counter-cyclical, providing automatic stabilizers both to the economy and to the institutions and individuals that participate in it. Medicaid is frequently discussed in these terms because some persons automatically become eligible when their incomes are lost or diminished during economic downturns. Thus, program enrollments and costs grow at times when state revenues may be reduced. Further, the determination of the federal match rate for the program drives more federal money to states whose incomes fall relative to the national economy.

The lags built into the federal medical assistance percentage (FMAP) calculation, however, often produce a pro-cyclical effect for many states.[3] The FMAP is

---

[3]This lag effect has long been recognized but not addressed by policy reforms. For example, during the severe recession of 1982, only four of the fourteen states suffering employment losses between 1979 and 1981 received FMAP increases in fiscal year 1982, but six experienced declines. The largest

based on a three-year moving average of per capita income and is published a year before it comes into effect. Thus, the FMAPs for federal fiscal year 2003 are based on per capita personal income for 1998–2000. States with longer-term secular shifts in wealth see this appropriately reflected in their FMAPs, but those with shorter cyclical shifts often see perverse results. State budget crises in recent years have led 18 states to consider cutting Medicaid eligibility, which would be likely to increase uninsurance in each state and further destabilize local health care providers and institutions (Smith et al., 2002).

Limits on State and Local Capacity to Raise Revenues and the Use of One-Time Revenues

States and localities have a number of constraints on their ability to raise new revenue sources to subsidize care for uninsured persons. Almost all states are required to balance their budgets annually, and many states have constitutional or statutory limits on tax rates or the rate of growth in tax revenues (Desonia, 2002). These governments are effectively prohibited from borrowing to finance operating expenditures and must finance these expenditures out of current tax and nontax (e.g., fees) revenue. States with low per capita income or depressed economies, characteristics that are positively related to uninsured rates, have even more constraints on financing health care for uninsured residents than do more prosperous states.

The entitlement nature of most state government support for health financing means that these programs tend to absorb whatever revenues may be available (Hovey, 1991). Once decisions for health entitlement programs have been made, substantial pressure is placed on the rest of state and local budgets. Medicaid cost pressures may or may not be met by commensurate parallel increases in spending. Governments will constrain Medicaid increases and increase revenues within their limited capacities to do so. For example, Alabama, with an uninsured rate of 13 percent, relies on a regressive tax structure (property and sales taxes) that has limited ability to raise revenues (Ormond and Wigton, 2002). Because its revenues are limited, Alabama's Medicaid program relies on federal supplemental payments (through disproportionate share hospital [DSH] and upper payment limit [UPL] payments) to a relatively greater extent than do other states. Alabama also uses tobacco settlement monies for a Medicaid Trust Fund.

Tobacco settlement dollars have been an important new revenue stream that has cushioned the effect that increased public spending related to uninsurance would otherwise have on states. However, this means that these revenue streams

---

FMAP increases went to states with increasing employment (Miller, 1985). The 1999–2001 personal income data used to calculate the FMAPs for fiscal year 2004 have already been published, and they will drive 2004 Medicaid grants regardless of state economic condition and the numbers of state residents eligible for the program at that time (Miller, 2002b).

are not available for other public purposes. Since the November 1998 Master Settlement Agreement between 46 states and the tobacco industry,[4] tobacco settlement payments (returning prior years' Medicaid expenditures for smokers) have provided states with almost $30 billion (2000–2002) (Dixon and Cox, 2002). These massive paybacks have allowed states to expand public financing of and eligibility for public insurance programs or for public hospital operating subsidies, among many health-related and unrelated uses. Public health and education efforts aimed directly at reducing smoking have been crowded out by the competing demands of programs that finance personal health care services, including Medicaid, SCHIP, and state-only insurance programs for medically indigent persons and families (Dixon and Cox, 2002). Over the four state fiscal years 2000 through 2003, 29 percent of tobacco settlement revenues to the states have been allocated to health services programs (exclusive of long-term care, which accounts for another 5 percent), while tobacco use prevention programs accounted for just 5 percent of the total (Dixon and Cox, 2002). States including Arizona, New Jersey, and New York have devoted significant proportions of their tobacco settlement revenues to health care—either to their Medicaid programs, to support for safety net providers, or to expand public coverage (Bovjberg and Ullman, 2002; Dixon and Cox, 2002). For example, New York has financed expanded coverage through its broad-based Health Care Reform Act of 2000 with a combination of tobacco settlement dollars and an increase in the cigarette tax; the programs intended to provide coverage are estimated to cost about $500 million over three and a half years (Coughlin and Lutzky, 2002).

Local governments (municipalities, counties, and special-purpose health or hospital districts) bear a large share of the direct financing of public hospital and clinic services. One study of local public financing for urban safety net hospitals (in Houston, Oakland, and Miami) finds that the dependence on local revenues made for unstable funding (Meyer et al., 1999). Furthermore, local revenue sources such as sales and property taxes fluctuate with the communities' changing economic fortunes (Clemmitt, 2000). The following vignettes exemplify both the diversity in local financing arrangements and their often provisional nature.

- An innovative program serving medically indigent and uninsured persons in Hillsborough County in south Florida generated a $6.6 million deficit (out of a $90 million budget) due to increased demands for care (Nguyen, 2002). In response, the County Commission raised taxes and reallocated dollars, in addition to tightening eligibility and cutting the generosity of benefits, to try to meet the needs of the approximately 19,000 persons currently enrolled. Rejecting a proposal to levy a one-cent gasoline tax, the commissioners decided to use $3.1 million in county reserve revenues, $2.5 million in property taxes that had been

---

[4]Four states—Florida, Minnesota, Mississippi, and Texas—had previously reached separate agreements with the industry (Dixon and Cox, 2002).

earmarked for road construction, and some funds from those used to pay for prisoners' health care to cover the program's deficit.

• In Texas, the need for indigent health care has outstripped the resources available (Pinkerton, 2002). During 2001, two of the larger counties that border Mexico exhausted the funding for health services programs mandated by the state. After spending local tax revenues and $4.6 million in state aid, Hidalgo County shuttered its program, resulting in the increased use of local emergency rooms for care. Cameron County trimmed services and instituted cost controls to save its $2.3 million program. Federal payments for uncompensated hospital care did not cover the full tab in local hospitals; the nearly 500-bed Providence Hospital in El Paso received $3 million in compensation for the estimated $10 million to $11 million it provided in free care in 2001.

• In the spring of 2001, Cincinnati's safety net arrangements were reported to be under increasing strain due to a growing number of uninsured persons (Cincinnati Business Courier, 2001). The city of Cincinnati had budgeted $13.4 million for health clinics, but one of the safety net providers in the city, the Cincinnati Health Network, citing empty financial reserves, was going to the city for another $300,000 to keep from having to turn away new uninsured patients.

• During 2001, the Kansas City Council debated whether to fund a $205.3 million public safety capital improvement plan by reducing or eliminating the general fund's support for indigent care at the Truman Medical Center and local community health centers (CHCs) (Jaffe, 2001).

Improvised Strategies to Address a Nationwide Problem

Federal health care financing policies provide only a part of the framework that states and localities must construct in order to meet their residents' needs for health services and insurance coverage. The programmatic structure of the federal Medicaid program places considerable fiscal demands on the states and at the same time offers states limited support to address the health care needs of uninsured residents. States and local governments, with highly disparate fiscal resources, health insurance coverage rates, and populations, have adopted a variety of revenue-raising and programmatic strategies to piece together programs of health care coverage and services. These public programs, and the community health care providers that depend on the financial support that they supply to serve low-income and uninsured residents, are far less stable and secure than such essential community services and resources should be, given our nation's wealth.

ECONOMIC BASE AND THE POTENTIAL FOR DEVELOPMENT

Health care accounts for a significant proportion of the economy nationally. In 1999, national health expenditures accounted for 13 percent of the gross domestic product (GDP), rising from less than 9 percent of the GDP in 1980 to slightly more than 13 percent in 1993, at which point the share stabilized (Cowan et al., 2001). Despite this prominent place in the national economy, much less is understood about how health care contributes to the economic vitality of particular communities and, more specifically, how uninsurance within a given community affects the level of health care expenditures and the local economy overall (Doeksen et al., 1997). The question of aggregate, national economic effects of uninsurance in the United States will be addressed in the Committee's next report on the economic costs related to uninsured populations. The discussion here sets out the Committee's hypotheses about the pathways by which uninsurance could affect local economies and communities' economic viability, particularly in rural areas.

How Uninsurance May Affect Communities' Economies

A community's uninsured rate reflects the availability of employment-based insurance coverage for individuals and their families and of public insurance programs such as Medicaid and SCHIP, the viability of the market for individual nongroup insurance policies, and the costs of health care and insurance premiums in the local market. Changes in any of these factors may affect a community's uninsured rate, and the concentration or clustering of uninsured persons in a community may in turn affect its social and economic foundations. An increasing or high uninsured rate, and the attendant high public costs, may discourage employers from locating or continuing to make their home in a community.

A high uninsured rate may both indicate and contribute to an area's economic challenges as it reflects the relative availability of employment-based coverage. For example, health insurance is likely to be less available in areas with a lower-waged labor force (IOM, 2001a). Although there is little direct evidence of the effects that a lack of health insurance may have on workplace productivity, there is some evidence of the lower health status of uninsured workers compared to their insured counterparts (Fronstin and Holtmann, 2000; Hadley, 2002). Furthermore, there is a growing body of research that finds the uneven availability of workplace health benefits keeps workers "locked in" to their jobs if they already have coverage through their employer (Gruber and Madrian, 2001). While such job lock may actually benefit the employer who offers health insurance in terms of worker retention, it may also inhibit the worker's propensity to move among jobs and employers, such that the local or regional economy is less dynamic and expansive than it might otherwise be.

The financial stress of relatively high local uninsured rates on health services arrangements is discussed at length in Chapter 3. While that chapter considered some of the consequences for access to and quality of care in the community, it did not address the aftermath of these effects for the economic base of the community. The health sector is a key part of most local economies, particularly in rural areas, where hospitals serve as social, historical, and civic, as well as economic, anchors. The following section focuses on the centrality of health care institutions and services in rural communities and economies to highlight the potential impact of high uninsured rates on communities. Rural communities are featured both because of the simpler model they offer for describing interrelationships among institutions, health care coverage and financing policies, and uninsurance and because the research literature is more extensive in this area. Despite the difficulty of tracing the broader economic impacts of uninsurance in metropolitan areas, the Committee finds it plausible that somewhat similar forces could be at work in urban communities.

Health Care and Uninsurance in Rural Economies

The economic effects of uninsurance on the viability of health care providers and institutions are easier to measure in rural than in urban areas because the scale and complexity of rural economies is less than those of urban economies. Rural residents on average are older and have lower incomes than do urban residents; consequently public financing, particularly through Medicare and Medicaid payments, is particularly important for the rural health services infrastructure (Cordes, 1998; Mueller et al., 1999). Medicare funding subsidizes access to care not only for Medicare beneficiaries but also for all community members (see Chapter 2 for more discussion). Recognition of Medicare's special role in financing rural health services is expressed with enhanced payments to designated sole community hospitals, through the DSH program and the Critical Access Hospital program (Poley and Ricketts, 2001). These dollars, spent locally, can be a source of new jobs, population growth (e.g., by making the community more attractive to retirees), tax revenues, and economic development (Cordes, 1998). For this reason, hospitals can represent a form of economic development that brings outside dollars into the community (Cordes et al, 1999). The public monies (through Medicare and Medicaid payments) spent on health services also attract additional private dollars spent by patients at local businesses (e.g., shopping, restaurants) in connection with medical or hospital visits. Local rural economies lose dollars spent on health care if residents travel out of the area to obtain services. The loss is amplified to the extent that traveling patients also spend their money on other goods and services outside their home communities, especially in more urban areas (Cordes, 1998; Doeksen et al., 1998; Scorsone et al., 2001).

One way to measure the importance of the health sector for rural economies is by means of an input–output model, with both overall employment and per capita income in a rural county dependent on the presence and size (or loss) of a hospital (Scorsone et al., 2001). Such models were developed in the 1980s to better understand the effects of changes in health care financing (specifically, the new Medicare prospective payment system for inpatient hospital services) on rural hospitals and economies during a period when many rural hospitals closed (Cordes et al., 1999; Poley and Ricketts, 2001). Researchers simulated changes in jobs, income, and tax revenues for a given county predicted by increases or decreases in payments to hospitals. Both spending by hospitals and spending by hospital employees as residents were taken into account in these simulation models. The estimated magnitude of the "multiplier effect" of the gain or loss of one hospital-based job varies by the size of the hospital.

Not surprisingly, according to these simulations, small, rural hospitals have smaller absolute effects (measured in terms of annual business sales, the number of full-time and part-time jobs, and hospital employee earnings) than do larger hospitals in urban areas. One study of rural hospitals finds a range of effects on the number of local jobs, with the smallest hospitals contributing 77 jobs and the largest more than 1,300 jobs (Cordes et al., 1999). Hospitals constitute one of the most influential economic sectors in rural areas, as trade and services in the other sectors are often influenced by the fate of a local hospital (Cordes et al., 1999). Rural hospitals are also more likely to close altogether than are larger hospitals in urban areas, so the relative impact on the local economy can be very great (Colgan, 2002). In rural counties, a hospital may be the second largest employer after the schools, with health-related jobs comprising between 10 and 20 percent of the local jobs (Doeksen, et al., 1997).

A higher-than-average uninsured rate and the corresponding burden of un-compensated care on the local hospital may threaten the survival of the institution and reduce the viability of the economic base of the community. The closure of a hospital may not be the only option for the community or hospital, however (Hartley and Lapping, 2000; Lapping and Hartley, 2000). For example, in Appa-lachia County, Kentucky, conversion of the local hospital into a clinic brought new funds into the community, as well as jobs and a new public insurance-based program intended to provide coverage to uninsured persons (Ziller and Leighton, 2000). The county's high uninsured rate was one of many interrelated factors that made continued operation of the hospital impractical. These factors included the modest tax base and high poverty level of the area and the tendency of insured residents to travel to a neighboring urban hospital with more up-to-date medical technology.

Rural hospital closings are associated with the loss of community physicians (Hartley et al., 1994). Many physicians rely on the hospital to structure an eco-nomically viable practice. Because physician practices also bring new jobs into a community, if a community loses them, the local economy may suffer as well, albeit to a more limited extent than with a hospital closing (Doeksen et al., 1997). According to the director of rural health programs for the Tennessee Hospital Association, a new doctor in a community may be expected to create five new jobs and $500,000 in income, which then will produce further economic activity locally (Raiford, 2002).

SOCIAL CONSEQUENCES OF UNINSURANCE: FIRST THOUGHTS

Health care providers in a community function as social institutions as well as sources of health services. What is known from existing literature about the social effects of uninsurance within a community? In previous sections of this chapter, the Committee has described how uninsurance can tap a community's store of economic resources or capital, resulting in financial strain on the health care system or, to reduce this strain, the raising of new tax or other revenues. Uninsurance may also strain social relationships among community members and local institutions. In the discussion that follows, the Committee identifies social effects as a new area of inquiry that may yield important findings about community uninsurance in the future. Two promising approaches to thinking about social effects, in terms of the intersection of uninsurance with measures of social capital and of income inequality, are briefly reviewed.

Health insurance, whether offered through an employer or publicly to groups left out of the employment-based system, is part of an implicit social contract in the United States (IOM, 2001a). The lack of insurance coverage represents a breach of that contract that, when experienced by large numbers of individuals in a community, may erode the social bonds that define and nurture functioning, healthy communities, as uninsured persons are made aware of their lesser claim on services and resources that are generally valued as essential to a dignified and secure life (Walzer, 1983; Miller, 1997; Faden and Powers, 1999). At the same time, less social cohesiveness and mutual trust within a community may be associated with greater uninsurance, for example, when employers or political jurisdictions do not offer health insurance to their workers and constituents.

There has been little empirical research about how community uninsurance might influence social relationships and what the variety of potential community effects might be that are associated in this way with uninsurance. Social connectedness or cohesion, for example, may promote access to health care by strengthening local health services arrangements, similar to the positive influence that such cohesion has been demonstrated to have on local government functioning (Hendryx et al., 2002; Shi et al., 2002). A relatively strong collective ethic may spur local leaders to raise funds for uncompensated hospital care, for example, or motivate the establishment of a free clinic to serve uninsured people. A community's values, history, and culture contribute to its success in responding to broader economic trends and market changes (Steinberg and Baxter, 1990). Steinberg and Baxter describe these responses in terms of what they call "mechanisms of accountability" that help build or foster the capability of communities to address social needs and respond to changing economic and fiscal environments. To the extent that community uninsurance diminishes these feelings of connectedness, access to health care for all community residents and the health of a community's population in the aggregate may be affected.

One way to observe and measure these social relationships is through the construct of social capital or cohesion. Social capital refers to the stocks of resources available through social relationships, as measured by indicators such as civic engagement, norms of reciprocity, and interpersonal trust between members of a community. Definitions of social capital are usually multidimensional and have both cognitive and social structural elements (Macinko and Starfield, 2001).[5] The more social capital that a community has, the greater is its ability to undertake collective action and to "realize common values and maintain the social controls that foster health" (Sampson and Morenoff, 2000). The process of mobilizing the community resources described as social capital can be thought of as a community's "collective efficacy," specifically, the level of mutual trust among community residents and the degree of shared confidence that residents can and will exert local social control for the public good (Sampson and Morenoff, 2000).

There are several plausible connections between uninsurance and social capital within a community:

• Low social capital may lead to greater uninsurance, for example, if a lack of social cohesion leads to decisions not to offer public coverage. Researchers have demonstrated an association between indicators of social capital at the state level and mortality rates (Kawachi et al., 1997) and poor self-rated health (Kawachi et al., 1998).

• Uninsurance may deplete a community's stock of social capital. This may be manifested in several ways. Lochner and colleagues (1999) propose four overlapping aspects of social capital: collective efficacy, a psychological sense of community, neighborhood cohesion, and community competence. For example, in a community with many uninsured persons or with a high uninsured rate, residents may experience a weakening of their beliefs or confidence in their ability to effectively take care of themselves or their community (*collective efficacy*), because of perceived or genuine difficulties in obtaining coverage or in gaining access to health services that health insurance usually facilitates.

• Social capital and uninsurance may function as markers or indicators of other social processes within the community, for example, social stratification and economic or income inequality. Some researchers have found an association between high degrees of income inequality and low social capital, measured by indicators of civic engagement and social trust. For example, areas with a high level of income inequality have a difficult time maintaining community bonds (Kawachi et al., 1997). Conversely, the erosion of social cohesiveness tends to lead to policies that widen the economic gap within communities (Kaplan et al., 1996).

---

[5]Although the precise definition of social capital is contested and continues to change (e.g., see Portes, 1998; Sobel, 2002), most versions encompass two components: the structural and the cognitive. The structural component of social capital includes the extent and intensity of associational links and activity in society (e.g., density of civic associations, measures of informal sociability, indicators of civic engagement). The cognitive component includes people's perceptions of trust, reciprocity, and sharing (Harpham et al., 2002). An additional distinction is commonly made between bonding and bridging social capital. Bonding capital refers to social cohesion within a group structure, while bridging capital refers to the type that links across different communities and groups (Narayan, 1999).

Another way to think about how uninsurance affects social relationships is to consider the phenomenon of income inequality within a community. For individuals and families, health insurance not only facilitates access to health services but also constitutes a component of socioeconomic status.[6] The lack of financial access to health care and relatively high out-of-pocket expenses (among the uninsured) may exacerbate existing inequalities in income and wealth among a community's residents. Kawachi and colleagues (1999) have proposed that greater income inequality in a community or society, through the mechanism of diminished social cohesion, leads to higher mortality (see also Kennedy et al., 1996; Kawachi and Kennedy, 1997a, 1999; Kawachi, 1999). Others have pointed out that income inequality also correlates with other community characteristics such as racial composition or individual educational attainment that may equally explain area variations in mortality rates (Mellor and Millyo, 2001, 2002; Deaton and Lubotsky, 2002).

The relative income inequality hypothesis posits that the range and steepness of the socioeconomic gradient among residents in a community can affect the health of all members of the community, not only those at risk for poor health due to poverty or other barriers to receipt of appropriate health care (Wilkinson, 1997). Three pathways have been proposed as ways that income inequality may adversely affect the health status of all community members, through

- the disparity or relative deprivation created between the interests of lower-income and higher-income persons (expressed in lower tax rates and levels of public spending on education and health services) (Kaplan et al., 1996);
- the erosion or diminution of social cohesion (e.g., trust in other community members and in the health care system); and
- stress invoked by social comparisons among community members (Kawachi and Kennedy, 1999).

Limited and mixed evidence points to a small adverse effect of community-level inequality on the health of all community members, independent of each individuals' social characteristics, across a variety of measures of income distribution (Kawachi and Kennedy, 1997b; Lynch et al., 1999; Kahn et al., 2000; Sampson and Morenoff, 2000). The size of relative inequalities in average household incomes at the state and county levels contributes to differences in age-adjusted mortality rates and chronic disease morbidity for a number of conditions. The size

---

[6]Uninsurance is closely related to household income, although there is a small "notch" effect for the working poor. That is to say, those with the lowest incomes (<100 percent of FPL) are more likely than those with slightly higher incomes (between 100 and 150 percent of FPL) to be covered through public insurance, while persons and families earning more than 200 percent of FPL annually are more likely to have private coverage (IOM, 2001a). For 2002, 100 percent of FPL is $8,860 for an individual and $15,020 for a family of three (USDHHS, 2002).

of the effect seen at the state and county levels tends to be small (Sampson and Morenoff, 2000).

The cross-sectional, observational nature of much of the evidence means that little can be said with certainty about the direction of causality between income inequality and health-related outcomes and the size of any effect (Macinko and Starfield, 2001). Social inequalities, health disparities, and uninsurance tend to cluster geographically, potentially amplifying the effects on each. The observed relationships between income inequality and health may be related to unmeasured influences on the patterns of residential location (Sampson and Morenoff, 2000; Shi, 2000; IOM, 2001a; Kawachi and Blakely, 2001). Measures of income inequality may also function as a proxy for another, unmeasured aspect of societal or economic inequality that adversely affects health in the aggregate, for example, the effect of economic growth or decline (Mellor and Milyo, 2001; Deaton, 2002). The Committee draws no conclusions about the role of disparities in health insurance status at the community level on population health but, rather, points to emerging developments in the social science literature that may someday allow for a more robust exploration of potential relationships between community uninsurance and the social dimensions of community life.

RESEARCH QUESTIONS

4.1 Effects of Local Uninsured Rates on Health Costs
Does the local uninsured rate, independent of other factors, affect the cost of health services and insurance premiums within the local market area?

Cross-sectional studies are the basis for our limited knowledge about how local uninsured rates contribute to the increasing cost of health services in local health services markets. Longitudinal small-area studies are needed to look at the hypothesized chains of events at the state and local levels to establish or disprove a causal relationship between uninsured rates and health insurance costs locally and to develop estimates of the size and strength of any such relationships.

4.2 Uninsurance and Tax Burdens
What is the burden on local taxpayers of uninsurance within states and localities? How does that burden compare to the tax burden that would be imposed if public insurance programs or subsidized coverage were expanded to reduce uninsured rates? How does the impact of public financing of health care vary across economic cycles?

As discussed in Chapter 2, public support for care for uninsured persons is substantial, yet documentation is inconsistent and exact estimates are difficult, if not impossible, to derive. More consistent reporting is needed across the states and localities of revenue and expenditure streams for financing the array of insurance-based and direct health services programs. A better understanding of state-level budget allocation decisions and the fiscal incentives operating in Medicaid and other programs that support care for uninsured persons could inform proposals to improve the target efficiency and equity of federal and state health financing programs. Specifically, programs of institutional support for uncompensated care, such as Medicare and Medicaid DSH payments, should be evaluated in terms of efficiency and equity.

A systematic analysis of the incidence of the federal, state, and local tax burdens for financing health care generally and for low-income and uninsured Americans in particular should be undertaken as part of any impact analysis of health care financing reform initiatives.

4.3 Uninsurance Effects on the Local Economy
Does the adverse financial impact of uninsurance on local health services and institutions extend to the local economy overall?

Finally, if little is known about the role that the health sector plays in rural economies, even less is known about the economic relationships that bind local health services to urban neighborhoods and metropolitan areas. Research is needed to identify the ways in which a changing uninsured population affects the financial viability of health care providers and institutions and to explicate the complicated series of financing relationships among public and private payers. Are there instances in which a high uninsured rate triggered a funding or political crisis that led to the transition of a local health care system toward a more efficient and effective use of limited resources? To what extent are an uninsured population's uncompensated health care expenses matched by public funds with the objective of keeping a local economy afloat?

SUMMARY

Although potential economic and social spillover effects of community uninsurance are not as well documented or described as the effects on access to health care, the Committee finds the preliminary evidence on economic consequences, and the promise of new research on social consequences, a compelling start. In Chapter 5, the Committee considers community effects related to population health.

5

Community Health and Uninsurance

Discussion of the evidence in previous chapters about community effects on access to care and on the economic and social foundations of local communities suggests that the health of the community itself may be compromised. The Committee hypothesizes that this may result from both the burden of disease related to the poorer health of uninsured community members and from spillover effects that can affect the insured as well as the uninsured. The mechanisms for this result can be as diverse as the spread of communicable diseases from unvaccinated or ill individuals and the paucity or loss of primary care service capacity as a result of physicians' location decisions, cutbacks in clinic staffing and hours, or outright closures, as described in previous chapters. Although it is easier to detect the impacts of high uninsurance on a community's health care providers and resources than on the health of a community's population, community-wide health effects can be inferred from studies of access, utilization, and disease incidence.

The intentional dispersal of anthrax through the U.S. mail in late 2001 revealed yet another way in which uninsurance could threaten community health, when the impaired access to care of uninsured persons means delays in detecting, treating, and monitoring the transmission of infectious disease linked to bioterrorism (Wynia and Gostin, 2002; IOM, forthcoming 2003). As public and policy attention turned to the country's readiness to respond to bioterrorist threats, the weaknesses of the highly fragmented public and private health care systems became apparent. This fragmentation and minimal capacity for communication across systems and types of care hamper the ability of a community to respond rapidly and effectively to an unfamiliar threat to the public's health.

As described in Chapter 3, community uninsurance is likely to lessen access to hospital emergency medical services for all members of a community, as one of several factors contributing to overcrowding and the diminished capacity of emergency departments (EDs) to absorb a sudden and large increase in the number of patients (U.S. Congress, 2001). This capability is key to a community's ability to respond to emergencies such as mass casualty events and certain types of biological and chemical terrorism (IOM, forthcoming 2003). As will be described in the pages that follow, unin-surance is also hypothesized to result in greater financial strains on state and local health departments, strains that may lead to the shifting of discretionary funds from population-based public health activities to the delivery of personal health services and cost-cutting measures such as the trimming of staff. Both types of responses weaken the ability of local health departments to respond to emergencies, particularly involving the spread of communicable diseases.

The case of the bioterrorism agent smallpox, a severe and often fatal infectious disease, illustrates how uninsurance may contribute to current weaknesses in emergency preparedness. Untreated, smallpox has a 30 percent or greater case-fatality rate among unvaccinated persons (Henderson et al., 1999). It can be spread through mass public exposure to aerosolized variola virus, by close personal contact and by contact with infected material (e.g., clothing). A person becomes infectious days after exposure to the virus, when rash, high fever, and other symptoms develop. Routine vaccination of the U.S. population ceased in 1972. Thirty years later, younger members of the population are likely not to have been vaccinated, and the long-term effectiveness of the vaccinations given before 1972 is unknown. The spread of smallpox can be checked through isolation of infected persons, if they are diagnosed and treated in a timely fashion, or through vaccination (Henderson et al., 1999). A mass vaccination campaign, whether in anticipation of or in response to the detection of a smallpox outbreak, would require staff and budget resources devoted to population-based public health activities. This would include the coordination of information, resources, and personnel across the health care sector, epidemiological surveillance and investigation of suspected or reported cases, laboratory testing of samples and medical supplies, and the training of staff to administer vaccines, track after-effects, and provide information to the public (Henderson et al., 1999; IOM, forthcoming 2003). While to date, limited federal funds have been made available to the states to assist in preparing for smallpox vaccination campaigns, it is anticipated that state and local health departments may have to reallocate funds from other programs in order to support vaccination (Connolly, 2002; Altman and O'Connor, 2003).

This chapter explores the implications for population health that flow from the Committee's hypothesis about community effects. Previous chapters describe both empirically confirmed and hypothesized effects of uninsurance on health care services, institutions, and resources and on communities' social and economic resources more broadly. In this chapter, the Committee traces these consequences through to their impact on the health of the community.

To understand the influence of uninsured populations on community health, it is more informative, yet more difficult, to examine cities and counties rather than states or regions. While marked local variation makes detection of hypothesized community effects more likely, uninsured rates and measures of health status are more readily available at the state level, where local variation tends to average out and health measures are often too crude to detect meaningful associations. While regional differences in health status across the United States are closely related to differences in demographic profiles and socioeconomic circumstances, the role of community uninsurance as a factor in this relationship has not been directly evaluated. In this chapter, the Committee reviews research that addresses the relationship between community uninsurance and population-level measures of access to and utilization of services. It also presents community-level (e.g., county or metropolitan statistical area [MSA]) data for the incidence of selected conditions and health outcome measures that merit further investigation.

This chapter has four sections. The first section examines the greater burden of disease and poorer health status in areas with relatively high uninsured rates and relatively low incomes. The second section considers the interrelationships between the capacity and performance of local public health agencies both in population health activities and as providers of last resort to medically indigent community residents. In the third and fourth sections, the Committee poses questions for further research to advance understanding of the relationships between uninsurance and a variety of measures and indicators of population health and provides a summary of the chapter.

GEOGRAPHIC AND SOCIOECONOMIC DISPARITIES IN HEALTH

Finding: Measured across states and metropolitan areas, persons from lower-income families, nearly one-third of whom are uninsured, are more likely to report fair or poor health status in areas with high uninsured rates.

Finding: Hospitalization rates for conditions amenable to early treatment on an ambulatory basis are higher in communities that include greater proportions of lower-income and uninsured residents, indicating both access problems and greater severity of illness.

Community uninsurance rates converge with a number of other factors that affect access to care and health status, such as the proportion of the population that is lower income and the proportion that consists of racial and ethnic minorities (Shi, 2000, 2001; IOM, 2001a, 2002a). Having a lower family income is consistently correlated with being uninsured (IOM, 2001a). About one-third (30.6 percent) of persons under age 65 in families earning less than 200 percent of the federal poverty level (FPL) are estimated to have been uninsured in 2001, over double the uninsured rate for the general population under age 65 (Fronstin, 2002). The relationship between family income and coverage is seen in the aggregate as well, in comparisons of poverty and uninsured rates among geographic regions (IOM, 2001a). Whereas having public health insurance coverage is most strongly correlated with both bad health and low income (since many adults gain Medicaid coverage because they are disabled or medically needy), uninsured persons on average have worse health status than do those with private coverage (IOM, 2002a). The variations in family income across geographic areas are also correlated with population-level measures of health and health outcomes such as having a regular source of care or hospitalization for conditions amenable to treatment on an outpatient basis.

In this section, the Committee explores the hypothesis that uninsurance affects a community's burden of disease. The independent influence or contribution of the local uninsured rate to the health status of insured residents is an important part of this story, yet one that has been insufficiently documented and tested. The studies that the Committee reviews in the discussion that follows do not include analytic adjustments allowing distinctions to be made among the relative influence on health-related outcomes of coverage status, income level, and other major covariates of uninsured rate. While the studies do not allow for the tracing of a definitive pathway for community effects, the Committee finds that the sheer number of uninsured persons in an area adds to the overall burden of disease and disability, as measured by self-reported health status and the number of preventable hospitalizations.

Geographic differences in self-reported health status across the states correlate with state uninsured rates (Holahan, 2002). It is not possible to conclude from such macro-level, cross-sectional statistics that high uninsured rates lead to poorer health. However, the worse measures of health in states with higher levels of uninsurance suggest unmet health care needs. Among 13 states surveyed in 1999, an unadjusted comparison indicates that children and adults in lower-income families (less than 200 percent of the federal poverty level [FPL]) are more likely to report fair or poor health status in states with higher uninsured rates, compared to lower-income children and adults in states with lower uninsured rates (Holahan, 2002). For lower-income children, whose overall average for fair or poor health is reported to be 8 percent, there is a range from a high of 12 percent for Texas (38 percent uninsured rate for lower-income children) and a low of 4 percent for Massachusetts (with its 15 percent uninsured rate for lower-income children).[1] For lower-income adults (under age 65), the overall average for self-reported fair or poor health status is 24 percent, ranging from a high of 27 percent for Texas (52 percent uninsured rate for lower-income adults) to a low of 16 percent for Wisconsin (33 percent uninsured rate for lower-income adults). State-level uninsured rates also correlate highly with the proportion of lower-income children and

---

[1]The uninsured rates described in this paragraph differ from those presented elsewhere in this report. They are estimated on the basis of data collected by the National Survey of America's Families, The Urban Institute, Washington, D.C.

adults who do not have a usual source of care, a measure of access (IOM, 2002a, 2002b).

For urban, suburban, and nonmetropolitan communities across the country, uninsured rates also correlate with the relative health status reported by residents. A nationally representative survey of 60 communities (a stratified, random sample of counties and groups of counties, data for 1996–1997) finds that, unadjusted for the multiple covariates of uninsured rate, residents of the 12 sites with the highest uninsured rates (average of 23 percent) are significantly less likely to report excellent or very good health (64.7 percent) and more likely to report being in good, fair, or poor health, compared to residents of the 12 sites with the lowest uninsured rates (average of 9 percent), where 73.5 percent report excellent or very good health (Cunningham and Ginsburg, 2001).

Health services researchers have proposed that potentially avoidable hospitalizations (sometimes described as ambulatory care-sensitive conditions) serve as an indicator of adequate access to primary and regular health care (Weissman et al., 1992; Billings et al., 1993, 1996; Millman, 1993; Bindman et al., 1995; Pappas et al., 1997; Gaskin and Hoffman, 2000; Falik et al., 2001; Kozak et al., 2001; IOM, 2002a, 2002b).[2] However, area-wide rates of potentially avoidable hospitalizations also measure the acuity of illness experienced within a population and reflect the efficiency with which health care is provided to the population as a whole. To the extent that the fraction of these hospitalizations that could have been avoided with earlier and appropriate care can be identified, the excess burden of illness (and excess costs of care) within the community can also be estimated.

Uninsured patients are more likely to experience avoidable hospitalizations than are privately insured patients when measured as the proportion of all hospitalizations (Pappas et al., 1997). Nationally, the proportion of hospitalizations that were potentially avoidable for persons younger than 65 has grown more substantially over the past two decades for uninsured persons than for those with Medicaid or private insurance, from 5.1 percent to 11.6 percent between 1980 and 1998 for the uninsured, compared with increases for Medicaid enrollees from 7.0 to 9.8 percent and for those with private insurance from 4.1 to 7.5 percent (Kozak et al., 2001).

Using ZIP-code area data to measure the proportion of lower-income residents and rates of potentially avoidable hospitalizations, studies consistently report substantially higher rates of these hospitalizations in lower-income areas (Billings et al., 1993, 1996; Millman, 1993; Bindman et al., 1995; Pappas et al., 1997).

---

[2]Both chronic and acute conditions have been identified and evaluated as ones for which prompt and appropriate treatment on an ambulatory basis can reduce the likelihood of hospitalization. Research constructs have included hospitalization for conditions such as pneumonia, dehydration, cellulitis, asthma, hypertension, chronic obstructive pulmonary disease, congestive heart failure, diabetes, perforated or bleeding ulcer, pyelonephritis, ruptured appendix, hypokalemia, vaccine-preventable conditions, and gangrene as ones indicative of inadequate primary and ongoing care.

Uninsurance is likely to contribute to these higher rates. One study, encompassing 164 ZIP-code areas in New York City, finds that age- and sex- adjusted rates of hospitalization for persons younger than 65 for asthma, congestive heart failure, diabetes, and pneumonia were five to six times higher in low-income areas (where more than 60 percent of the population had household incomes under $15,000) than in high-income areas (where less than 17.5 percent of the population had household incomes under $15,000) (Billings et al., 1993). A second study performed a similar analysis for 18 MSAs, 15 in the United States and 3 in Ontario, Canada. This analysis reveals disparities in rates of potentially avoidable hospitalizations within U.S. metropolitan areas that were from 200 to more than 300 percent greater in low-income ZIP-code areas than in high-income areas. In contrast, the disparities within Canadian metropolitan areas were much lower (rates for the three metropolitan areas were 40 to 60 percent greater in low-income as compared high-income local areas) (Billings et al., 1996). The authors attribute the difference in experience between U.S. and Canadian metropolitan areas in part to the greater financial access of lower-income residents to primary and ambulatory care available under the Canadian health care system.

A third national study examines rates of potentially avoidable hospitalizations (adjusted for age and sex) in relation to median income within ZIP-code areas (Pappas et al., 1997). The authors estimate that designated conditions accounted for between 3 million and 5 million hospitalizations in 1990 (12 to 19 percent of all hospitalizations in that year, excluding those related to childbirth and for psychiatric conditions); see footnote 2 for a list of these conditions. They used the rates of hospitalization for these designated conditions that residents in areas with the highest median household incomes ($40,000 or more) experienced as the baseline rates below which such hospitalizations could not be reduced. The authors then calculated that almost 30 percent of such hospitalizations (between 844,000 and 1.4 million) could represent excessive prevalence and severity of illness within lower-income neighborhoods.

The higher hospitalization rates for conditions that can be managed on an outpatient basis (if access to and quality of care are good) that occur in communities with proportionately more uninsured and lower-income residents highlight the costliness of uninsurance in terms of dollars as well as health. Individual suffering and disability could be avoided with greater access to appropriate ambulatory care services. In addition, timely and adequate care for uninsured residents could lead to offsetting reductions in the demands on the resources of community facilities and public budgets that currently provide hospital care.

PUBLIC HEALTH AND COMMUNITY UNINSURANCE

Finding: Because areas with relatively high uninsured rates are likely to have greater burdens of disability and disease, their needs for

population-based public health services are expected to be greater and the accompanying financial pressures on state and local health departments considerable.

Finding: State and local public health programs are adversely affected when funds are diverted to support personal health services for uninsured persons. Budgets for population-based public health activities, such as disease and immunization surveillance, community-based health education and behavioral interventions, and environmental health, which benefit all members of a community, frequently are squeezed by demands on health departments to provide or pay for safety net services for the uninsured.

Finding: The transformation of public health agencies into assurers rather than providers of health services is likely to leave uninsured members of the community disproportionately disadvantaged with respect to the receipt of privatized services.

Public health, as practiced by health departments, includes the key functions of assessing population health, developing policy solutions for problems identified, and ensuring that problems are addressed by the solutions devised (IOM, 1988). Many health departments also care for uninsured residents who have difficulty gaining access to care in other settings. About a third of local health departments surveyed in the early 1990s reported that they offered general primary care services (NACCHO, 2001). A more recent survey finds that more than one-quarter of local health departments serve as the only safety-net provider in their community (Keane et al., 2001a)

The national consensus-based planning document *Healthy People 2010* (USDHHS, 2000) identifies ensuring access to personal health services as one of ten essential activities of health departments. Particularly in rural areas, health departments can be central sites for the delivery of personal health services, even though many rural counties do not have fully staffed public health departments and may not offer much in the way of health services (NACCHO, 2001). Yet health departments do much more than fill in some of the many gaps in the U.S. personal health care delivery system, and public health involves much more than the provision of health services to uninsured people.

Historically, there have been tensions between the public health and medical care professionals and constituencies over the relative shares of resources devoted to population-based health-oriented activities (e.g., injury prevention) on the one hand and the provision of health services to members of medically underserved groups, including uninsured persons, on the other (IOM, 1988, forthcoming 2003; Baker et al., 1994). In many parts of the country, health department officials have expressed their perceptions of being caught between the increasing demand and need for care of growing numbers of uninsured persons and diminished budgets (IOM, 1988; Lewin and Altman, 2000). These pressures are felt not only within health departments but also by other providers in the health care system (see Chapter 2 for further discussion).

In the 1990s, these tensions were sharpened by the privatization of services and functions at many health departments, a development brought about by the advent of Medicaid managed care contracting by many states and by local health departments seeking greater cost-effectiveness and efficiencies through contracting for personal health services delivery (Goldberg, 1998; Martinez and Closter, 1998; Keane et al., 2001c; Mays et al., 2001).

The transition of state Medicaid programs from fee for service to managed care contracting has added financial pressures on health departments, pressures that may result in decreased access to health department services for all members of a community (Koeze, 1994; Ormond et al., 2000a). Local health departments have experienced losses of revenue when Medicaid enrollees have been assigned for care to private health plans or networks for care that do not include the health department. They have tended to receive less favorable reimbursement than under fee-for-service arrangements and have had diminished capacity to support the delivery of personal health services to uninsured persons as a result (Goldberg, 1998; Martinez and Closter, 1998). For example, through the 1980s, Medicaid reimbursement for immunizations and screening and health assessment services (under the Early and Periodic Screening, Diagnosis, and Treatment [EPSDT] program) was an important revenue source for local health departments delivering well-child care to all of their clients, uninsured as well as Medicaid beneficiaries (Martinez and Closter, 1998; Slifkin et al., 2000). In response to the infusion of federal Medicaid dollars for these services during the 1980s, states cut back or simply did not increase their direct support of health department activities. With the loss in the 1990s of fee-for-service reimbursements for these health department services consequent to Medicaid managed care contracts with private health plans for EPSDT services, together with cuts in real-dollar terms in their budgets, local health departments have been pressed to reduce their level of service provision (Ormond and Lutzky, 2001; IOM, forthcoming 2003).

In an effort to improve cost-effectiveness and quality of care, many health departments have privatized the delivery of certain personal health services (Keane et al., 2001b, 2001c).[3] Many services that were once delivered predominantly in public health clinic settings—for example, immunizations and treatment of sexually transmitted diseases (STDs) and tuberculosis (TB)—are or can be delivered effectively within other primary care settings. For example, as both childhood and adult immunization services have been integrated into private and public health

---

[3]Although health department services and programs are often the providers of last resort for uninsured persons, these programs generally are not as successful as other ambulatory care providers in giving the continuity of care or medical home that is a hallmark of quality health services (IOM, 2001a).

insurance plans, the role of local health departments in directly providing immu-nizations in special clinics and campaigns has shifted to quality assurance in private practitioners' offices and in health plans, surveillance of immunization rates, and the promotion of professional best practices among private plans and practitioners (Slifkin et al., 2000; Smith et al., 2000).[4]

With this privatization has come the growth of health departments' roles as *assurers* of population health, rather than as direct service providers themselves, with an expanded role for states and localities in overseeing and facilitating the delivery of population-based public health services within private health plans (IOM, 2000, forthcoming 2003). However, for uninsured individuals, a shift to private sector primary care and the loss of dedicated public health sites for care may result in diminished access to this care because private practitioners and especially health plan services may not be readily accessible to the uninsured. A survey of a random sample of local health department directors, stratified by the size of their jurisdiction, finds that a majority believe that their uninsured constitu-ents cannot rely on privatized services alone and that the directors do not see themselves as able to promote quality of or access to care for privatized services (Keane et al., 2001a). Thus, the transformation of public health agencies into *assurers* rather than *providers* of health services is likely to leave the uninsured within the community out of the equation and disproportionately disadvantaged with respect to the receipt of privatized services.

The Committee hypothesizes that health departments have often tried to address the unmet health needs of a sizable or growing uninsured population by shifting discretionary funds toward the delivery of health services at the expense of population-based public health programs (e.g., injury control, disease surveillance, environmental health) and that this shifting, absent new revenue sources to finance care delivery, is likely to have adverse effects on the community. The Committee bases its thinking on the conclusions of two Institute of Medicine (IOM) Com-mittees that have evaluated the status of public health, one from the vantage point of the 1980s and the other more recently (forthcoming 2003). Both reach similar conclusions, based on site visits and interviews with public health officials as well as on a limited research literature.

• According to the IOM Committee on the Future of Public Health, "the direct provision by health departments of personal health care to patients who are unwanted by the private sector absorbs so much of the limited resources available to public health—money, human resources, energy, time, and attention—that the price is higher than it appears. Maintenance functions—those community-wide public services that are truly ill-suited to the private sector—become stunted

---

[4]See the special supplement to the *American Journal of Preventive Medicine* (Smith et al., 2000) on the history of, trends in, and current policies regarding immunization programs for a fuller account of these reforms.

because they cannot compete, and key functions such as assessment and policy development wither because they are not seen as life-and-death matters." (IOM, 1988, p. 52).

• The IOM Committee on Assuring the Health of the Public in the 21st Century, in its recent report states: "The committee finds that as in 1988, the continued lack of a nationwide strategy to assure adequate financing of personal medical, preventive, and health promotion services will continue to place undue burdens on the public health system and to fragment the provision of personal health services to those most in need of comprehensive, integrated approaches. Also, if the number of uninsured continues to increase, this may require the diversion of resources urgently needed for population health efforts to the health care assurance component of the governmental public health system" (IOM, forthcoming 2003, p. 154).

Vaccine-Preventable and Communicable Disease

Finding: The strength of the local health department and the adequacy of its funding are likely to influence how community uninsurance affects the health of all community members. The incidence and prevalence of vaccine-preventable and communicable diseases are expected to be higher in areas with high uninsured rates where health departments have been chronically short of funding.

In the following discussion of childhood immunization and communicable diseases (including STDs, HIV/AIDS, and TB), the Committee examines how public health efforts in these areas are affected by and related to uninsurance within communities. The examples of childhood immunization rates and reportable conditions illustrate how the concentration of ill health in areas with higher uninsured rates may be amplified by these high rates. Despite the decline in the incidence of many infectious diseases in urban and suburban areas over the past decade (Andrulis et al., 2002), these conditions are common in communities facing other challenges related to the lower socioeconomic status of their residents, as discussed earlier in this chapter. Likewise, despite national and state public health efforts to maintain high levels of childhood immunizations, these rates also vary substantially among communities and are lower in lower-income urban counties and areas with less health insurance coverage (Santoli et al., 2000).

Communicable disease control is a traditional core function of health departments, to prevent their spread throughout the population, for example, through the tracing and notification of persons with whom an infected individual has come in contact. For both immunization rates and communicable diseases, the health consequences of uninsurance are intertwined with the long-term underfunding of health departments, which traditionally have led in managing immunization programs and detecting and treating communicable diseases. The Committee hypothesizes that the presence of sizable uninsured populations that do not have reliable access to services provided either by health departments or by practitioners in the private sector means that both population immunization levels and communicable disease rates are likely to be worse than they otherwise would be if everyone in the United States had health insurance.

The section that follows includes illustrative discussions of potential population health effects of uninsurance related to childhood immunization levels, STDs (syphilis, gonorrhea, and chlamydia), and TB, diseases that are both preventable and curable if diagnosed and treated in a timely fashion. The incidence and prevalence of these diseases reflect the level of public resources devoted to prevention, screening, contact tracing, and successful treatment. HIV/AIDS is an important part of the story (e.g., syphilis and gonorrhea leave a person more vulnerable to HIV infection, and HIV-positive persons are more likely to contract TB) and is also discussed below.

Immunization Rates

Underimmunization increases the vulnerability of entire communities to outbreaks of diseases such as measles, pertussis (whooping cough), and rubella (IOM, 2000). The history of childhood immunization and federal immunization policy since the development of the polio vaccine in the 1950s has been one of cyclical efforts and sporadic attention (Johnson et al., 2000; Roper, 2000; Smith, 2000). When attention to this public health issue wanes, outbreaks occur. The latest and deadliest major outbreak of measles occurred between 1989 and 1991 in several major U.S. cities, including Chicago, Los Angeles, Milwaukee, and Washington, D.C. (Johnson et al., 2000). During 1989 and 1990, a total of 43,000 cases of measles were reported and more than 100 deaths were attributed to this disease (IOM, 2000; see Box 5.1).

Local, state, and federal public health agencies and programs have as central missions ensuring full immunization coverage of the nation's children for a range of childhood illnesses and promoting the immunization of adults for influenza, pneumonia, and other diseases (IOM, 2000). These goals depend in ever-greater measure upon immunization within health insurance programs such as Medicaid, the State Children's Health Insurance Program (SCHIP), employment-sponsored plans, and Medicare (DeBuono, 2000; Fairbrother et al., 2000; Sisk, 2000). As a result, both childhood and adult immunization levels are positively correlated with having either public or private health insurance as compared with being uninsured.

The completely federally financed Vaccines for Children (VFC) program provides childhood vaccines free to private primary care practitioners, federally qualified health centers, and public clinics for administration to uninsured children, Medicaid-eligible children, and in clinical settings, children whose private insurance does not cover immunizations (IOM, 2000). Established in 1994, this program provides vaccines to about one-third of all children in the United States between birth and age 18 (CDC, 2002b). Notably, VFC is the Centers for Disease

BOX 5.1
The Measles Epidemic, 1989–1991

In 1983, a record low number of measles cases was reported in the United States, 1,497 cases. This was a reduction of 97 percent from the more than 57,000 cases reported in 1977. (A vaccine for measles became widely available in 1965.) This success was not sustained, however. In 1984 and 1985, outbreaks occurred among older children who had entered school before the vaccine was routinely used. In 1986, a new pattern emerged, with outbreaks among preschool children, concentrated in inner city, low-income neighborhoods in 20 counties across the United States.

These sporadic outbreaks of measles became epidemic between 1989 and 1991. Unimmunized and underimmunized preschoolers became a reservoir for the disease, which spread rapidly through several cities, including Chicago, Dallas, Houston, Los Angeles, Milwaukee, New York, and Washington, D.C. Within two years, 43,000 cases of measles were reported and 101 deaths were attributed to the disease.

The measles epidemic led to the creation of a federal Interagency Coordinating Committee in 1991 to improve access to immunization services and to the federal Infant Immunization Initiative in 1992. It also provided impetus for the passage of the VFC program as part of the Omnibus Budget Reconciliation Act of 1993 to reduce financial barriers for private practitioners to administer, and thus for children to receive, immunizations.

SOURCE: IOM, 2000.

Control and Prevention's (CDC) largest public–private partnership, reaching children through arrangements with 33,000 private practice sites (primarily physicians' offices) and 10,000 public clinics (CDC, 2002b). By making free vaccines available to physicians in private practice for administration to uninsured and Medicaid-enrolled children, the VFC program keeps children in their medical homes for immunizations and avoids fragmentation of their care by eliminating the need to make referrals to public immunization clinics.

Although VFC is an important programmatic improvement in securing the immunization of uninsured children, achieving childhood immunization goals is facilitated when children have public or private health insurance. Insurance increases the likelihood that children will have a regular source of care and receive routine preventive services (IOM, 2002b). When New York State expanded children's insurance prior to the enactment of SCHIP, the statewide immunization rate rose from 83 to 88 percent for all children between 1 and 5 years of age (Rodewald et al., 1997). The increase was greatest among those children that had been uninsured and those who had had a recent gap in coverage of longer than six months. At the same time, immunization visits to primary care practitioners' offices increased by 27 percent and those to public health department immunization clinics decreased by 67 percent (Rodewald et al., 1997).

Despite the efforts of the past decade to expand sources of federal financial support for childhood immunization services in children's medical homes, the 8.5 million children who currently do not have health insurance (Mills, 2002) are at increased risk of not receiving immunizations. Because uninsured families and children tend to live in neighborhoods with higher-than-average uninsured rates and are likely to go without immunizations, influenced by a host of related factors such as lower family income and lower parental educational attainment, all who live in these communities are more likely to be exposed to disease outbreaks such as the ones that culminated in the measles epidemic of 1989–1991. Because a community's level of childhood immunization is influenced by many factors that vary along with uninsurance rates (e.g., family income) and also by the scope and effectiveness of the local public immunization program, direct links between uninsurance and immunization levels are difficult to evaluate statistically. As an illustration of the general relationship, however, Table C.5 (Appendix C) displays the relative rankings of 28 metropolitan counties on up-to-date immunization rates for 2-year-olds for a basic series of four vaccines and on uninsured rates. Data are for 1997.

Sexually Transmitted Diseases

Sexually transmitted diseases are not confined to uninsured persons, but because uninsured persons are less likely to receive a timely diagnosis or treatment, the consequences can be particularly severe (IOM, 2002a). The Committee hypothesizes that these consequences may include continued transmission of the disease to other members of the community. Like many other conditions, STDs are more common among lower-income persons, and the extent to which they are diagnosed and treated depends on the capacity and responsiveness of community providers in serving such patients (IOM, 1997; CDC, 2000). Often, local health departments operate clinics devoted to STDs and their clientele tends to be uninsured persons (Landry and Forrest, 1996; Celum et al., 1997). If funding for local health department specialty services (e.g., STD clinics, family planning) is reduced because of mandated priorities or when other claims on public budgets take precedence (such as the state share of Medicaid program costs or public hospital operations), STDs may go undetected and untreated and their incidence and prevalence in the community at large may increase. Syphilis, gonorrhea, and chlamydia, three of the most serious and common STDs, are bacterial infections that are treatable with antibiotics once diagnosed (CDC, 2000). See Boxes 5.2, 5.3, and 5.4 for brief descriptions of these 3 diseases. If not treated, they are transmissible, so their incidence rates are indicators of the relative effectiveness of local public and personal health care services (CDC, 2000).

Although there are federal funds to support state and local programs for the diagnosis, contact tracing, and treatment of these STDs, federal grants do not meet the full need for such services. In the context of diminishing state and local funding to subsidize direct services delivery to medically indigent persons, the

BOX 5.2
Syphilis

During the 1990s the incidence of primary and secondary syphilis in the United States dropped significantly, with the number of cases reported in 2000 the lowest since record keeping began in 1941—5,979 reported cases, or a rate of 2.2 cases per 100,000 persons (CDC, 2001c; Lukehart and Holmes, 1998). This chronic, systemic infection is most often transmitted sexually, although it may also be conveyed nonsexually and in utero as congenital syphilis (Lukehart and Holmes, 1998). When it first appears, it can be treated with antibiotics. If untreated, it will become latent and later develop into secondary and tertiary forms with an array of severe adverse health outcomes (CDC, 2001c). Tracing, informing, and treating the partners of persons with infectious syphilis are critical to preventing spread of the disease because about 50 percent of all sexual partners of a person with infectious syphilis become infected themselves. The disease can be detected by screening during pregnancy (Lukehart and Holmes, 1998).

Despite the declining incidence of syphilis nationally, the South remains the epicenter for this STD, particularly in urban and suburban areas, and African Americans as a group in this region continue to be disproportionately affected—a pattern reflecting the influence of demographic and socioeconomic circumstances and difficulties gaining access to health care (CDC, 2001c; Andrulis et al., 2002). Syphilis is also known to facilitate transmission of the virus that causes AIDS (Lukehart and Holmes, 1998). In 1999, the federal government began a national campaign to eradicate syphilis entirely.

BOX 5.3
Gonorrhea

Gonorrhea is the most common of the reportable diseases in the United States, with a stable case rate in recent years of about 132 cases per 100,000 persons (Holmes and Morse, 1998). Patterns of incidence for gonorrhea resemble those for syphilis. There are marked ethnic and racial disparities, although, as with syphilis, biases tied to reporting from public clinics may overstate the degree of these differences. Reported rates range from 28 per 100,000 persons for non-Hispanic whites and 70 per 100,000 persons for Hispanics to 827 per 100,000 persons for African Americans (Holmes and Morse, 1998). In addition, youth, single marital status, and low socioeconomic status are each associated with greater likelihood of getting gonorrhea.

While the incidence and prevalence of this STD reflect the presence of sexual and health-related behavioral risk factors, they also serve as indicators of local access to care (Holmes and Morse, 1998). Once transmitted, gonorrhea can become infectious within days and not exhibit symptoms. Public health outreach, interviews, and contact tracing must be carried out quickly if they are to be effective in preventing the spread of disease. Treatment is relatively inexpensive and may be as simple as one dose or a short course of antibiotics (CDC, 2001c). Incompletely treated, gonorrhea strains may mutate into drug-resistant versions. It is estimated that one-third of the strains found in the United States are resistant to penicillin or tetracycline, two common antibiotics used to treat this infection (Holmes and Morse, 1998).

BOX 5.4
Chlamydia

Chlamydia is frequently hard to detect, with an estimated incidence of 3 million cases annually, of which just one-sixth are reported (CDC, 2001a). This bacterial infection is easily treated and cured, when diagnosed. Untreated, it can cause pelvic inflammatory disease (PID), infertility, and tubal pregnancies. As many as 40 percent of women with untreated chlamydial infections develop PID, which in turn is related to infertility and chronic severe pelvic pain. Women infected with chlamydia are at much higher risk (three to five times greater than those not infected) of acquiring HIV infection.

Because of its prevalence and the fact that 75 percent of the women and 50 percent of the men infected with chlamydia have no symptoms, screening is the most effective approach to controlling this disease. Adolescent girls between 15 and 19 years of age account for 46 percent of reported infections, and women ages 20 to 24 account for another 33 percent (CDC, 2001a). The CDC recommends screening all sexually active girls and women under 20 years of age at least annually, and annual screening of women 20 years and older who have one or more risk factors for chlamydia (e.g., new or multiple sex partners, lack of barrier contraception).

Within the past decade, a collaborative federal prevention program has established demonstration projects across the United States that involve family planning providers, STD and primary health care programs, and public health laboratories to provide screening and treatment services. However, given the large at-risk population, targeted screening programs cannot control the spread of this disease. Screening and treatment within primary care programs and health plans present greater opportunities to address this health problem. One randomized trial of chlamydia screening and treatment in a health maintenance organization achieved a 56 percent reduction in the incidence of PID among the screened group within a year of the screening (CDC, 2001a).

IOM report *The Hidden Epidemic: Confronting Sexually Transmitted Diseases* also concludes that there is a need for "a secure source of funding for STD-related services for uninsured persons," including federal categorical support, to maintain and improve on national progress in stemming the prevalence of STDs (Eng and Butler, 1997). State and local governments pay for clinical services, contributing a little more than half (58 percent) of the operating funds for specialized STD clinics, with much variation among localities (Eng and Butler, 1997). The Committee posits that because uninsured persons are less likely to gain access to private sector health services, they are also more likely to have undetected or untreated STDs and, as a result, may be more likely to infect someone else.

For uninsured persons, the key site of care for STDs is the local health department STD clinic. Other sites for care include other community-based clinics (e.g., community health centers, family planning clinics, school health centers), private physician offices, and hospitals (Landry and Forrest, 1996). Public STD clinics are found in most counties and cities and in every major city and every state. The size of these clinics, the services provided, the quality of care, and the funding streams that support these clinics vary considerably from location to location (Eng and Butler, 1997). STD clinics function in a safety-net capacity, providing a high volume of care and much of the specialized care (e.g., screening, contact tracing and notification of partners who may have been infected by a patient, short-term treatment) for these diseases nationally and serving patients who seek privacy or have difficulties gaining access to care because they are uninsured or because there are no knowledgeable local providers (Eng and Butler, 1997). Clients' access to STD clinic services is more often limited by clinic capacity than by the price of services, as sliding-scale payment arrangements are common and patients pay little or none of the costs of care (Eng and Butler, 1997).

A 1995 survey of five urban STD clinics around the country found that clinic clients are likely to be uninsured (58 percent), under 25 years of age (51 percent), members of ethnic and racial minority groups (64 percent), less well educated (55 percent with a high school diploma or fewer years of schooling), and low income (67 percent earning less than $20,000 a year) (Celum et al., 1997). Symptoms of an STD were most likely to be the motivator to visit the clinic, followed by concerns about the cost of care. Fully 66 percent of those surveyed were diagnosed with an STD as a result of their visit (Celum et al., 1997). Data on funding and services provided at public STD clinics and other community clinics that offer STD-related services are limited, and even less is known about experiences in the private sector, where the majority of STD cases are diagnosed (Eng and Butler, 1997).

A recent IOM study points to the lack of coordination among providers and institutions serving a common population and the importance of coordination in both cities (where STD clinics have very high caseloads) and rural areas (where clinics may have limited hours or services due to lower demand or fewer funds) (Eng and Butler, 1997). The fragmented and unstable nature of public funding and lack of coordination in the provision of STD services particularly affect uninsured populations that disproportionately rely on public clinic services. Poorly coordinated care can lead to incomplete treatment or no treatment (Eng and Butler, 1997). Lack of health insurance coverage may mean that an insured partner receives treatment while an uninsured partner does not. The relationship between lack of access to care and continued infectiousness among persons with syphilis, gonorrhea, or chlamydia is clear. The Committee hypothesizes that community uninsurance, coupled with lack of public resources to pay for or deliver coordinated STD services, may contribute indirectly to the spread of disease within the community.

HIV/AIDS

Infection with the human immunodeficiency virus (HIV) constitutes an on-going global epidemic. In 2000, an estimated 800,000 to 900,000 people in the United States were living with HIV infection or AIDS, the more advanced form of the infection (CDC, 2001c). Almost 20 percent of all persons with HIV infection are uninsured (Kates and Sorian, 2000). Persons who are HIV positive and uninsured are more likely to be unaware of their infectious state than are seropositive persons with health insurance, either public or private (Bozzette et al., 1998). As a result, one health consequence of community uninsurance may be a greater risk of the transmission of the virus that causes HIV/AIDS especially for members of groups that are already at greater risk for becoming infected (e.g., persons from lower-income families or households, members of ethnic and racial minority groups, injection drug users).

The Committee's second report, *Care Without Coverage*, documents numerous adverse health consequences for uninsured adults who are HIV positive, including greater morbidity and mortality (IOM, 2002a). These findings reflect the greater difficulties that uninsured persons have in obtaining access to health services, a regular source of care, and quality care that meets professional and clinical standards (IOM, 2002a).

• Uninsured adults are less likely to receive primary and preventive services that include screening.
• They are much less likely to receive the combination antiretroviral therapy, highly active antiretroviral therapy (HAART), with either protease inhibitors or nonnucleoside reverse transcriptase inhibitors, that is the clinical standard of care for HIV/AIDS (HIV/AIDS Treatment Information Service, 2002).
• They are likely to experience greater delays in starting treatment after having been diagnosed, as measured by a first office visit and waiting time until the start of antiretroviral therapy.
• They are less likely to receive the regular care that is integral to the clinical standard of care for HIV/AIDS, are less likely to receive needed health services, and are more likely to stop drug therapy.

While part of the difficulty in gaining access to timely and appropriate care is linked to the site of care for uninsured patients (Sorvillo et al., 1999), another aspect of the problem is the difficulty that uninsured persons who are HIV positive face in obtaining public coverage before they have developed full-blown AIDS (Kates and Sorian, 2000). Health insurance is a key facilitator of access to care for persons with HIV because of the cost of therapy. In recent years, lifesaving combination antiretroviral therapy has transformed HIV from a usually deadly disease into a chronic illness that may be managed over years but at a cost of roughly $20,000 annually for persons who have not yet developed AIDS (Kates and Sorian, 2000). Although uninsured persons can and do obtain care from community health centers, academic medical centers, public hospitals, and other providers that participate in safety-net arrangements, effective treatment of HIV, to lower the chances that a person will develop AIDS, requires regular care and coordination of care across providers, both of which are more difficult to do in safety net settings, given limited funds and other resources (Kates and Sorian, 2000).

Most HIV-positive persons with Medicaid or Medicare, or other publicly subsidized coverage (e.g., through a state high-risk pool as a medically uninsurable person), have obtained this coverage only through being certified as disabled (Kates and Sorian, 2000). Medicaid coverage is available to persons who meet income and categorical eligibility standards in their state of residence, while Medicare coverage, which does not include prescription drug coverage, may be available after a 29-month waiting period (KFF, 2000). Some states have federal program waivers that allow them to provide Medicaid coverage as soon as someone is diagnosed with HIV (KFF, 2000).

Because of the existing barriers to public coverage, a particularly vulnerable group of people—uninsured persons who are HIV positive—is left at risk of not being diagnosed or adequately treated at the point at which they are most likely to transmit the virus. There are discretionary public funds for HIV care available to the states and certain designated metropolitan areas through the federal Ryan White program (Kates and Sorian, 2000). These funds are used by states and localities to fund some limited early intervention services, treatment, wraparound services (e.g., transportation, outreach, health education), and prescription drugs for uninsured and underinsured persons with HIV disease. Thus, uninsured persons may not necessarily have to rely on charity care or pay out of pocket for all expenses associated with diagnosing and treating HIV. States vary in how they use Ryan White funds, so the experiences of uninsured persons in obtaining access to screening and therapy for HIV-positive status depend on how the funds are allocated within states according to priorities set by planning councils and the state. In the case of prescription drug benefits under Title II of the Ryan White CARE Act (AIDS Drug Assistance Programs), all states participate in this program but many have waiting lists for potential enrollees (Aldrige et al., 2002).

Tuberculosis

Tuberculosis is a preventable and treatable contagious disease whose spread may be exacerbated by uninsurance within a community. A bacterial respiratory infection that usually settles in the lungs, TB is transmitted through contact in close quarters, often by sneezing or coughing. The disease may be latent or active and is more likely to be conveyed in its active phase. For close contacts of persons with TB, the case rate is 700 per 100,000 persons (Geiter, 2000). In contrast with STDs and HIV infection, whose transmission requires intimate contact, TB is spread in public settings such as schools, workplaces, hospitals, and clinics. People may be completely unaware of their exposure to and potential for contracting the disease.

Although the incidence of TB has declined over time, it has been increasingly geographically concentrated within the largest cities (greater than 500,000 population), although prevalence data are not available consistently to compare the experiences of specific communities (Geiter, 2000). Previously closely associated with the prevalence of HIV/AIDS and disproportionately seen in homeless persons, persons affected by substance abuse, and prison populations, in recent years TB has become more of a concern for low-income immigrant communities in urban areas, along the southwestern U.S. border with Mexico, and in other medically underserved communities (Geiter, 2000; CDC, 2001b; Kershaw, 2002). Of the 17,531 reported TB cases in the United States in 1999, 43 percent were among foreign-born persons, with people born in Mexico accounting for 1,753 cases (almost a quarter of the foreign-born cases) (CDC, 2001b).

Timely diagnosis and appropriate treatment are integral to stemming the transmissibility of tuberculosis, particularly when latent, given the relatively low number of active cases (IOM, 2000). Inadequate access to primary and follow-up care has contributed to the increase in drug-resistant tuberculosis, which poses a public health threat (CDC, 1999). This not only results in greater suffering and risks for the patient but also creates greater risks of infection for those with whom the patient comes in contact. Even more so than for STDs, the control of this disease rests with health departments and success is directly related to the adequacy and continuity of public funding. Screening, contact tracing and notification, and treatment are all labor intensive. This is particularly true for treatment, which requires up to a year's worth of daily medication, with multiple pills taken at different times each day. To ensure compliance, the standard of care—directly observed therapy—involves a public health worker watching the patient take his or her medication (Geiter, 2000). As the number of TB cases has declined nationally, TB control programs have had to compete for public dollars that have been redirected to other health issues, even though the disease has not been eradicated (Geiter, 2000).

Immigrants from Mexico and binational U.S. residents have a greater risk of TB because of the higher rate of the disease in Mexico (CDC, 2001a). Legal immigrants seeking permanent residence are screened for infectious TB before entering the United States and may enter the country with either active but noninfectious disease or latent disease, with instructions to report to a health department at their destination for follow-up treatment (Geiter, 2000). Undocumented immigrants are unlikely to have been tested.

Immigrants to the United States are both more likely to be exposed to TB and less likely to be diagnosed and treated in a timely manner. Recent immigrants are more likely than long-term U.S. residents to encounter difficulties in gaining access to care. Their generally lower incomes and exclusion from Medicaid mean that they are much less likely to have health insurance coverage (Hudman, 2000; IOM, 2001a; Ku and Matani, 2001). Recent immigrants are at the highest risk for developing TB, and this risk declines with increasing length of stay: 30 percent of all TB cases among foreign-born persons occur in the person's first year within the United States and 56 percent of all cases occur in the first five years (Geiter, 2000). In this way, immigrant communities with high uninsured rates can experience tuberculosis as a spillover health consequence, and all members of the community may be exposed.

Urban areas around the United States have experienced an increase in TB case rates due to growth in the size of foreign-born populations from countries with higher rates than the United States. New York City, for example, has the highest TB rate of any city nationally, with 1,261 new cases of the disease reported in 2001. In parts of New York City, tuberculosis has made a resurgence, following a decline after HIV/AIDS-related TB was addressed in the mid-1990s (Kershaw, 2002). During the 1990s, the city saw a shift from 18 to 64 percent of new TB cases annually occurring among foreign-born residents (Kershaw, 2002). Compared to the 1992 rate of 240 cases per 100,000 persons in Central Harlem, the rate in immigrant communities is considerably lower—for example, 36 cases per 100,000 persons in the Queens neighborhood of Corona. The rate for Corona, however, is more than twice New York City's average case rate of 16 cases per 100,000 persons and is seven times the national average.

Tuberculosis case rates are somewhat lower but no less a threat to public health along the 2,000-mile U.S.–Mexico border, where the mobility of local residents and the immigration of seasonal agricultural workers have brought greater-than-average risk for contracting TB (CDC, 2001b). The majority of TB cases reported between 1993 and 1998 were U.S.-born citizens. Persons born in Mexico, however, accounted for just over 40 percent of all cases reported in Arizona, New Mexico, and Texas (CDC, 2001b). The TB case rates for border cities in Texas are high. For 1998–1999, per 100,000 population, the case rates of TB were 23 in Laredo, 22 in Brownsville, 70 in Matamoros, 15 in McAllen, and 10 in El Paso, Texas (CDC, 2001b).

For the border region, higher rates of communicable and chronic diseases reflect a mix of circumstances that contribute to a lack of access to health care. Poverty rates are high, and the rapid economic and population growth has not been matched by increases in public or private health care services capacity (Pinkerton, 2002). Uninsured rates in border counties range between 25 and 35 percent and are believed to be even higher among residents of semirural *colonias*, where one survey put the uninsured rate at 64 percent (Pinkerton, 2002). Border hospitals that treat TB patients are at a financial disadvantage. As rural facilities, they deliver a relatively lower volume of services and receive lower payments from programs such as Medicaid, compared with urban, higher-volume hospitals. At the same time, they incur significant amounts of uncompensated care and may not receive reimbursement for nonemergency services delivered to uninsured recent immigrants, who are not eligible for Medicaid coverage (CDC, 2001b; Pinkerton, 2002). For TB patients, migratory living patterns and cultural and language differences are likely to make access to care and successful completion of treatment difficult. For border health departments, effective TB control will require greater coordination with Mexican health officers of outreach, partner notification and contact tracing, screening, and treatment (CDC, 2001b).

As is the case with childhood immunizations, multiple covariates are likely to

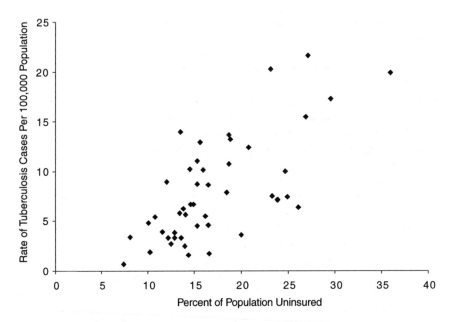

FIGURE 5.1 Urban uninsurance and tuberculosis case rates, 1997.
NOTES: Data points represent the following cities: Akron, OH; Albuquerque, NM;
Atlanta, GA; Austin, TX★; Baltimore, MD; Birmingham, AL; Boston, MA★; Buffalo,
NY★; Charlotte, NC★; Chicago, IL; Cincinnati, OH★; Cleveland, OH; Columbus, OH;
Dallas, TX; Dayton, OH; Denver, CO; Detroit, MI; Fort Worth, TX; Houston, TX;
Indianapolis, IN; Jacksonville, FL; Jersey City, NJ; Kansas City, MO★; Louisville, KY;
Memphis, TN★; Miami, FL; Milwaukee, WI; Minneapolis, MN★; Nashville, TN; New
Orleans, LA; New York City, NY; Newark, NJ; Norfolk, VA★; Oakland, CA; Oklahoma
City, OK; Omaha, NE★; Philadelphia, PA; Phoenix, AZ★; Richmond, VA; Rochester,
NY; Sacramento, CA; San Antonio, TX; San Francisco, CA; St. Louis, MO★; Tampa, FL;
Tulsa, OK; and Washington, DC.★
★These cities represent multicounty areas, while disease rates are for the central county
unless otherwise indicated.
SOURCES: Brown et al., 2000; CDC, 2002a.

influence the relationship between community uninsurance and TB case rates.
Figure 5.1 illustrates the simple, unadjusted correlation between TB case rates and
uninsured rates for 47 large MSAs (where both rates are available) for 1997. This
fairly large and statistically significant correlation (Spearman coefficient = 0.63,
$p < .001$) between reported cases of TB and uninsured rates is likely to be
overstated due to the presence of unmeasured covariates with uninsured rate.[5]
Even if this substantial correlation does not support the conclusion that uninsurance

---

[5]See Table C.5 in Appendix C for the uninsured and TB case rates used in this figure.

is a major causal factor in the incidence of TB, it nonetheless indicates an increased risk for the community at large with respect to the transmission of TB.

RESEARCH QUESTIONS

5.1 Health Status Within the Community at Large
Does the local uninsured rate, independent of other factors, affect the health status of community residents overall? Are particular groups within the general population more affected than others?

A number of cross-sectional studies have documented the worse health status and access to care of lower-income populations in localities and states with relatively high uninsured rates. However, these studies neither confirm nor reject the hypothesis that high rates of uninsurance locally have deleterious effects on health and access to care among those with coverage. Longitudinal studies could shed some light on this question. Do changes in the uninsured rate over time lead to changes in the health status of insured people as well as to changes in the health of those lacking coverage? Race, ethnicity, and socioeconomic status need to be controlled analytically in such studies, as they influence health outcomes and covary with uninsured status (IOM, 2002a; Smedley et al., 2002).

5.2 Public Health Departments and Services, Including Emergency Preparedness
Does demand for personal health care services by uninsured residents adversely affect the availability of public health services within localities and states? Does the presence of substantial uninsured populations within communities adversely affect emergency preparedness and the community's ability to respond effectively to bioterrorism and other mass casualty events?

The Committee's findings about the likely reduced access to hospital emergency medical services and trauma care in areas with high uninsured rates allude to a related community effect, emergency preparedness. Our nation's capability to respond to casualties on a broad scale, including bioterrorism, is a function of its public health capacity, which depends on adequate and consistent funding for public health activities and health departments at the state and local level nationally. To the extent that uninsurance contributes to the under-funding of public health programs that perform these functions, uninsurance may weaken emergency preparedness. The influence of the presence of many uninsured people on public health preparedness and the ability of the public health programs to contain bioterrorism also need to be examined.

State and local health departments do not now offer a reliable source of information for tracking expenditures for and resources devoted to personal health care and public health services, either for insured or uninsured residents (IOM, forthcoming 2003). The issue of states' allocations of federal and own-source health dollars between public health activities and personal health services merits closer and regular evaluation. To do this would require more systematic and standardized accounting and reporting of state and local health spending than currently exists (IOM, 2000, forthcoming 2003). In view of the increasing demands being placed upon state and local health departments in the areas of emergency preparedness and disease surveillance in the context of bioterrorism, the need for such information is urgent.

5.2 Population Health (Burden of Disease), Including Spillover Effects of Communicable and Chronic Diseases

Does the local uninsured rate, independent of other factors, influence the spread or prevalence of communicable diseases?

The lack of information relating local health insurance coverage rates to health indicators precludes definitive statements about the effects of uninsurance on population health. Have preventable infectious disease rates declined in communities that have substantially reduced the number of uninsured? How concentrated or diffused are the spillover effects on population health of uninsurance within the community? Are those who are affected similar to the uninsured population on several social, geographic, or economic dimensions, or is population health widely affected throughout the community?

Surveys and statistics that report on both health insurance and health status at the county, city, and neighborhood levels are needed. In order to assess the effects of relatively low coverage rates on the incidence and prevalence of tuberculosis, HIV disease, and other STDs, for example, one must know local uninsured rates as well as the case rates for at-risk populations at the county and city levels. Any direct relationship cannot be detected with the aggregate statistics for STD case rates and for uninsured rate that are now available.

Chronic diseases can also have spillover effects, and their exacerbation by lack of health insurance has not been examined. For example, research on the interaction of severe mental illness and uninsurance could lead to a better understanding of the social and economic, as well as the health-related, costs that result. In *Care Without Coverage*, the Committee reports that nearly 20 percent of adults with severe mental illnesses are uninsured and as a result are less likely than insured adults to receive appropriate care (McAlpine and Mechanic, 2000; IOM, 2002a). One example of a spillover effect related to the lack of appropriate treatment of severe mental illness is imprisonment (President's Commission, 2002). The costs associated with the lack of treatment due to lack of coverage are likely to be considerable and could be estimated.

SUMMARY

The research reviewed in this chapter points to a number of potential, but not fully documented, relationships between measures of population health within communities and communities' uninsured rates. It is likely that the poorer health and lesser access to care of uninsured community members affects the health of a community's populations overall, through the several mechanisms outlined in this chapter. The uninsured themselves and those who live with and near them are undoubtedly the most directly affected. Because detailed local health status, health outcomes, and insurance coverage data are not available together, or available for enough localities to discern differences among them that could be attributed to the extent of local uninsurance, these findings are qualitative and suggestive rather than definitive.

Conclusion 1. A community's high uninsured rate has adverse consequences for the community's health care institutions and providers. These consequences reduce access to clinic-based primary care, specialty services, and hospital-based care, particularly emergency medical services and trauma care.

Conclusion 2. Research is needed to more clearly define the size, strength, and scope of adverse community effects that are plausible consequences of uninsurance. These include potentially deleterious effects on access to primary and preventive health care, specialty care, the underlying social and economic vitality of communities, public health capacity, and the overall population health.

Research Agenda

The Context for Community Effects

2.1 What are the unmet needs for care of uninsured persons and families? Do they differ geographically, both within and among states?

2.2 What are the sources of public support for care to uninsured persons? How much does each source contribute and how efficiently are the funds allocated?

2.3 To what extent does uncompensated care by doctors, hospitals, and other entities support care for uninsured persons? To what degree do private cross-subsidies subsidize care of uninsured persons?

Access to Care

3.1 Does the local uninsured rate, independent of other factors, affect residents' access to care throughout the community?

3.2 How does the local uninsured rate affect the availability of primary and preventive services for the community's insured as well as uninsured residents?

3.3 How does the local uninsured rate affect the availability of specialty services, including emergency medical services and trauma care for the community's insured as well as uninsured residents?

3.4 How does the local uninsured rate, in conjunction with public institutional support such as disproportionate share hospital payments, affect hospital service offerings, financial stability, and decisions to close?

3.5 How does uninsurance within communities affect the quality of care available to and provided to all residents, insured and uninsured alike?

Economic and Social Effects

4.1 Does the local uninsured rate, independent of other factors, affect the cost of health services and insurance premiums within the local market area?

4.2 What is the burden on local taxpayers of uninsurance within states and localities? How does that burden compare to the tax burden that would be imposed if public insurance programs or subsidized coverage were expanded to reduce uninsured rates? How does the impact of public financing of health care vary across economic cycles?

4.3 Does the adverse financial impact of uninsurance on local health services and institutions extend to the local economy overall?

Community Health

5.1 Does the local uninsured rate, independent of other factors, affect the health status of community residents overall? Are particular groups within the general population more affected than others?

5.2 Does demand for personal health care services by uninsured residents adversely affect the availability of public health services within localities and states? Does the presence of substantial uninsured populations within communities adversely affect emergency preparedness and the community's ability to respond effectively to bioterrorism and other mass casualty events?

5.3 Does the local uninsured rate, independent of other factors, influence the spread or prevalence of communicable diseases?

6

Summary: Conclusions and Research Agenda

The Committee has presented a series of hypotheses and findings related to the effects that uninsurance may have on a community as a whole. This report has traced connections between health services oriented toward those without health insurance and those who have coverage; among public insurance programs, uninsured rates, and their effects on health care providers and institutions; and between public health activities and personal health care. *A Shared Destiny* relates a story that is important but not simple. The point of the story *is* simple, however: over 41 million uninsured persons and 58 million members of uninsured families are spread broadly and widely across communities in the United States, where their uninsured status is likely to have an impact on population health and on the American health care enterprise in which we all participate. The examination of community effects ties together aspects of health policy that are usually compartmentalized, requiring new approaches to research that will clarify the true costs and consequences of uninsurance at the local level.

The Committee draws two conclusions based on its expert judgement and its review of illustrative findings from the limited body of relevant evidence that has been identified.

Conclusion 1. A community's high uninsured rate has adverse consequences for the community's health care institutions and providers. These consequences reduce access to clinic-based primary care, specialty services, and hospital-based care, particularly emergency medical services and trauma care.

Conclusion 2. Research is needed to more clearly define the size,

strength, and scope of adverse community effects that are plausible consequences of uninsurance. These include potentially deleterious effects on access to primary and preventive health care, specialty care, the underlying social and economic vitality of communities, public health capacity and overall population health.

Community impacts of uninsurance have rarely been studied directly. As a result, in this report the Committee has worked from its conceptual framework to devise hypotheses about community effects, drawing illustrative inferences from quantitative and, more often, qualitative studies that do not directly address questions about community effects. Much of the research reviewed in this report represents early efforts in new fields of inquiry. This research uses new data sources, research constructs, and models of interactions among people, their health, and structural features of communities and institutions. The limited amount and preliminary nature of much of the evidence considered in this report leads the Committee to its call for further investigations of these impacts. In the sections of the chapter that follow, a research agenda is outlined, pulling together the specific research questions presented at the end of the earlier chapters.

Following an initial section about the conceptual framework, the structure of the following research agenda parallels that of Chapters 2 through 5 of the report.

A RESEARCH AGENDA FOR COMMUNITY EFFECTS

Conceptual Framework for Community Effects

The Andersen-Aday behavioral model of access to health care serves as a point of departure for the conceptual framework the Committee has developed for its series of reports. In *A Shared Destiny,* the conceptual framework highlights the individual, family, and community-level resources, characteristics, and needs that are hypothesized to influence outcomes at the community level and the hypothesized pathways for these effects. The Committee's framework is a first attempt to theorize and document community effects, and in this report it has served at least as much as a plan for future research as it has the framework within which to assess the limited literature available. Additional conceptual and empirical work is needed to fashion a more useful model, particularly one that can address the following concerns:

• the validity and explanatory value of the proposed pathways or mechanisms by which uninsurance produces community effects;
• the role of the framework's feedback loops, or the process of adaptation to change by community residents, health care providers, and other actors, in modulating or otherwise contributing to the proposed mechanisms for community effects or the effects themselves; and

- the identity and relative influence of individual, family, and community-level factors that may make for different experiences of community effects by different groups within communities.

The Context for Community Effects: The Financing and Delivery of Health Services

2.1 Local Patterns of Unmet Need and Utilization by Uninsured Persons
What are the unmet needs for care of uninsured persons and families? Do they differ geographically, both within and among states?

Basic to much of the proposed research in this report is the need for reliable and current local estimates of uninsured rate and measures of the dispersion or concentration of uninsured persons within local health services markets and among the providers within a market. Until the late 1990s most estimates of uninsured rate, were available only at the national, state, or major metropolitan statistical area (MSA) level, most notably through the U.S. Census Bureau's March Current Population Survey (CPS).[1] In recent years, the Health Resources and Services Administration's State Planning Grant program, together with the State Health Access Data Assistance Center (SHADAC), has facilitated the creation of uninsured rate surveys at the county or regional level within states, although these estimates tend not to be comparable across surveys. Enhanced data collection and coordination of existing surveys is needed, as well as the development of new methods to allow generation of more precise and reliable local uninsured rates and for the comparison of these estimated rates across jurisdictions.

A local uninsured rate can be the basis for estimating the unmet need or health services utilization of uninsured persons, but more direct measures are preferable. Programs to provide and pay for uninsured care are often stretched to their resource limits, with existing dollars outstripped by the perceived health needs of this population (Lewin and Altman, 2000; Felt-Lisk et al., 2001; IOM, forthcoming 2003). Evaluative research is needed to understand how uninsurance at a local level influences the organization and delivery of health care. How have communities that have been substantially effective in meeting the needs for health care of uninsured and other underserved populations met those needs, and what financing and services strategies have they employed?

2.2 Public Subsidy of Health Services Delivered to Uninsured Persons
What are the sources of public support for care to uninsured persons? How much does each source contribute and how efficiently are the funds allocated?

---

[1]Appendix B in the Committee's first report, *Coverage Matters*, reviews the major surveys that give estimates of uninsured rates (IOM, 2001).

The Committee relies on Hadley and Holahan's recent publication (2003) for a working set of rough estimates about the extent of public subsidy. More complete and consistent documentation of existing federal, state, and local supports for the provision of care to uninsured persons is needed. The levels of such payments to hospitals are substantial and may even be adequate to cover the costs of uncompensated hospital care for those completely without health insurance (Hadley and Holahan, 2003). However, more research is needed to identify administrative barriers and inefficiencies in the allocation of funds that result in inadequate or poorly targeted subsidies for the care for uninsured persons. For example, the formulas used to calculate Medicare and Medicaid disproportionate share hospital (DSH) payment rates do not take the number of uninsured patients into account. It is difficult if not impossible to compare Medicaid spending across the states related to DSH payments because many states in effect match the federal grant with monies raised from hospitals themselves (e.g., hospital taxes, intergovernmental transfers from public hospitals) and the states collect and classify data on these payments differently.

2.3 Private Subsidy of Care Delivered to Uninsured Persons

To what extent does uncompensated care by doctors, hospitals, and other entities support care for uninsured persons? To what degree do private cross-subsidies subsidize care of uninsured persons?

It is widely assumed that private payers (e.g., employers, insurers) and private sector health care providers (e.g., nonprofit hospitals, physician practices) cross-subsidize the costs of care for uninsured patients. However, the size of this subsidy is difficult to estimate and the mechanisms through which this uncompensated care is subsidized are complex and not explicitly addressed or documented in the research literature. To the extent that private cross-subsidies occur, what are the implications for health care costs, for local businesses and employers who offer employment-based coverage, and to economic activity in the community?

The literature on hospital cost-shifting presents a useful approach to proposed research on private cross-subsidy. One way to gauge the extent of cross-subsidy, for example, is depicted in Figure 2.1 in Chapter 2, which compares the contributions of uncompensated care, Medicare margins, and private payer surpluses to hospitals' total margins over time. A longitudinal analysis of changes in payment-to-cost ratios or prices for each payer to an individual provider, correlated with changes in the provider's total margin and in the cost of unreimbursed care provided to uninsured persons, would yield more precise information about the amount and sources of private subsidy (Dobson, 2002; Morrissey, 2002). Both quantitative and qualitative studies would likely be needed to tease out the extent of private cross-subsidy, with much regional and market variation related to the market position of both insurers and health care providers (e.g., ability to negotiate discounted charges, anticipated revenue from a hospital's patient case mix, the amount of hospital revenues across which an uncompensated care burden could be spread).

Effects of Uninsurance on Access to Care Within Communities

3.1 Access to Care Across the Community
Does the local uninsured rate, independent of other factors, affect residents' access to care throughout the community?

Existing studies of the relationship between community uninsurance (state or MSA uninsured rate) and access to care offer preliminary evidence that, particularly for lower-income and uninsured populations, higher local uninsured rates are associated with worse access to care. These provocative findings should be corroborated with additional studies that include more refined measures of access as outcome variables. Well-controlled, longitudinal study designs could allow researchers to tease out the difference between the effects of the uninsured population exerting an *aggregate* influence on local health services (e.g., because the uninsured constitute a large portion of the population being studied) compared with having an *ecological* impact (e.g., the independent effect of uninsured rate on access to care for insured persons). Is the supply of services in more affluent urban neighborhoods and suburbs affected by proximity to large or small populations of uninsured persons, and how?

3.2 Access to Primary and Preventive Services
How does the local uninsured rate affect the availability of primary and preventive services for the community's insured as well as uninsured residents?

Because primary and preventive services are often considered elective by patients (unlike emergency medical services and hospital inpatient care), use of these services may fall off more quickly when patients lack the financial means to pay for care. When the number or proportion of uninsured patients increases within a primary care practice, the combination of decreasing patient utilization and an increasing proportion of uninsured visits may also adversely affect the financial position of the practice. As a result, primary care practices may become financially unviable. A conservative estimate of the amount of charity care that physicians provide annually to uninsured patients is roughly $5 billion (Hadley and Holahan, 2003). Better information about the distribution and impact of the burden of providing uncompensated care among physician practices and its implications for the availability of high-quality, stable primary care services is needed in order to understand the dimensions of the problems that uninsurance poses for communities.

3.3 Access to Specialty Care, Including Emergency Medical Services
How does the local uninsured rate affect the availability of specialty services, including emergency medical services and trauma care for a community's insured as well as uninsured residents?

The legal duty of hospital emergency departments (EDs) and trauma units to screen and medically stabilize all patients regardless of ability to pay is one source of financial stress on hospitals. What is less clear, however, is how important the financial demands of providing care to uninsured patients are compared with other reasons for emergency department overcrowding and causes of financial strain (Tsai et al., forthcoming 2003). Further study is needed to understand the degree to which ED overcrowding and financial instability could be ameliorated by reductions in the number of uninsured persons, the restructuring of financial subsidies for their care, or the strategic diversion of emergency department patients to alternative sites for primary care. In addition, more research is needed to understand the degree to which administrative and staffing decisions made within hospitals (e.g., the specialized services offered such as psychiatric inpatient care) reduce community access and what alternatives exist to address the problem without jeopardizing the financial health of hospitals.

While emergency medical services and trauma care provide some of the strongest evidence about access to specialty care, the Committee's findings about the difficulty community health center physicians have obtaining referrals for their uninsured and other patients, and about hospital-based specialty services, suggest that further investigation of the availability throughout a community to a wide range of specialty services is merited. How does the institutional setting (e.g., academic health center) influence or moderate the effect of uninsurance on access to other specialty services? And what impacts does uninsurance have on the other related missions of these institutions, for example, medical education in academic health centers?

3.4 Access to Hospital-Based Services
How does the local uninsured rate, in conjunction with public institutional support such as disproportionate share hospital payments, affect hospital service offerings, financial stability, and decisions to close?

The limitations and preliminary findings of the Committee's commissioned analyses of hospital services and financial margins suggest a number of ways that community effects on access to care might be explored. Perhaps most important is the examination of strategic or competitive responses of hospital administrators and their boards to local market conditions, including the decisions of competing hospitals to expand or shrink inpatient capacity and boost or trim the provision of services, and the relationship between these responses and individual hospital financial margins. More refined studies, based on market areas smaller than MSAs, are needed to understand better the impacts of uninsured populations on hospital services and operations. For example, findings for rural areas that the concentration of uninsured patients may lessen the size of the effect of local uninsured rate on inpatient capacity, services, and margins of all hospitals in the county, on average, suggest that such concentration of uncompensated care caseload among a few providers may be beneficial to the health care system as a whole. On the other hand, concentrating all care for uninsured persons in one facility, such as a county hospital, may both limit access to care, compared with more dispersed safety net arrangements, and lead to poor quality of care. Further research is needed to assess the overall effect of concentration and dispersion on access to hospital-based care.

Although there were hundreds of hospital closures during the 1980s and 1990s, there has been little documentation of the role that a community's uninsured rate may have played in these closures. Most studies of hospital closings do not directly address the influence of uninsurance because of the limited information about local uninsured rates and hospital payer mix. Closures of public hospitals are of particular concern because these hospitals serve as providers of last resort. Studies that examine reasons for these closings and the impacts of these closings or conversions are needed.

3.5 Quality of Care
How does uninsurance within communities affect the quality of care available to and provided to all residents, insured and uninsured alike?

An important and under-examined potential impact of uninsurance within a community is on the quality of care available and provided to all residents. The Committee's earlier reports documented problems of quality (based on measures of process and outcomes) in the care of uninsured patients. This report focuses more holistically on the impact on providers' performance overall when uninsured patients or uncompensated care overwhelm or impair their capacity to provide quality services. No studies have directly assessed the correlation of community uninsured rates with hospital or physician quality of care.

There are at least two areas in which high uninsured rates could adversely affect quality of care for all patients. First, if high uninsured rates influence hospital margins, this could lead to cutbacks in nursing staff, which in turn threaten quality of care (Needleman et al., 2002). Second, if high uninsured rates contribute significantly to emergency department overcrowding at certain facilities, these hospitals may deliver poorer quality of care during times of patient overload. Detailed studies at the level of the patient are needed to understand the relationship between overcrowding and quality of care.

Economic and Social Implications of Uninsurance Within Communities

4.1 Increases in Local Health Care Costs
Does the local uninsured rate, independent of other factors, affect the cost of health services and insurance premiums within the local market area?

Cross-sectional studies are the basis for our limited knowledge about whether and how local uninsured rates contribute to the increasing cost of health services in health services markets. Longitudinal small-area studies are needed to look at the hypothesized chains of events at the state and local levels to establish or disprove the causal relationship between uninsured rates and health insurance costs and to develop estimates of the size and strength of any such relationships.

4.2 Budget Implications for States and Localities

What is the burden on local taxpayers of uninsurance within states and localities? How does that burden compare to the tax burden that would be imposed if public insurance programs or subsidized coverage were expanded to reduce uninsured rates? How does the impact of public financing of health care vary across economic cycles?

Public support of care for uninsured persons is substantial, yet documentation is inconsistent and precise estimates are difficult to derive. More consistent reporting is needed across states and localities of revenue and expenditure streams for financing the array of insurance-based and direct health services programs now operating across the nation. Greater knowledge of the budget allocation process and decisions made at the state level between funding Medicaid and the programs that support direct care for uninsured persons, and between health care and other public services, could inform proposals to improve the equity and target efficiency of federal and state health financing programs. Specifically, programs of institutional support for uncompensated care such as the Medicare and Medicaid DSH payments need to be evaluated in light of these goals.

A systematic analysis of the existing federal, state, and local tax burdens for financing health care generally and for low-income and uninsured Americans in particular should be undertaken as part of any impact analysis of health financing reform initiatives.

4.3 Economic Base and the Potential for Development

Does the adverse financial impact of uninsurance on local health services and institutions extend to the local economy overall?

More research is needed to understand the relationship between community uninsurance and the social and economic life of communities. In-depth, longitudinal case studies of communities could be employed to investigate the role played by health insurance coverage or the lack of it. For example, areas that have undergone dramatic social or economic change, such as the economic decline of communities reliant on manufacturing and their subsequent adaptations and economic recovery, might be worthwhile sites to study.

If little is known about the role that the health sector plays in rural economies, even less is known about the economic relationships that bind local health services to urban neighborhoods and larger market areas. Research is needed to identify the ways in which a changing uninsured population affects the financial viability of health care providers and institutions, elucidating the complicated series of financial relationships among public and private payers. Can a high uninsured rate trigger a funding or political crisis that leads to the transition of a local health care system toward a more efficient and effective use of limited resources? To what extent are an uninsured population's unreimbursed health care expenses matched by public support with the objective of keeping a local economy afloat?

Uninsurance and Community Health

5.1 Health Status Within the Community at Large
Does the local uninsured rate, independent of other factors, affect the health status of community residents overall? Are particular groups within the general population more affected than others?

A number of cross-sectional studies have documented the worse health status and access to care of lower-income populations in localities and states with relatively high uninsured rates. However, these studies neither confirm nor reject the hypothesis that high rates of uninsurance locally have deleterious effects on the health and access to care among those with coverage. Longitudinal studies could shed some light on this question. Do changes in the uninsured rate over time lead to changes in the health status of insured people as well as to changes in the health of those lacking coverage? Race, ethnicity, and socioeconomic status need to be controlled analytically in such studies, as they influence health outcomes and covary with uninsured status (IOM, 2002a; Smedley et al., 2002).

5.2 Public Health Departments and Services, Including Emergency Preparedness
Does demand for personal health care services by uninsured residents adversely affect the availability of public health services within localities and states? Does the presence of substantial uninsured populations within communities adversely affect emergency preparedness and the community's ability to respond effectively to bioterrorism and other mass casualty events?

The Committee's findings about the relationship between uninsurance and likely reduced access to hospital emergency medical services and trauma care allude to a related community effect on emergency preparedness. Our nation's capability to respond to casualties on a broad scale, including bioterrorism, is a function of its public health capacity, which depends on adequate and consistent funding for public health activities and health departments at the state and local level nationally. To the extent that uninsurance contributes to the under-funding of public health programs that perform these functions, uninsurance may weaken emergency preparedness. The influence of the presence of many uninsured people on public health preparedness and the ability of the public health programs to contain bioterrorism acts also need to be examined.

State and local health department budgets do not now offer a reliable source of information for tracking expenditures for and resources devoted to personal health care and public health services, either for insured or uninsured residents (IOM, forthcoming 2003). The issue of states' allocations of federal and own-source health dollars between public health activities and personal health services merits closer and more regular evaluation. To do this would require more systematic and standardized accounting and reporting of state and local health spending than currently exists (IOM, 2000, forthcoming 2003). In view of the increasing demands being placed upon state and local health departments in the areas of emergency preparedness and disease surveillance in the context of bioterrorism, the need for such information is urgent.

5.3 Population Health (Burden of Disease), Including Spillover Effects of Communicable and Chronic Diseases
Does the local uninsured rate, independent of other factors, influence the spread or prevalence of communicable diseases?

A lack of information relating local health insurance coverage rates to health indicators precludes definitive statements about the effects of uninsurance on population health. Have preventable infectious disease rates declined in communities that have substantially reduced the number of uninsured? How concentrated or diffused are the spillover effects on population health of uninsurance within the community? Are those who are affected similar to the uninsured population on several social, geographic, or economic dimensions, or is population health affected widely throughout the community?

Surveys and statistics that report on both health insurance and health status at the county, city, and neighborhood levels are needed. In order to assess the effects of relatively low insurance coverage rates on the incidence and prevalence of tuberculosis, HIV disease, and other sexually transmitted diseases, for example, one must know local uninsured rates as well as the case rates for at-risk populations at the county and city levels. Any direct relationship cannot be detected with the aggregate statistics for case rates and for uninsured rate that are now available.

Chronic diseases can also have spillover effects, and their exacerbation by lack of health insurance has not been examined. For example, research on the interaction of severe mental illness and uninsurance could lead to a better understanding of the social and economic, as well as the health-related, costs that result. In *Care Without Coverage*, the Committee reported that nearly 20 percent of adults with severe mental illnesses are uninsured and as a result are less likely than insured adults to receive appropriate care (McAlpine and Mechanic, 2000; IOM, 2002). One example of a spillover effect related to the lack of appropriate treatment of severe mental illness is imprisonment (President's Commission, 2002). The costs associated with the lack of treatment due to lack of coverage are likely to be considerable, and could be estimated.

CONCLUSION

What we don't know *can* hurt us. There is much that is not understood about the relationships between health services delivery and financing mechanisms and even less about how the current structure and performance of the American health care enterprise affect communities' economies and the quality of social and political life in this country. Because policy makers and researchers have not asked or examined these questions through comprehensive and systematic research and analysis, there is a limited body of evidence of mixed quality on community effects.

The Committee believes, however, that it is both mistaken and dangerous to assume that the prevalence of uninsurance in the United States harms only those who are uninsured. It calls for further research to examine the suggested effects of uninsurance at the community level but nonetheless believes there is sufficient evidence to justify the adoption of policies to address the lack of health insurance in the nation (Corrigan et al., 2002). Rather, the call for more research is to say that, as long as we as a nation tolerate the status quo, we should more fully understand the implications and consequences of our stalemated national health policy.

A

Conceptual Framework for Assessing the Consequences of Uninsurance for Communities

The conceptual framework used in this report, and the variations on this framework described in Chapter 2, are closely related to the conceptual framework introduced in the Committee's first report, *Coverage Matters* (IOM, 2001a). In the paragraphs that follow, the Committee's initial framework is described and its modification for use in this report is clarified.

Figure A.1 depicts the conceptual framework used in *Coverage Matters*. The framework is based on Andersen's model of access to health services, which incorporates ideas from the behavioral sciences to understand the process of health services delivery and health-related outcomes for individuals (Andersen and Aday, 1978; Andersen and Davidson, 2001). In addition, it draws on an economic model of insurance status and the impact of out-of-pocket costs on health care demand.

To describe the roles of factors at the individual, family, and community levels (e.g., an individual's health insurance status) that influence both the process of services delivery and the consequences of health care experiences, the framework uses Andersen's grouping of variables into three categories: (1) resources that foster or enable the process of obtaining health care; (2) personal or community characteristics that favor or predispose action related to obtaining health care; and (3) needs for health care, as articulated by those in need, determined by health care providers, or identified by researchers and decision makers. Arrows and spatial relationships among the boxes in Figure A.1 indicate hypothesized causal and temporal relationships.

To depict the economic consequences of uninsurance, the Committee creates links within Andersen's framework among determinants of health insurance and such factors as family economic well-being, the institutional viability of health services, and community-level socioeconomic conditions. This expansion allows the Committee to assess hypothesized interactions between economics and health. The Committee recognizes that insurance is one of many factors that can influence the physical, social, and economic health of communities and their health care arrangements.

CONCEPTUAL FRAMEWORK INTRODUCED IN COVERAGE MATTERS

The left panel of Figure A.1 addresses the main economic forces affecting the insured or uninsured status of individuals and families. Individual- and family-level characteristics include financial resources, categorical eligibility for public health insurance, labor market determinants of employment-based insurance, and the requisite skills to enroll and maintain coverage. Community-level factors include public program eligibility standards, labor market characteristics that determine the availability of employment-based health insurance, and the commercial market for individual health insurance.

The center panel of Figure A.1 is based almost directly on Andersen's model of access to health care (Andersen and Davidson, 2001). The boxes labeled "individual and family level" and "community level" contain individual- and aggregate-level variables, respectively, believed to influence how people obtain access to health care. Community-level variables are ecologic or aggregate measures to describe the context or environment within which individuals and their families seek and use health care. For example, the community's morbidity rate for whooping cough might indicate the need for an immunization campaign. Because health care services are provided and consumed locally, the term community refers to a geographic grouping.

Implicit in the categories of resources, characteristics, and needs are judgments about how much a particular variable may be susceptible to change. Variables labeled "resources" are considered, at least theoretically, to be more open to change. Those termed "characteristics" are considered less flexible or manipulable, and those called "needs" comprise a mixed or heterogeneous grouping, with some needs being more changeable than others.

As a whole, community-level and individual- and family-level variables describe many *potential* scenarios for accessing health care. The variables within the box labeled "health care" describe how these potentials may be realized, with particular attention to the role of health insurance coverage. The process of health care delivery is characterized in terms of three types of variables: (1) personal health practices (e.g., dietary habits, physical exercise), (2) use of health services (e.g., number and kind of physician visits within a year), and (3) processes of care (e.g., adherence to clinical practice guidelines). The Committee focuses most of its attention on the literature concerning the processes of services delivery and the utilization of health services while recognizing that personal health practices may be influenced by insurance coverage and access to care.

The right panel of Figure A.1 describes the ways in which the committee

177

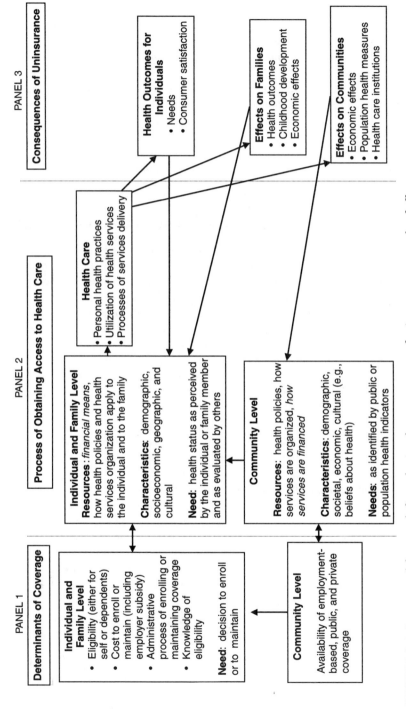

FIGURE A.1 A conceptual framework for evaluating the consequences of uninsurance—a cascade of effects. NOTE: Italics indicate terms that include direct measures of health insurance coverage.

anticipates that health insurance status may affect the health, economic, and social characteristics of individuals, families, and communities by means of access to and the process of health care delivery. These effects of *realized access* to health care cascade from the smallest unit of analysis, the individual, to increasingly larger units, first the family and then the community. The consequences linked to health insurance influence community-level and individual- and family-level variables that describe the process of obtaining access to health care and also of gaining or losing health insurance coverage. This last panel should make it clear that the process is dynamic with multiple feedbacks. For example, employment status and income affect family insurance status, which affects current and future health status. Health status, in turn, can influence future employment status, bringing us full circle.

CONCEPTUAL FRAMEWORK FOR THIS REPORT

Figure A.2 depicts a version of Figure A.1 modified to reflect the focus of the Committee in this report. The modified version draws on the same theories and conceptual approaches to health insurance as does the initial version in Figure A.1. It focuses on part of the second and third panels of Figure A.1, to emphasize hypothesized community effects and pathways believed to lead to community effects. The left panel of Figure A.2, containing a box labeled "health care" corresponds to the center panel of Figure A.1, while the right panel of Figure A.2 corresponds to both the third panel of Figure A.1 (labeled "consequences of uninsurance") and the box labeled "community-level determinants of coverage" in the left panel of Figure A.1. Where both frameworks are similar, the text description is shortened in Figure A.2.

The health, social, and economic consequences of delayed or forgone health care for uninsured individuals and families (as depicted in the two boxes labeled "adverse health outcomes for uninsured" and "adverse economic effects") can result in a greater burden of disease and disability for the community overall as well as erosion of the capacity for timely and appropriate health services delivery in the community. To the extent that uninsured individuals and their families obtain health services, the uncompensated care burden on local providers and facilities (as depicted in the box labeled "lower revenues for providers and facilities") serves as another pathway to community effects because it is hypothesized to lead to (1) pressures to increase public spending to subsidize care for uninsured persons, (2) increased costs for health care and for health insurance, and (3) financially destabilized local health services. As a result, *all* members of the community may experience diminished access to and quality of health services, as well as a greater burden of disease and disability.

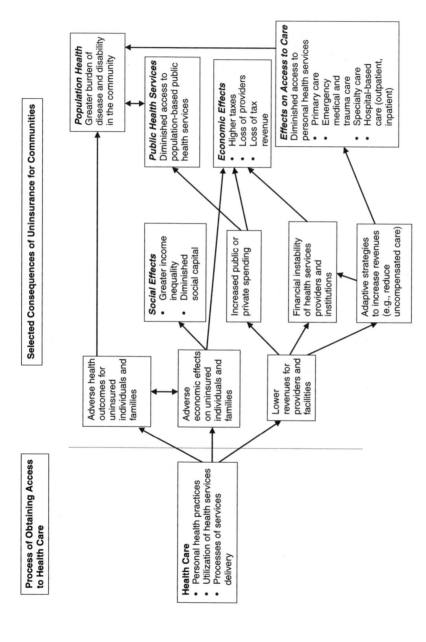

FIGURE A.2 A conceptual framework for community effects.

B

Geographic Differences in Uninsured Rates

The marked variation in uninsured rates among states and localities allows for comparisons to detect the impacts that uninsurance may have on community health services, social institutions, economic bases, and population health. Because covariates of uninsured rates, for example, per capita income, also contribute to potential community effects, the discussion that follows describes the economic, social, and demographic characteristics of states and localities that underpin differences related to health care services, economic resources, and insurance coverage. Following a discussion of the Census Bureau's March Supplement to the Current Population Survey (CPS), the basis for most of the uninsured rate estimates referred to in this report, a brief overview of uninsured rates across the country is presented, with attention to differences among regions, states, cities, and counties and to disparities among urban, suburban, and rural areas.

Individual-level measurements of insurance status, aggregated to the community level of interest (e.g., metropolitan statistical area [MSA], state, ethnic or racial minority group) are a simple and concise way to characterize uninsurance within a community.[1] The CPS is the basis for annual estimates of insurance coverage by

---

[1] Another way to think about the influence that an uninsured population might have on a community is in terms of the *shortfall* or *gap* between the health needs of uninsured persons and the community resources available and used to meet those needs. Taking this approach requires not only estimates of uninsurance but also measures of unmet need for care among uninsured people in a community, their actual utilization (or effective demand) for care, the relationship between these two measures, and the response of health care institutions and service providers to these factors. Given the limitations of existing data and studies, virtually all studies to date of community effects and this report rely for the most part on the uninsured rate as a measure of the likely relative impact of uninsurance on a given community.

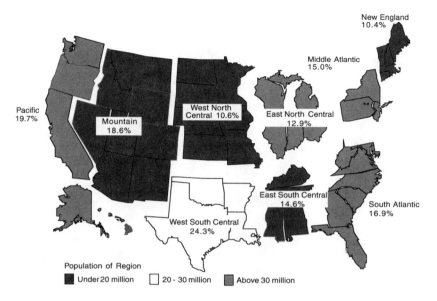

FIGURE B.1 Probability of being uninsured for population under age 65, by census region, 2001.
SOURCE: Fronstin, 2002, estimates based on March 2001 Current Population Survey.

type of coverage and of persons uninsured for the previous calendar year since the late 1970s (Levit et al., 1992). During 2001, there were an estimated 41 million civilian, noninstitutionalized uninsured persons in the United States, approximately 16.5 percent of the population under age 65 (Mills, 2002). There is considerable geographic variation in the distribution of uninsured persons regionally and from state to state; see Figures B.1 and B.2 and Tables C.1, C.2, and C.3 in Appendix C.

Using CPS-derived estimates of uninsured rates to compare geographically defined communities involves acknowledging some important methodological limitations related to the sample sizes of the CPS survey and the period of time over which coverage status is measured. For example, while the Committee's focus would ideally be on communities no larger than a city or rural county, and perhaps an even smaller area, and on comparisons among areas on a yearly basis, the relatively small sample sizes of the CPS survey mean that the smallest type of community for which uninsured rates are estimated is the MSA of more than 500,000 population. To attain sufficient statistical reliability, these MSA-level estimates are based on a three-year average.

In addition, uninsured rates differ according to the length of time (denominator) over which the number of uninsured persons (numerator) is measured because of transitions into and out of coverage. For example, the 2001 California Health Interview Survey includes three sets of estimates for uninsured rates in the state,

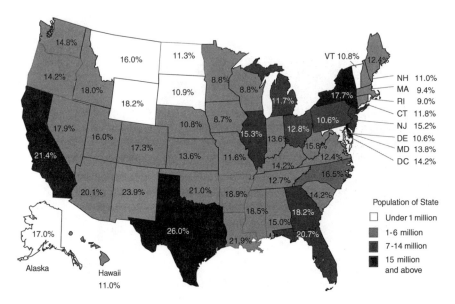

FIGURE B.2 Probability of being uninsured for population under age 65, by state, 2001. SOURCE: Fronstin, 2002, estimates based on March 2001 Current Population Survey.

each of which gives a different picture of uninsurance: persons who report being uninsured at the time of the survey, or a point estimate (average 15 percent uninsured rate for persons under age 65, or about 4.5 million people); persons reporting uninsured status at any time in the previous 12 months (average 21 percent uninsured rate, 6.2 million people); and persons uninsured for the entire 12 months preceding the survey interview (12 percent, or 3.6 million people) (Brown et al., 2002). Many more people experience being uninsured for relatively short times than are captured in the point estimates made on the basis of data from the Census Bureau's annual CPS (IOM, 2001a; Short, 2001). The median duration of an uninsured spell is between five and six months (Bennefield, 1998). Both the length and the frequency of uninsured periods vary with the source of coverage and among different populations. For example, persons covered under individual policies are more likely to experience an uninsured period compared to persons with employment-based coverage, and persons experiencing long periods of uninsurance are more likely to be lower income (earning less than 200 percent of the federal poverty level [FPL]) (IOM, 2001a).

SOURCES OF GEOGRAPHIC VARIATION IN UNINSURED RATES

Estimates of uninsured rates are available for regions or counties within most states. These estimates have been developed using a few different approaches. This work has been facilitated by the State Health Access Data Assistance Center (SHADAC) at the University of Minnesota, to respond to federal interest in devising more accurate estimates for the purposes of allocating State Children's Health Insurance Program (SCHIP) funds. Unlike CPS estimates of uninsured rates, these approaches yield estimates that are not directly comparable from state to state but rather are useful to illustrate the diversity of situations that exist within and among states. Much of the information that follows comes from states' own health-related surveys, generated as part of their Health Resources and Services Administration State Planning Grant projects. These surveys may poll a sample of state residents directly, use a proxy measure such as the number of self-pay hospital discharges to estimate the size of an uninsured population, or create an analytic model to predict an area's uninsured rate, based on data from variables such as unemployment rate that are known to be closely related to uninsured rate (SHADAC, 2002). Some of the larger states may have chosen to rely on CPS samples if they are considered large enough to give reliable estimates for regions, particularly metropolitan areas, within the state.

There is much variation in the dispersion and concentration of uninsured populations across regions, states, counties, and cities, and across rural, suburban, and urban areas. Regional, state, and within-state differences in uninsured rates reflect diversity in rates of employment-based coverage and the extent to which public programs and the individual health insurance markets cover persons who are not eligible for or do not participate in employment-based plans.[2] These rates also vary in keeping with other socioeconomic and demographic characteristics of local populations.

Regional differences in economic base set the stage for differences in unin-sured rates (Diehr et al., 1991; Holahan, 2002). In parts of Appalachia and along the southwestern border of the United States, for example, higher uninsured rates reflect the lower average incomes and higher number of employers that tend not to offer employment-based coverage to their workers.

• *Appalachia*: Ohio's southeastern counties are home to about one-fifth of the state's uninsured population but have the highest uninsured rates in the state, 14.2 percent uninsured on average, compared to the state's 11 percent average uninsured rate (figures for 1998; Dorsky, 2000). Both unemployment rates and average weekly income are strong predictors of uninsured rates in Ohio.
• *Southwestern border*: For Texas, federal CPS data give the highest uninsured rate estimates for the border counties, although 75 percent of uninsured persons

---

[2]See the Committee report, *Coverage Matters: Insurance and Health Care* (IOM, 2001a), for a fuller discussion of the determinants of differing rates of health insurance coverage by type and of uninsured rates geographically.

live in nonborder parts of the state and are more likely to live in urban areas (State of Texas, 2002).

One of the few studies that has looked specifically at the role of the local economic base examines the experiences of adults under age 65 in 29 larger Wisconsin counties (Marsteller et al., 1998). Modeling each county's uninsured rate as a function of the local economy, population demographic characteristics, and characteristics of the health services market, the authors find that the local unemployment rate is a key predictor of a county's uninsured rate, tempered by relative economic fortunes (e.g., whether in a recession or an upturn in the business cycle) (Marsteller et al., 1998).

Differences in state public policies—specifically the Medicaid program, state insurance regulations, and to a lesser extent state, high-risk insurance pools (where they exist)—contribute to differences in uninsured rates (Cunningham and Kemper, 1998; Marsteller et al., 1998; Brown et al., 2000; Trenholme and Kung, 2000). For Medicaid, the breadth and generosity of benefits, eligibility rules, administrative difficulties in enrolling and maintaining enrollment, and extent of crowd-out of private coverage differ from state to state; each of these considerations influences a state's uninsured rate. The proportion of a state's population that is eligible for Medicaid also depends on the relative size of its low-income population or how income is distributed within the state (Holahan, 2002).

One way to measure the relative influence of state and local funding on uninsured rates is to compare the need for public coverage, or the proportion of persons without employment-based coverage, with the proportion of this need met through public coverage (e.g., Medicaid, SCHIP) (Holahan, 2002). A regression analysis of 50 states using three-year moving averages of uninsured rates (1997–1999) finds that differences among the states in their proportion of residents without employment-based coverage contribute to differences in state uninsured rates. For low-income populations (persons in families earning less than 200 percent of FPL), differences among the states in their proportion of low-income residents with public coverage also contribute to differences in state uninsured rates (Holahan, 2002). In 13 states during the same time period, states varied fourfold in their level of spending per low-income person (Holahan, 2002).

A state's fiscal effort can make a difference in its uninsured rate. In two states with comparable proportions of residents lacking employment-based coverage (22 percent for Colorado and 18 percent for Minnesota), a greater fiscal effort by the State of Minnesota (45 percent of persons without employment-based coverage enrolled in public insurance) compared to Colorado (19 percent of persons without employment-based coverage enrolled in public coverage) resulted in an uninsured rate of 10 percent for Minnesota, compared with 17 percent for Colorado (Holahan, 2002).

Geographic differences in coverage rates also reflect the distinctive social, economic, and demographic profiles of communities and how these profiles intersect with the likelihood that members of constituent population groups (e.g., young adults, foreign-born residents, lower-waged workers) will be offered or will be able to afford to purchase private or public coverage. For example, in Florida, rural, ethnically diverse counties with smaller populations have the highest uninsured rates, as does urban Dade county, while the lowest uninsured rates are in counties with smaller cities and suburban populations and relatively low proportions of African American and Hispanic residents (Lazarus et al., 2000).

Within a locality or health services market, the presence of a diversity of culturally or linguistically defined communities also has implications for health, health services delivery, and community effects. Recent immigrants, members of racial and ethnic minority groups (e.g., Cuban, Filipino, African American, American Indian, and Alaska Native), and language minorities may have special service needs and patterns of utilization and insurance coverage, either for the group as a whole or for populations within the group. For example, across a low-income (less than $15,000 annually) cohort of 77 Spanish-speaking, Mexican American residents of El Paso, care-seeking patterns appear to be influenced both by insurance status (more than 60 percent report being uninsured) and by the accessibility of the local health care system, where there is a shortage of primary care providers (Parchman, 2002).

Finally, uninsured rates reflect differences in population density (Ormond et al., 2000b; IOM, 2001a; Rowley, 2002). Although uninsured rates nationally are about the same for rural and urban areas on average, and greater numbers of uninsured persons live in urban areas (given their greater population size overall), there is a diversity of patterns within states. Suburbs often have lower uninsured rates than the central urban neighborhoods of the major cities that they adjoin as well as lower rates than neighboring rural counties.

- In some states, uninsured persons are relatively uniformly dispersed, so that the uninsured rates for different counties or regions do not differ appreciably from the average uninsured rate for the state. For example, Vermont's 14 counties have uninsured rates similar to the state's overall rate of 8.4 percent (State of Vermont, 2001). In contrast, Florida's 67 counties range from 12 percent uninsured to 30 percent uninsured, with many significantly different from the state's overall rate of 16.8 percent uninsured (Lazarus et al., 2000; 1999 data).
- For many states, rural areas have fewer numbers of uninsured persons but higher uninsured rates, compared with more urban regions. In Oregon, urban Clackamus, Multnomah, and Washington Counties are home to almost 40 percent of the state's uninsured population, but the highest uninsured rates are in the rural Gorge and Southwest regions (State of Oregon, 2001).
- Where a state's urban areas have higher uninsured rates than rural areas, the cities tend to be large and ethnically diverse and to have higher uninsured rates in their central cores compared to MSAs or suburban jurisdictions alone. For example, in Minnesota, the seven counties that comprise the Twin Cities MSA have a 5.3 percent uninsured rate similar to the state's 5.4 percent uninsured rate overall. Excluding the populations of the central cities Minneapolis and St. Paul

(with uninsured rates of 11.0 and 9.5 percent, respectively) substantially lowers the uninsured rate for the rest of the MSA, to 3.9 percent uninsured (Gildemeister et al., 2002).

NATIONAL COMPARISONS

Two national studies use different data sets to compare uninsured rates among sites around the nation. The first uses estimates from the CPS in a survey of the 85 largest metropolitan areas in the United States (1998), finding a range of uninsured rates for 1998 between 7 percent (Akron, Ohio; Harrisburg, Pennsylvania) and 37 percent (El Paso, Texas) (Brown et al., 2000). Brown and colleagues use the MSA-level uninsured rates as an explanatory factor in a cross-sectional study of access to health care within communities. The second study compares 60 large, small, and nonmetropolitan areas (1996–1997) and finds a similarly broad range of uninsured rates, from 4.7 percent (Rochester, New York) to 28.9 percent (Miami, Florida), with the mean uninsured rate for the 12 sites with the highest rates (23.2 percent) almost three times the average for the 12 sites with the lowest rates, 8.6 percent (Cunningham and Ginsburg, 2001) (see Figure B.3 which depicts uninsured rates at a sample of these sites). The 12 sites with the lowest uninsured rates

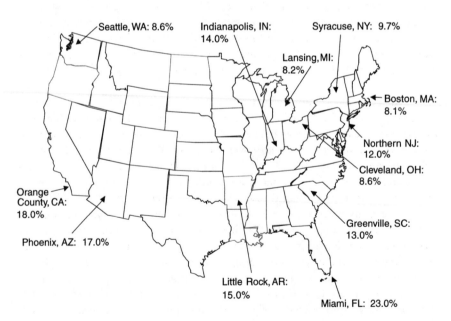

FIGURE B.3 Uninsured rates for persons under 65 years in selected urban areas, 2000–2001.
SOURCE: Estimates from the Community Tracking Study, Center for Studying Health System Change.

are all either northeastern or midwestern metropolitan areas of more than 200,000 population, while the sites with high uninsured rates tend to be more heterogeneous and scattered across the South and West. In this analysis, differences among the sites are most strongly related to differences in the characteristics of individual residents (33 percent of the variation, mostly reflecting differences in racial or ethnic makeup, income level, and level of educational attainment), with differences related to job characteristics (e.g., number of workers in a family, whether full or part time work) accounting for 26 percent of the variation and differences in state policies regarding public insurance and social services of lesser influence (about 13 percent of the variation) (Cunningham and Ginsburg, 2001). Additional data about regional differences in employer characteristics, for example, the proportion of low-waged jobs or smaller-sized firms, both of which are associated with lower offer rates for employment-based coverage, might clarify the relative importance of these factors in shaping regional differences in uninsured rates.

Comparisons among states and regions are difficult to make using CPS estimates because the factors that covary with uninsured rates may be markedly different in different states and regions. In the Committee's first report, *Coverage Matters*, a multivariate analysis allows for these comparisons through the use of "equalized" estimates. Differences among states' uninsured rates diminish considerably if variations in the socioeconomic, demographic, and health status characteristics of each state's residents are taken into account (IOM, 2001a).

The Committee's analysis in *Coverage Matters* is a type of thought experiment that estimates what states' uninsured rates would be if every state had the same socioeconomic, demographic, and health characteristics. Given the limits of any statistical model, one would not expect the differences among the states to disappear entirely with these adjustments, and indeed they do not. The remaining variation in uninsured rates—from 8.3 percentage points lower than the national average of 17.5 percent (for Hawaii) to 7.4 percentage points higher than the average (for New Mexico)—appears to exist independently of, and cannot be accounted for by, these measured characteristics.

Making this adjusted comparison nonetheless substantially revises estimates for some regions. For example, the four southwestern border states, all with uninsured rates 5 to 12 percentage points above the national average of 17.5 percent, would have much lower uninsured rates if the measured characteristics of their states' populations matched those of the nation overall. New Mexico and Texas would have uninsured rates about 40 percent lower than those they actually do, and California would have an uninsured rate slightly below the nation's average rate rather than one almost 5 percentage points higher (IOM, 2001a). For seven states, this analysis yields a higher adjusted uninsured rate estimate, with increases ranging from 37 percent (for West Virginia) to more than twice as high (for Washington).

In the "equalized" analysis described above, the factors that are analytically taken into account (e.g., race and ethnicity, income, educational attainment, immigrant status) contribute to the distinctiveness of each state's circumstances.

Because the statistical adjustments in the analysis that the Committee originally performed mask the distinctiveness of local factors that are of policy interest, this report focuses on a number of these factors themselves, as they appear together within localities.

C

Data Tables

TABLE C.1 Sources of Coverage, Distribution of the Uninsured Population Under Age 65, and Uninsured Rates, by Census Region of Residence, 2001

	No. in Population (<65 yrs) (millions)	Distribution of Population (%)	No. with Employment-Based Coverage (est.) (millions)	Employment-Based Coverage Rate (%)	No. with Individually Purchased Coverage (est.) (millions)
By Census Region					
Totals	247.5	100	162.3	65.6	16.4
New England	12.0	4.8	8.7	72.8	0.7
Middle Atlantic	34.1	13.8	23.4	68.7	1.7
East North Central	39.2	15.8	28.3	72.2	2.3
West North Central	16.6	6.7	11.9	71.4	1.6
South Atlantic	45.2	18.3	29.5	65.1	3.1
East South Central	14.8	6.0	9.4	63.2	0.9
West South Central	28.0	11.3	16.2	57.8	1.8
Mountain	16.6	6.7	10.6	64.1	1.2
Pacific	41.1	16.6	24.4	59.3	3.3
By Region					
Totals	247.5	100	162.3	65.6	16.4
Northeast	46.1	18.6	32.1	69.6	2.4
Midwest	55.8	22.5	40.2	72.0	3.9
South	88.0	35.6	55.1	62.6	5.8
West	57.7	23.3	35.0	60.6	4.4

NOTE: Numbers may not add to 100 due to respondents reporting more than one source of coverage and due to rounding.
SOURCES: Fronstin, 2002, estimates from March 2001 Current Population Survey.

Individually Purchased Coverage Rate (%)	No. with Public Coverage (est.) (millions)	Public Coverage Rate (%)	No. of Uninsured (est.) (millions)	Distribution of Uninsured (%)	Uninsured Rate (%)
6.6	37.9	15.3	40.9	100	16.5
5.7	1.8	14.9	1.2	2.9	10.4
5.0	5.0	14.8	5.1	12.5	15.0
5.9	4.8	12.3	5.1	12.5	12.9
9.4	2.2	13.3	1.8	4.4	10.6
6.8	7.3	16.1	7.6	18.6	16.9
6.2	3.2	21.8	2.2	5.4	14.6
6.3	4.2	15.0	6.8	16.6	24.3
7.1	2.4	14.4	3.1	7.6	18.6
7.9	6.9	16.8	8.1	19.8	19.7
6.6	37.9	15.3	40.9	100	16.5
5.2	6.8	14.8	6.3	15.4	13.7
7.0	7.0	12.5	6.9	16.9	12.4
6.6	14.7	16.7	16.6	40.6	18.9
7.6	9.3	16.1	11.2	27.4	19.4

TABLE C.2 Distribution of Uninsured Population Under Age 65 and
Uninsured Rates, by Designation as Residing in Urban or Nonurban
(Rural) Areas, 2001.

	No. in Population (<65 yrs) (millions)	Distribution of Population (%)	No. with Employment-Based Coverage (est.) (millions)	Employment-Based Coverage Rate (%)	No. with Individually Purchased Coverage (est.) (millions)
By designation as metropolitan statistical area (MSA) or non-MSA					
Totals	247.5	100	162.3	100	16.4
MSA	202.8	82	134.6	66.4	13.0
Non-MSA	44.7	18	27.6	61.7	3.4

NOTE: Numbers may not add to 100% due to respondents reporting more than one source of coverage and due to rounding, MSA = metropolitan statistical area.
SOURCE: Fronstin, 2002, estimates from March 2001 Current Population Survey.

Individually Purchased Coverage Rate (%)	No. with Public Coverage (est.) (millions)	Public Coverage Rate (%)	No. of Uninsured (est.) (millions)	Distribution of Uninsured (%)	Uninsured Rate (%)
100	37.9	100	40.9	100	16.5
6.4	29.5	14.5	33.4	82	16.5
7.6	8.4	18.8	7.5	18	16.8

TABLE C.3 Distribution of Uninsured Population Under Age 65 and Uninsured Rates, by State of Residence, 2001

	No. in Population (<65 years) (millions)	Distribution in Population (%)	No. of Uninsured (est.) (millions)	Distribution of Uninsured (%)	Uninsured Rate (%)
Totals	247.5	100	40.9	100	16.5
Alabama	3.8	2	0.6	1	15.0
Alaska	0.6	0	0.1	0	17.0
Arizona	4.7	2	0.9	2	20.1
Arkansas	2.3	1	0.4	1	18.9
California	31.1	13	6.7	16	21.4
Colorado	4.0	2	0.7	2	17.3
Connecticut	2.9	1	0.3	1	11.8
Delaware	0.7	0	0.1	0	10.6
District of Columbia	0.5	0	0.1	0	14.2
Florida	13.6	6	2.8	7	20.7
Georgia	7.5	3	1.4	3	18.2
Hawaii	1.0	0	0.1	0	11.0
Idaho	1.2	0	0.2	1	18.0
Illinois	10.9	4	1.7	4	15.3
Indiana	5.2	2	0.7	2	13.6
Iowa	2.5	1	0.2	1	8.7
Kansas	2.2	1	0.3	1	13.6
Kentucky	3.5	1	0.5	1	14.2
Louisiana	3.8	2	0.8	2	21.9
Maine	1.1	0	0.1	0	12.4
Maryland	4.7	2	0.6	2	13.8
Massachusetts	5.5	2	0.5	1	9.4
Michigan	8.7	4	1.0	2	11.7
Minnesota	4.5	2	0.4	1	8.8
Mississippi	2.5	1	0.5	1	18.5
Missouri	4.9	2	0.6	1	11.6
Montana	0.8	0	0.1	0	16.0
Nebraska	1.5	1	0.2	0	10.8
Nevada	1.9	1	0.3	1	17.9
New Hampshire	1.1	0	0.1	0	11.0
New Jersey	7.2	3	1.1	3	15.2
New Mexico	1.6	1	0.4	1	23.9
New York	16.4	7	2.9	7	17.7
North Carolina	7.1	3	1.2	3	16.5
North Dakota	0.5	0	0.1	0	11.3
Ohio	9.7	4	1.2	3	12.8
Oklahoma	2.9	1	0.6	2	21.0
Oregon	3.1	1	0.4	1	14.2
Pennsylvania	10.5	4	1.1	3	10.6
Rhode Island	0.9	0	0.1	0	9.0
South Carolina	3.5	1	0.5	1	14.2
South Dakota	0.6	0	0.1	0	10.9

TABLE C.3 Continued

	No. in Population (<65 years) (millions)	Distribution in Population (%)	No. of Uninsured (est.) (millions)	Distribution of Uninsured (%)	Uninsured Rate (%)
Tennessee	5.0	2	0.6	2	12.7
Texas	19.0	8	4.9	12	26.0
Utah	2.1	1	0.3	1	16.0
Vermont	0.5	0	0.1	0	10.8
Virginia	6.2	2	0.8	2	12.4
Washington	5.2	2	0.8	2	14.8
West Virginia	1.5	1	0.2	1	15.8
Wisconsin	4.6	2	0.4	1	8.8
Wyoming	0.4	0	0.1	0	18.2

SOURCE: Fronstin, 2002, estimates from March 2001 Current Population Survey.

TABLE C.4 Combined Federal Medicare and Medicaid Disproportionate Share Hospital (DSH) Payments by State, 1998

	Population <65 yrs, 1998 (millions)	No. of Uninsured, 1998 (millions)	Uninsured Rate, 1998 (%)	No. of Medicaid, 1998 (millions)	Medicaid Rate, 1998 (%)
Total	238.6	43.9	18.4	24.9	10.4
Alabama	3.7	0.7	19.5	0.4	10.0
Alaska	0.6	0.1	18.6	0.0	7.0
Arizona	4.3	1.2	27.2	0.4	8.6
Arkansas	2.2	0.5	21.8	0.2	9.3
California	29.9	7.3	24.4	3.8	12.8
Colorado	3.6	0.6	16.5	0.1	3.6
Connecticut	2.9	0.4	14.3	0.2	7.4
Delaware	0.7	0.1	17.1	0.1	9.7
District of Columbia	0.4	0.1	19.2	0.1	22.0
Florida	11.9	2.5	21.3	1.0	8.6
Georgia	6.9	1.3	19.5	0.9	12.8
Hawaii	1.0	0.1	11.6	0.1	11.1
Idaho	1.1	0.2	19.7	0.1	9.4
Illinois	11.0	1.8	16.6	1.0	9.0
Indiana	5.2	0.8	16.1	0.3	5.7
Iowa	2.4	0.3	10.9	0.2	7.0
Kansas	2.2	0.3	12.2	0.2	8.5
Kentucky	3.4	0.5	16.1	0.4	10.9
Louisiana	3.8	0.8	21.5	0.5	13.2
Maine	1.1	0.2	14.6	0.1	9.3
Maryland	4.4	0.8	18.9	0.1	3.4
Massachusetts	5.3	0.6	11.7	0.7	13.7
Michigan	8.9	1.3	14.9	1.1	12.1
Minnesota	4.3	0.4	10.3	0.4	8.8
Mississippi	2.4	0.6	23.1	0.2	9.9
Missouri	4.7	0.6	12.1	0.5	9.9
Montana	0.8	0.2	22.0	0.1	10.8
Nebraska	1.5	0.2	10.3	0.2	10.3
Nevada	1.7	0.4	23.7	0.1	4.1
New Hampshire	1.1	0.1	12.5	0.1	8.9
New Jersey	7.2	1.3	18.0	0.4	6.0
New Mexico	1.6	0.4	24.0	0.2	13.6
New York	16.0	3.2	19.7	2.4	15.3
North Carolina	6.5	1.1	17.1	0.7	10.1
North Dakota	0.6	0.1	16.6	0.0	7.3
Ohio	9.8	1.2	11.8	1.0	9.9
Oklahoma	2.8	0.6	21.4	0.2	7.8
Oregon	3.0	0.5	16.1	0.4	14.1
Pennsylvania	10.3	1.2	12.1	1.1	11.0

Sum No. (Uninsured and Medicaid), 1998 (millions)	Sum % (Uninsured and Medicaid), 1998 (%)	Sum %/ Total, (%)	Combined Federal Medicare and Medicaid DSH payment, 1998 (millions)	Combined DSH/Sum No. ($$)	Combined DSH/ Sum No./ Total (%)
68.8	28.8	100	19,844	288	100
1.1	29.5	102	490	445	155
0.1	25.6	89	18	180	63
1.6	35.8	124	169	106	37
0.7	31.1	108	26	37	13
11.1	37.2	129	3,314	299	104
0.7	20.1	70	199	284	99
0.6	21.7	75	403	672	233
0.2	26.8	93	14	70	24
0.2	41.2	143	73	365	127
3.5	29.9	104	693	198	69
2.2	32.3	112	555	252	88
0.2	22.7	79	20	100	35
0.3	29.1	101	9	30	10
2.8	25.6	89	421	150	52
1.1	21.8	76	172	156	54
0.5	17.9	62	33	66	23
0.5	20.7	72	60	120	42
0.9	27.0	94	266	296	103
1.3	34.7	120	853	656	228
0.3	23.9	83	139	463	161
0.9	22.3	77	197	219	76
1.3	25.4	88	619	476	165
2.4	27.0	94	449	187	65
0.8	19.1	66	99	124	43
0.8	33.0	115	256	320	111
1.1	22.0	76	740	673	234
0.3	32.8	114	3	10	3
0.4	20.6	72	21	53	18
0.5	27.8	97	94	188	65
0.2	21.4	74	129	645	224
1.7	24.0	83	1,130	665	231
0.6	37.6	131	25	42	14
5.6	35.0	122	2,527	451	157
1.8	27.2	94	585	325	113
0.1	23.9	83	4	40	14
2.2	21.7	75	759	345	120
0.8	29.2	101	62	78	27
0.9	30.2	105	49	54	19
2.3	23.1	80	734	319	111

Continued

TABLE C.4 Continued

	Population <65 yrs, 1998 (millions)	No. of Uninsured, 1998 (millions)	Uninsured Rate, 1998 (%)	No. of Medicaid, 1998 (millions)	Medicaid Rate, 1998 (%)
Rhode Island	0.8	0.1	11.5	0.1	8.5
South Carolina	3.4	0.6	17.5	0.3	8.4
South Dakota	0.6	0.1	16.4	0.0	6.4
Tennessee	5.0	0.7	14.4	1.0	20.1
Texas	18.0	4.9	27.0	1.7	9.4
Utah	1.9	0.3	15.1	0.1	7.4
Vermont	0.5	0.1	11.0	0.1	16.1
Virginia	5.8	0.9	16.0	0.3	5.4
Washington	5.2	0.7	13.5	0.6	11.5
West Virginia	1.4	0.3	20.9	0.2	16.8
Wisconsin	4.5	0.6	13.2	0.4	8.5
Wyoming	0.4	0.1	19.0	0.0	6.5

SOURCES: Fronstin, 2000; Wynn et al., 2002.

Sum No. (Uninsured and Medicaid), 1998 (millions)	Sum % (Uninsured and Medicaid), 1998 (%)	Sum %/ Total, (%)	Combined Federal Medicare and Medicaid DSH payment, 1998 (millions)	Combined DSH/Sum No. ($$)	Combined DSH/ Sum No./ Total (%)
0.2	20.0	69	66	330	115
0.9	25.9	90	539	599	208
0.1	22.8	79	4	40	14
1.7	34.5	120	142	84	29
6.6	36.4	126	1,854	281	98
0.4	22.5	78	15	38	13
0.2	27.1	94	31	155	54
1.2	21.4	74	242	202	70
1.3	25.0	87	386	297	103
0.5	37.7	131	114	228	79
1.0	21.7	75	42	42	15
0.1	25.5	89	0	0	0

TABLE C.5 Estimated Vaccination Coverage of 4:3:1:3[a] Series Among
Children 19–35 Months of Age and Uninsured Rates for Selected Urban Areas,
1997

Area	Population	Uninsured Rate (%)	Rank, % Population Uninsured	Vaccination Coverage Rate (%)	Rank, Vaccination Coverage
United States	267,784,000	16.1		76 (± 0.8)	
Birmingham, AL	784,113	16.5	14	82 (± 4.3)	3
Phoenix, AZ	2,478,253	26.1	23	72 (± 4.8)	18
Los Angeles, CA	8,223,152	31.5	27	71 (± 5.5)	19
San Diego, CA	2,405,871	21.9	20	78 (± 4.3)	7
San Jose, CA	1,460,505	16.3	13	73 (± 4.8)	17
District of Columbia– MD–VA–WV	4,186,038	15.3	12	73 (± 5.4)	15
Miami, FL	1,752,653	26.9	24	75 (± 5.0)	12
Jacksonville, FL	918,873	18.7	16	70 (± 5.1)	21
Atlanta, GA	3,340,844	18.7	17	75 (± 4.9)	11
Chicago, IL	6,912,774	15.3	11	68 (± 5.5)	24
Indianapolis, IN	1,334,459	12.9	3	81 (± 4.5)	4
New Orleans, LA	1,162,705	20.8	19	69 (± 6.0)	23
Boston, MA	4,642,418	15.3	10	86 (± 3.6)	1
Baltimore, MD	2,169,524	14.6	8	83 (± 4.7)	2
Detroit, MI	3,911,274	13.4	5	65 (± 4.6)	26
Newark, NJ	1,693,870	18.8	18	66 (± 6.3)	25
New York, NY	7,734,663	27.1	25	75 (± 5.1)	10
Cleveland, OH	1,902,126	13.8	6	73 (± 5.3)	16
Columbus, OH	1,308,928	16.6	15	74 (± 5.0)	14
Philadelphia, PA	4,258,856	14.9	9	78 (± 5.1)	6
Nashville, TN	1,017,287	14.5	7	77 (± 4.6)	9
Knoxville, TN	566,821	13.3	4	70 (± 5.3)	22
San Antonio, TX	1,352,127	23.9	21	79 (± 4.8)	5
Houston, TX	3,576,686	29.5	26	64 (± 6.1)	28
Dallas, TX	2,874,219	24.7	22	74 (± 5.4)	13
El Paso, TX	642,947	37.1	28	65 (± 5.3)	27
Seattle, WA	2,077,951	12.0	2	77 (± 4.6)	8
Milwaukee, WI	1,283,147	8.1	1	70 (± 4.9)	20

[a] 4:3:1:3 = four or more doses of diptheria, tetanus, and pertussis vaccine; three or more doses of
poliovirus vaccine; one or more doses of a measles-containing vaccine; and three or more doses of
Haemophilus influenzae type b vaccine.
SOURCES: Brown et al., 2000; IOM, 2000.

TABLE C.6 Urban Uninsurance and Tuberculosis Case Rates, 1997

City	Population	Uninsured rate (%)	Rank, % Population Uninsured	Rate of Cases of Tuberculosis per 100,000 Population	Rank, Disease Rate
Akron, OH	591,371	7.4	47	0.7	48
Albuquerque, NM	601,564	20.0	13	3.6	38
Atlanta, GA	3,340,844	18.7	15	10.7	12
Austin, TX[a]	985,589	23.3	10	7.5	20
Baltimore, MD	2,169,524	14.6	28	6.7	25
Birmingham, AL	784,113	16.5	19	8.6	18
Boston, MA[a]	4,642,418	15.3	24	4.5	35
Buffalo, NY[a]	981,723	11.6	42	3.9	36
Charlotte, NC[a]	1,198,149	12.0	41	8.9	16
Chicago, IL	6,912,774	15.3	25	11.0	11
Cincinnati, OH[a]	1,409,692	12.5	39	2.7	43
Cleveland, OH	1,902,126	13.8	33	6.2	28
Columbus, OH	1,308,928	16.6	18	1.7	46
Dallas, TX	2,874,219	24.7	7	10.0	15
Dayton, OH	824,271	14.4	30	1.6	47
Denver, CO	1,722,414	12.2	40	3.3	40
Detroit, MI	3,911,274	13.4	36	5.8	29
Fort Worth, TX	1,416,768	23.8	9	7.1	23
Houston, TX	3,576,686	29.5	2	17.3	4
Indianapolis, IN	1,334,459	12.9	37	3.3	41
Jacksonville, FL	918,873	18.7	16	13.7	7
Jersey City, NJ	479,900	35.9	1	19.9	3
Kansas City, MO[a]	1,515,994	13.6	34	3.3	42
Louisville, KY	870,766	12.9	38	3.8	37
Memphis, TN[a]	975,937	15.6	23	12.9	9
Miami, FL	1,752,653	26.9	4	15.5	5
Milwaukee, WI	1,283,147	8.1	46	3.4	39
Minneapolis, MN[a]	2,486,355	10.1	45	4.8	33
Nashville, TN	1,017,287	14.5	29	10.2	13
New Orleans, LA	1,162,705	20.8	12	12.4	10
New York City, NY	7,734,663	27.1	3	21.6	1
Newark, NJ	1,693,870	18.8	14	13.2	8
Norfolk, VA[a]	1,395,298	10.8	43	5.4	32
Oakland, CA	2,010,788	13.5	35	14.0	6
Oklahoma City, OK	918,493	18.4	17	7.9	19
Omaha, NE[a]	616,156	10.2	44	1.9	45
Philadelphia, PA	4,258,856	14.9	27	6.7	26
Phoenix, AZ[a]	2,478,253	26.1	5	6.4	27
Richmond, VA	833,770	14.0	32	2.5	44
Rochester, NY	946,829	16.2	21	5.5	31
Sacramento, CA	1,327,441	15.9	22	10.1	14

continued

TABLE C.6 Continued

City	Population	Uninsured Rate (%)	Rank, % Population Uninsured	Rate of Cases of Tuberculosis per 100,000 Population	Rank, Disease Rate
San Antonio, TX	1,352,127	23.9	8	7.1	24
San Francisco, CA	1,423,697	23.1	11	20.3	2
St. Louis, MO[a]	2,340,329	14.1	31	5.6	30
Tampa, FL	1,737,127	24.9	6	7.4	21
Tulsa, OK	676,107	16.5	20	4.6	34
Washington, DC[a]	4,186,038	15.3	26	8.7	17

[a]These cities represent multicounty areas, while disease rates are for the central county unless otherwise indicated.

SOURCES: Brown et al., 2000; CDC, 2002a.

D

Commissioned Papers

The Impact of Uninsured Populations on the Availability of Hospital Services and Financial Status of Hospitals in Urban Areas

Darrell J. Gaskin and Jack Needleman

ABSTRACT

Objective: To identify the effects of the percentage of uninsured persons in a community on the availability of hospital services for the entire community.

Data and Study Design: Our analysis focuses on the 85 largest metropolitan statistical areas (MSAs) during the 1990s and relies on data from the March Current Population Survey, the American Hospital Association's (AHA) Survey of Hospitals and Medicare Cost Reports. We estimate the impact of the uninsured rate on hospital margins and four measures of hospital service availability, i.e., capacity, services to vulnerable populations, community services, and high–tech services. We estimate two sets of regression models, MSA-level and hospital-level models.

Findings: We find that as the uninsured rate increased the availability of some hospital services declined. The results of the MSA and hospital level analyses aare consistent for the measures of capacity, services to vulnerable populations and community services. The uninsured rate was negatively related to beds per capita in the MSA and the average hospital size. The availability of services for vulnerable populations and community services and the propensity for hospitals to offer these services is negatively associated with the percentage of uninsured residents. The results for hi-tech services for the MSA- and hospital-level analyses are not congruent. The results from the MSA-level analysis suggest that the uninsured rate is negatively associated with the availability of some high-tech services. However, the results of the hospital-level analysis suggest that as the uninsured rate increases, hospitals are more likely to offer some high-tech services, specifically extracorporeal shock-wave lithotripsy (ESWL), angioplasty, and magnetic resonance imaging (MRI). The results of the MSA- and hospital-level analyses also differ for hospitals' financial health. The MSA level results suggest that hospitals are negatively impacted by the rate of uninsurance. The hospital-level results suggest that there is no association.

Conclusion: Our findings suggest that the lack of health insurance not only creates an access to care problem for uninsured individuals but also reduces the availability of hospital services to the entire community.

INTRODUCTION

An estimated 41 million Americans or 16.5 percent of the population under age 65 lacked health insurance in 2001 (Mills, 2002). The lack of health insurance has a significant impact on the health and well-being of uninsured persons. A number of studies have shown that uninsured persons have less access to health care services and as a result have worse health outcomes and lower overall health status (IOM, 2002a; 2002b). The uninsured are less likely to receive preventive and screening services compared to persons with health insurance. Uninsured persons with chronic conditions are less likely to receive appropriate care to manage their health conditions (Mandelblatt et al., 1999; Powell-Griner et al., 1999; Zambrana et al, 1999; Ayanian et al., 2000; Cummings et al., 2000; Breen et al., 2001). Compared to insured persons, uninsured persons are less likely to have a usual source of care and less likely to seek care when they felt they needed it (IOM, 2001a). When hospitalized, the uninsured receive fewer services, are more likely to receive substandard care than insured patients, and are at greater risk of dying during the hospital stay or soon after discharge (Hadley et al., 1991; Burstin et al., 1992; Haas and Goldman, 1994; Blustein et al., 1995). Persons without health insurance have poorer heath outcomes for an episode of illness and higher overall mortality rates (Ayanian et al., 1993; Blustein et al., 1995; Canto et al., 2000; Roetzheim et al., 2000).

While research has shown the persons who are uninsured face significant barriers to health care, little is known about how the overall percentage of those without health insurance, i.e., the uninsured rate, affects access to care for their community. Theoretically, the size and scope of the health care delivery system in a community is determined by the intersection of the demand for health care in a community with health care providers' ability and willingness to offer services. Because insurance pays for a large proportion of health care services, the distribution of community residents by source of payment will partially determine their demand for health care services. In particular, health insurance coverage does tend to increase individuals' demand for health care services. Uninsured persons use fewer health care services than do similar insured persons. Also, hospitals, physicians and other health care providers receive substantially less reimbursement for the care provided to uninsured patients compared to similar insured patients. Consequently, a high uninsured rate should reduce overall demand for health services in a community.

We are concerned particularly about the impact of uninsurance on the availability of hospital services. Several studies have shown that market forces that have depressed demand for hospital services have had an impact on the size of the hospital delivery system. For example, Medicare's transition from a cost-based reimbursement system to prospective payment and its subsequent reduction in growth of hospital payment rates resulted in lower hospital utilization, a reduction in the intensity of hospital services, and encouraged a reduction in hospital size (Coulam and Gaumer, 1991; Hodgkin and McGuire, 1994). The introduction of managed care also reduced demand for hospital services. Several studies have demonstrated that increased HMO penetration is associated with reduction in hospital utilization, hospital beds, slower hospital cost inflation, and slower revenue growth (Miller and Luft, 1994; Chernew, 1995; Robinson, 1996; Gaskin and Hadley, 1997). Dranove and colleagues (1986) have modeled the impact of managed care penetration on hospitals, and they conclude that downward pressure on hospital prices would result in a reduction in hospital capacity. Given these major changes in the nature of demand for hospital services, hospital behavior in less concentrated markets has transformed from non-price competition to price competition. Prior to the implementation of Medicare prospective payment and the growth of managed care, the empirical evidence indicated that hospitals in less concentrated markets competed on the basis of technology, amenities, and services, e.g., Luft's so called "medical arms race" (Robinson and Luft, 1985; Luft et al., 1986; Noether, 1988; Frech, 1996). However, studies based on data from the late 1980s and early 1990s present strong evidence of price competition in hospital markets (Robinson and Luft, 1988; Zwanziger and Melnick, 1988; Melnick et al., 1992; Keeler et al., 1999). Hospitals in less concentrated areas charged significantly lower prices compared with those in more concentrated areas.

We postulate that similar to other market forces that reduce the demand for hospital services, high uninsured rates will be associated with reduction in hospital capacity. This potentially can have a negative spillover effect on insured patients. For example, if a hospital is unable to maintain its trauma center because of a high uninsured rate, an ambulance may have to carry insured patients further to obtain trauma care. In this study we attempt to identify the effects of the percentage of uninsured persons in a community on the availability of hospital services for the entire community. In particular, we address the following questions: (1) Are hospitals smaller in communities with high uninsured rates? (2) Are hospitals less likely to offer particular types of services in communities with uninsured rates? (3) Does the availability of hospital services for the entire community decline as the percentage of uninsured persons on a community increases? (4) Does uninsurance negatively affect the financial status of hospitals?

CONCEPTUAL FRAMEWORK

As stated above, we hypothesize that the uninsured rate is negatively related to the demand for hospital services. Specifically, as the uninsured rate increases, the overall demand for hospital services by insured patients decreases while the overall demand for hospital services by uninsured patients (i.e., charity or discount care) increases. Uninsured patients, however, tend to use less hospital care than do insured patients for similar health care needs because of their limited financial resources. As a result, an increase in the uninsured rate should lower and flatten the demand for hospital services in a geographic market. For simplification, assume that hospitals serve two types of patients: insured and uninsured. Payment rates for treating insured patients are typically greater than average costs. Reimbursements for treating uninsured patients are typically less than average cost. Assume hospitals have a cost structure that exhibits increasing or constant returns to scale, that is, total cost increases with the volume of services at an increasing rate. Empirically, hospitals exhibit scale economies up to a moderate size, 150 to 250 beds (Folland et al., 2001). Beyond this size the evidence is mixed regarding whether hospitals experience constant or decreasing returns to scale. Assume that the typical urban hospital operates at volume levels where marginal cost equals average cost. Hospitals use their marginal cost to determine their supply of hospital services. They equate marginal costs with either marginal revenues or average revenues depending upon their market structure (Tirole, 1998). Hospitals that are monopolies or part of oligopolies will set marginal costs equal to marginal revenues. Hospitals that are in monopolistic competitive markets will set their marginal costs equal to average revenues (Chamberlin, 1962).

For simplification, suppose that the distribution of each hospital's patients by source of payment is equal to the distribution of persons in the market by insurance status. In such a market, as the uninsured rate increases, the percentage of uninsured patients treated by each hospital increases and therefore their average and marginal revenues decline. Consequently, each hospital will reduce its supply of services. Obviously, this is a simplification that does not reflect most hospital markets because hospitals differ with respect to serving the uninsured in their geographic markets. However, the general notion that an increase in the uninsured rate places downward pressure on the supply of hospital services is correct.

Now relax the assumption that hospitals care for uninsured patients proportionally to their presence in the market area. Suppose in some markets there are safety-net hospitals that provide a disproportionate share of the care to the uninsured while other hospitals provide less than a proportionate share of uninsured patients. In such a market, an increase in the uninsured rate would have a larger effect on safety-net hospitals than on other hospitals. However, if as the uninsured rate increases, non–safety-net hospitals in the community become proportionately more involved in the care for the uninsured, then these hospitals will be more affected by the change in demand.

Another assumption implicit in our model is that uninsured and insured patients use hospitals for the same mix of services. However, suppose there is a set of hospital services that the uninsured are more likely to use than insured patients. For these services, hospitals' profits will tend to be lower than profits associated with other hospital services because of their payer mix. Therefore, we expect that hospitals will cut back on services that the uninsured are more likely to use as the uninsured rate increases.

The discussion above assumed that each hospital bases its decisions on its own revenue and cost structure. The framework can also be extended to consider strategic interactions among hospitals in multi-hospital markets. Hospitals facing demand for services from uninsured or nonpaying patients for specific services may prefer to shift these patients to other hospitals. Where this cannot be accomplished directly, an option is to not provide the service or restrict the size of the service by reducing beds available for the service. This will shift uninsured patients to other hospitals but can also increase the travel time and inconvenience for insured patients to obtain the service. In markets where care for the uninsured is concentrated in a few safety net hospitals, this effect may be small. In markets where care for the uninsured is more widely shared or where there are fewer hospitals, these strategic interactions may reduce the availability of services beyond the level needed to adjust for the lower demand from the uninsured.

DATA

This study relies primarily on three databases:

- The March Current Population Survey (CPS)
- the AHA Annual Survey of Hospitals and
- the Medicare Cost Reports

We used data from the March CPS from 1990 to 2000 to calculate the percentage of uninsured residents in the 85 largest MSAs. See the addendum for the list of MSAs. We focus on the 85 largest MSAs because they had large enough subsamples in the CPS data to yield reliable estimates of the uninsured rate. The size of the subsamples range from 143 to 6,148 with a mean of 900, standard deviation of 145, and a median of 623. To improve the accuracy of our estimates, we calculated the percentage of uninsured persons in an MSA by combining data for 3 years, i.e., the current year and the years before and after. The analysis focuses on the years 1991, 1994, 1996, and 1999. In addition, we calculated the percentage of the MSA's population covered by Medicare and Medicaid using the CPS data.

To measure the availability of hospital services, we used data from the AHA Survey of Hospitals for the years 1991, 1994, 1996, and 1999. In particular, we used four measures of hospital service availability: hospital capacity, services to vulnerable populations, high tech services, and community services. To measure capacity we used the number of hospital beds, medical/surgical beds, psychiatric beds, intensive care unit (ICU) beds, and beds devoted to patients diagnosed with alcoholism, drug abuse, or chemical dependency. Five services for vulnerable populations were examined: psychiatric outpatient services, psychiatric emergency room services, psychiatric inpatient services, outpatient, and rehabilitation services for persons diagnosed with alcoholism, drug abuse, or chemical dependency, and services for patients diagnosed with HIV-AIDS. Nine high-tech services were examined. Four require investments in beds as well as in equipment and personnel: trauma center, neonatal intensive care unit, transplant services, and burn units. Five involve investments in equipment and personnel: magnetic resonance imaging (MRI), radiation therapy, angioplasty, single photo emission computerized tomography (SPECT), and extracorporeal shock-wave lithotripsy (ESWL). Three community services were examined: community outreach centers, transportation services, and Meals on Wheels. We have data on these three services only for 1994, 1996, and 1999 because AHA did not collect information on them in 1991. For each of the 17 services, we created a variable that indicates whether the hospital or one of its subsidiaries provided the service. If the hospital reported that it provided the service locally through a partner in its health system, network, or a joint venture, we did not designate this hospital as a provider of the service. This eliminated some double counting. Consider a local health system that consists of an academic health center (AHC) hospital and three community hospitals, a configuration common in New York City (Salit et al., 2002). Suppose the AHC hospital has a burn unit but the community hospitals do not have one. The AHC hospital would report that it provided the service at the hospital. The community hospitals would report that they provided the service locally through the health system. To avoid counting this burn unit four times, we only recognized those that are provided at the hospital or a subsidiary. Ideally, we would use the number of beds provided or volume of visits to measure the magnitude of these services. However, this information is not available for all of the services on the AHA survey.

To measure hospital financial status, we used hospital margins calculated from the Medicare Cost Reports. Other hospital characteristics used in the analysis were ownership status, teaching status based on the residents-to-bed ratio, and the percentage of the hospital inpatient days that were covered by Medicaid. When modeling the hospital service availability, we obtained the hospital characteristics from the AHA data and when modeling hospital financial status, we obtained these hospital characteristics from the Medicare Cost Reports.

In these analyses we controlled for four health care market factors: hospital market competition, HMO penetration, local costs, and overall demand. To control for the level of hospital competition, we calculated a Herfindahl index, which is equal to the sum of the squares of the market shares, using staffed hospital beds. We obtained HMO penetration data from InterStudy. We used the HCFA wage index as a measure of cost. To control for overall demand adjusting for geographic convenience, we used population density (Porell and Adams, 1995).

METHODOLOGY

We conducted MSA- and hospital-level analysis on three sets of variables: hospital beds, hospital services, and hospital margins.

Beds

In the MSA level analysis, we regressed beds per capita for total beds, medical-surgical beds, beds in intensive care units, psychiatric inpatient beds, and beds for treatment of alcohol and chemical dependency on the percent of uninsured residents in the MSA, the other MSA characteristics, (i.e., percent Medicaid, percent Medicare, percent HMO enrollment, level of hospital competition, hospital wage index, and population density) and year categorical variables to control for fixed time effects. We estimated these models using generalized least squares with robust standard errors, controlling for clustering at the MSA level. We gave greater weight to larger MSAs by using the average MSA population as a weight in the regression analysis.

We conducted hospital-level regressions of the natural log of beds in each of the five bed categories on the MSA-level variables, plus controls for hospital characteristics such as ownership, teaching status, size, and percent Medicaid patients. We used a general estimating equations framework to construct random effects regression models controlling for unobserved hospital and time effects. We prefer random effects models because the uninsured rate does not vary substantially over time within an MSA, and within MSA variation over the time period we examine is unlikely to drive hospital behavior. For psychiatric beds and alcohol/chemical dependency beds, because a high proportion of hospitals did not provide beds for the service, we used random effect negative binominal count models. For each model, we calculated standard errors using the Huber-White correction and weighted each hospital by its average number of beds during the study period. Since hospitals are nested within MSAs, we adjusted the estimated standard errors to reflect MSA clustering. We also verified that the models were homoscledastic with respect to the uninsured rate using the Breusch-Pagan Test (Greene, 2000).

Services

For the MSA analysis, we regressed the proportion of hospitals offering specific services on the percent of uninsured in the MSA and the other MSA-level variables described above. We also conducted this regression weighting the proportion of hospitals offering the service by total hospital beds in these hospitals. This weighted analysis gives larger hospitals offering the service more importance and implicitly uses as the dependent variable the proportion of hospital beds in the MSA that are in hospitals offering the service. In both regressions, we estimated these models with robust standard errors and weighted each MSA by its population size.

For the hospital-level analysis, we estimated random effect logistic regression models that controlled for hospital-specific effects for each service. The MSA- and hospital-level variables were those described above, with adjustments for clustering at the MSA level.

Margin

To determine whether the uninsured rate affected the financial status of hospitals, we estimated MSA-level and hospital-level models. For the MSA-level model, the aggregate margin was the dependent variable. This is a measure used by the Medicare Payment Advisory Commission (MedPAC) to characterize the financial health of a category of hospitals. Aggregate margin equals total hospital revenues in the MSA, minus total hospital expenses in the MSA, divided by total revenues. The independent variables were the percent of uninsured residents in the MSA, the percent Medicaid and Medicare enrollees, the percent of public and for-profit hospitals in the MSA, hospital wage index, population density, and year categorical variables to control for fixed time effects.

For the hospital-level models, we used the total hospital margin as the dependent variable. Because of outliers, we excluded observations with margins below the third percentile and above 97th percentile. The independent variables in this model were the uninsured rate, the other MSA characteristics, and the hospital characteristics. Similar to the other hospital-level models, we estimated random effects controlling for unobserved hospital and time effects, weighting by hospital beds and calculating robust standard errors using the Huber-White correction.

RESULTS

Means and standard deviations for the percent uninsured at the MSA level, beds per 100,000 population, the proportion of hospitals offering each service (unweighted), and percentage of beds in hospitals with each service (weighted), and MSA-level margin are presented in Table D.1. The regression coefficients on the proportion of uninsured in the MSA for regressions on beds, services, and margins are presented in Table D.2. Results from regressions of services using the unweighted and weighted availability measure are both presented. Hospital-level regressions are presented in Table D.3.

Proportion of Uninsured

On average 12.2 percent of the total population in the 85 MSAs studied was uninsured in 1999. The range varied from 6.2 percent uninsured in Allentown-

TABLE D.1 Means and Standard Deviations for Percent Uninsured in MSA and Dependent Variables

Variable	Unweighted			Weighted		
	N	Mean	SD	N	Mean	SD
Percent Uninsured in MSA	340	14.6	5.3			
Beds per 100,000 Population						
Total	340	316.2	106.6			
Medical-Surgical	340	173.2	78.0			
ICU	340	29.7	10.3			
Psychiatric	340	18.5	12.1			
Alcohol and chemical dependence	340	3.9	4.3			
		%	%		%	%
Services for Vulnerable Populations						
Psychiatric inpatient	340	39.6	18.1	340	59.2	21.6
Psychiatric emergency	340	40.5	19.4	340	58.4	22.1
Psychiatric outpatient	340	32.5	16.7	340	49.3	21.8
Alcohol and chemical dependence	340	25.8	16.7	340	37.8	22.4
AIDS	340	54.1	21.0	340	73.7	18.9
High Technology Services						
Trauma	340	22.3	13.8	340	38.5	19.8
NICU	340	25.8	12.6	340	42.9	17.9
Transplant	340	16.5	11.2	340	32.2	17.3
Burn	340	5.2	4.9	340	11.1	11.0
MRI	340	47.2	20.6	340	66.2	23.3
Radiation therapy	340	37.2	15.3	340	61.0	18.5
Angioplasty	340	34.2	14.9	340	60.4	18.8
SPECT	340	41.2	16.8	340	57.3	19.4
ESWL	340	14.5	10.7	340	26.0	19.0
Community Services						
Community outreach	255	56.9	17.8	255	75.4	17.5
Transportation	255	24.8	15.6	255	33.7	22.0
Meals on Wheels	255	12.3	12.7	255	14.2	15.7
Margin	340	3.4	4.8			

TABLE D.2 Regression Coefficients of Beds, Services, and Margin on Percentage of Uninsured in Metropolitan Area and Other Variables, MSA-Level Regressions

Variable	N	Coefficients and Standard Errors (SE) for Percent Uninsured in MSA			
		Unweighted Regression		Weighted Regression	
		Coefficient	SE	Coefficient	SE
Beds per 100,000 Population					
Total	339	−2.67	$(1.27)^a$		
Medical-surgical	339	−2.00	$(0.82)^a$		
ICU	339	−0.12	(0.13)		
Psychiatric	339	−0.61	$(0.17)^c$		
Alcohol and chemical dependence	339	−0.19	$(0.04)^c$		
Services for Vulnerable Populations					
Psychiatric inpatient	339	−1.10	$(0.26)^c$	−1.10	$(0.29)^c$
Psychiatric emergency	339	−1.40	$(0.27)^c$	−1.30	$(0.29)^c$
Psychiatric outpatient	339	−1.27	$(0.22)^c$	−1.36	$(0.26)^c$
Alcohol and chemical dependence	339	−1.13	$(0.22)^c$	−1.31	$(0.31)^c$
AIDS	339	−0.47	$(0.20)^a$	−0.20	(0.21)
High Technology Services					
Trauma	339	−0.62	$(0.21)^b$	−0.63	$(0.24)^b$
NICU	339	0.26	(0.19)	0.61	$(0.23)^b$
Transplant	339	−0.19	(0.17)	−0.32	(0.23)
Burn	339	−0.17	$(0.04)^c$	−0.17	(0.13)
MRI	339	−0.14	(0.19)	0.10	(0.22)
Radiation therapy	339	−0.33	(0.19)	−0.14	(0.26)
Angioplasty	339	0.24	(0.18)	0.46	$(0.21)^a$
SPECT	339	−0.65	$(0.23)^b$	−0.32	(0.19)
ESWL	339	0.22	(0.13)	0.24	(0.22)
Community Services					
Community outreach	255	−1.15	$(0.23)^c$	−0.77	$(0.24)^b$
Transportation	255	0.10	(0.29)	0.37	(0.38)
Meals on Wheels	255	−0.52	$(0.21)^a$	−0.42	(0.28)
Margin	340	−0.14	$(0.04)^b$		

[a] $p < 0.05$
[b] $p < 0.01$
[c] $p < 0.001$

NOTES: Regressions of beds and services include percent MSA Medicaid, percent MSA Medicare, HMO penetration, Herfindahl index, population density, CMS wage index, and dummies for years 1994, 1996, and 1999. Regressions of margin include percent MSA Medicaid, percent MSA Medicare, percent hospitals in MSA for-profit, percent hospitals in MSA public, percent hospitals in MSA major teaching hospitals, and dummies for years 1994, 1996, and 1999.

TABLE D.3 Regression Coefficients of Beds, Services, and Margin on Percentage of Uninsured in Metropolitan Area and Other Variables, Hospital Level Regressions

Variable	N	Coefficient	SE
		Coefficients and Standard Errors (SE) for Percent Uninsured in MSA	
Log (Beds in Hospital)			
Total	7157	-0.0070	(0.0027)[b]
Medical-surgical	6261	-0.0103	(0.0045)[a]
ICU	6261	0.0082	(0.0040)[a]
Psychiatric	6261	-0.0103	(0.0004)[c]
Alcohol and chemical dependence	6261	-0.0163	(0.0006)[c]
Services for Vulnerable Populations			
Psychiatric inpatient	6261	-0.022	(0.013)
Psychiatric emergency	6261	-0.030	(0.016)
Psychiatric outpatient	6261	-0.024	(0.016)
Alcohol and chemical dependence	6261	-0.041	(0.018)[a]
AIDS	6261	-0.020	(0.016)
High Technology Services			
Trauma	6261	0.005	(0.017)
NICU	6261	0.041	(0.016)[b]
Transplant	6261	0.007	(0.017)
Burn	6261	-0.020	(0.016)
MRI	6261	0.051	(0.033)
Radiation therapy	6261	0.006	(0.016)
Angioplasty	6261	0.045	(0.019)[a]
SPECT	6261	0.002	(0.014)
ESWL	6261	0.022	(0.021)
Community Services			
Community outreach	4493	-0.009	(0.016)
Transportation	4493	0.024	(0.020)
Meals on Wheels	4493	-0.039	(0.029)
Margin	6459	0.027	(0.059)

[a] $p<0.05$
[b] $p<0.01$
[c] $p<0.001$

NOTES: Regressions of beds and services include percent MSA Medicaid, percent MSA Medicare, HMO penetration, Herfindahl index, population density, CMS wage index, and dummies for years 1994, 1996, and 1999. Regressions of margin include percent MSA Medicaid, percent MSA Medicare, percent hospitals in MSA for-profit, percent hospitals in MSA public, percent hospitals in MSA major teaching hospitals, and dummies for years 1994, 1996, and 1999. Standard errors are adjusted for hospital and MSA level clustering.

Bethlehem, Pennsylvania and Harrisburg, Pennsylvania, to 26.6 percent uninsured in Jersey City, New Jersey. During the 1990s, the average uninsured rate fell 3.8 percentage points. Most of these MSAs, 76 of 85, experienced a decline in the uninsured rate during the 1990s. Almost a third had declines of greater than 5 percentage points. Of those MSAs in which the uninsured rate increased, the largest occurred in San Francisco, which increased from 14.8 to 18.7 percent, and Jersey City, which increased from 22.7 to 26 percent.

Beds

Across the 85 metropolitan areas in this analysis, there were 316 beds per 100,000 population. More than half of these were in medical-surgical beds. Approximately 10 percent of beds were in ICUs. There were far fewer psychiatric and alcohol and chemical dependence treatment beds (18.5 and 3.9 per 100,000 respectively), but there is much wider variation across MSAs in the supply of these beds than in any other category.

In the MSA-level regressions, there is evidence that beds per capita and all categories of beds studied except ICU beds were lower where the proportion of the population uninsured is higher. In the hospital-level regressions, for all bed categories except ICU beds, hospitals offer fewer beds where the local uninsured rate is higher. An increase in the uninsured rate of 5.3 percentage points, one standard deviation, is associated with a 4.5 percent decrease in beds overall, a 6.1 percent decrease in medical–surgical beds, a 17.5 percent decrease in psychiatric beds, and 25.8 percent decrease in alcohol and chemical dependence beds at the mean level of beds per capita.

Services for Vulnerable Populations

With respect to services for vulnerable populations, AIDS services are the most common. Over half the hospitals offer these services, and nearly three-quarters of hospital beds are in hospitals that offer these services. Psychiatric inpatient and emergency services are available in approximately 40 percent of hospitals (with 60 percent of the beds), while psychiatric outpatient and alcohol and chemical dependence treatment are available in between one–quarter to one-third of hospitals.

In the MSA-level regressions, the availability of all three psychiatric services and alcohol and chemical dependence services are found to be lower in metropolitan areas with higher uninsurance, with an increase in the uninsured rate of 5.3 percent associated with 5.8 to 7.4 percent fewer hospitals offering the service. AIDS services are also lower, although statistically significant only in the unweighted regression. In hospital-level regressions, there is a negative association between all these services and the uninsured rate, but only the association with alcohol and chemical dependency services is statistically significant.

High-Technology Services

Bed-based high-technology services (trauma, neonatal ICU [NICU], transplant, and burn) were much less commonly available than services for vulnerable populations, with the proportion of hospitals offering such services varying from 25.8 percent for NICU to 5.2 percent for burn. Because these services were more likely to be offered by larger hospitals, the proportion of beds in hospitals offering these services varied from 42.9 percent for NICU to 11.1 percent for burn care.

Among these four services, in the MSA-level regressions, trauma services are less likely to be available in communities with higher uninsured rates, a finding observed in both the unweighted and weighted regressions. (In the hospital-level regression, the results are of the opposite sign but not statistically significant.) The estimates of the negative impact of MSA uninsured rate on the MSA-level analysis of burn service availability are consistent in the unweighted and weighted model, but only statistically significant for the unweighted model. There is no statistically significant association of transplant services and uninsured rates in any model. The availability of NICU services is higher in MSAs with higher uninsured rates, a finding that is statistically significant in the weighted MSA regression and hospital-level regression.

High-technology services that do not have dedicated beds associated with them were much more likely to be provided by hospitals. With the exception of lithotripsy (present on average in only 14.5 percent of the hospitals in our sample), approximately 30 to 50 percent of the hospitals provided the services we studied. The proportion of beds in hospitals with these services varied from 57.3 percent for SPECT to two-thirds for MRI. We find no consistent pattern of association between the availability of other high-technology services and uninsured rates in the regression analysis.

Community Services

The frequency with which the community services we studied were provided by hospitals varied widely. Community outreach was the most common, present in 60 percent of the hospitals in our sample and in hospitals with 75 percent of beds, on average. Transportation services were provided by one-quarter of the hospitals in our sample and Meals on Wheels by 12 percent.

In the MSA-level regressions, a smaller proportion of hospitals are likely to provide community outreach services in MSAs with high uninsured rates. This is true whether availability is measured in terms of the proportion of hospitals or the proportion of beds. The results in the hospital level regressions are consistent with this finding but not statistically significant.

There is some evidence that hospitals in communities with high uninsured rates are less likely to offer Meals on Wheels, but no evidence of lower levels of transportation services.

Hospital Margins

The average hospital margin in our MSAs was 3.4 percent. There is wide variation among aggregate MSA margins. We observe no statistically significant association in either the MSA or hospital-level regressions of margin on uninsured rates.

DISCUSSION

In our analysis, we find inconsistent results between the MSA and hospital-level models. Within MSAs, the impact of uninsured patients on hospital decisions to offer services may differ across institutions in ways that our hospital-level models do not currently capture. We place more weight on the MSA-level models. The hospital-level models indicate how average individual hospitals may respond to increased demand for hospital care from the uninsured as measured by the MSA-wide uninsured rate. However, it is unlikely that the overall market response is merely the weighted average of individual hospital responses in the market. This would assume that hospitals neither behave strategically nor respond to the actions of their competitors. For example, a safety-net hospital may eliminate a high-tech service because they cannot support it with its payer mix. However, this may pave the way for a competing hospital to offer the service. The competing hospital, because of its location, amenities, and reputation in the market, may be able to attract more privately insured patients, thus making the service financially solvent. The competing hospital may have higher aggregate volume that can improve quality and lower per-patient costs associated with the service, and this might be a positive aspect of consolidation. Alternatively, the shift of the service away from hospitals that serve the uninsured might reduce its availability to the uninsured and insured populations who use that hospital, a negative consequence of the shift. None of this is observable in the hospital-level models. The MSA-level models allow us to observe the overall association of uninsurance and the availability of hospital services, net of the strategic behavior by individual hospitals.

There are also inconsistencies between the unweighted and weighted MSA-level models of service availability. The unweighted models examine the proportion of *hospitals* offering the service; the weighted model, the proportion of *beds* in hospitals with the service. This gives greater weight to larger hospitals. Implicitly this presumes that a service offered by a large hospital will more likely be larger and have a greater impact on the geographic market than the same service offered at a smaller facility.

A possible explanation for the weak association we observe between margins and the uninsured rate is the presence of other revenue sources that support hospital care of the uninsured in some MSAs. For example, hospitals in Maryland, Massachusetts, New Jersey, and New York received some state and local subsidy from charity care or indigent care pools. These funds offset financial losses due to care for the uninsured and improve hospital margins. Their presence may cloud the statistical association between uninsured rates and hospital margins. State and local governments are more likely to establish these revenue sources in communities with high uninsured rates. We may not have adequately controlled for the existence of these alternate revenue sources in our analyses.

The lack of an association between margins and the uninsured rate for urban hospitals differs from our finding for rural hospitals. There, we find a consistent association of lower margins with higher uninsured admissions. We believe these contrasting findings reflect a difference in strategies between urban hospital administrators and rural hospital administrators when faced with financial pressure due to the uninsured rate. Urban hospital administrators are more likely to reduce or eliminate services in order to maintain the overall financial health of the institution. Compared to their rural counterparts, urban hospital administrators are more likely to employ this strategy because there may be other alternatives for the service in their metropolitan area. Although overall capacity for the service is reduced, the community does not lose the service completely. Conversely, in rural areas, the hospital may be the sole provider of that service in the geographic area. This reality may encourage rural hospital administrators to maintain services when faced with low (or even negative) margins.

With the exception of trauma care, we did not find a strong association between the uninsured rate and the availability of high-tech services. A possible explanation is that uninsured persons do not have good access to elective hospital services. For some of these high-tech services, particularly when provided on an outpatient basis, patients need a physician referral. For the most part, uninsured patients will only get referred to these services if they are admitted to the hospital through the emergency room and the hospital-assigned physician orders the services. Consequently, hospitals are better able to control their patient mix by source of payment for their high-tech services. This ensures that these services will not incur losses due to high demand from uninsured patients. Of the high-tech services in our study, only trauma units and to some extent burn units do not present this access problem for the uninsured. Because trauma care patients are emergent and their admission is not discretionary or readily controlled by hospital policies, trauma units can incur losses due to large volumes of uninsured patients. Hospital administrators must take this into account in deciding whether to offer trauma care. Hence, the availability of trauma care is sensitive to the uninsured rate.

Notwithstanding these inconsistencies and limitations in the analysis, in this analysis, we find robust associations between MSA uninsured rates and availability of psychiatric and alcohol and substance abuse services. We find this association in our MSA- and hospital-level analyses of beds and services. We find some evidence of an association of uninsured rates and the provision of trauma services and community outreach services by hospitals and weaker evidence of an impact on burn services and Meals on Wheels. The common feature of these services (with the exception of Meals on Wheels services) is that they have the potential to bring into the hospital uninsured patients whose care may be expensive. The presence of higher numbers of uninsured persons in a market may discourage hospitals from offering services for fear that they will not be reimbursed for a significant portion of the care they provide.

ADDENDUM
85 LARGEST U.S. METROPOLITAN STATISTICAL AREAS

Akron, OH
Albany, NY
Albuquerque, NM
Allentown, PA
Ann Arbor, MI
Atlanta, GA
Austin-San Marcos, TX
Bakersfield, CA
Baltimore, MD
Bergen-Passaic, NJ
Birmingham, AL
Boston, MA-NH
Buffalo-Niagara, NY
Charlotte, NC-SC
Chicago, IL
Cincinnati, OH-KY-IN
Cleveland, OH
Columbus, GA-AL
Columbus, OH
Dallas, TX
Dayton, OH
Denver, CO
Detroit, MI
El Paso, TX
Fort Lauderdale, FL
Fort Worth, TX
Fresno, CA
Grand Rapids, MI
Greensboro, NC

Greenville, SC
Harrisburg, PA
Hartford, CT
Honolulu, HI
Houston, TX
Indianapolis, IN
Jacksonville, FL
Jersey City, NJ
Kansas City, MO-KS
Knoxville, TN
La Vegas, NV-AZ
Los Angeles, CA
Louisville, KY-IN
Memphis, TN-AR-MS
Miami, FL
Middlesex, NJ
Milwaukee, WI
Minneapolis, MN-WI
Monmouth, NJ
Nashville, TN
Nassau-Suffolk, NY
New Orleans, LA
New York, NY
Newark, NJ
Norfolk, VA-NC
Oakland, CA
Oklahoma City, OK
Omaha, NE-IA
Orange County, CA

Orlando, FL
Philadelphia, PA-NJ
Phoenix-Mesa, AZ
Pittsburgh, PA
Portland, OR-WA
Providence, RI-MA
Raleigh, NC
Richmond, VA
Riverside-San Bernardino, CA
Rochester, NY
Sacramento, CA
Salt Lake City, UT
San Antonio, TX
San Diego, CA
San Francisco, CA
San Jose, CA
Seattle, WA
St. Louis, MO-IL
Syracuse, NY
Tacoma, WA
Tampa, FL
Tucson, AZ
Tulsa, AZ
Ventura, CA
Washington, DC-MD-VA-WV
West Palm Beach, FL
Youngstown, OH

The Impact of Uninsured Discharges on the Availability of Hospital Services and Hospital Margins in Rural Areas

Jack Needleman and Darrell J. Gaskin

ABSTRACT

Objective: To identify the effects of the percentage of uninsured persons in a rural community on the availability of hospital services for the entire community.

Data and Study Design: Our analysis focuses on rural counties in seven states: CA, MA, NJ, NY, PA, WA, and WI. We use data on state hospital discharges for 1991, 1994, and 1996 to calculate the proportion of discharges of county residents that were either self-pay or charity care. Data from the Medicare Cost Reports and American Hospital Association's (AHA) Survey of Hospitals were used to estimate the impact of the uninsured rate on hospital margins and four measures of hospital service availability, i.e., capacity, services to vulnerable populations, community services, and high-tech services. We estimate county-level models.

Findings: We find some evidence that in counties with higher proportions of uninsured patients who are not concentrated in a subset of hospitals, hospitals are less likely to offer psychiatric inpatient services. We also find some evidence that there are fewer intensive care unit (ICU) and psychiatric beds. There is a consistent association of higher uninsured admissions and a lower likelihood of hospitals offering high-technology services, although the association is statistically significant only for transplant, magnetic resonance imaging (MRI), radiation therapy, and lithotripsy (ESWL) services. There is strong evidence that hospital margins are lower in counties with higher proportions of uninsured discharges.

Conclusion: Admissions of uninsured patients in rural counties are associated with lower hospital financial status and less availability of psychiatric and high-technology services.

INTRODUCTION

Prior research has shown that the lack of health insurance coverage is a barrier to care for the uninsured and can lead to negative health outcomes. The uninsured receive about two-thirds of the care obtained by comparable insured population (Long and Marquis, 1994; Marquis and Long, 1994-1995). However, little is known about how the presence of uninsured persons affects the health care delivery system in their communities. According to the AHA, hospitals provided over $18 billion in uncompensated care in 1997. Most of this care was provided as charity to low-income persons who lacked health insurance coverage (Weissman et al., 1999). Providing hospital care to patients who are inadequately insured can be a financial burden to hospitals. This financial stress could affect hospitals' ability to deliver services to the broader community. Needleman (2000) identifies three ways this financial stress could affect hospitals care for the entire community: (1) cutbacks in services, (2) reductions in quality, and (3) closures of facilities. In particular, he argues that hospitals that are faced with a high demand for charity care may respond by reducing staff, cutting back hours, increasing waiting times and eliminating services. Potentially these types of changes can affect the hospitals' ability to provide high-quality services. Theoretically, it follows that if the financial stress due to high demand for charity care is great enough, hospitals would eventually have to close due to a lack of resources.

In the 1980s, approximately 700 hospitals closed. While there have been numerous studies on the determinants of hospital closures, none have examined the role of hospital's payer mix or community uninsurance. However, researchers have found a relationship between hospital closures and three community characteristics that are correlated with high uninsured rates: the percentage of residents who are low-income or minority and high unemployment rates.

In a similar study that focuses on hospitals in the 85 largest metropolitan statistical areas (MSAs) during the 1990s, we present evidence that high uninsured rates were associated with reductions in hospital services. The uninsured rate was negatively related to beds per capita in the MSA and the average hospital size. In addition, the availability of services for vulnerable populations and community services and the propensity for hospitals to offer these services was negatively associated with the uninsured rate.

In this study, we examine the effect of uninsurance on rural hospitals. In 1999, 18.9 percent of residents of rural areas lacked health insurance coverage

(NCHS, 2001). How does their presence affect the availability of hospital services in rural areas? Similar to urban hospitals, we expect the overall effect to be negative. However, there should be some differences. When faced with financial pressure, rural hospital administrators may try to offer a full range of services to meet the broad needs of their communities because residents have few alternatives. In contrast, urban hospital administrators may be more likely to maintain niche "specialty" services in the face of financial pressure because there are more alternatives in their communities for basic or routine hospital services.

Detailed data on the number of uninsured persons or the uninsured rate at the county or hospital market level are not available. (See Appendix B of this report for further discussion of data and measurement issues for local uninsured rates.) As a surrogate for the uninsured rate, we use the proportion of hospital discharges from a county that is uninsured (Rask, 1994; Turner and Campbell, 1999). We examine whether there is an association between the proportion of uninsured hospital discharges among a rural county's residents and lesser availability of hospital services in the county. Our specific research questions are

• Are there fewer hospital beds per capita in rural counties with high proportions of uninsured discharges?
• Does the availability of hospital services for the entire county decline as the proportion of uninsured discharges in the county increases?
• Does the proportion of uninsured discharges negatively affect the financial status of hospitals?
• Does the impact of the proportion of uninsured discharges on the hospital delivery system decline as hospital care for the uninsured become more concentrated in a few hospitals?

CONCEPTUAL FRAMEWORK

As stated above, we hypothesize that the uninsured rate is negatively related to the demand for hospital services. Several studies have shown that market forces that have depressed demand for hospital services have had an impact on the size of the hospital delivery system. For example, Medicare's transition from a cost-based reimbursement system to prospective payment and the subsequent reduction in the growth of Medicare hospital payment rates resulted in lower hospital utilization, a reduction in the intensity of hospital services, and encouraged a reduction in hospital size (Coulam and Gaumer, 1991; Hodgkin and McGuire, 1994). The introduction of managed care also reduced demand for hospital services. Several studies have demonstrated that increased HMO penetration is associated with reduction in hospital utilization, hospital beds, slower hospital cost inflation, and slower revenue growth (Miller and Luft, 1994; Chernew, 1995; Robinson, 1996; Gaskin and Hadley, 1997). Dranove and colleagues (1986) modeled the impact of managed care penetration on hospitals, and they concluded that downward pressure on hospital prices would result in a reduction in hospital capacity.

For simplicity, assume that hospitals serve two types of patients, insured and uninsured, and that every hospital in the market serves each type of patient proportionate to their presence in the hospital market area. Payment rates for treating insured patients are typically greater than average cost. Reimbursement rates for treating uninsured patients are typically less than average cost. If, at the volumes at which the rural hospital operates, the cost structure exhibits increasing returns to scale (e.g., total cost increases with the volume of services at a decreasing rate), cost-minimizing hospitals will operate at volume levels where marginal cost is less than average cost (Folland et al., 2001). In choosing the volume of services they provide, hospitals will equate marginal costs with marginal revenues where average revenues exceed average costs depending upon their market structure (Tirole, 1988). Hospitals that are monopolies or part of oligopolies will set marginal costs equal to marginal revenues. Hospitals that are in monopolistic competitive markets will compete until their average costs equal average revenues (Chamberlin, 1962). In such a market, as the uninsured rate increases, average and marginal revenues at each hospital decline. In response, each hospital will reduce its supply of services. This implies that overall market supply will decline as the overall demand curve shifts downward. Also, because there are more uninsured patients, the need for hospital services at discounted rates (or for free) will increase. As shown in Figure D.1, this results in a downward rotation of the demand curve for hospital services.

In some markets, there are safety-net hospitals that provide a disproportionate share of the care to the uninsured while other hospitals provide less than their proportionate share of the market for uninsured patients. In such a market, an increase in the uninsured rate would have a larger effect on safety-net hospitals than on other hospitals, if the safety-net hospitals absorbed the increase in the demand for care for uninsured patients. However if, as the uninsured rate increases, non–safety net hospitals in the co mmunity become proportionately more involved in the care for the uninsured, then these hospitals will be more affected by the change in demand.

Another assumption implicit in our model is that the uninsured and insured patients use the hospital for the same mix of services. However, suppose there is a set of hospital services that the uninsured are more likely to use than insured patients. Profits for these services will tend to be lower than profits associated with other hospital services because of their payer mix. Therefore, we expect that hospitals will cut back on services that the uninsured are more likely to use as the uninsured rate increases. In rural areas, this will often have a negative spillover effect on insured patients in county. Because rural communities have few alternative providers, insured patients may have to travel long distances to obtain services dropped by their local hospital.

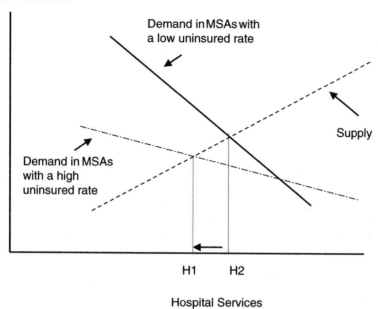

FIGURE D.1 The impact of uninsurance rate on the demand and supply of hospital services.

DATA

Data for this study come from four sources:

- state hospital discharge data from seven states
- the AHA Annual Survey of Hospitals
- the Medicare Cost Reports and
- the Area Resource File compiled by the Bureau of Health Professions

We used hospital discharge data from California, Massachusetts, New Jersey, New York, Pennsylvania, Washington, and Wisconsin for 1991, 1994, and 1996. These states were chosen because they distinguished whether patients' expected source of payment was self pay or charity care.

Our analysis focuses on the availability of hospital services in 168 rural counties in our seven states: 23 counties in California, 25 in Florida, 2 in Massachusetts, 21 in New York, 29 in Pennsylvania and 23 in Washington and 45 in Wisconsin. We defined rural counties as those that were not located within an MSA. Of the 168 counties, 56 percent have only one hospital and 69 percent were located

TABLE D.4 Comparison of Counties Included in Analysis to All U.S. Rural Counties

	Sample	U.S.
Number	168	2,369
Average County Population, 1997	46,229	22,250
Population Density (people per square mile)	55.9	44.1
Per Capita Income, 1998	$20,748	$18,917
Poverty Rate (percent), 1997	13.5	16.0
Percent Adjacent to Metropolitan Area	69.6	43.4

adjacent to an MSA. As shown in Table D.4, compared to U.S. rural counties as a whole, the counties included in this analysis have larger populations, are more densely populated, have somewhat higher per capita income, and are more likely to be adjacent to metropolitan areas.

We identified patients from rural counties using their county of residence information in the discharge database. For each rural county, we calculated the proportion of discharges originating in that county where the expected sources of payment were self-pay or charity, Medicaid, Medicare, or HMO. For ease of exposition, we refer to these proportions as the county's percent of uninsured discharges, Medicaid discharges, Medicare discharges, and HMO discharges, respectively. We used these measures as proxies for the rate of insurance coverage for hospital care in the county. The percentage of uninsured discharges indicates the amount of inpatient services provided to uninsured persons relative to the entire inpatient market. This is a reasonable proxy for uninsured persons' share of the demand for hospital services.

To measure the availability of hospital services, we used data from the AHA Survey of Hospitals for the years 1991, 1994, and 1996. We used four measures of hospital service availability: hospital capacity, services to vulnerable populations, community services, and high-tech services. To measure capacity we used the number of hospital beds, medical-surgical beds, psychiatric beds, ICU beds, and beds devoted to patients diagnosed with alcoholism, drug abuse, or chemical dependency. Five services for vulnerable populations were examined: psychiatric outpatient services, psychiatric emergency room services, psychiatric inpatient services, outpatient and rehabilitation services for persons diagnosed with alcoholism, drug abuse, or chemical dependency, and services for patients diagnosed with HIV-AIDS. Eight high-tech services were examined. Three require investments in beds, in addition to equipment and personnel: trauma center, neonatal intensive care unit (NICU), and transplant services. Five involve investments in equipment and personnel: magnetic resonance imaging (MRI), radiation therapy, angioplasty, single photo emission computerized tomography (SPECT), and extracorporeal shock-wave lithotripsy (ESWL). Three community services were examined: community outreach centers, transportation services, and Meals on Wheels. We have data on these services for 1994 and 1996 only because the AHA did not collect this information in 1991. For each of the 16 services, we create a variable that indicates whether the hospital or one of its subsidiaries provided the service. If the hospital indicated that it provided the service locally through a partner in its health system, network, or a joint venture, we did not designate this hospital as a provider of the service. This eliminated some double counting. To measure hospital financial status, we used hospital margins calculated from the Medicare Cost Reports.

In our analyses, we are specifically interested in how the relative concentration of uninsured discharges affects the availability of hospital services. To measure the relative concentration of uninsured discharges we calculated two Herfindahl indexes, which equal the sum of the squares of the market shares. The first measures the concentration of *all* hospital discharges in the county and the second measures the concentration of *uninsured* discharges in the county. We then divided the Herfindahl index for uninsured discharges by the Herfindahl index for all discharges. In counties where this ratio equals one, the uninsured discharges are no more concentrated within a subset of hospitals than are all discharges. In counties where this ratio exceeds one, the uninsured discharges are more concentrated than all discharges. This is an indication that one or a few hospitals in area have assumed a disproportionate role in providing these counties' safety-net services. We include in our regression the main effect of percent uninsured, main effect of the concentration ratio, and the interaction of the concentration ratio with percent uninsured. Our hypothesis is that the county-level effect of the uninsured percentage will be smaller where the uninsured are concentrated.

We examine the interaction of this ratio with the county's percentage uninsured discharges to determine whether relative concentration dampens the effect of uninsured discharges on the availability of hospital services. To facilitate the interpretation of the coefficients on the percentage of uninsured discharges, the main effect of the relative concentration ratio, and the interaction term, we centered the relative concentration ratio on its mean. We examine the overall effect of percent of uninsured discharges in counties with low and high concentration of uninsured discharges by summing the coefficient on the percent uninsured discharges with the product of the coefficient on the interaction term and relative concentration ratio evaluated at the three distinct points. Specifically, we interpreted the effects of uninsured discharges at the 25th percentile (counties where the uninsured discharges are dispersed relative to all discharges), at the mean (which is equivalent to the main effect of the percent uninsured measure), and the 75th percentile (counties where the uninsured are concentrated relative to all discharges).

In addition, we controlled for three other health care market factors. To control for the level of hospital competition, we used the Herfindahl index for all discharges. We use the HCFA wage index as a measure of cost and population density as a measure of overall demand adjusted for geographic convenience (Porell and Adams, 1995).

METHODS

To address our research questions, we analyzed three sets of variables: hospital beds, hospital services, and hospital margins.

Beds

We regressed beds per capita in each county in the following categories: total beds, medical–surgical beds, beds in ICUs, psychiatric inpatient beds, and beds for treatment of alcohol and chemical dependency, on the percent of uninsured discharges in the county, relative concentration of uninsured, other county characteristics (i.e., percent Medicaid discharges, percent Medicare discharges, percent HMO discharges, level of hospital competition, hospital wage index, and population density), and year categorical variables to control for fixed time effects. We estimated these models using generalized least squares with robust standard errors, controlling for clustering at the county level. We gave greater weight to larger counties by using the average county population as a weight in the regression analysis.

Services

We regressed the proportion of hospitals offering specific services on the percent of uninsured discharges in the county, relative concentration of uninsured, and the other county- level variables described above. Because this formulation of the dependent variable does not distinguish the size of the service, we estimated a second set of models using a weighted proportion of hospitals offering specific services. To give larger hospitals offering the specific services more importance, we recalculated this dependent variable using hospital beds as weights. In both regressions, we estimated these models with robust standard errors, and controlled for clustering at the county level. Results from both models are comparable, and we report results only from the weighted regression.

Margin

To determine whether the percentage of uninsured discharges negatively affects the financial status of hospitals, we estimated a model with aggregate margin as the dependent variable. The aggregate margin is a measure used by MedPAC to characterize the financial health of a category of hospitals. It equals total hospital revenues in the county minus total hospital expenses in the county divided by total revenues. The independent variables were the percent of uninsured discharges in the county, the percents Medicaid and Medicare discharges, the percents of public and for-profit hospitals in the county, hospital wage index, population density, and year categorical variables to control for fixed time effects.

RESULTS

Means and standard deviations for the percent of discharges for uninsured patients, beds per 100,000 population, the proportion of hospitals offering each service, (unweighted) percentage of beds in hospitals with each service (weighted), and county-level hospital margins for the rural counties in this analysis are presented in Table D.5. The regression coefficients on the proportion of discharges for the uninsured and the interaction of the percentage of uninsured and uninsured concentration ratios for the regressions on beds, services, and margins are presented in Table D.6. Table D.6 also includes the coefficient on percent uninsured at the 25th and 75th percentile of the relative concentration index and the statistical significance of these coefficients.

Proportion of Uninsured

The proportion of discharges for patients without insurance in the rural counties studied averaged 4.4 percent. This is substantially lower than the percent of uninsured in rural counties, and reflects the fact that the uninsured are younger than the average person in the population and therefore less likely to be hospitalized. (Persons over age 65, virtually all of whom have coverage through Medicare, are disproportionately represented among hospital discharges.) The variation in the proportion of discharges from the uninsured is very large. The standard deviation for the proportion of uninsured is 4.4, as large as the mean, with a range from 0 to 8.8 percent.

Beds

In the 168 counties in this study, there are an average of 423.3 hospital beds per 100,000 population, with wide variation across the counties (standard deviation = 392.3). The average number of beds per capita and variation in beds is larger among these rural counties than was observed in metropolitan areas (Gaskin and Needleman, 2003). Forty-four percent are medical or surgical beds. ICU beds represent only 4 percent of the beds. There are fewer psychiatric and alcohol and chemical dependence beds (10.0 and 4.2 beds per 100,000, respectively) with wide variation across the counties.

There is some evidence that beds per capita are influenced by the percent uninsured in the county. The coefficients on the percent uninsured are consistently negative, although statistically significant only for ICU beds. There is a statistically significant association of ICU beds with percent uninsured at all three levels of uninsured concentration tested. In addition, for psychiatric beds there is a statistically significant association of percent uninsured and bed supply at low levels of concentration of the uninsured (see Table D.6).

TABLE D.5 Means and Standard Deviations for Percent Uninsured Discharges and Dependent Variables

Variable	Unweighted			Weighted		
	N	Mean	SD	N	Mean	SD
Percent Uninsured Discharges	426	4.4	4.4			
Beds per 100,000 Population						
Total	422	423.3	392.3			
Medical-Surgical	396	186.8	146.5			
ICU	396	17.8	22.1			
Psychiatric	396	10.0	19.1			
Alcohol and chemical dependence	396	4.2	16.0			
		%	%		%	%
Services for Vulnerable Populations						
Psychiatric inpatient	396	21.7	37.2	396	23.7	39.0
Psychiatric emergency	396	35.1	43.7	396	37.4	44.9
Psychiatric outpatient	396	15.7	33.5	396	16.5	34.5
Alcohol and chemical dependence	396	17.3	33.1	396	17.7	34.1
AIDS	400	39.6	44.1	396	42.4	45.9
High-Technology Services						
Trauma	396	16.1	33.4	396	16.6	34.1
NICU	426	2.7	12.9	422	3.7	16.7
Transplant	400	6.0	21.8	396	6.4	22.8
MRI	396	20.1	36.0	396	21.3	37.4
Radiation therapy	400	13.4	29.9	396	15.5	32.6
Angioplasty	396	3.6	16.0	396	4.5	18.5
SPECT	396	20.6	36.6	396	21.6	37.8
ESWL	396	6.6	21.9	396	7.4	23.8
Community Services						
Community outreach	258	51.8	44.4	258	52.5	45.1
Transportation	258	9.9	25.0	258	10.5	27.1
Meals on Wheels	258	18.9	35.2	258	18.5	35.8
Margin	414	1.8	5.9	410	2.0	5.8

Services for Vulnerable Populations

With respect to services for vulnerable populations, AIDS services are the most common, with nearly 40 percent of hospitals (with 42.4 percent of the beds) offering these services. Psychiatric emergency services are available in approximately 35 percent of hospitals (with 37 percent of beds), while psychiatric inpatient, outpatient, and alcohol and chemical dependence treatment are available in approximately one-in-five to one-in-six hospitals.

For all services for vulnerable populations except AIDS services, the coefficient on percent uninsured, although not statistically significant, is negative. For both psychiatric inpatient and psychiatric emergency services there is a statistically significant association of the interaction of the uninsured concentration and percent uninsured on the proportion of hospitals offering this service. At the lower level of concentration, there is a statistically significant association of percent uninsured with availability of inpatient psychiatric services.

High-Technology Services

Bed-based high-technology services (trauma, NICU, and transplant) are much less commonly available than services for vulnerable populations, with the proportion of hospitals offering such services varying from 16.1 percent for trauma to 2.7 percent for NICU.

Among these three services, transplant services are less likely to be available in communities with lower concentrations of uninsured and higher uninsured rates. For trauma and NICU services, while the coefficients on percent uninsured are negative, they are not statistically significant.

High-technology services that do not have dedicated beds associated with them vary in their availability in these rural counties. The two imaging services studied—MRI and SPECT—are available in approximately 20 percent of hospitals. Radiation therapy is available in one out of seven hospitals. Lithotripsy and angioplasty are available in relatively few hospitals (6.6 and 3.6 percent of hospitals, respectively). With the exception of SPECT, there is a negative association between these services and the percent uninsured in the county. The association with percent uninsured is statistically significant for MRI and lithotripsy services across the range of uninsured concentrations and statistically significant for radiation therapy when the concentration of the uninsured is low.

Community Services

Community outreach services were available from approximately half the hospitals in our sample. By contrast, Meals on Wheels services were only available from 19 percent and transportation services from only 10 percent. Provision of Meals on Wheels services was negatively associated with percent uninsured in counties where the concentration of uninsured were low.

Hospital Margins

The average county hospital margin in our sample is 1.8 percent, with a standard deviation of 5.9 percentage points, reflecting the substantial variation across counties in margins. We observe statistically significant associations between

TABLE D.6 Regression Coefficients of Beds, Services, and Margin on Percent Uninsured and Interaction of Percent Uninsured With Uninsured Concentration, County-Level Regressions (Weighted)

Variable	N	Percent Uninsured	SE
Beds per Capita			
Total	411	−2.31	(3.08)
Medical-Surgical	411	−1.80	(1.18)
ICU	386	−0.45[a]	(0.22)
Psychiatric	386	−0.37	(0.21)
Alcohol and chemical dependence	386	−0.17	(0.12)
Services for Vulnerable Populations			
Psychiatric inpatient	386	−0.91	(0.59)
Psychiatric emergency	386	−0.77	(0.63)
Psychiatric outpatient	386	−0.67	(0.46)
Alcohol and chemical dependence	386	−0.16	(0.54)
AIDS	389	0.71	(0.90)
High-Technology Services			
Trauma	386	−0.85	(0.57)
NICU	411	−0.35	(0.30)
Transplant	386	−0.49	(0.28)
MRI	386	−1.67[c]	(0.51)
Radiation therapy	389	−0.90	(0.51)
Angioplasty	386	−0.43	(0.27)
SPECT	386	0.61	(0.84)
ESWL	386	−0.91[a]	(10.36)
Community Services			
Community outreach	255	−0.48	(0.70)
Transportation	255	0.22	(0.56)
Meals on Wheels	255	−0.58	(0.51)
Margin	402	−0.17[b]	(0.06)

[a] $p<0.05$
[b] $p<0.01$
[c] $p<0.001$

Percent Uninsured × Uninsured Concentration	SE	25th Percentile of Uninsured Concentration	75th Percentile of Uninsured Concentration
0.56	(1.07)	−2.75	−2.15
1.10	(0.50)[a]	−2.66	−1.48
0.11	(0.07)	−0.54[a]	−0.42[a]
0.34	(0.07)[c]	−0.64[a]	−0.28
0.10	(0.05)	−0.25	−0.14
0.60	(0.18)[c]	−1.38[a]	−0.73
0.64	(0.22)[b]	−1.28	−0.59
0.03	(0.14)	−0.69	−0.66
0.00	(0.20)	−0.16	−0.16
0.04	(0.30)	0.68	0.73
0.18	0.19	−1.00	−0.80
0.15	(0.12)	−0.46	−0.30
0.60	(0.08)[c]	−0.96[b]	−0.32
0.41	(0.17)[a]	−1.99[c]	−1.56[b]
0.66	(0.18)[c]	−1.41[a]	−0.71
−0.10	(0.11)	−0.35	−0.46
−0.11	(0.30)	0.69	0.57
0.18	(0.12)	−1.04[a]	−0.86[a]
1.13	0.85	−1.37	−0.16
−0.19	(0.37)	0.37	0.16
0.88	(0.67)	−1.27[a]	−0.33
0.07	(0.02)[b]	−0.22[b]	−0.15[a]

NOTES: Regressions of beds and services include percent county Medicaid, percent county Medicare, percent county HMO, Herfindahl index, ratio of uninsured Herfindahl index to total Herfindahl index, population density, CMS wage index, and dummies for years 1994 and 1996. Regressions of margin include percent county Medicaid, percent county Medicare, percent county HMO, percent hospitals in county for-profit, percent hospitals in county public, Herfindahl index, ratio of uninsured Herfindahl index to total Herfindahl index (the uninsured concentration), county population density, and dummies for years 1994, 1996, and 1999.

higher proportions of uninsured admissions and lower margins across the range of uninsured concentrations.

DISCUSSION

In this analysis of hospitals in rural counties, we find some evidence that in counties with higher proportions of uninsured patients and low concentration of these patients across hospitals, hospitals are less likely to offer psychiatric inpatient services. We also find some evidence that there are fewer psychiatric and ICU beds. There is a consistent association of higher uninsured admissions with a lower likelihood of hospitals offering high-technology services, although the association is statistically significant only for transplant, MRI, radiation therapy, and lithotripsy services. There is strong evidence that hospital margins are lower in counties with higher proportions of uninsured admissions.

The findings on beds and services for vulnerable populations generally parallel those in our analysis of metropolitan areas, although in this analysis we find fewer statistically significant associations with bed supply and services for vulnerable populations. Specifically, in the metropolitan analysis, we find statistically significant associations with psychiatric outpatient services, alcohol and chemical dependence services, and beds that we do not observe here.

Likewise, the findings on high technology services are similar, with most services in both samples displaying a negative association with uninsured admissions. However, for only a few services are the associations statistically significant and, with the exception of transplant services, the services for which the associations are statistically significant differ across the two samples.

One feature shared by several of the services for which we observe statistically significant associations with uninsured admissions—inpatient psychiatric services and transplant—is that they have the potential to bring into the hospital uninsured patients whose care may be expensive. The presence of higher numbers of uninsured in a market may discourage hospitals from offering services for fear that they will not be reimbursed for a significant portion of the care they provide.

For some of these services, a statistically significant association is only observed at low levels of concentration of the uninsured among the hospitals serving the county. The fact that we observe higher average rates of offering beds or services when care for the uninsured is more concentrated in counties may reflect strategic interactions among hospitals. This illustrates the variability among rural counties in their capacity to maintain hospital services and the impact of higher uninsured rates on hospitals in these counties. One limitation of this study is that it includes principally rural counties in the north and Pacific west. It should be replicated in a broader cross-section of rural hospitals, especially those in the south and southwest.

In sharp contrast to the findings in metropolitan areas, for rural counties and hospitals we find a consistent association of lower margins to higher uninsured admissions. This may reflect rural hospital administrators' preference to maintain services when faced with low (or even negative) margins. This strategy, while preserving a rural hospital's ability to serve its community in the short-term, has implications for hospital's ability to provide, maintain, and improve services in the future. Because of lower margins, rural hospitals in areas with high uninsured rates may have difficulty maintaining and replacing their physical plant, investing in new technologies, and expanding their scope of services to meet new community health needs. The lower margins may account in part for the lower likelihood of offering specific costly, high-technology services. Lower margins may also affect quality or staffing in ways that are not observable in this analysis.

E

Glossary

Ambulatory Care All types of health services that are provided on an outpatient basis, in contrast to services provided in the home or to inpatients. Although many inpatients may be ambulatory, the term usually implies that the patient must travel to a location to receive services that do not require an overnight stay. Ambulatory care settings may be either mobile (when the facility is capable of being moved to different locations) or fixed (when the person seeking care must travel to a fixed service site). [*]

Ancillary Services Supplemental services, including laboratory, radiology, physical therapy, and inhalation therapy, that are provided in conjunction with medical or hospital care.[*]

Bad Debts Income lost to a provider (or institution) because of the failure of patients to pay amounts owed. Bad debts may sometimes be recovered by increasing charges to paying patients. Some cost-based reimbursement programs reimburse certain bad debts. The impact of the loss of revenue from bad debts may be partially offset for proprietary institutions by the fact that tax is not payable on income not received.[*]

Catchment Area A geographic area defined and served by a health program or institution such as a hospital or community mental health center that is delineated

---

[*]Adapted from the Academy for Health Services Research and Health Policy glossary at http://www.academyhealth.org/publications.glossary.pdf. Accessed February 4, 2002.

on the basis of such factors as population distribution, natural geographic boundaries, and accessibility of transportation. By definition, all residents of the area needing the services of the program are usually eligible for them, although eligibility may depend on additional criteria.*

Charge-to-Cost Ratio The markup on the underlying cost of a service.

Charity Care Generally, physician and hospital services provided to persons who are unable to pay for the cost of services, especially those who are low income, uninsured, and underinsured. A high proportion of the costs of charity care is derived from services for children and pregnant women (e.g., neonatal intensive care). *

Community Health Center (CHC) An ambulatory health care program (defined under section 330 of the Public Health Service Act) usually serving a catchment area that has scarce or nonexistent health services or a population with special health needs; sometimes known as a neighborhood health center. Community health centers attempt to coordinate federal, state, and local resources in a single organization capable of delivering health and related social services to a defined population. Although such a center may not provide all types of health care directly, it usually takes responsibility to arrange all health care services needed by its patient population. *

Contractual Allowance The difference between hospital charges and the amount actually paid by a third-party payer.

Conversion, Hospital Conversion A transaction in which all or part of the assets of a health care organization undergo a shift in ownership status (nonprofit, public, or for-profit) through sale, lease, joint venture, or operating or management agreements. *

Cost-Based Reimbursement Payment made by a health plan or payer to health care providers based on the actual costs incurred in the delivery of care and services to plan beneficiaries. This method of paying providers is still used by some plans; however, cost-based reimbursement is being replaced by prospective payment and other payment mechanisms. *

Cost-Shifting Recouping the cost of providing uncompensated care by increasing revenues from some payer(s) to offset losses and lower net payments from others.

Critical Access Hospital (CAH) A rural hospital designation established by the Medicare Rural Hospital Flexibility Program enacted as part of the Balanced

Budget Act of 1997. Rural hospitals meeting criteria established by their state may apply for CAH status. Designated hospitals are reimbursed based on cost (rather than prospective payment), must comply with federal and state regulations for CAHs, and are exempt from certain hospital staffing requirements. *

Cross-Subsidization Payments made for services rendered to one individual or group are used to cover shortfalls in individual payments for services rendered to another individual or group.

Disproportionate Share Adjustment, Hospital (DSH) A payment adjustment under Medicare's prospective payment system or under Medicaid for hospitals that serve a relatively large volume of low-income patients. *

Federally Qualified Health Center (FQHC) A health center in a medically underserved area that is eligible to receive cost-based Medicare and Medicaid reimbursement and to provide direct reimbursement to nurse practitioners, physician assistants, and certified nurse midwives. Federal legislation creating the FQHC category was enacted in 1989. *

Graduate Medical Education (GME) Medical education after the receipt of the M.D. or equivalent degree, including the education received as an intern, resident (which involves training in a specialty), or fellow, as well as continuing medical education. The Centers for Medicare and Medicaid Services partially finances GME through Medicare direct and indirect payments. *

Health Professions Shortage Area (HPSA) An area or group designated by the U.S. Department of Health and Human Services as having an inadequate supply of health care providers. HPSAs can include (1) an urban or rural geographic area, (2) a population group for which access barriers can be demonstrated to prevent group members from using local providers, or (3) medium- and maximum-security correctional institutions and public or nonprofit private residential facilities. *

High-Risk Pool A subsidized health insurance pool organized by some states as an alternative for individuals who have been denied health insurance because of a medical condition or whose premiums are rated significantly higher than the average due to health status or claims experience. It is commonly operated through an association composed of all health insurers in a state. The Health Insurance Portability and Accountability Act of 1996 allows states to use high-risk pools as an "acceptable alternative mechanism" that satisfies the statutory requirements for ensuring access to health insurance coverage for certain individuals.

Hill-Burton Act Coined from the names of the principal sponsors of P.L. 79-725 (the Hospital Survey and Construction Act of 1946). This program provided federal support for the construction and modernization of hospitals and other health facilities. Hospitals that have received Hill-Burton funds incur an obligation to provide a certain amount of charity care. *

Indigent Care Health services provided to the poor or those unable to pay. Since many indigent patients are not eligible for federal or state programs, the costs which are covered by Medicaid are generally recorded separately from indigent care costs. *

Margins, Operating Revenues from sales minus current costs of goods sold. *

Medically Indigent Persons who cannot afford needed health care because of insufficient income and/or lack of adequate health insurance. *

Medically Underserved Population A population group experiencing a short-age of personal health services that may or may not reside in a Health Professions Shortage Area or be defined by its place of residence. Thus, migrants, American Indians, or the inmates of a prison or mental hospital may constitute such a population. The term is defined and used to give priority for federal assistance (e.g., the National Health Service Corps). *

National Health Service Corps A program administered by the U.S. Depart-ment of Health and Human Services that places physicians and other providers in health professions shortage areas by providing scholarship and loan repayment incentives. Since 1970, Corps members have worked in community health cen-ters, migrant centers, Indian health facilities, and other sites targeting underserved populations. *

Overcrowding, Emergency Department A situation in which the demand for service exceeds the ability to provide care within a reasonable time, causing physicians and nurses to feel too rushed to provide quality care (Derlet and Richards, 2000).

Primary Care The provision of integrated, accessible health care services by clinicians who are accountable for addressing a large majority of personal health care needs, developing a sustained partnership with patients, and practicing in the context of family and community (Donaldson et al., 1996).

Prospective Payment, Prospective Payment System (PPS) Any method of paying hospitals and other health programs in which amounts or rates of payment are established in advance for a defined period (usually a year). Institutions are paid these amounts regardless of the costs they actually incur. These systems of payment are designed to introduce a degree of constraint on charge or cost increases by setting limits on amounts paid during a future period. In some cases, such systems provide incentives for improved efficiency by sharing savings with institutions that perform at lower than anticipated costs. Prospective payment contrasts with the method of payment originally used under Medicare and Medicaid (as well as other insurance programs) in which institutions were reimbursed for actual expenses incurred. [*]

Quality of Care The degree to which health services for individuals and populations increase the likelihood of desired health outcomes and are consistent with current professional knowledge (IOM, 1990, p. 21).

Rural Health Clinic (RHC) A public or private hospital, clinic, or physician practice designated by the federal government as in compliance with the Rural Health Clinics Act (P.L. 95-210). The practice must be located in a medically underserved area or a health professions shortage area and use physician assistants and/or nurse practitioners to deliver services. A rural health clinic must be licensed by the state and provide preventive services. [*]

Rural Health Clinics Act Establishes a reimbursement mechanism to support the provision of primary care services in rural areas. P.L. 95-210 was enacted in 1977 and authorizes the expanded use of physician assistants, nurse practitioners, and certified nurse practitioners; extends Medicare and Medicaid reimbursement to designated clinics; and raises Medicaid reimbursement levels to those set by Medicare. [*]

Social Capital A research construct with either or both cognitive and social structural elements that refers to the stocks of resources available through social relationships, as measured by indicators such as civic engagement, norms of reciprocity, and interpersonal trust (Macinko and Starfield, 2001).

Social Cohesion The degree of perceived or operationalized social connectedness or integration among a group of people, sometimes measured as social capital (see Kawachi and Kennedy, 1997a).

Sole Community Hospital (SCH) A hospital (1) that is more than 50 miles from any similar hospital; (2) 25 to 50 miles from a similar hospital and isolated from it at least one month a year (e.g., by snow), or the exclusive provider of services to at least 75 percent of its service area populations; (3) 15 to 25 miles from any similar hospital and isolated from it at least one month a year; or (4) designated as an SCH under previous rules. The Medicare diagnosis related group (DRG) program makes special optional payment provisions for SCHs, most of which are rural, including providing that their rates are set permanently so that 75 percent of their payment is hospital specific and only 25 percent is based on regional DRG rates. [*]

Specialist A physician, dentist, or other health professional who is specially trained in a certain branch of medicine or dentistry related to specific services or procedures (e.g., surgery, radiology, pathology); certain age categories of patients (e.g., geriatrics); certain body systems (e.g., dermatology, orthopedics, cardiology); or certain types of diseases (e.g., allergy, periodontics). Specialists usually have advanced education and training related to their specialties. *

Specialty Care Services provided by medical specialists who generally do not have first contact with patients (e.g., cardiologists, urologists, dermatologists). In the United States, there has been a trend toward self-referral by patients for these services, rather than referral by primary care providers. *

Tertiary Care Services provided by highly specialized providers (e.g., neurologists, thoracic surgeons, intensive care units). Such services frequently require highly sophisticated equipment and support facilities. The development of these services has largely been a function of diagnostic and therapeutic advances attained through basic and clinical biomedical research. *

Uncompensated Care Service provided by physicians and hospitals for which no payment is received from the patient or from third-party payers. Some costs of these services may be covered through cost shifting. Not all uncompensated care results from charity care. It also includes bad debts from persons who are not classified as charity cases but who are unable or unwilling to pay their bills. *

F

Biographical Sketches

COMMITTEE ON THE CONSEQUENCES OF UNINSURANCE SUBCOMMITTEE ON COMMUNITY EFFECTS OF UNINSURED POPULATIONS

Mary Sue Coleman, Ph.D., *Co-chair,* is president of the University of Michigan. She is professor of biological chemistry in the University of Michigan Medical School and professor of chemistry in the College of Literature, Science and the Arts. She previously was president of the University of Iowa and president of the University of Iowa Health Systems (1995–2002). Dr. Coleman served as provost and vice president for academic affairs at the University of New Mexico (1993–1995) and dean of research and vice chancellor at the University of North Carolina at Chapel Hill (1990–1992). She was both faculty member and Cancer Center administrator at the University of Kentucky in Lexington for 19 years, where her research focused on the immune system and malignancies. Dr. Coleman is a member of the Institute of Medicine (IOM) and a fellow of the American Association for the Advancement of Science. She serves on the Iowa Governor's Strategic Planning Council, the Board of Trustees of the Universities Research Association, the Board of Governors of the Warren G. Magnuson Clinical Center at the National Institutes of Health, and other voluntary advisory bodies and corporate boards.

Arthur L. Kellermann, M.D., M.P.H., *Co-chair,* is professor and director, Center for Injury Control, Rollins School of Public Health, Emory University, and professor and chairman, Department of Emergency Medicine, School of

Medicine, Emory University. Dr. Kellermann has served as principal investigator or co-investigator on several research grants, including federally funded studies of handgun-related violence and injury, emergency cardiac care, and the use of emergency room services. Among many awards and distinctions, he is a fellow of the American College of Emergency Physicians (1992), is the recipient of a meritorious service award from the Tennessee State Legislature (1993) and the Hal Jayne Academic Excellence Award from the Society for Academic Emergency Medicine (1997), and was elected to membership in the Institute of Medicine (1999). In addition, Dr. Kellermann is a member of the Editorial Board of the journal *Annals of Emergency Medicine*, and has served as a reviewer for the *New England Journal of Medicine*, the *Journal of the American Medical Association*, and the *American Journal of Public Health*.

Ronald M. Andersen, Ph.D. is the Fred W. and Pamela K. Wasserman Professor of Health Services and professor of sociology at the University of California at Los Angeles School of Public Health. He teaches courses in health services organization, research methods, evaluation, and leadership. Dr. Andersen received his Ph.D. in sociology at Purdue University. He has studied access to medical care for his entire professional career of 30 years. Dr. Andersen developed the Behavioral Model of Health Services Use that has been used extensively nationally and internationally as a framework for utilization and cost studies of general populations as well as special studies of minorities, low income, children, women, the elderly, oral health, the homeless, and the HIV-positive population. He has directed three national surveys of access to care and has led numerous evaluations of local and regional populations and programs designed to promote access to medical care. Dr. Andersen's other research interests include international comparisons of health services systems, graduate medical education curricula, physician health services organization integration, and evaluations of geriatric and primary care delivery. He is a member of the Institute of Medicine and was on the founding board of the Association for Health Services Research. He has been chair of the Medical Sociology Section of the American Sociological Association. In 1994 he received the association's Leo G. Reeder Award for Distinguished Service to Medical Sociology; in 1996 he received the Distinguished Investigator Award from the Association for Health Services Research; and in 1999 he received the Baxter Allegiance Health Services Research Prize.

John Ayanian, M.D., M.P.P. is associate professor of medicine and health care policy at Harvard Medical School and Brigham and Women's Hospital, where he practices general internal medicine. His research focuses on quality of care and access to care for major medical conditions, including colorectal cancer and myocardial infarction. He has extensive experience in the use of cancer registries to assess outcomes and evaluate the quality of cancer care. In addition, he has studied the effects of race and gender on access to kidney transplants and on quality of care for other medical conditions. Dr. Ayanian is deputy editor of the journal *Medical*

Care, a Robert Wood Johnson Foundation Generalist Physician Faculty Scholar, and a fellow of the American College of Physicians.

David W. Baker, M.D., M.P.H.★ is associate professor of medicine and chief, Division of General Internal Medicine, Feinberg School of Medicine, Northwestern University in Chicago, Illinois. His research has focused on access to health care and health care delivery for vulnerable populations. He is currently principal investigator for a study examining health outcomes for the uninsured among a national sample of adults 51–61 years old in the Health and Retirement Study. He is also principal investigator for a study examining trends in mortality rates for patients hospitalized in northeast Ohio. Other areas of interest include the effect of limited reading ability and language barriers on patients' health care use and the cost-effectiveness of screening patients for early heart disease. He has served on the Cuyahoga County Access to Care Coalition, the Cuyahoga County Community Health Assessment Project, and the Ohio Department of Health State Health Resources Plan Task Force.

Regina M. Benjamin, M.D., M.B.A.★ is associate dean for rural health at the University of South Alabama (USA) in Mobile, Alabama, where she administers the USA-Telehealth and the Alabama-Area Health Education Center programs. In addition, she is a clinical professor at the University of Alabama-Birmingham. She established and operates the Bayou La Batre Rural Health Clinic in Bayou La Batre, Alabama. In 1998 she was the United States recipient of the Nelson Mandela Award for Health and Human Rights. In 1995, Dr. Benjamin was elected to the American Medical Association Board of Trustees, making her the first physician under age 40 and the first African American woman to be elected. She serves on the Board of Physicians for Human Rights, as well as a number of professional and philanthropic boards and commissions. Dr. Benjamin is a diplomate of the American Board of Family Practice and a fellow of the American Academy of Family Physicians. She was a Kellogg National Fellow and a Rockefeller Next Generation Leader. Dr. Benjamin was named by *Time Magazine* as one of the "Nation's 50 Future Leaders Age 40 and Under." She was featured in a *New York Times* article, "Angel in a White Coat," "Person of the Week" on ABC's *World News Tonight* with Peter Jennings, "Woman of the Year" by *CBS This Morning,* and on the December 1999 cover of *Clarity Magazine*. She previously served as a member of the Committee on Cancer Research Among Minorities and the Medically Underserved.

Robert J. Blendon, M.B.A., Sc.D. is currently professor of health policy and political analysis at both the Harvard School of Public Health and the John F. Kennedy School of Government and has received outstanding teaching awards

---

★Member, Subcommittee on the Community Effects of Uninsured Populations.

from both institutions. He also directs the Harvard Opinion Research Program and the Henry J. Kaiser National Program on the Public, Health and Social Policy, which focuses on the better understanding of public knowledge, attitudes, and beliefs about major domestic public policy issues. Dr. Blendon also co-directs the Washington Post-Kaiser Family Foundation (KFF) survey project, which was nominated for a Pulitzer Prize, and a new project for National Public Radio and KFF on American attitudes toward health and social policy, which was cited by the *National Journal* as setting a new standard of public opinion surveys in broadcast journalism. From 1987 to 1996, Dr. Blendon served as chair of the Department of Health Policy and Management at the Harvard School of Public Health and as deputy director of the Harvard University Division of Health Policy Research and Education. Prior to his Harvard appointment, Dr. Blendon was senior vice president at The Robert Wood Johnson Foundation. He was senior editor of a three-volume series, *The Future of American Health Care,* and is a member of the Institute of Medicine, the advisory committee to the director of the Centers for Disease Control and Prevention, and the editorial board of the *Journal of the American Medical Association.* Dr. Blendon is a graduate of Marietta College and received his master's of business administration and doctoral degrees from the University of Chicago and the Johns Hopkins School of Public Health, respectively.

Sheila P. Davis, B.S.N., M.S.N., Ph.D. is associate professor, Department of Adult Health, in the School of Nursing at the University of Mississippi Medical Center. She is also vice president of Davis, Davis & Associates, a health management consultant company. Her research focuses on minority health issues, especially cardiovascular risk among ethnic populations. Dr. Davis is the founder and chair of the Cardiovascular Risk Reduction in Children Committee at the University of Mississippi. This is a multidisciplinary committee (physicians, nurses, dietician, health educator, college administrator, nurse practitioners, etc.) committed to reducing cardiovascular risks in children. Dr. Davis is a member of the American Nurses' Association and has written numerous publications on the profession and the experiences of ethnic minorities in the health professions. She is author of a faith-based program Healthy Kid's Seminar, which is used to promote adoption of healthy life-style choices by children.

George C. Eads, Ph.D. is vice president of Charles River Associates (CRA), Washington, D.C., office and is an internationally known expert in the economics of the automotive and airlines industries. Prior to joining CRA, Dr. Eads was vice president and chief economist at General Motors Corporation. He frequently represented the corporation before congressional committees and federal regulatory agencies. He has served as a member of the President's Council of Economic Advisers and as a special assistant to the assistant attorney general in the Antitrust Division of the U.S. Department of Justice. Dr. Eads has published numerous books and articles on the impact of government on business and has taught at several major universities, including Harvard and Princeton.

Sandra R. Hernández, M.D. is chief executive officer (CEO) of The San Francisco Foundation, a community foundation serving the five Bay Area counties. It is one of the largest community foundations in the country. Dr. Hernández is a primary care internist who previously held a number of positions within the San Francisco Department of Public Health, including director of the AIDS Office, director of community public health, county health officer, and finally director of health for the City and County of San Francisco. She was appointed to and served on President Clinton's Advisory Commission on Consumer Protection and Quality in the Healthcare Industry. Among the many honors and awards bestowed on her, Dr. Hernandez was named by *Modern Healthcare* magazine as one of the top ten health care leaders for the next century. Dr. Hernández is a graduate of Yale University, Tufts School of Medicine, and the JFK School of Government at Harvard University. She is on the faculty of University of California at San Francisco School of Medicine and maintains an active clinical practice at San Francisco General Hospital in the AIDS Clinic.

Ichiro Kawachi, M.D., Ph.D. is director of the Harvard Center for Society and Health at the Harvard School of Public Health, where he also holds an appointment as associate professor of health and social behavior. Dr. Kawachi's current research ranges from the psychosocial predictors of health and illness (job stress, social networks and support, and psychological factors) to the investigation of more distal societal influences on population health (income distribution, social capital, and gender inequality). Dr. Kawachi is the recipient of a Robert Wood Johnson Investigator Award in Health Policy Research for his work on income distribution, social capital, and health. He recently coedited the first textbook on social epidemiology as well as a reader on income inequality and health. Dr. Kawachi is a member of the Research Advisory Committee of the Pan American Health Organization–WHO, and also acted as a consultant to the World Bank on social capital and health. For the past three years, he has served as a core member of the MacArthur Foundation Network on Socioeconomic Status and Health. Dr. Kawachi is also senior editor of the international journal *Social Science & Medicine*.

Ronda Kotelchuck, M.R.P. is executive director of the Primary Care Development Corporation (PCDC), a public–private partnership initiative to build primary care centers in New York City's underserved communities. Prior to PCDC, she worked for the New York City Health and Hospitals Corporation (HHC) where, as vice president for corporate planning and intergovernmental

---

*Member, Subcommittee on the Community Effects of Uninsured Populations.

relations, she spearheaded HHC's 1989 strategic plan, financial restructuring, and Communicare program, a city initiative that expanded community-based primary care. Ms. Kotelchuck previously worked for the New York City Financial Control Board and the Greater Boston Health Systems Agency. She speaks and has written broadly on health care topics. She is a fellow of the New York Academy of Medicine. Ms. Kotelchuck received her B.A. from Lewis and Clark College and her M.R.P. from Cornell University.

Willard G. Manning, Ph.D. is professor in the Department of Health Studies, Pritzker School of Medicine, and in the Harris School of Public Policy, at the University of Chicago. His primary research focus has been the effects of health insurance and alternative delivery systems on the use of health services and health status. He is an expert in statistical issues in cost-effectiveness analysis and small area variations. His recent work has included examination of mental health services use and outcomes in a Medicaid population, and cost-effectiveness analysis of screening and treating depression in primary care. Dr. Manning is a member of the Institute of Medicine.

James J. Mongan, M.D. is president and CEO of Partners HealthCare, Inc. and was previously president of Massachusetts General Hospital. Dr. Mongan served as assistant surgeon general in the Department of Health and Human Services, as former associate director for health and human resources, Domestic Policy Staff, the White House; and as former deputy assistant secretary for health policy, Department of Health, Education and Welfare. Dr. Mongan is chair of the Task Force on the Future of Health Insurance for Working Americans, a nonpartisan effort of the Commonwealth Fund to address the implications of the changing U.S. workforce and economy for the availability and affordability of health insurance, is a member of the Kaiser Family Foundation Board and the Kaiser Commission on the Medicaid and the Uninsured.

Keith Mueller, Ph.D.★ is director of the Nebraska Center for Rural Health Research and a professor in the Department of Preventive and Societal Medicine (section chief, Health Services Research and Rural Health Policy) at the University of Nebraska Medical Center. Dr. Mueller's doctoral training is in political science, with additional post-doctorate training in health services research. He was the 1996–1997 President of the National Rural Health Association and is a member of the Health Delivery Panel of the Rural Policy Research Institute. His research interests include policy analysis, access to care among the uninsured, and managed care.

★Member, Subcommittee on the Community Effects of Uninsured Populations.

Christopher Queram, M.A.* has been CEO of the Employer Health Care Alliance Cooperative (The Alliance) of Madison, Wisconsin, since 1993. The Alliance is a purchasing cooperative owned by more than 175 member companies that contracts with providers, manages and reports data, performs consumer education, and designs employer and provider quality initiatives. Prior to his current position, Mr. Queram served as vice president for programs at Meriter Hospital, a 475-bed hospital in Madison. Mr. Queram is a member of the Board of the National Business Coalition on Health and served as board chair for the past two years. He was a member of the President's Advisory Commission on Consumer Protection and Quality in the Health Care Industry. Mr. Queram served as a member of the Planning Committee for the National Quality Forum and continues as convenor of the Purchaser Council of the Forum. He is a member of the Wisconsin Board on Health Information and the Board of the Wisconsin Private Employer Health Care Coverage program. He holds a master's degree in health services administration from the University of Wisconsin at Madison and is a fellow in the American College of Healthcare Executives.

Shoshanna Sofaer, Ph.D. is the Robert P. Luciano Professor of Health Care Policy at the School of Public Affairs, Baruch College, in New York City. She completed her master's and doctoral degrees in public health at the University of California, Berkeley; taught for six years at the University of California, Los Angeles School of Public Health; and served on the faculty of George Washington University Medical Center, where she was professor, associate dean for Research of the School of Public Health and Health Services, and director of the Center for Health Outcomes Improvement Research. Dr. Sofaer's research interests include providing information to individual consumers on the performance of the health care system; assessing the impact of information on both consumers and the system; developing consumer-relevant performance measures; and improving the responsiveness of the Medicare program to the needs of current and future cohorts of older persons and persons with disabilities. In addition, Dr. Sofaer studies the role of community coalitions in pursuing public health and health care system reform objectives and has extensive experience in the evaluation of community health improvement interventions. She has studied the determinants of health insurance status among the near-elderly, including early retirees. Dr. Sofaer served as co-chair of the Working Group on Coverage for Low Income and Non-Working Families for the White House Task Force on Health Care Reform in 1993. Currently, she is co-chair of the Task Force on Medicare of the Century Foundation in New York City, a member of the IOM Board of Health Care Services, and a member of the Health Systems Study Section of the Agency for Healthcare Research and Quality.

---

*Chair, Subcommittee on the Community Effects of Uninsured Populations.

Mary B. Tierney, M.D.* is senior primary care advisor at the American Institutes for Research in Washington, D.C. She also has hospital privileges at the Children's National Medical Center in Washington, D.C. Dr. Tierney previously was an associate clinical professor of child health and development at the George Washington University School of Medicine. Formerly, she was chair, Department of Pediatrics at the Public Benefits Corporation of the District of Columbia. She is a member of the American Academy of Pediatrics and is featured in Who's Who in American Women. Dr. Tierney's research interests includes clinical child development, special needs children, Medicaid and State Children's Health Insurance Program policy, quality assurance, and public health.

Stephen J. Trejo, Ph.D. is associate professor in the Department of Economics at the University of Texas at Austin. His primary research focus has been in the field of labor economics. He has examined the response of labor market participants to the incentives created by market opportunities, government policies, and the institutional environment. Specific research topics include the economic effects of overtime pay regulation; immigrant labor market outcomes and welfare recipiency; the impact of labor unions on compensation, employment, and work schedules; the importance of sector-specific skills; and the relative economic status of Mexican Americans.

Reed V. Tuckson, M.D.* is senior vice president of Consumer Health and Medical Care Enhancement at United Health Group. Formerly, he was senior vice president, Professional Standards, at the American Medical Association. Dr. Tuckson was President of Charles R. Drew University, School of Medicine and Science from 1991 to 1997. From 1986 to 1990, he was commissioner of public health for the District of Columbia. Dr. Tuckson serves on a number of health care, academic, and federal boards and committees and is a nationally known lecturer on topics concerning community-based medicine, the moral responsibilities of health professionals, and physician leadership. He currently serves on the IOM Roundtable on Research and Development of Drugs, Biologics, and Medical Devices and is a member of the Institute of Medicine.

Edward H. Wagner, M.D., M.P.H., F.A.C.P. is a general internist–epidemiologist and Director of the W.A. (Sandy) MacColl Institute for Healthcare Innovation at the Center for Health Studies (CHS), Group Health Cooperative. He is also professor of health services at the University of Washington School of Public Health and Community Medicine. Current research interests include the development and testing of population-based care models for diabetes, frail elderly, and other chronic illnesses; the evaluation of the health and cost impacts of chronic disease and cancer interventions; and interventions to prevent disability and re-

---

*Member, Subcommittee on the Community Effects of Uninsured Populations.

duce depressive symptoms in older adults. Dr. Wagner has written two books and more than 200 journal articles. He serves on the editorial boards of *Health Services Research* and the *Journal of Clinical Epidemiology* and acts as a consultant to multiple federal agencies and private foundations. He recently completed a stint as senior advisor on managed care initiatives in the Director's Office of the National Institutes of Health. As of June 1998, he directs Improving Chronic Illness Care (ICIC), a national program of The Robert Wood Johnson Foundation. The overall goal of ICIC is to assist health systems improve their care of chronic illness through quality improvement and evaluation, research, and dissemination. Dr. Wagner is also principal investigator of the Cancer Research Network, a National Cancer Institute funded consortium of 10 health maintenance organizations (HMOs) conducting collaborative cancer effectiveness research.

Mary Wakefield, R.N., Ph.D. ★ is Director, Center for Rural Health, at the University of North Dakota and was previously professor and director of the Center for Health Policy, Research, and Ethics at George Mason University. Previously, Dr. Wakefield served as chief of staff for two U.S. senators. During her tenure on Capitol Hill, she co-chaired the Senate Rural Health Caucus Staff Organization. In this capacity, she was directly involved with a wide range of rural health policy issues including recruitment and retention of health care providers, reimbursement, emergency services, telemedicine, rural research, and interdisciplinary education. Dr. Wakefield serves on many health-related advisory boards, and in March 1997, she was appointed to President Clinton's Advisory Commission on Consumer Protection and Quality in the Health Care Industry. Dr. Wakefield previously served as a member of the Committee on Quality of Health Care in America.

Lawrence Wallack, Dr.P.H. is professor of public health and director, School of Community Health, at Portland State University. He is also emeritus professor of public health, University of California, Berkeley. Dr. Wallack's primary interest is in the role of mass communications, particularly the news media, in shaping public health issues. His current research is on how public health issues are framed in print and broadcast news. He is principal author of *Media Advocacy and Public Health: Power for Prevention and News for a Change: An Advocate's Guide to Working with the Media*. He is also co-editor of *Mass Communications and Public Health: Complexities and Conflicts*. Dr. Wallack has published extensively on topics related to prevention, health promotion, and community interventions. Specific content areas of his research and intervention work have included alcohol, tobacco, violence, handguns, sexually transmitted diseases, cervical and breast cancer, affirmative action, suicide, and childhood lead poisoning. Dr. Wallack is a member of the IOM Committee on Communication for Behavior Change in the 21st Century: Improving the Health of Diverse Populations.

★Member, Subcommittee on the Community Effects of Uninsured Populations.

Institute of Medicine Staff

Wilhelmine Miller, M.S., Ph.D. is a senior program officer in the Division of Health Care Services. She served as staff to the Committee on Immunization Finance Policy and Practices, conducting and directing case studies of health care financing and public health services. Prior to joining the IOM, Dr. Miller was an adjunct faculty member in the Departments of Philosophy at Georgetown University and Trinity College, teaching political philosophy, ethics, and public policy. She received her doctorate from Georgetown, with studies and research in bioethics and issues of social justice. In 1994–1995, Dr. Miller was a consultant to the President's Advisory Committee on Human Radiation Experiments. Dr. Miller was a program analyst in the Department of Health and Human Services for 14 years, responsible for policy development and regulatory review in areas including hospital and HMO payment, prescription drug benefits, and child health. Her M.S. from Harvard University is in health policy and management.

Dianne Miller Wolman, M.G.A. joined the Health Care Services Division of the Institute of Medicine in 1999 as a senior program officer. She directed the study that resulted in the IOM report *Medicare Laboratory Payment Policy: Now and in the Future,* released in 2000. Her previous work experience in the health field has been varied and extensive, focused on finance and reimbursement in insurance programs. She came from the U.S. General Accounting Office, where she was a senior evaluator on studies of the Health Care Financing Administration, its management capacity, and its oversight of Medicare contractors. Prior to that, she was a reimbursement policy specialist at a national association representing non-profit providers of long-term care services. Her earlier positions included policy analysis and management in the Office of the Secretary in the Department of Health and Human Services and work with a peer review organization, a governor's task force on access to health care, and a third-party administrator for very large health plans. In addition, she was policy director for a state Medicaid rate-setting commission. She has a bachelor's degree in sociology from Brandeis University and a master's degree in government administration from Wharton Graduate School, University of Pennsylvania.

Lynne Page Snyder, Ph.D., M.P.H. is a program officer in the IOM's Division of Health Care Services. She came to IOM from the U.S. Department of Health and Human Services, where she worked as a public historian, documenting and writing about past federal activities in medicine, health care, and public health. In addition, she has worked for the Social Science Research Council's Committee on the Urban Underclass and served as a graduate fellow at the Smithsonian Institution's National Museum of American History. She has published on twentieth-century health policy, occupational and environmental health, and minority health. Current research interests include long-term care, health literacy, and access to care by low-income seniors. She earned her doctorate in the history and sociology of science from the University of Pennsylvania (1994), working under Rosemary Stevens, and received her M.P.H. from the Johns Hopkins School of Hygiene and Public Health (2000).

Tracy McKay, B.A. is a research associate in the IOM Division of Health Care Services. She has worked on several projects, including the National Roundtable on Health Care Quality; Children, Health Insurance, and Access to Care; Quality of Health Care in America; and a study on non-heart-beating organ donors. She has assisted in the research for the National Quality Report on Health Care Delivery, Immunization Finance Policies and Practices, and Extending Medicare Coverage for Preventive and Other Services and helped develop this project on the consequences of uninsurance from its inception. Ms. McKay received her B.A. in sociology from Vassar College in 1996.

Ryan Palugod, B.S. is a senior program assistant in the IOM Division of Health Care Services. Prior to joining the project staff in 2001, he worked as an administrative assistant with the American Association of Homes, Services for the Aging. He graduated with honors from Towson University with a degree in health care management in 1999.

Consultants to the Committee on the Consequences of Uninsurance

Darrell J. Gaskin, Ph.D. is deputy director of the Center for Health Disparities Solutions and research scientist in the Department of Health Policy and Management at the Johns Hopkins Bloomberg School of Public Health. Prior to joining the Hopkins faculty, he was a research professor at Georgetown University's Institute for Health Care Research and Policy. He is an expert in the areas of access to care for the low-income and uninsured and the health care safety net. Dr. Gaskin is the principal investigator for a study funded by the Commonwealth Fund entitled "The Impact of Managed Care and Medicaid Payment Changes on Urban Safety Net Hospitals." Dr. Gaskin is also involved in the IOM's ongoing study of academic health center hospitals and their missions. He is a staff member of the Commonwealth Fund Task Force on Academic Health Centers. Dr. Gaskin's other research interests include the impact of market forces and public policy on physicians' behavior, hospitals' provision of mental health care and patients' treatment decision making. Dr. Gaskin recently received the Academy of Health Services Research and Health Policy 2002 Article-of-the-Year Award for his *Health Services Research* article entitled, "Are Urban Safety Net Hospitals Losing Low-Risk Medicaid Maternity Patients."

Jack Needleman, Ph.D. is assistant professor of economics and health policy in the Department of Health Policy and Management at Harvard University. Dr. Needleman's research examines the impact of changes in the health care market and regulation on health care providers and consumers. Recent work looks at the future of public hospitals and clinics, the impact of the Balanced Budget Act on safety net hospitals, market change and access to inpatient psychiatric services for Medicaid and uninsured patients, the relationship of nurse staffing and hospital quality, and quality of care for Medicaid beneficiaries with diabetes. Dr. Needleman has done extensive research on nonprofit and for-profit hospitals, including the extent and impact of changes in hospital ownership from nonprofit or public to for-profit corporations. He teaches and conducts program evaluation. Dr. Needleman has a Ph.D. in public policy from Harvard University.

References

Aaron, Henry J. 2002. The Unsurprising Surprise of Renewed Health Care Cost Inflation. *Health Affairs* Web Exclusive: W85-W87.

Academy for Health Services Research and Health Policy. 2000. *Glossary of Terms Commonly Used in Health Care*. Accessed February 4, 2002. Available at: http://www.academyhealth.org/publications.glossary.pdf.

Aldridge, Chris, Danielle David, Arnold Doyle, Jennifer Kates, et al. 2002. National ADAP Monitoring Project. Annual Report. Accessed October 5, 2002. Available at: http://www.atdn.org/access/adap/adap2002.pdf.

Altman, Drew E., and Larry Levitt. 2002. The Sad History of Health Care Cost Containment as Told in One Chart. *Health Affairs* Web Exclusive: W83-W84.

Altman, Lawrence K., and Anahad O'Connor. 2003. Health Officials Fear Local Impact of Smallpox Plan. *New York Times*. Accessed January 6, 2003. Available at: http://nytimes.com/2003/01/05/national/05VACC.html.

Andersen, Ronald. 1995. Revisiting the Behavioral Model and Access to Medical Care: Does It Matter? *Journal of Health and Social Behavior* 36(3):1-10.

Andersen, Ronald, and Lu Ann Aday. 1978. Access to Medical Care in the U.S.: Realized and Potential. *Medical Care* 16(7):533-546.

Andersen, Ronald, and Odin W. Anderson. 1999. National Medical Expenditure Surveys. Genesis and Rationale. Pp. 11-30 in *Informing American Health Care Policy. The Dynamics of Medical Expenditure and Insurance Surveys, 1977-1996*, Alan C. Monheit, Renate Wilson, and Ross H. Arnett, eds. San Francisco: Jossey-Bass.

Andersen, Ronald M., and Pamela Davidson. 2001. Improving Access to Care in America: Individual and Contextual Indicators. In: *Changing the U.S. Health Care System: Key Issues in Health Services, Policy and Management*, Ronald Andersen, Thomas Rice, and Gerald Kominski, eds. San Francisco, CA: Jossey-Bass.

Andersen, Ronald M., Hongjian Yu, Roberta Wyn, Pamela L. Davidson, et al. 2002. Access to Medical Care for Low-Income Persons: How Do Communities Make a Difference? *Medical Care Research and Review* 59(4):384-411.

Andrulis, Dennis, Lisa M. Duchon, and Hailey Maier Reid. 2002. *Healthy Cities, Healthy Suburbs: Progress in Meeting Healthy People Goals for the Nation's 100 Largest Cities and Their Suburbs.* Brooklyn, NY: SUNY Downstate Medical Center.

Ansell, David A., and Robert L. Schiff. 1987. Patient Dumping. Status, Implications, and Policy Recommendations. *Journal of the American Medical Association* 257(11):1500-1502.

Arizona Daily Star. 2002. A Political Emergency. Accessed September 30, 2002. Available at: http://www. azstarnet.com/star/mon/2093editborderhealthcos.html.

Asplin, Brent R., and R.K. Kropp. 2001. A Room with a View: On-Call Specialist Panels and Other Health Policy Challenges in the Emergency Department. *Annals of Emergency Medicine* 37(5):500-503.

Associated Press. 2001. Arizona Lawmakers Approve Bill To Cover Dialysis, Chemotherapy for Undocumented Immigrants. Accessed December 21, 2001. Available at: http://www.kaiser-network.org/daily_reports/ print_report.cfm?DR_ID=8712&dr_cat=3.

Associated Press. 2002. In Face of Overcrowding, Phoenix Emergency Rooms Diverting Patients to Other Facilities. Accessed August 13, 2002. Available at: http://www.kaisernetwork.org/daily_reports/rep_index.cfm?hint=3&DR_ID=12868.

Ayanian, John Z., Betsy A. Kohler, Toshi Abe, and Arnold M. Epstein. 1993. The Relation Between Health Insurance Coverage and Clinical Outcomes Among Women With Breast Cancer. *New England Journal of Medicine* 329(5):326-331.

Ayanian, John Z., Joel S. Weissman, Eric C. Schneider, Jack A. Ginsburg, et al. 2000. Unmet Health Needs of Uninsured Adults in the United States. *Journal of the American Medical Association* 284(16):2061-2069.

Baker, David W., Carl D. Stevens, and Robert H. Brook. 1994. Regular Source of Ambulatory Care and Medical Care Utilization by Patients Presenting to a Public Hospital Emergency Department. *Journal of the American Medical Association* 271(24):1909-1912.

Bamezai, Anil, Jack Zwanziger, Glenn A. Melnick, and Joyce M. Mann. 1999. Price Competition and Hospital Cost Growth in the United States (1989-1994). *Health Economics* 8(3):233-243.

Baxter, Raymond J., and Robert E. Mechanic. 1997. The Status of Local Health Care Safety Nets. *Health Affairs* 16(4):7-23.

Bazzoli, Gloria J., Patricia J. Meersman, and Cheeling Chan. 1996. Factors That Enhance Continued Trauma Center Participation in Trauma Systems. *Journal of Trauma-Injury Infection & Critical Care* 41(5):876-885.

Bennefield, Robert L. 1998. Dynamics of Economic Well-Being: Health Insurance, 1993 to 1995. Who Loses Coverage and for How Long? *Census Bureau Current Population Reports. Household Economic Studies*, P70-64. Washington, DC: U.S. Census Bureau.

Billings, John, Lisa Zeital, Joanne Lukomnik, Timothy S. Carey, et al. 1993. Impact of Socioeconomic Status on Health Use in New York City. *Health Affairs* 12(1):162-173.

Billings, John, Geoffery M. Anderson, and Laurie S. Newman. 1996. Recent Findings on Preventable Hospitalizations. *Health Affairs* 15(3):239-249.

Billings, John, Nina Parikh, and Tod Mijanovich. 2000. *Emergency Room Use: The New York Story.* New York: The Commonwealth Fund.

Bindman, Andrew B., Kevin Grumbach, Dennis Keane, Loren Rauch, et al. 1991. Consequences of Queuing for Care at a Public Hospital Emergency Department. *American Journal of Public Health* 266(8):1091-1096.

Bindman, Andrew B., Kevin Grumbach, Dennis Osmand, Miriam Komaromy, et al. 1995. Preventable Hospitalizations and Access to Care. *Journal of the American Medical Association* 274(4):305-311.

Bitterman, Robert. 2002. Explaining the EMTALA Paradox. *Annals of Emergency Medicine* 40(5):470-475.

Blanchfield, Bonnie B., and Emily Randall. 2000. *Data Sources to Study Uncompensated Care Provided by Hospitals.* Bethesda, MD: Project HOPE Walsh Center for Rural Health Analysis.

Blendon, Robert J., John T. Young, and Catherine M. DesRoches. 1999. The Uninsured, the Working Uninsured, and the Public. *Health Affairs* 18(6):203-211.

Blendon, Robert J., Linda H. Aiken, Harold E. Freeman, Bradford L. Kirkman-Liff, et al. 1986. Uncompensated Care by Hospitals or Public Insurance for the Poor. Does It Make a Difference? *New England Journal of Medicine* 314(18):1160-1163.

Blumstein, James F. 1986. Providing Hospital Care to Indigent Patients: Hill-Burton as a Case Study and a Paradigm. Pp. 94-107 In: *Uncompensated Hospital Care. Rights and Responsibilities*, Frank A Sloan, James F. Blumstein, and James M. Perrin, eds. Baltimore: Johns Hopkins University Press.

Blustein, Jan, Raymond R. Arons, and Steven Shea. 1995. Sequential Events Contributing to Variations in Cardiac Revascularization Rates. *Medical Care* 33(8):864-880.

Bonnie, Richard J., Carolyn E. Fulco, and Cathryn T. Liverman, eds. 1999. *Reducing the Burden of Injury. Advancing Prevention and Treatment*. Washington, DC: National Academy Press.

Borden, Kevin, Matt Haney, Renee Markus Hodin, and Kim Shellenberger. 2001. *Don't Lien on Me: Why the State's Medical Indigency Care Program Is Unhealthy for Idahoans*. Boston, MA: The Access Project.

Bovbjerg, Randall R., Alison Evans Cuellar, and Jon Holahan. 2000a. *Market Competition and Uncompensated Care Pools*. Washington, DC: The Urban Institute.

Bovbjerg, Randall R., Jill A. Marsteller, and Frank C. Ullman. 2000b. *Health Care for the Poor and Uninsured After a Public Hospital's Closure or Conversion*. Washington, DC: The Urban Institute.

Bovbjerg, Randall R., and Frank C. Ullman. 2002. *Recent Changes in Health Policy for Low-Income People in New Jersey*. Washington, DC: The Urban Institute.

Bozzette, Samuel A., Sandra H. Berry, Naihua Duan, Martin R. Frankel, et al. 1998. The Care of HIV-Infected Adults in the United States. *The New England Journal of Medicine* 339(26):1897-1904.

Breen, Nancy, Diane Wagener, Martin L. Brown, William Davis, et al. 2001. Progress in Cancer Screening Over a Decade. Results of Cancer Screening from the 1987, 1992, and 1998 National Health Interview Surveys. *Journal of the National Cancer Institute* 93(22):1704-1713.

Brewster, Linda R., Liza S. Rudell, and Cara S. Lesser. 2001. *Emergency Room Diversions: A Symptom of Hospitals Under Stress*. Issue Brief 38, Findings from HSC. Washington, DC: Center for Studying Health System Change.

Brown, E. Richard, Roberta Wyn, and Stephanie Teleki. 2000. *Disparities in Health Insurance and Access to Care of Residents Across U.S. Cities*. Los Angeles, CA: Regents of the University of California.

Brown, E. Richard, Ninez Ponce, Thomas Rice, and Shana Alex Lavarreda. 2002. *The State of Health Insurance in California: Findings from the 2001 California Health Interview Survey*. Los Angeles, CA: UCLA Center for Health Policy Research.

Bruen, Brian, Teresa Coughlin, Stuart Guterman, and Amy Lutzky. 2001. *The Medicaid DSH Program and Providing Health Care Services to the Uninsured: A Look at Five Programs*. Washington, DC: The Urban Institute.

Buchmueller, Thomas C., and Paul J. Feldstein. 1996. Hospital Community Benefits Other Than Charity Care: Implications for Tax Exemption and Public Policy. *Hospital & Health Services Administration* 41(4):461-471.

Bureau of Primary Health Care. 2001. *Experts With Experience, 1990-2000*. Bethesda, MD: Health Resources and Services Administration.

———. 2002. Uniform Data System (UDS) National Rollup Report, National Summary for 2001. Accessed October 28, 2002. Available at: ftp://ftp.hrsa.gov/bphc/pdf/uds.

Burstin, Helen R., Stuart R. Lipsitz, and Troyen A. Brennan. 1992. Socioeconomic Status and Risk for Substandard Medical Care. *Journal of the American Medical Association* 268(17):2383-2387.

California Endowment. N.d. *About the California Endowment*. Accessed December 2, 2002. Available at: http://www.calendow.org/about/about.htm.

California HealthCare Foundation. 2001. *Health Care in California: Improving Delivery and Financing Systems.* Foundation Report 1999-2001. Accessed December 2, 2002. Available at: http://www.chcf.org/aboutchcf/.

California Wellness Foundation. N.d. *Origins of the California Wellness Foundation.* Accessed December 2, 2002. Available at: http://www.tcwf.org/about/history.htm.

Campbell, Ellen S., and Michael W. Ahern. 1993. Have Procompetitive Changes Altered Hospital Provision of Indigent Care? *Health Economics* 2(3):281-289.

Canto, John G., William J. Rogers, William J. French, Joel M. Gore, et al. 2000. Payer Status and the Utilization of Hospital Resources in Acute Myocardial Infarction. *Archives of Internal Medicine* 160(6):817-823.

Carlson, Barbara L., Jill Eden, Daniel O'Connor, and Jerilynn Regan. 2001. Primary Care of Patients Without Insurance by Community Health Centers. *Journal of Ambulatory Care Management* 24(2):47-59.

Catholic Health Association. 2002. *A Commitment to Caring. The Role of Catholic Hospitals in the Health Care Safety Net.* Accessed November 18, 2002. Available at: http://www.chausa.org/PUBLICPO/SAFETYNET.ASP.

Celum, Connie L., Gail Bolan, Melissa Krone, Karen Code, et al. 1997. Patients Attending STD Clinics in an Evolving Health Care Environment: Demographics, Insurance Coverage, Preferences for STD Services, and STD Morbidity. *Sexually Transmitted Diseases* 24(10):599-605.

Centers for Disease Control and Prevention (CDC). 1999. Tuberculosis Elimination Revisited: Obstacles, Opportunities, and a Renewed Commitment. Advisory Council for the Elimination of Tuberculosis. *Morbidity and Mortality Weekly Report* 48(RR-9).

———. 2000. *Tracking the Hidden Epidemics. Trends in STDs in the United States.* Atlanta, GA: U.S. Department of Health and Human Services. Accessed December 31, 2002. Available at: www.cdc.gov/nchstp/dstd/Stats_Trends/Trends2000.pdf.

———. 2001a. *Chlamydia in the United States.* Atlanta, GA: U.S. Department of Health and Human Services. Accessed November 4, 2001. Available at: http://www.cdc.gov/nchstp/dtsd/Fact_Sheets/chlamydia_facts.htm.

———. 2001b. Preventing and Controlling Tuberculosis Along the U.S.-Mexico Border. *Morbidity and Mortality Weekly Report* 50(RR-1):1-6.

———. 2001c. *Sexually Transmitted Disease Surveillance, 2000.* Atlanta, GA: U.S. Department of Health and Human Services.

———. 2002a. *Table 28. Tuberculosis Cases and Case Rates Per 100,000 Population: Metropolitan Statistical Areas with ≥500,000 Population, 1997 and 1996.* Atlanta, GA: National Center for HIV, STD, and TB Prevention, Centers for Disease Control and Prevention, U.S. Department of Health and Human Services.

———. 2002b. *Vaccines for Children Program.* Atlanta, GA: U.S. Department of Health and Human Services. Accessed October 2, 2002. Available at: http://www.cdc.gov/nip/vfc/Provider/ProvidersHomePage.htm.

Chamberlin, Edward. 1962. *The Theory of Monopolistic Competition: A Re-Orientation of the Theory of Value.* 8th ed. Cambridge, MA: Harvard University Press.

Chernew, Michael. 1995. The Impact of Non-IPA HMOs on the Number of Hospitals and Hospital Capacity. *Inquiry* 34(3):205-216.

Chernew, Michael, David Cutler, and Patricia Seliger Keenan. 2002. *Rising Health Care Costs and the Decline in Insurance Coverage.* Ann Arbor, MI: Economic Research Initiative on the Uninsured.

Cincinnati Business Courier. 2001. Cincinnati's Health Care System Buckling Under Weight of Uninsured. Accessed April 24, 2001. Available at: http://www.kaisernetwork.org/daily_reports/rep_hpolicy.cfm#4244.

Clancy, Thomas V., L. N. Misick, Deborah L. Covington, M. Paige Churchill, et al. 1994. The Financial Impact of Intentional Violence on Community Hospitals. *Journal of Trauma* 37(1):1-4.

Clement, Jan P. 1997-1998. Dynamic Cost-Shifting in Hospitals: Evidence from the 1980s and 1990s. *Inquiry* 34(4):340-350.

Clement, Jan P., Dean G. Smith, and John R. Wheeler. 1994. What Do We Want and What Do We Get from Not-for-Profit Hospitals? *Hospital & Health Services Administration* 39(2):159-178.

Clemmitt, Marcia. 2000. Perspectives. Frayed Connections: Can Funding Health Centers Save the Safety Net? *Medicine & Health* 54(34): Suppl. 1-4.

Coburn, Andrew F. 2002. *Insurance Coverage in Rural Populations and Places*. Washington, DC: Unpublished presentation to the IOM Committee on the Consequences of Uninsurance.

Cohn, Jonathan. 2002. The White House Abandons L.A. Ill Treatment. *The New Republic*. November 20,

Colgan, Charles S. 2002. *The Economic Effects of Rural Hospital Closures*. Portland, ME: Edmund S. Muskie School of Public Service, University of Southern Maine. Unpublished paper.

Commonwealth Fund. 2001. *A Shared Responsibility. Academic Health Centers and the Provision of Care to the Poor and Uninsured*. New York, NY: The Commonwealth Fund, Task Force on Academic Health Centers.

Connolly, Ceci. 2002. Smallpox Plan May Force Other Health Cuts. *Washington Post*. December 24.

Conover, Christopher J. 1998. *Health Care for the Medically Indigent of South Carolina. Final Report*. Raleigh, NC: North Carolina Center for Health Policy, Law and Management, Duke University.

Conover, Christopher J., and Hester H. Davies. 2000. *The Role of TennCare in Health Policy for Low-Income People in Tennessee*. Occasional Paper No. 33. Washington, DC: The Urban Institute.

Cooper, Philip F., and Barbara S. Schone. 1997. More Offers, Fewer Takers for Employer-Based Health Insurance: 1987 and 1996. *Health Affairs* 16(6):142-149.

Cordes, Sam M. 1998. Health Care and the Rural Economy. *Forum for Applied Research and Public Policy* 13(2):90-93.

Cordes, Sam M., Evert Van der Sluis, Charles Lamphear, and Jerry Hoffman. 1999. Rural Hospitals and the Local Economy: A Needed Extension and Refinement of Existing Empirical Research. *Journal of Rural Health* 15(2):189-201.

Cornwell, Edward E. I., Thomas V. Berne, Howard Belzberg, Juan Asensio, et al. 1996. Health Care Crisis from a Trauma Center Perspective. *Journal of the American Medical Association* 276(12):940-944.

Corrigan, Janet M., Ann Greiner, and Shari M. Erickson, eds. 2002. *Fostering Rapid Advances in Health Care. Learning from System Demonstrations*. Washington, DC: The National Academies Press.

Coughlin, Teresa, and David Liska. 1997. *The Medicaid Disproportionate Share Hospital Payment Program: Background and Issues*. Washington, DC: The Urban Institute.

Coughlin, Teresa A., and Amy W. Lutzky. 2002. *Recent Changes in Health Policy for Low-Income People in New York*. State Update. Washington, DC: The Urban Institute.

Coughlin, Teresa A., and Stephen Zuckerman. 2002. *States' Use of Medicaid Maximization Strategies to Tap Federal Revenues: Program Implications and Consequences*. Discussion Paper 02-09. Washington, DC: The Urban Institute.

Coughlin, Teresa A., Leighton Ku, and Johnny Kim. 2000. *Reforming the Medicaid Disproportionate Share Hospital Program in the 1990s*. Washington, DC: The Urban Institute.

Coulam, Robert F., and Gary L. Gaumer. 1991. Medicare's Prospective Payment System: A Critical Appraisal. *Health Care Financing Review* 14(3):45-77.

Cowan, Cathy A., Helen C. Lazenby, Anne B. Martin, Patricia A. McDonnell, et al. 2001. National Health Expenditure, 1999. *Health Care Financing Review* 22(4):77-110.

Cummings, Doyle M., Lauren Whetstone, Amy Shende, and David Weismiller. 2000. Predictors of Screenings Mammography: Implications for Office Practice. *Archives of Family Medicine* 9(9):870-875.

Cunningham, Peter. 2002. *Mounting Pressures: Physicians Serving Medicaid Patients and the Uninsured, 1997-2001*. Tracking Report No. 6. Results from the Community Tracking Study. Washington, DC: Center for Studying Health System Change.

Cunningham, Peter, and Ha T. Tu. 1997. A Changing Picture of Uncompensated Care. *Health Affairs* 14(4):167-175.

Cunningham, Peter J., and Peter Kemper. 1998. Ability to Obtain Medical Care for the Uninsured: How Much Does It Vary Across Communities? *Journal of the American Medical Association* 280(10): 921-927.

Cunningham, Peter J., Jerome M. Grossman, Robert F. St. Peter, and Cara S. Lesser. 1999. Managed Care and Physicians' Provision of Charity Care. *Journal of the American Medical Association* 281(12):1087-1192.

Cunningham, Peter J., and Paul B. Ginsberg. 2001. What Accounts for Differences in Uninsurance Rates Across Communities? *Inquiry* 38(10):6-21.

Cunningham, Robert. 1996. Perspectives. CHCs' Loss of Medicaid Stealth Subsidy Jeopardizes Uninsured. *Medicine & Health* 50(29 Suppl.):1-4.

Cutler, David M. 2002. *Employee Costs and the Decline in Health Insurance Coverage.* Boston: Harvard University and National Bureau of Economic Research.

Dailey, J. T., H. Teter, and R. Adams Cowley. 1992. Trauma Center Closures: A National Assessment. *Journal of Trauma* 33(4):539-546.

Davis, Karen, Karen Scott Collins, and Allyson Hall. 1999. Community Health Centers in a Changing U.S. Health Care System. *The Commonwealth Fund Policy Brief:*1-8.

Davison, David. 2001. Is Philanthropy Dying at the Hospital? Accessed October 28, 2002. Available at: http://philanthropyroundtable.org/magazines/2001/august/davison.html.

Deaton, Angus. 2002. Policy Implications of the Gradient of Health and Wealth. *Health Affairs* 21(2):13-30.

Deaton, Angus, and Darren Lubotsky. 2002. *Mortality, Inequality, and Race in American Cities and States.* Princeton, NJ: Center for Health and Wellbeing, Princeton University.

DeBuono, Barbara A. 2000. Vaccine Coverage: Access and Administration. *American Journal of Preventive Medicine* 19(3 Suppl.):21-23.

Derlet, Robert W. 1992. ED Overcrowding in New York City. *Journal of Emergency Medicine* 10(1):93-94.

———. 2002. Overcrowding in Emergency Departments: Increased Demand and Decreased Capacity. *Annals of Emergency Medicine* 39(4):430-432.

Derlet, Robert W., and John R. Richards. 2000. Overcrowding in the Nation's Emergency Departments: Complex Causes and Disturbing Effects. *Annals of Emergency Medicine* 35(1):63-68.

Derlet, Robert W., John R. Richards, and Richard L Kravitz. 2001. Frequent Overcrowding in U.S. Emergency Departments. *Academic Emergency Medicine* 8(2):151-155.

Desai, Kamal R., Gary J. Young, and Carol Vandeusen Lukas. 1998. Hospital Conversions From For-Profit to Nonprofit Status: The Other Side of the Story. *Medical Care Research and Review* 55(3):298-308.

Desai, Kamal R., Carol Vandeusen Lukas, and Gary J. Young. 2000. Public Hospitals: Privatization and Uncompensated Care. *Health Affairs* 19(2):167-172.

Desonia, Randy. 2002. *Running on Empty: The State Budget Crisis Worsens.* Issue Brief No. 783. Washington, DC: National Health Policy Forum, The George Washington University.

Diehr, Paula, Carolyn W. Madden, Allen Cheadle, Donald L. Patrick., et al. 1991. Estimating County Percentages of People Without Health Insurance. *Inquiry* 28(4):413-419.

Diez-Roux, Ana V. 2001. Commentary. Investigating Neighborhood and Area Effects on Health. *American Journal of Public Health* 91(11):1783-1789.

Dixon, Lee, and James Cox. 2002. State Management and Allocation of Tobacco Settlement Revenues. Washington, DC: National Conference of State Legislatures.

Dobson, Al. 2002. Cost-Shifting: An Integral Aspect of U.S. Health Care Finance. Washington, DC: Unpublished presentation at AcademyHealth meeting, "When Public Payment Declines Does Cost-Shifting Occur? Hospital and Physician Responses."

Doeksen, Gerald A., Tom Johnson, and Chuck Willoughby. 1997. *Measuring the Economic Importance of the Health Sector on a Local Economy: A Brief Literature Review and Procedures to Measure Local Impacts.* Mississippi State, MS: The Southern Rural Development Center.

Doeksen, Gerald A., Tom Johnson, Diane Biard-Holmes, and Val Schott. 1998. A Healthy Health Sector Is Crucial for Community Economic Development. *Journal of Rural Health* 14(1):66-72.

Donaldson, Molla, Karl D. Yordy, Kathleen N. Lohr, and Neal A. Vanselow, eds. 1996. *Primary Care: America's Health in a New Era*. Washington, DC: National Academy Press.

Dorsky, Dave. 2000. *Uninsured Rates in Ohio by County, 1998*. Columbus, OH: Ohio Department of Health.

Dranove, David, Mark Satterthwaite, and Jody L. Sindelar. 1986. The Effect of Injecting Price Competition into the Hospital Market: The Case of Preferred Provider Organizations. *Inquiry* 23(4):419-431.

Dranove, David, and William D. White. 1998. Medicaid-Dependent Hospitals and Their Patients: How Have They Fared? *Health Services Research* 33(2 pt 1):163-85.

Draper, Debra A., Linda R. Brewster, Lawrence D. Brown, Lance Heineccius, et al. 2001a. *Financial Pressures Continue to Plague Hospitals. Northern New Jersey*. Washington, DC: Center for Studying Health System Change.

Draper, Debra A., Linda R. Brewster, Lawrence D. Brown, Carolyn A. Watts, et al. 2001b. *Rapid Population Growth Attracts National Firms. Phoenix, Arizona*. Community Report, Third Visit, 2000-2001. Washington, DC: Center for Studying Health System Change.

Duarte, Carmen. 2001. Kolbe's Bill Seeks Immigrant Care Reimbursement. *Arizona Daily Star*, p. A1. Accessed June 19, 2001. Available at: http://www.azstarnet.com/star/tue/10619BORDER. html.

Duncan, R. P. 1992. Uncompensated Hospital Care. *Medical Care Review* 49(3):265-330.

Duncan, R. P., and Kerry E. Kilpatrick. 1987. Unresolved Hospital Charges in Florida. *Health Affairs* 6(1):157-166.

Dunham, N. C., David A. Kindig, S. Lastiri-Quiros, Margaret T. Barham, et al. 1991. Uncompensated and Discounted Medicaid Care Provided by Physician Group Practices in Wisconsin. *Journal of the American Medical Association* 265(22):2982-2986.

Dunn, Daniel L., and Michael Chen. 1994. Uncompensated Hospital Care Payment and Access for the Uninsured: Evidence from New Jersey. *Health Services Research* 29(1):113-130.

Eads, George C. 1977. The Demise of the Concept of Cross-Subsidy in U.S. Domestic Air Transportation Reasons and Implications. *Research Seminar Series*. Canadian Transport Commission.

Eastman, A. B., Charles L. Rice, David G. Bishop, and J. David Richardson. 1991. An Analysis of the Critical Problem of Trauma Center Reimbursement. *Journal of Trauma* 31(7):920-925.

Ehrenreich, Barbara. 1989. *Fear of Falling*. New York: Pantheon Books.

Eng, Thomas R., and William T. Butler, eds. 1997. The Hidden Epidemic: Confronting Sexually Transmitted Diseases. Washington, DC: National Academy Press.

Erikson, Jane. 2002. Everyone May Get Access to Coverage. *Arizona Daily Star*, p. A-1. Accessed February 4, 2001. Available at: http://www.azstarnet.com/star/sun/10204 HEALTHY ARIZONAFOLO.html.

Etheredge, Lynn. 2000. *On the Archeology of Health Care Policy. Periods and Paradigms, 1975–2000*. Special Report, The Robert Wood Johnson Health Policy Fellowships Program. Washington, DC: Institute of Medicine.

Faden, Ruth, and Madison Powers. 1999. *Incrementalism: Ethical Implications of Policy Choices*. Washington, DC: The Henry J. Kaiser Family Foundation .

Fagnani, Lynne, and Jennifer Tolbert. 1999. *The Dependence of Safety Net Hospitals and Health Systems on the Medicare and Medicaid Disproportionate Share Hospital Payment Programs*. New York: The Commonwealth Fund.

Fairbrother, Gerry, Hanns Kuttner, Wilhelmine Miller, R. Hogan, et al. 2000. Findings from Case Studies of State and Local Immunization Programs. *American Journal of Preventive Medicine* 19(3 Suppl.):54-77.

Fairbrother, Gerry, Heidi Park, and Michael Gusmano. 2002. *How Community Health Centers Are Coping with Their Uninsured Caseloads*. National Association of Community Health Centers 27th Policy and Issues Forum. Washington, DC. New York: The Commonwealth Fund.

Falik, Marilyn, Jack Needleman, Barbara L. Wells, and Jodi Korb. 2001. Ambulatory Care, Sensitive Hospitalizations, and Emergency Visits: Experiences of Medicaid Patients Using Federally Qualified Health Centers. *Medical Care* 39(6):555-561.

Fath, John J., Adelaide A. Ammon, and Max M. Cohen. 1999. Urban Trauma Care Is Threatened by Inadequate Reimbursement. *American Journal of Surgery* 177(5):371-374.

Felt-Lisk, Suzanne, Megan McHugh, and Embry Howell. 2001. *Study of Safety Net Provider Capacity to Care for Low-Income Uninsured Patients. Final Report.* Washington, DC: Mathematica Policy Research.

Fenz, Caton. 2000. *Providing Health Care to the Uninsured in Texas: A Guide for County Officials.* Boston: The Access Project.

Fields, W. W., Brent R. Asplin, Gregory L. Larkin, Catherine A. Marco, et al. 2001. The Emergency Medical Treatment and Labor Act As a Federal Health Care Safety Net Program. *Academic Emergency Medicine* 8(11):1064-1069.

Finerfrock, William. 2002. *Introduction.* Washington, DC: National Association of Rural Health Clinics.

Finger, Anne L. 1999. Caring for the Uninsured. How America's Doctors Are Making a Difference. *Medical Economics* 76(24):118-120, 123-124, 129-130.

Fleming, Arthur W., R.P. Sterling-Scott, G. Carabello, I. Imari-Williams, et al. 1992. Injury and Violence in Los Angeles, Impact on Access to Health Care and Surgical Education. *Archives of Surgery* 127(6):671-676.

Folland, Sherman, Allen C. Goodman, and Miron Stano. 2001. *The Economics of Health and Health Care.* 3rd ed. Upper Saddle River, NJ: Prentice Hall.

Forrest, Christopher B., and Ellen-Marie Whelan. 2000. Primary Care Safety-Net Delivery Sites in the United States. *Journal of the American Medical Association* 284(16):2077-2083.

Frank, Richard G., and David S. Salkever. 1991. The Supply of Charity Services by Nonprofit Hospitals: Motives and Market Structure. *RAND Journal of Economics* 13(2):430-445.

Frech, H. E. III. 1996. *Competition and Monopoly in Medical Care.* Washington, DC: AEI Press.

Friedman, Emily. 1987. Problems Plaguing Public Hospitals: Uninsured Patient Transfers, Tight Funds, Mismanagement, and Misperception. *Journal of the American Medical Association* 257(14):1856-1857.

Fronstin, Paul. 2000. *Sources of Health Insurance and Characteristics of the Uninsured: Analysis of the March 1999 Current Population Survey.* Issue Brief 217. Washington, DC: Employee Benefit Research Institute.

Fronstin, Paul. 2002. *Sources of Health Insurance and Characteristics of the Uninsured: Analysis of the March 2002 Current Population Survey.* Issue Brief 252. Washington, DC: Employee Benefit Research Institute.

Fronstin, Paul, and Alphonse G. Holtmann. 2000. Productivity Gains from Employment-Based Health Insurance. *The Economic Costs of the Uninsured: Implications for Business and Government,* Washington, DC: Employee Benefit Research Institute.

Gabel, Jon. 1999. Job-Based Health Insurance, 1977-1998: The Accidental System Under Scrutiny. *Health Affairs* 18(6):62-74.

Gale, John, and Andrew Coburn. 2001. *The Role of Rural Health Clinics in the Delivery of Services to Low Income and Underserved Populations: Results from a National Survey.* Atlanta, GA: Presentation at the Academy for Health Services Research and Health Policy Annual Meeting.

Gaskin, Darrell J. 1999. Safety Net Hospitals: Essential Providers of Public Health and Specialty Services. New York: The Commonwealth Fund.

Gaskin, Darrell J., and Jack Hadley. 1997. The Impact of HMO Penetration on the Rate of Hospital Cost Inflation, 1985-1993. *Inquiry* 34(3):205-216.

Gaskin, Darrell J., and Catherine Hoffman. 2000. Racial and Ethnic Differences in Preventable Hospitalizations Across 10 States. *Medical Care Research and Review* 57(Suppl. 1):85-107.

Gaskin, Darrell J., Jack Hadley, and Victor G. Freeman. 2001. Are Urban Safety-Net Hospitals Losing Low-Risk Medicaid Maternity Patients. *Health Services Research* 36(1 pt. 1):25-51.

Gaskin, Darrell J., and Jack Needleman. 2002. *The Impact of Uninsured Populations on the Availability of Hospital Services and Financial Status of Hospitals.* Baltimore, MD: The Johns Hopkins Bloomberg School of Public Health.

Geiter, Lawrence, ed. 2000. *Ending Neglect: The Elimination of Tuberculosis in the United States.* Washington, DC: National Academy Press.

Gildemeister, Stefan, Julie Sonier, and April Todd-Malmlov. 2002. *Minnesota's Uninsured: Findings from the 2001 Health Access Survey.* St. Paul, MN: Minnesota Department of Health; University of Minnesota School of Public Health.

Goldberg, Bruce W. 1998. Managed Care and Public Health Departments: Who Is Responsible for the Health of the Population? *Annual Reviews in Public Health* 19:527-537.

Goldstein, Amy. 2002. States' Budget Woes Fuel Medicaid Cuts. Poor Lose Coverage and Services. *The Washington Post.* Accessed October 10, 2002. Available at: www.washingtonpost.com/wp-dyn/articles/A9653-2002Oct10.html.

Grantmakers in Health. 2001. 43 Million and Counting: Facing Up to the Problem of the Uninsured. Accessed December 2, 2002. Available at: http://www.gih.org/usr_doc/49508.pdf.

Grantmakers in Health. 2002a. All Health Care Is Local: Community Efforts to Cover the Uninsured. Accessed December 2, 2002. Available at: http://www.gih.org/usr_doc/uninsured_finding.pdf.

Grantmakers in Health. 2002b. *Assets for Health. Findings from the 2001 Survey of New Health Foundations.* Washington, DC: Grantmakers in Health.

Gray, Bradford H., ed. 1986. *For-Profit Enterprise in Health Care.* Washington, DC: National Academy Press.

Grazman, D. N., and Michael R. Cousineau. 2000. Privatizing Indigent Health Services in Los Angeles County: Understanding the Effects on Community-Based Providers. *Health Services Management Research* 13(3):187-199.

Greene, William H. 2000. *Econometric Analysis.* 4th ed. Upper Saddle River, NJ: Prentice Hall.

Gribbin, August. 2002. Hospitals Feel Pain of Mexico Crossings. *Washington Times.* Accessed March 18, 2002. Available at: http://www.washtimes.com/national/20020318-97583307.htm.

Gruber, Jonathan. 1994. The Effect of Competitive Pressure on Charity: Hospital Responses to Price Shopping in California. *Journal of Health Economics* 13(2):183-212.

Gruber, Jonathan, and Bridgitte C. Madrian. 2001. *Health Insurance, Labor Supply, and Job Mobility: A Critical Review of the Literature.* Ann Arbor, MI: University of Michigan.

Grumbach, Kevin, Dennis Keane, and Andrew Bindman. 1993. Primary Care and Public Emergency Department Overcrowding. *American Journal of Public Health* 83(3):372-378.

Haas, Jennifer S., and Lee Goldman. 1994. Acutely Injured Patients with Trauma in Massachusetts: Differences in Care and Mortality by Insurance Status. *American Journal of Public Health* 84(10):1605-1608.

Hadley, Jack. 2002. *Sicker and Poorer: The Consequences of Being Uninsured.* Washington, DC: The Kaiser Family Foundation.

Hadley, Jack, and Judith Feder. 1985. Hospital Cost Shifting and Care for the Uninsured. *Health Affairs* 4(3):67-80.

Hadley, Jack, Earl P. Steinberg, and Judith Feder. 1991. Comparison of Uninsured and Privately Insured Hospital Patients. *Journal of the American Medical Association* 265(3):374-379.

Hadley, Jack, Stephen Zuckerman, and Lisa I. Iezzoni. 1996. Financial Pressure and Competition. Changes in Hospital Efficiency and Cost-Shifting Behavior. *Medical Care* 34(3):205-219.

Hadley, Jack, Bradford H. Gray, and Sara R. Collins. 2001. *A Statistical Analysis of the Impact of Nonprofit Hospital Conversions on Hospitals and Communities, 1985-1996.* New York: The Commonwealth Fund.

Hadley, Jack, and John Holahan. 2003. How Much Medical Care Do the Uninsured Use and Who Pays for It? *Health Affairs* Web Exclusive:1/W66-W81.

Harpham, Trudy, Evalyn Grant, and E. Thomas. 2002. Measuring Social Capital Within Health Surveys: Key Issues. *Health Policy and Planning* 17(1):106-111.

Hartley, David, Lois Quam, and Nicole Lurie. 1994. Urban and Rural Differences in Health Insurance and Access to Care. *Journal of Rural Health* 10(2):98-108.

Hartley, David, and Mark B. Lapping. 2000. *Case Report. Old West County Montana.* Portland, ME: Maine Rural Health Research Center.

Hawkins, Daniel R., and Sara Rosenbaum. 1998. The Challenges Facing Health Centers in a Changing Healthcare System. Pp. 99-122 in: *The Future U.S. Healthcare System: Who Will Care for the Poor and Uninsured?* Stuart H. Altman, Uwe E. Reinhardt, and Alexandra E. Shields, eds. Chicago, IL: Health Administration Press.

Health Insurance Association of America. N.d. *Source Book of Health Insurance Data, 1982-1983.* Washington, DC: Health Insurance Association of America.

Health Insurance Association of America. 2002. *New Survey Results Show Health Insurance Tax Credits Could Help Millions.* Washington, DC: Health Insurance Association of America.

Heffler, Stephen, Katharine Levit, Shiela Smith, Cynthia Smith, et al. 2001. Health Spending Growth Up in 1999; Faster Growth Expected in the Future. *Health Affairs* 20(2):193-203.

Henderson, Donald A., Thomas V. Inglesby, John G. Bartlett, Michael S. Ascher, et al. 1999. Smallpox as a Biological Weapon. Medical and Public Health Management. *Journal of the American Medical Association* 281:2127-2137.

Hendryx, Michael S., Melissa M. Ahern, Nicholas P. Lovrich, and Arthur H. McCurdy. 2002. Access to Health Care and Community Social Capital. *Health Services Research* 37(1):87-103.

Herring, Bradley J. 2001. *Does Access to Charity Care for the Uninsured Crowd Out Private Health Insurance Coverage?* New Haven, CT: Institution for Social and Policy Studies, Yale University.

HIV/AIDS Treatment Information Service. 2002. *Guidelines for the Use of Antiretroviral Agents in HIV-Infected Adults and Adolescents. Developed by the Panel on Clinical Practices for Treatment of HIV Infection.* Washington, DC: U.S. Department of Health and Human Services, The Henry J. Kaiser Family Foundation.

Hodgkin, Dominic, and Thomas G. McGuire. 1994. Payment Levels and Hospital Response to Prospective Payment. *Journal of Health Economics* 13(1):1-29.

Hoerger, Thomas J. 1991. 'Profit" Variability in For-Profit and Not-for-Profit Hospitals. *Journal of Health Economics* 10(3):259-289.

Holahan, John. 2002. *Variations Among States in Health Insurance Coverage and Medical Expenditures: How Much Is Too Much?* Discussion Paper 02-07. Washington, DC: The Urban Institute.

Holahan, John, and Johnny Kim. 2000. Why Does the Number of Uninsured Americans Continue to Grow? *Health Affairs* 19(4):188-196.

Holahan, John, and Mary Beth Pohl. 2002. *Changes in Insurance Coverage: 1994-2000 and Beyond.* Washington, DC: The Kaiser Commission on Medicaid and the Uninsured.

Holmes, King K., and Stephen A. Morse. 1998. Gonococcal Infections. Pp. 915-922 in: *Harrison's Principles of Internal Medicine*, 14th ed. Anthony S. Fauci et al.,eds. New York: McGraw-Hill.

Hovey, Harold A. 1991. Who Pays When State Health Care Costs Rise? Pp. 71-129 in *State Governments: The Effects of Health Care Program Expansion in a Period of Fiscal Stress*, Advisory Council on Social Security. Washington, DC: Advisory Council on Social Security.

Howell, Embry M. 2001. The Impact of the Medicaid Expansions for Pregnant Women: A Synthesis of the Evidence. *Medical Care Research and Review* 58(1):3-30.

Hudman, Julie. 2000. *Immigrants' Health Care: Coverage and Access.* Pub No. 2203. Washington, DC: The Henry J. Kaiser Family Foundation.

Hurtado, Margarita P., Elaine K. Swift, and Janet M. Corrigan, eds. 2001. *Envisioning the National Health Care Quality Report.* Washington, DC: National Academy Press.

Idaho State Planning Grant. 2002. *HRSA Planning Grants. Final Report.* Boise, ID: Idaho Department of Commerce.

Institute of Medicine. 1988. *The Future of Public Health.* Washington, DC: National Academy Press.

———. 1990. *Medicine: A Strategy for Quality Assurance.* Washington, DC: National Academy Press.

———. 2000. *Calling the Shots: Immunization Finance Policies and Practices.* Washington, DC: National Academy Press.

————. 2001a. *Coverage Matters: Insurance and Health Care.* Washington, DC: National Academy Press.

————. 2001b. *Crossing the Quality Chasm; A New Health System for the 21st Century.* Washington, DC: National Academy Press.

————. 2002a. *Care Without Coverage: Too Little, Too Late.* Washington, DC: National Academy Press.

————. 2002b. *Health Insurance Is a Family Matter.* Washington, DC: National Academies Press.

————. Forthcoming 2003. *The Future of the Public's Health in the 21st Century.* Washington, DC: National Academies Press.

Jacobs, Lawrence, Theodore Marmor, and Jonathan Oberlander. 1999. The Oregon Health Plan and the Political Paradox of Rationing: What Advocates and Critics Have Claimed and What Oregon Did. *Journal of Health Politics, Policy and Law* 24(1):161-180.

Jaffe, Anna. 2001. Indigent Care Financing on the Block. *Kansas City Business Journal.* Accessed May 11, 2001. Available at: http://kansascity.bcentral.com/kansascity/stories/2001/05/14/story1.html.

Johnson, Kay A., Alice Sardell, and Barbara Richards. 2000. Federal Immunization Policy and Funding: A History of Responding to Crises. *American Journal of Preventive Medicine* 19(3 Suppl.):99-113.

Johnson, Loren A., and Robert W. Derlet. 1996. Conflicts Between Managed Care Organizations and Emergency Departments in California. *Western Journal of Medicine* 164(2):137-142.

Johnson, Loren A., Todd B. Taylor, and Roneet Lev. 2001. The Emergency Department On-Call Backup Crisis: Finding Remedies for a Serious Public Health Problem. *Annals of Emergency Medicine* 37(5):495-499.

Kahn, Rene S., Paul H. Wise, Bruce P. Kennedy, and Ichiro Kawachi. 2000. State Income Inequality, Household Income, and Maternal Mental and Physical Health: Cross Sectional National Survey. *British Medical Journal* 321(7272):1311-1315.

Kaiser Commission on Medicaid and the Uninsured (KCMU). 2002. *Medicaid Update: What Changes Are States Considering in the Face of Fiscal Pressures?* Washington, DC: Kaiser Commission on Medicaid and the Uninsured.

Kaiser Family Foundation (KFF). 2000. *Medicaid's Role for Persons With HIV/AIDS.* Accessed October 5, 2002. Available at: http://www.kff.org/content/2000/1588/Mcaidhivfs.PDF.

Kamoie, Brian E. 2000. EMTALA: Reaching Beyond the Emergency Room to Expand Hospital Liability. *Journal of Health Law* 33(1):25-55.

Kane, Carol. 2002. *Physician Marketplace Report. Physician Provision of Charity Care, 1988-1999.* Chicago: American Medical Association, Center for Health Policy Research.

Kane, Nancy M., and William H. Wubbenhorst. 2000. Alternative Funding Policies for the Uninsured: Exploring the Value of Hospital Tax Exemption. *Milbank Quarterly* 78(2)150, 185-212.

Kaplan, George A., Elsie R. Pamuk, John W. Lynch, Richard D. Cohen, et al. 1996. Inequality in Income and Mortality in the United States: An Analysis of Mortality and Potential Pathways. *British Medical Journal* 312(7037):999-1003.

Kates, Jennifer, and Richard Sorian. 2000. *Financing HIV/AIDS Care: A Quilt with Many Holes.* Menlo Park, CA: Kaiser Family Foundation.

Katz, Aaron, Robert E. Hurley, Leslie Jackson, Timothy K Lake, et al. 2000. *Provider Systems Thrive in Robust Economy. Indianapolis, Indiana.* Washington, DC: Center for Studying Health System Change.

Katz, Aaron, Robert E. Hurley, Leslie Jackson, Timothy K. Lake, et al. 2001. *Insurers Consolidate, Hospitals Struggle Financially. Syracuse, New York.* Washington, DC: Center for Studying Health System Change.

Kawachi, Ichiro. 1999. Social Capital and Community Effects on Population and Individual Health. Pp. 120-130 in: *Socioeconomic Status and Health in Industrial Nations. Social, Psychological, and Biological Pathways,* Nancy E. Adler, Michael Marmot, Bruce S. McEwan, and Judith Stewart, eds. New York: New York Academy of Sciences.

Kawachi, Ichiro, and Bruce P. Kennedy. 1997a. Health and Social Cohesion: Why Care About Income Inequality? *British Medical Journal* 314(7086):1037-1040.

———. 1997b. The Relationship of Income Inequality to Mortality: Does the Choice of Indicator Matter? *Social Science & Medicine* 45(7):1121-1127.

———. 1999. Income Inequality and Health: Pathways and Mechanisms. *Health Services Research* 34(1 Pt. 2):215-227.

Kawachi, Ichiro, and Tony A. Blakely. 2001. When Economists and Epidemiologists Disagree... *Journal of Health Politics, Policy and Law* 26(3):533-541.

Kawachi, Ichiro, Bruce P. Kennedy, Kimberly Lochner, and Deborah Prothrow-Stith. 1997. Social Capital, Income Inequality, and Mortality. *American Journal of Public Health* 87(9):1491-1498.

Kawachi, Ichiro, Bruce P. Kennedy, and Roberta Glass. 1998. Social Capital and Self-Rated Health: A Contextual Analysis. *American Journal of Public Health* 89(8):1187-1193.

Kawachi, Ichiro, Bruce P. Kennedy, and Richard G. Wilkinson. 1999. *Income Inequality and Health: A Reader* . New York: The New Press.

Keane, Christopher, John Marx, and Edmund Ricci. 2001a. Local Health Departments' Changing Role in Provision and Assurance of Safety Net Services. Accessed December 2, 2002. Available at: http://www.hrsa.gov/financeMC/LHDabstract.pdf.

Keane, Christopher, John Marx, and Edmund Ricci. 2001b. Perceived Outcomes of Public Health Privatization: A National Survey of Local Health Department Directors. *The Milbank Quarterly* 79(1):115-137.

Keane, Christopher, John Marx, and Edmund Ricci. 2001c. Privatization and the Scope of Public Health: A National Survey of Local Health Department Directors. *American Journal of Public Health* 91(4):611-617.

Keeler, Emmett B., Glenn A. Melnick, and Jack Zwanziger. 1999. The Changing Effects of Competition on Non-Profit and For-Profit Hosptial Pricing Behavior. *Journal of Health Economics* 18(1):69-86.

Kellermann, Arthur L. 1991. Too Sick to Wait. *Journal of the American Medical Association* 266(8):1123-1125.

———. 1994. Nonurgent Emergency Department Visits. *Journal of the American Medical Association* 271(24):1953-1954.

Kellermann, Arthur L., and Bela B. Hackman. 1990. Patient 'Dumping' Post-COBRA. *American Journal of Public Health* 80(7):864-867.

Kellogg Foundation. 2002. *More Than a Market: Making Sense of Health Care Systems.* Battle Creek, MI: The W.K. Kellogg Foundation.

Kennedy, Bruce P., Ichiro Kawachi, and Deborah Prothrow-Stith. 1996. Income Distribution and Mortality: Cross Sectional Ecological Study of the Robin Hood Index in the United States. *British Medical Journal* 312(7037):1004-1007.

Kershaw, Sarah. 2002. The New Front in the Battle Against TB. *New York Times.* Accessed on May 20, 2002. Available at: http:// nytimes.com/2002/05/20/nyregion/20TUBE.html.

Koeze, Jeffrey S. 1994. Paying for Public Health Services in North Carolina. *Popular Government* 60(2):11-20.

Kohn, Linda T., Janet M. Corrigan, and Molla S. Donaldson, eds. 1999. *To Err Is Human: Building a Safer Health System.* Washington, DC: National Academy Press.

Komaromy, Miriam, Nicole Lurie, and Andrew B. Bindman. 1995. California Physicians' Willingness to Care for the Poor. *Western Journal of Medicine* 162(2):127-132.

Kozak, Lola J., Margaret J. Hall, and Maria F. Owings. 2001. Trends in Avoidable Hospitalizations, 1980-1998. *Health Affairs* 20(2):225-232.

Krumholz Harlan M., Jersey Chen., Saif S. Rathore, Yongfei Wang, et al.. Forthcoming 2003. Regional Variation in the Treatment and Outcomes of Myocardial Infarction: Investigating New England's aAdvantage. *American Heart Journal.*

Ku, Leighton, and Teresa A. Coughlin. 1995. Medicaid Disproportionate Share and Other Special Financing Programs. *Health Care Financing Review* 16(3):27-54.

Ku, Leighton, and Sheetal Matani. 2001. Left Out: Immigrants' Access to Health Care and Insurance. *Health Affairs* 20(1):247-256.

Landry, David J., and Jacqueline D. Forrest. 1996. Public Health Departments Providing Sexually Transmitted Disease Services. *Family Planning Perspectives* 28(6):261-266.

Lapping, Mark B., and David Hartley. 2000. *Case Report. Great Plains County North Dakota.* Portland, ME: Maine Rural Health Research Center.

Larrubia, Evelyn. 2002. Supervisors OK Limited Health Services Cuts. Spending: Plan to Address a Looming Funding Shortfall Leaves Toughest Decisions for New Agency Director. *Los Angeles Times.* Accessed January 30, 2002. p. B4. Available at: http://www.latines.com/news//local//a-000007535jm30.story?col1/a%2Dheadlines%2DCalifornia.

Lazarus, William, Brady Foust, and Ben Hitt. 2000. *The Florida Health Insurance Study. Volume 6: The Small Area Analysis.* Tallahassee, FL: The State of Florida, Agency for Health Care Administration.

Leichter, H. M. 1999. Oregon's Bold Experiment: Whatever Happened to Rationing? *Journal of Health Politics, Policy and Law* 24(1):147-160.

Levit, Katherine R., Gary L. Olin, and Suzanne W. Letsch. 1992. Americans' Health Insurance Coverage, 1980-91. *Health Care Financing Review* 14(1):31-57.

Lewin Group. 2002. *Emergency Department Overload: A Growing Crisis.* Washington, DC: American Hospital Association, American College of Emergency Physicians.

Lewin, Marion Ein, and Stuart Altman, eds. 2000. *America's Health Care Safety Net. Intact but Endangered.* Washington, DC: National Academy Press.

Lewis, Irving J. 1983. Evolution of Federal Policy on Access to Health Care, 1965 to 1980. *Bulletin of the New York Academy of Medicine* 59(1):9-20.

Lipson, Debra J., and Naomi Naierman. 1996. Effects of Health System Changes On Safety-Net Providers. *Health Affairs* 15(2):33-48.

Lochner, Kimberly, Ichiro Kawachi, and Bruce P. Kennedy. 1999. Social Capital: A Guide to Its Measurement. *Health and Place* 5(4):259-270.

Long, Stephen H., and M. Susan Marquis. 1994. The Uninsured 'Access Gap' and the Cost of Universal Coverage. *Health Affairs* 13(2):211-220.

Luft, Hal S., James C. Robinson, Deborah W. Garnick, S.C. Maerki, et al. 1986. The Role of Specialized Clinical Services in Competition Among Hospitals. *Inquiry* 23(1):83-94.

Lukehart, Sheila A., and King K. Holmes. 1998. Syphilis. Pp. 1023-1033 in *Harrison's Principles of Internal Medicine*, 14th ed. Anthony S. Fauci, Eugene Braunwald, Kurt J. Isselbacher, Jean D. Wilson, et al., eds. New York: McGraw-Hill.

Lurie, Nicole. 2002. Measuring Disparities in Access to Care. Pp. 99-147 in: *Guidance for the National Healthcare Disparities Report.* Elaine K. Swift, ed. Washington, DC: The National Academies Press.

Lutzky, Amy W., and Stephen Zuckerman. 2002. *Recent Changes in Health Policy for Low-Income People in California.* Washington, DC: The Urban Institute.

Lutzsky, Amy W., Jon Holahan, and Joshua M. Wiener. 2002. *Health Policy for Low-Income People: Profiles of 13 States.* Washington, DC: The Urban Institute.

Lynch, John W., George A. Kaplan, Elise R. Pamuk, Richard D. Cohen, et al. 1999. Income Inequality and Mortality in Metropolitan Areas of the United States. Pp. 69-81 in: *The Society and Population Health Reader. Income Inequality and Health,* Ichiro Kawachi, Bruce P. Kennedy, and Richard G. Wilkinson, eds. New York: The New Press.

Macinko, James, and Barbara Starfield. 2001. The Utility of Social Capital in Research on Health Determinants. *Milbank Quarterly* 79(3):387-427.

Malone, Ruth E., and Daniel Dohan. 2000. Emergency Department Closures: Policy Issues. *Journal of Emergency Nursing* 26(4):380-383.

Mandelblatt, Jeanne S., Karen Gold, Ann S. O'Malley, Kathryn Taylor, et al. 1999. Breast and Cervix Cancer Screening Among Multiethnic Women: Role of Age, Health, and Source of Care. *Preventive Medicine* 28(4):418-425.

Mann, Joyce M., Glenn A. Melnick, Anil Bamezai, and Jack Zwanziger. 1995. Managing the Safety Net: Hospital Provision of Uncompensated Care in Response to Managed Care. *Advances in Health Economics and Health Services Research* 15:49-77.

Mann, Joyce M., Glenn A. Melnick, Anil Bamezai, and Jack Zwanziger. 1997. A Profile of Uncompensated Hospital Care, 1983-1995. *Health Affairs* 16(4):223-232.

Mark, Tami L., and Michael Cheng. 1997. *The Community Impact of Hospital Mergers and Conversions.* Bethesda, MD: Project Hope Center for Health Affairs.

Markus, Anne, Dylan Roby, and Sara Rosenbaum. 2002. *A Profile of Federally Funded Health Centers Serving a Higher Proportion of Uninsured Patients.* Washington, DC: The Kaiser Commission on Medicaid and the Uninsured.

Marmor, Theodore. 2000. *The Politics of Medicare.* 2nd ed. New York: Hawthorne.

Marquis, M. Susan, and Stephen H. Long. 1994-1995. The Uninsured Access Gap: Narrowing the Estimates. *Inquiry* 31(4):405-414.

Marsteller, Jill A., Len M. Nichols, Adam Badawi, Bethany Kessler, et al. 1998. Variations in the Uninsured State and County Level Analyses. Accessed May 1, 2001. Available at: http://www.urban.org/health/variatfr.html.

Martinez, Rose M., and Elizabeth Closter. 1998. *Public Health Departments Adapt to Medicaid Managed Care.* Issue Brief No. 16. Washington, DC: Center for Studying Health System Change.

Matherlee, Karen. 2001. *Mission Possible? Maintaining the Safety Net in Urban and Rural Colorado.* Washington, DC: National Health Policy Forum.

Mays, Glen P., Paul K. Halverson, and Rachel Stevens. 2001. The Contributions of Managed Care Plans to Public Health Practice: Evidence from the Nation's Largest Local Health Departments. *Public Health Reports* 116(Suppl. 1):50-67.

McAlearney, John S. 2002. The Financial Performance of Community Health Centers, 1996–1999. *Health Affairs* 21(2):219-225.

McAlpine, Donna D., and David Mechanic. 2000. Utilization of Specialty Mental Health Care Among Persons With Severe Mental Illness: The Roles of Demographics, Need, Insurance, and Risk. *Health Services Research* 35(1):277-282.

McCaig, Linda F., and Nghi Ly. 2002. *National Hospital Ambulatory Medical Care Survey: 2000 Emergency Department Summary.* Advance Data from Vital and Health Statistics, No. 32. Hyattsville, MD: National Center for Health Statistics.

McManus, Michael. 2001. *Emergency Department Overcrowding in Massachusetts: Making Room in Our Hospitals.* Waltham, MA: The Massachusetts Health Policy Forum.

Medicare Payment Advisory Commission (MedPAC). 2001. *Report to the Congress: Medicare in Rural America.* Washington, DC: MedPAC.

———. 2002a. *Report to the Congress: Medicare Payment Policy.* Washington, DC: MedPAC.

———. 2002b. *Report to the Congress: Assessing Medicare Benefits.* Washington, DC: MedPAC.

Mellor, Jennifer M., and Jeffrey Milyo. 2001. Reexamining the Ecological Association Between Income Inequality and Health. *Journal of Health, Politics, Policy and Law* 26(3):487-522.

———. 2002. Income Inequality and Health Status: Evidence from the Current Population Survey. *Journal of Human Resources* 37(3):510-539.

Melnick, Glenn A., Joyce Mann, and I. Golan. 1989. Uncompensated Emergency Care in Hospital Markets in Los Angeles County. *American Journal of Public Health* 79(4):514-516.

Melnick, Glenn A., Jack Zwanziger, Anil Bamezai, and R. Pattison. 1992. The Effects of Market Structure and Bargaining Position on Hospital Prices. *Journal of Health Economics* 11(3):217-233.

Meyer, Jack A., Mark Legnini, Emily K. Fatula, and Larry S. Stepnick. 1999. *The Role of Local Governments in Financing Safety Net Hospitals: Houston, Oakland, and Miami.* Occasional Paper, 25. Washington, DC: The Urban Institute.

MGT of America. 2002. *Medical Emergency: Costs of Uncompensated Care in Southwest Border Counties.* Washington, DC: United States/Mexico Border Counties Coalition.

Miller, Robert H., and Harold S. Luft. 1994. Managed Care Plan Performance Since 1980. A Literature Analysis. *Journal of the American Medical Association* 271(19):1512-1519.

Miller, Victor. 1985. Recent Changes in Federal Grants and State Budgets. Pp. 44-64 in: *The Health Policy Agenda. Some Critical Questions.* Marion Ein Lewin, ed. Washington, DC: American Enterprise Institute.

———. 2001. *Health Centers Expansion.* Issue Brief 01-34. Washington, DC: Federal Funds Information for States.

———. 2002a. *Medicaid Cliff Looms for Disproportionate Share Hospital Payments.* Issue Brief 02-23. Washington, DC: Federal Funds Information for States.

———. 2002b. *The States, Medicaid, and Health Care Spending.* Washington, DC: Unpublished presentation to the IOM Committee on the Consequences of Uninsurance.

Miller, Wilhelmine. 1997. *Egalitarianism and Self-Respect.* Washington, DC: Unpublished Ph.D. dissertation, Georgetown University.

Millman, Michael, ed. 1993. *Access to Health Care in America.* Washington, DC: National Academy Press.

Mills, Robert J. 2002. *Health Insurance Coverage: 2001.* Current Population Reports. P60-220. Washington, DC: U.S. Department of Commerce, Economics and Statistics Administration, U.S. Census Bureau.

Morrisey, Michael A. 1993. Hospital Pricing: Cost-Shifting and Competition. *EBRI Issue Brief* 137:1-17.

———. 1994. *Cost Shifting in Health Care. Separating Evidence From Rhetoric.* Washington, DC: The AEI Press.

———. 1996. Hospital Cost Shifting, A Continuing Debate. *EBRI Issue Brief* 180:1-13.

———. 2002. Cost Shifting…Again? Washington, DC: Unpublished presentation at AcademyHealth meeting, "When Public Payment Declines Does Cost-Shifting Occur? Hospital and Physician Responses."

Mueller, Keith J., Andy Coburn, and Sam M. Cordes. 1999. The Changing Landscape of Health Care Financing and Delivery: How Are Rural Communities and Providers Responding? *The Milbank Quarterly* 77(4):485-510.

Narayan, Deepa. 1999. *Bonds and Bridges: Social Capital and Poverty.* Washington, DC: The World Bank.

National Association of Community Health Centers (NACHC). 2002. *President Bush Signs Community Health Center Legislation into Law.* Accessed November 14, 2002. Available at: http://www.nachc.com/advocacy/Reauth_Enactment.asp.

National Association of County and City Health Officials (NACCHO). 2001. *Local Public Health Agency Infrastructure: A Chartbook.* Accessed October 26, 2001. Available at: http://www.nacco.org/general428.cfm.

National Association of Rural Health Clinics (NARHC). N.d. *Rural Health Clinics Act – PL 95-210. An Overview.* Accessed October 1, 2002. Available at: http://www.narhc.org/Program%20Overview.htm

National Association of State Budget Officers and the Reforming States Group. 2001. *1998-1999 State Health Care Expenditure Report.* New York: The Milbank Memorial Fund; National Association of State Budget Officers; Reforming States Group.

National Center for Health Statistics (NCHS). 2001. *Urban and Rural Health Chartbook. Health, United States, 2001.* Hyattsville, MD: National Center for Health Statistics.

Needleman, Jack. 1999. For-Profit Conversions. Nonprofit to For-Profit Conversions by Hospitals, Health Insurers, and Health Plans. *Public Health Reports* 114(2):108-119.

———. 2000. *Community Impacts of Uninsurance.* Washington, DC: Unpublished paper prepared for the IOM Committee on the Consequences of Uninsurance.

———. 2001. The Role of Nonprofits in Health Care. *Journal of Health Politics, Policy and Law* 26(5):1125-30.

Needleman, Jack, Jeffrey Lamphere, and Deborah Chollet. 1999. Uncompensated Care and Hospital Conversions in Florida. *Health Affairs* 18(4):125-133.

Needleman, Jack, and Darrell J. Gaskin. 2002. *The Impact of Uninsured Discharges on the Availability of Hospital Services and Hospital Margins in Rural Areas.* Boston: Harvard School of Public Health.

Needleman, Jack, Peter I. Buerhaus, Soeren Mattke, Maureen Stewart, et al. 2002. Nurse-Staffing Levels and the Quality of Care in Hospitals. *New England Journal of Medicine* 346(22):1715-1722.

Nguyen, Dong-Phuong. 2002. County Finds Funds for Indigent Care. Hillsborough's Model Program to Provide Health Care for the Poor Survives as County Commission Provides a Bailout Uncompensated Care and Hospital Conversions in Florida. *St. Petersburg Times Online.* Accessed January 31, 2002. Available at: http://www.sptimes.com/2002/01/31/news_pf/TampaBay/County_finds_funds_fo.shtml.

Nicholson, Sean. 2002. *Medicare Hospital Subsidies. Money in Search of a Purpose.* Washington, DC: The American Enterprise Institute Press.

Nicholson, Sean, Mark V. Pauly, Lawton R. Burns, Agnieshka Baumwritter, et al. 2000. Measuring Community Benefits Provided by For-Profit and Nonprofit Hospitals. *Health Affairs* 19(6):168-177.

Noether, Monica. 1988. Competition Among Hospitals. *Journal of Health Economics* 7(3):259-284.

Norton, Stephen A., and Deborah J. Lipson. 1998. *Portraits of the Safety Net: The Market, Policy Environment, and Safety Net Response.* Occasional Paper No. 19. Washington, DC: The Urban Institute.

Numbers, Ronald L. 1985. The Third Party: Health Insurance in America. Pp. 233-247 in: *Sickness and Health in America. Readings in the History of Medicine and Public Health* . 2nd ed. Judith Leavitt and Ronald Numbers, eds. Madison, WI: University of Wisconsin Press.

Ormond, Barbara A., and Amy Westpfahl Lutzky. 2001. *Ambulatory Care for the Urban Poor: Structure: Financing, and System Stability.* Occasional Paper No. 49. Washington, DC: The Urban Institute.

Ormond, Barbara A., and Alyssa Wigton. 2002. *Recent Changes in Health Policy for Low-Income People in Alabama.* State Update 13. Washington, DC: The Urban Institute.

Ormond, Barbara A., Susan Wallin, and Susan M. Goldenson. 2000a. *Supporting the Rural Health Care Safety Net.* Occasional Paper No. 36. Washington, DC: The Urban Institute.

Ormond, Barbara A., Stephen Zuckerman, and Aparna Lhila. 2000b. Rural/Urban Differences in Health Care Are Not Uniform Across States. Series B, B-11. Washington, DC: The Urban Institute. Accessed March 26, 2001. Available at: http://newfederalism.urban.org/html/series_b/b11/b11.html.

Pappas, Gregory, Wilbur C. Hadden, Lola Jean Kozak, and Gail F. Fisher. 1997. Potentially Avoidable Hospitalizations: Inequities in Rates Between U.S. Socioeconomic Groups. *American Journal of Public Health* 87(5):811-816.

Parchman, Michael L. 2002. *Cross-Border Utilization of Health Care on the U.S.-Mexico Border.* Washington, DC: Unpublished presentation at the 2002 Annual Meeting of the Academy for Health Services Research and Health Policy.

Pilote Louise, Robert M. Califf, Shelly Sapp, Dave P. Miller, et al. 1995. Regional Variation Across the United States in the Management of Acute Myocardial Infarction. *New England Journal of Medicine* 333(19):565-572.

Pinkerton, James. 2002. Health Care: Crisis at the Border. Poverty, Lack of Doctors Cloud Area's Future. *Houston Chronicle (TX).* Accessed May 5, 2002. Available at: http://www.chron.com/cs/CDA/story.hts/topstory/1396674.

Poley, Stephanie T., and Thomas C. Ricketts. 2001. *Fewer Hospitals Close in the 1990s: Rural Hospitals Mirror This Trend.* Chapel Hill, NC: North Carolina Rural Health Research and Policy Analysis Program, Cecil G. Sheps Center for Health Services Research, UNC-Chapel Hill.

Porell, Frank W., and E. Katherine Adams. 1999. Hospital Choice Models: A Review and Assessment of Their Utility for Policy Impact Analysis. *Medical Care Research & Review* 52(2):158-195.

Portes, Alejandro. 1998. Social Capital: Its Origins and Applications in Modern Sociology. *Annual Review of Sociology* 24(1):1-24.

Powell, Jennifer H. 2002. Hospitals Dread Loss of Aid to Uninsured. *Boston Herald,* p. 023. October 21.

Powell-Griner, Eve, Julie Bolen, and Shayne Bland. 1999. Health Care Coverage and Use of Preventive Services Among the Near Elderly in the United States. *American Journal of Public Health* 89(6):882-886.

President's New Freedom Commission on Mental Health (President's Commission). 2002. Interim Report of the President's New Freedom Commission on Mental Health. Washington, DC: Executive Office of the President.

Prinz, Timothy S., Kathryn Haslanger, Derek DeLia, Steven Fass, et al. 2000. *Hospital Markets, Policy Change, and Access to Care for Low-Income Populations in New York.* New York: United Hospital Fund.

Raiford, David. 2002. Rural Docs in Demand. Recruitment Top Priority Among Local Non-Urban Hospital Firms. *Nashville Business Journal* (Nashville, TN). Accessed May 3, 2002. Available at: http://www.bizjournals.com/industries/health_care/hospitals/2002/05/06/nashville_story3.html.

Rajan, Shruti. 1998. Publicly Subsidized Health Insurance: A Typology of State Approaches. *Health Affairs* 17(3):101-117.

Ramirez, Margaret. 2001. Study: Hospital Care Suffering. Competition Bad for Poor, Uninsured. *Newsday* (New York). Accessed May 8, 2001. Available at: http://www.newsday.com/news/skybot/city/tuesday/nd3668.htm.

Rask, Kevin N., and Kimberly J. Rask. 2000. Public Insurance Substituting for Private Insurance: New Evidence Regarding Public Hospitals, Uncompensated Care Funds, and Medicaid. *Journal of Health Economics* 19(1):1-31.

Rask, Kimberly. 1994. Hospital Discharge Data and The Uninsured. *Journal of Health Care for the Poor and Underserved* 5(4):275-279.

Rask, Kimberly J., Mark V. Williams, Ruth M. Parker, and S.E. McNagny. 1994. Obstacles Predicting Lack of a Regular Provider and Delays in Seeking Care for Patients at an Urban Public Hospital. *Journal of the American Medical Association* 271(24):1931-1933.

Redman, Eric. 1973. *The Dance of Legislation.* New York: Simon and Schuster.

Reed, Marie C., Peter J. Cunningham, and Jeffrey J. Stoddard. 2001. *Physicians Pulling Back from Charity Care.* Issue Brief No. 42, Findings from HSC. Washington, DC: Center for Studying Health System Change.

Reuter, James, and Darrell Gaskin. 1997. Academic Health Centers in Competitive Markets. *Health Affairs* 16: 242-252.

Rhee, Peter M., David Grossman, Frederick Rivara, Charles Mock, et al. 1997. The Effect of Payer Status on Utilization of Hospital Resources in Trauma Care. *Archives of Surgery* 132(4):399-404.

Riccardi, Nicholas. 2002a. County's Dilemma: Cost Vs. Care. Health: L.A. Supervisors Weigh Clinic Closures Against the Commitment to Serve the Poor and Uninsured—A Thankless Balancing Act. *Los Angeles Times*, p. B1. Accessed June 24, 2002. Available at: http://www. latimes.com/news/local/la-000044258jun24.story?coll=la%2Dheadlines%2Dcalifornia.

———. 2002b. State Balks Over L.A.'s Health Cuts. Finance: County's Request for a $1.4-Billion Federal Bailout Stalls While the Davis Administration Seeks a Reevaluation of Plans to Shutter 11 Clinics. *Los Angeles Times*, p. B1. Accessed August 10, 2002. Available at: http://www. latimes.com/news/local/la-me-health10aug10.story?coll=la-headlines-california.

Riccardi, Nicholas, Evelyn Larrubia, and Garrett Therolf. 2002. Health Care Takes Deep Cuts. Budget: County Supervisors Vote to Close 11 of 18 Clinics, Pare 5,000 Jobs and End Inpatient Services at High Desert Hospital. *Los Angeles Times*, p. B1. Accessed June 27, 2002. Available at: http://www.latimes.com/news/local/la-me-health27jun27.story?coll=la%2Dheadlines%2Dcalifornia.

Richards, John R., Misty L. Navarro, and Robert W. Derlet. 2000. Survey of Directors of Emergency Departments in California on Overcrowding. *Western Journal of Medicine* 172(6):385-388.

Ricketts, Thomas C. 2002. *Community Capacity to Improve Population Health: How Can We Measure It?* Chapel Hill, NC: Unpublished paper prepared for The Robert Wood Johnson Foundation.

Robinson, James C. 1996. Decline in Hospital Utilization and Cost Inflation Under Managed Care in California. *Journal of the American Medical Association* 276(13):1060-1064.

Robinson, James C., and Harold S. Luft. 1985. The Impact of Hospital Market Structure on Patient Volume, Average Length Stay, and the Cost of Care. *Journal of Health Economics* 4(4):333-356.

———. 1988. Competition, Regulation, and Hospital Costs, 1982 to 1986. *Journal of the American Medical Association* 260(18):2676-2681.

Rodewald, Lance E., Peter G. Szilagyi, Jane Holl, Laura R. Shone, et al. 1997. Health Insurance for Low-Income Working Families. *Archives of Pediatric and Adolescent Medicine* 151(8):798-803.

Roetzheim, Richard G., Naazneen Pal, Eduardo C. Gonzalez, Jeanne M. Ferrante, et al. 2000. Effects of Health Insurance and Race on Colorectal Cancer Treatments and Outcomes. *American Journal of Public Health* 90(11):1746-1754.

Roper, William L. 2000. Breaking the 'Immunization Cycle'. *American Journal of Preventive Medicine* 19(3 Suppl.):113-115.

Rosenbaum, Sara, Sara Wilensky, Peter Shin, and Dylan Roby. 2002. *Managed Care and Community Health Centers: An Overview and Analysis*. Washington, DC: The George Washington University School of Public Health and Health Services, Center for Health Services Research and Policy.

Rosenberg, Charles. 1987. *The Care of Strangers. The Rise of America's Hospital System*. New York, NY: Basic Books.

Rowley, Thomas. 2002. *The Rural Uninsured: Highlights from Recent Research*. Washington, DC: U.S. Department of Health and Human Services, Health Resources and Services Administration, Office of Rural Health.

Rubin, Lillian B. 1994. *Families on the Fault Line*. New York: HarperCollins Publishers.

Rundall, Thomas G., Shoshanna Sofaer, and Wendy Lambert. 1988. Uncompensated Hospital Care in California: Private and Public Hospital Respnses to Competitive Market Forces. *Advances in Health Economics and Health Research* 9:113-33.

Rundle, Rhonda L. 2002. Garthwaite Aims To Revamp Los Angeles Health System. *Wall Street Journal*. Accessed July 15, 2002. Available at: http://online.wsj.com/article/0,,SB10266822 22606127840-search,00.html?collection=wsjie/2day&vql-string=%28Los+Angeles%29%3 Cin%3E%28article%2Dbody%29.

Salit, Sharon A., Steve Fass, and Mark Nowak. 2002. Out of the Frying Pan: New York City Hospitals in an Age of Deregulation. *Health Affairs* 21(1):127-139.

Sampson, Robert J., and Jeffrey D. Morenoff. 2000. Paper Contribution 1. Public Health and Safety in Context: Lessons From Community-Level Theory on Social Capital. In: *Promoting Health. Intervention Strategies From Social and Behavioral Research*. Washington, DC: National Academy Press.

Santoli, Jeanne M., Sabeena Setia, Lance E. Rodewald, Dennis O'Mara, et al. 2000. Immunization Pockets of Need. Science and Practice. *American Journal of Preventive Medicine* 19(3S):89-98.

Sardell, Alice. 1988. *The U.S. Experiment in Social Medicine: The Community Health Center Program, 1965-1986*. Pittsburgh, PA: University of Pittsburgh Press.

Saywell, Robert M. Jr., John R. Woods, Jr., George H. Rodman, A.W. Nyhuis, et al. 1989a. Financial Analysis of Inner-City Helicopter Service: Charges Versus Collections. *Annals of Emergency Medicine* 18(1):21-25.

Saywell, Robert M. Jr., Terrell W. Zollinger, D.K. Chu, C.A. MacBeth, et al. 1989b. Hospital and Patient Characteristics of Uncompensated Hospital Care: Policy Implications. *Journal of Health Politics, Policy and Law* 14(2):287-307.

Schiff, Robert L., David A. Ansell, James E. Schlosser, Ahamed H. Idris, et al. 1986. Transfers to a Public Hospital. *New England Journal of Medicine* 314(9):552-557.

Schlesinger, Mark. 1997. Paradigms Lost: The Persisting Search for Community in U.S. Health Policy. *Journal of Health Politics, Policy and Law* 22(4):937-992.

Schneider, Andy. 2002. *The Medicaid Resource Book*. Washington, DC: The Kaiser Commission on Medicaid and the Uninsured.

Schur, Claudia L., and Sheila J. Franco. 1999. Access to Health Care. Pp. 25-37 in: *Rural Health in the United States*, Thomas C. Ricketts III, ed. New York: Oxford University Press.

Scorsone, Eric A., Sharon Garcia, and Bethany Adams. 2001. *Economic Impact of Knox County Hospital.* Lexington, KY: Kentucky Rural Health Works.

Seifert, Robert. 2002. *The Uncompensated Care Pool: Saving The Safety Net.* Waltham, MA: The Massachusetts Health Policy Forum.

Selzer, Don, Gerardo Gomez, Lewis Jacobson, Todd Wischmeyer, et al. 2001. Public Hospital-Based Level I Trauma Centers: Financial Survival in the New Millenium. *The Journal of Trauma, Injury, Infection, and Critical Care* 51(2):301-307.

Sengupta, Somini. 2001. Health Agency Seeks to Close 27 Clinics. *New York Times.* Accessed May 15, 2001. Available at: http://www.nytimes.com/2001/05/15/nyregion/15CLIN.html.

Shi, Leiyu. 2000. Vulnerable Populations and Health Insurance. *Medical Care Research and Review* 57(1):110-134.

Shi, Leiyu. 2001. The Convergence of Vulnerable Characteristics and Health Insurance in the US. *Social Science and Medicine* 53(4):519-529.

Shi, Leiyu, Robert M. Politzer, Jerri Regan, Deborah Lewis-Idema, et al. 2001. The Impact of Managed Care on the Mix of Vulnerable Populations Served by Community Health Centers. *Journal of Ambulatory Care Management* 24(1):51-66.

Shi, Leiyu, Barbara Starfield, Robert Politzer, and Jerri Regan. 2002. Primary Care, Self-Rated Health, and Reductions in Social Disparities in Health. *Health Services Research* 37(3):529-550.

Short, Pamela F. 2001. *Counting and Characterizing the Uninsured.* Ann Arbor, MI: Economic Research Initiative on the Uninsured.

Shortell, Stephen M., and Ellen F. Hughes. 1988. The Effects of Regulation, Competition, and Ownership on Mortality Rates Among Hospital Inpatients. *New England Journal of Medicine* 318(17):1100-7110.

Siegel, Bruce. 1996. Re-Engineering the Public Hospital System: Saving the Safety Net. *Bulletin of the New York Academy of Medicine* 73(2):357-369.

Sisk, Jane E. 2000. The Best and Worst of Times: Use of Adult Immunizations. *American Journal of Preventive Medicine* 19(3 Suppl.):26-28.

Slifkin, Rebecca T., Pam Silberman, and Susan Reif. 2000. *The Effect of Market Reform on Rural Public Health Departments.* Working Paper 65. Chapel Hill, NC: Cecil G. Sheps Center for Health Services Research, University of North Carolina at Chapel Hill.

Smedley, Brian D., Adrienne Y. Stith, and Alan R. Nelson, eds. 2002. *Unequal Treatment: Confronting Racial and Ethnic Disparities in Health Care.* Washington, DC: National Academies Press.

Smith, David R. 2000. Immunization in the New Millenium: Meeting the Challenge to Realize the Promise. *American Journal of Preventive Medicine* 19(3 Suppl.):1-4.

Smith, David R., Wilhelmine Miller, Hanns Kuttner, and William L. Roper, eds. 2000. *American Journal of Preventive Medicine* 19(3 Suppl.).

Smith, Vernon, Eileen Ellis, Kathy Gifford, Rekha Ramesh, et al. 2002. *Medicaid Spending Growth: Results from a 2002 Survey.* Pub. No. 4064. Washington, DC: The Henry J. Kaiser Family Foundation.

Sobel, Joel. 2002. Can We Trust Social Capital? *Journal of Economic Literature* 40(1):139-154.

Sorvillo, Frank, Peter Kerndt, Sylvia Odem, M. Castillon, et al. 1999. Use of Protease Inhibitors Among Persons with AIDS in Los Angeles County. *AIDS Care* 11(2):147-155.

Spencer, Christine S. 1998. Do Uncompensated Care Pools Change the Distribution of Hospital Care to the Uninsured? *Journal of Health Politics, Policy and Law* 23(1):53-73.

Starr, Paul. 1982. *The Social Transformation of American Medicine.* New York: Basic Books.

State Health Access Data Assistance Center (SHADAC). 2002. *Overview of Approaches for Estimating Uninsurance Rates at the Sub-State Level.* Issue Brief No. 5. Minneapolis, MN: State Health Access Data Assistance Center.

State of Idaho. 2002. *Idaho State Planning Grant.* Boise, ID: Idaho Department of Commerce.

State of New Mexico. 2000. *County Funded Health Care Report. State Fiscal Year 1999.* Santa Fe, NM: New Mexico Health Policy Commission.

State of New Mexico. 2002. *County Funded Health Care Report. State Fiscal Year 2001*. Santa Fe, NM: New Mexico Health Policy Commission.

State of Oregon. 2001. *Oregon HRSA State Planning Grant. Final Report to the Secretary*. Salem, OR: Oregon Health Policy and Research, HRSA Universal Care Planning Project.

State of Texas. 2002. *Texas State Planning Grant. Final Report to the Secretary. U.S. Department of Health and Human Services*. Austin, TX: Texas Department of Insurance.

State of Texas Comptroller's Office. 2000. *Texas Estimated Health Care Spending on the Uninsured*. Austin, TX: The State of Texas.

State of Vermont. 2001. *Profile of the Vermont Uninsured Population*. Issue Brief No. 1. Montpelier, VT: Vermont Department of Banking, Insurance, Securities and Health Care Administration.

Steinberg, Caroline R., and Raymond J. Baxter. 1998. Accountable Communities: How Norms And Values Affect Health System Change. *Health Affairs* 17(4):149-157.

Steinhauer, Jennifer. 2001a. After 5 Years of Fiscal Success, City Public Hospitals Face Deficit. *New York Times*. Accessed May 23, 2001. Available at: http://www.nytimes.com/2001/05/23/nyregion/23HEAL.html

Steinhauer, Jennifer. 2001b. 15 School Health Clinics Scheduled for Closing Get a Reprieve. *New York Times*. Accessed June 1, 2001. Available at: http://www.nytimes.com/2001/06.01/nyregion/01CLIN.html.

Stevens, Robert and Rosemary Stevens. 1974. *Welfare Medicine in America. A Case Study of Medicaid*. New Haven, CT: Yale University Press.

Stevens, Rosemary. 1989. *In Sickness and In Wealth: America's Hospitals in the Twentieth Century*. New York: Basic Books.

Stock, Lawrence M., Georgienne E. Bradley, Roger J. Lewis, David W. Baker, et al. 1994. Patients Who Leave Emergency Departments Without Being Seen by a Physician: Magnitude of the Problem in Los Angeles County. *Annals of Emergency Medicine* 23(2):294-298.

Strunk, Bradley C., Paul B. Ginsburg, and Jon R. Gabel. 2002. Tracking Health Care Costs: Growth Accelerates Again in 2001. *Health Affairs* Web Exclusive:W299-W310. Available at: http://www.healthaffairs.org/WebExclusives/2106Strunk.pdf.

Sutton, Janet, Bonnie B. Blanchfield, Andrew Singer, and Meredith J. Milet. 2001. *Is the Rural Safety Net at Risk? Analyses of Charity and Uncompensated Care Provided by Rural Hospitals in Washington, West Virginia, Texas, Iowa, and Vermont*. Bethesda, MD: The Project HOPE Walsh Center for Rural Health Analysis.

Swift, Elaine K.(ed.). 2002. *Guidance for the National Healthcare Disparities Report*. Washington, DC: National Academies Press.

Taheri, Paul A., David A. Butz, and Lazar J. Greenfield. 1999. Paying a Premium: How Patient Complexity Affects Costs and Profit Margins. *Annals of Surgery* 229(6):807-811; discussion 811-814.

Taylor, Pat, Lynn Blewitt, Michelle Brasure, Kathleen Call Thiede, et al. 2001. *Small Town Health Care Safety Nets. Preliminary Report on a Pilot Study*. Washington, DC: Health Resources and Services Administration, Office of Rural Health Policy.

Taylor, Todd B. 2001. Emergency Services Crisis of 2000—The Arizona Experience. *Academic Emergency Medicine* 8(11):1107-1108.

Tilly, Jane, Frank C. Ullman, and Julie Chesky. 2002. *Recent Changes in Health Policy for Low-Income People in Michigan*. State Update 18. Washington, DC: The Urban Institute.

Tirole, Jean. 1988. *The Theory of Industrial Organization*. Cambridge, MA: MIT Press.

Trenholm, Christopher, and Susanna Kung. 2000. Disparities in State Health Insurance Coverage: A Matter of Policy or Fortune? Princeton, NJ: Mathematica Policy Research, Inc.

Trocchio, Julie. 1996. What Are True Community Benefits? *Health Progress* 77(5):34-37.

Tsai, Alexander C., Joshua H. Sarver, Rita K. Cydulka, and David K. Baker. Forthcoming 2003. Declining Payments for Emergency Department Care, 1996-1998. *Annals of Emergency Medicine*.

Turner, Carolyn, and Ellen Campbell. 1999. Counting the Uninsured Using State-Level Hospitalization Data. *Public Health Reports* 114:149-156.

United Hospital Fund. 2002. Mission Possible? New York City's Municipal Hospitals in an Era of Declining Resources. *Hospital Watch* 13(1).

U.S. Congress. U.S. House of Representatives. 2001. *National Preparedness: Ambulance Diversions Impede Access to Emergency Rooms.* Prepared for Rep. Henry A. Waxman. Washington, DC: Committee on Government Reform, Special Investigations Division, Minority Staff. Accessed May 23, 2002. Available at: http://www.house.gov/reform/min/maj/maj_terrorism_diversions.htm.

U.S. Department of Health and Human Services. 2000. *Healthy People 2010: Understanding and Improving Health.* 2nd ed. Washington, DC: U.S. Government Printing Office.

———. 2002. *The 2002 HHS Poverty Guidelines.* Accessed March 15, 2002. Available at: http://aspe.hhs.gov/poverty/02poverty.htm.

U.S. General Accounting Office. 2000. 1993. *Emergency Departments: Unevenly Affected by Growth and Change in Patient Use.* Washington, DC: U.S. Government Printing Office.

———. 2000. *Community Health Centers. Adapting to Changing Health Care Environment Key to Continued Success.* GAO/HEHS-00-39. Washington, DC: U.S. Government Printing Office.

———. 2001. *Health Centers and Rural Clinics. Payments Likely to Be Constrained Under Medicaid's New System.* GAO-01-577. Washington, DC: U.S. Government Printing Office.

Wall, Susan. 1998. Transformations in Public Health Systems. *Health Affairs* 17(3):64-80.

Walzer, Michael. 1983. *Spheres of Justice: A Defense of Pluralism and Equality.* New York: Basic Books.

Weiner, Saul. 2001. 'I Can't Afford That!' Dilemmas in the Care of the Uninsured and Underinsured. *Journal of General Internal Medicine* 16(6):412-418.

Weinick, Robin, John Billings, and Helen Burstin. 2002. What is the Role of Primary Care in Emergency Department Overcrowding? Accessed June 27, 2002. Available at: http://www.kaisernetwork.org/health_cast/uploaded_files/WeinickED.pdf.

Weiss, Eve, Kathryn Haslanger, and Joel C. Cantor. 2001. Accessibility of Primary Care Services in Safety Net Clinics in New York City. *American Journal of Public Health* 91(8):1240-1245.

Weissman, Joel S., Carol Van Deusen Lukas, and Arnold M. Epstein. 1992. Bad Debt and Free Care in Massachusetts Hospitals. *Health Affairs* 11(2):148-161.

Weissman, Joel S., Paul Dryfoos, and Katharine London. 1999. Income Levels of Bad-Debt and Free-Care Patients in Massachusetts Hospitals. *Health Affairs* 18(4):156-166.

Weissman, Joel, Manjusha Gokhale, Ernest Moy, Eric G. Campbell, et al. 2002. Access to Care for Uninsured Patients in Academic Health Centers. *Academy for Health Services Research and Health Policy Annual Meeting.* Washington, DC: Academy for Health Services Research and Health Policy.

Wilkinson, Richard G. 1997. Socioeconomic Determinants of Health. Health Inequalities: Relative or Absolute Material Standards. *British Medical Journal* 314(7080):591-595.

Wynia, Matthew K., and Lawrence Gostin. 2002. The Bioterrorist Threat and Access to Health Care. *Science* 296(5573):1613.

Wynn, Barbara O., Theresa Coughlin, Serhiy Bondarenko, and Brian Bruen. 2002. *Analysis of the Joint Distribution of Disproportionate Share Hospital Payments.* Washington, DC: RAND Corporation.

Young, Gary J., Kamal R. Desai, and Carol Van Deusen Lukas. 1997. Does the Sale of Nonprofit Hospitals Threaten Health Care for the Poor? *Health Affairs* 16(1):137-141.

Young, Gary J., and Kamal R. Desai. 1999. Nonprofit Hospital Conversions and Community Benefits: New Evidence From Three States. *Health Affairs* 18(5):146-155.

Young, Gary P., Michelle B. Wagner, Arthur L. Kellermann., Jack Ellis, et al. 1996. Ambulatory Visits to Hospital Emergency Departments. Patterns and Reasons for Use. *Journal of the American Medical Association* 276(6):460-465.

Yudkowski, Beth K., Suk-Fong S. Tang, and Alicia M. Siston. 2000. *Pediatrician Participation in Medicaid/SCHIP.* Elk Grove Village, IL: American Academy of Pediatrics.

Zambrana, Ruth E., Nancy Breen, Sarah A. Fox, and Mary L. Gutierrez-Mohamed. 1999. Use of Cancer Screening Services by Hispanic Women: Analyses by Subgroup. *Preventive Medicine* 29(6 Pt. 1):466-477.

Ziller, Erika, and Al Leighton. 2000. *Case Report. Appalachia County Kentucky*. Portland, ME: Maine Rural Health Research Center.

Zuckerman, Stephen, Gloria Bazzoli, Amy Davidoff, and Anthony LoSasso. 2001a. How Did Safety-Net Hospitals Cope in the 1990s? *Health Affairs* 20(4):159-168.

Zuckerman, Stephen, Genevieve M. Kenney, Lisa Dubay, Jennifer Haley, et al. 2001b. Shifting Health Insurance Coverage 1997-1999. *Health Affairs* 20(1):169-177.

Zwanziger, Jack, and Glenn A. Melnick. 1988. The Effects of Hospital Competition and the Medicare PPS Program on Hospital Cost Behavior in California. *Journal of Health Economics* 7(4):301-320.

Zwanziger, Jack, Glenn A. Melnick, and Anil Bamezai. 1994. Costs and Price Competition in California Hospitals, 1980-1990. *Health Affairs* 13(4):118-126.

———. 2000. Can Cost Shifting Continue in a Price Competitive Environment? *Health Economics* 9(3):211-226.